AFTER
CIVIL
RIGHTS

AFTER CIVIL RIGHTS

Racial Realism in the New American Workplace

JOHN D. SKRENTNY

PRINCETON UNIVERSITY PRESS ■ PRINCETON AND OXFORD

Library of Congress Cataloging-in-Publication Data
Skrentny, John David.
After civil rights : racial realism in the new American workplace / John D. Skrentny.
pages cm
Includes bibliographical references and index.
ISBN 978-0-691-15996-6 (hardcover : alk. paper) 1. Discrimination in employment—
United States. 2. Race discrimination—United States. 3. Civil service—United States.
4. Civil rights—United States. I. Title.
HD4903.5.U58S5697 2013
331.13'30973–dc23
2013013184

British Library Cataloging-in-Publication Data is available

This book has been composed in Fairfield LT Std

Printed on acid-free paper. ∞

Printed in the United States of America

For Minh

CONTENTS

LIST OF FIGURES AND TABLES

Figures

Tables

After spending several years researching and writing about the historical development of minority rights legislation in the United States, I learned something new. I learned that not everyone was as passionate about the history of American policy as I was. It turned out that many people were more interested in what was happening now, in the contemporary United States, than what had happened in the past. They wanted to know more about where we were going than about how we arrived at where we were.

Eventually I came to share their interest. I had studied the history of affirmative action in employment for African-Americans in my first book, which focused on the years between 1965 and 1975. In my second, I sought to show how other groups won new rights during the same period, including nonblack racial minorities, women, immigrants, the disabled, and others. It makes sense now to write a third book to bring the story of minority rights development up to date, at least as it regards the important topic of employment, and as it regards people whom employers tend to categorize on the basis of their race, national origin, or immigrant status.

More specifically, the purpose of this book is, first, to reveal changes that are going on in employment practices across a broad spectrum of job sectors as regards race. I call this management strategy racial realism. It refers to employer perceptions that workers vary by race in their ability to do certain jobs and contribute to organizational effectiveness, and/or in the kinds of signals their racial backgrounds send to customers and citizens. Though racial realism benefits whites, hardly anyone openly advocates for employers to manage their workplaces in ways that leverage whiteness. The racial realism that employers, advocates, activists, and political leaders regularly talk about is the kind that benefits nonwhites.

A second goal of this book is to show how these employment practices are or (mostly) are not authorized by law, and to point some ways toward reform. I wish to show that despite the partisan nature of so many policy debates in America, these changes are not partisan, and that in words and actions, both political parties have shown support for them. In some small way, I hope also that by calling attention to these new realities, the book will encourage advocates to take true ownership of them—to acknowledge that they might claim to support color-blind classical liberalism in

some contexts, but they also support racial realism, and to acknowledge
that racial realism has downsides as well as upsides. Only then can we
ensure that employment practices are in line with the consensus value of
equal opportunity.

Writing a book about what is happening "now" in American employment and law presents several challenges to someone used to writing
about the past. First, "now" is obviously a moving target, requiring con-
stant updates. Second, an early strategy—interviewing employers about
their beliefs and practices—had to be abandoned because too many employers were either unwilling to talk openly and directly about these topics or unwilling to talk at all. Their reluctance is almost certainly related
to a major point of the book—that racial realism is still far away from civil
rights law as currently interpreted. Third, the effort to be comprehensive
in mapping what was going on "now" and also policy-oriented means that
a rigorous causal argument is not possible. While the introductory chapter presents a causal story to account for the rise of racial realism in the
last few decades, and while I believe that story to be accurate, the book
does not attempt to rigorously test that argument.

This book took a very long time to write. Describing it as "a book
about race, law, and employment in America," as I often did, perhaps
makes it sound narrow in its focus. In fact, it required learning vast new
literatures, because in each section I sought to show how employers and
advocates think of and use racial realism, to give some sense of how widespread the phenomenon is, to present material on whether social science
research supports employers' racial realism, and then to assess what the
law has to say about it. It is not easy to be expert in all of these literatures,
but I did my best to present the state of knowledge in each of them.

During this long process, I benefited from the wise counsel of many,
many scholars and research assistants. I apologize to those whom I neglect to mention below. The basic idea for the book was developed in
conversations with Paul Frymer, perhaps the only person in America
who is as fascinated with Section 703(e) of Title VII of the Civil Rights
Act of 1964 as I am. We presented some early material at conferences
at Harvard Law School and the University of Connecticut Law School,
and published a piece together in the *Connecticut Law Review*. I also
benefited from audience comments when I presented various pieces of
this research before scholars at meetings of the American Sociological
Association, the Association for the Study of Law, Culture and the Hu-
manities, and the Association of American Law Schools, and also at semi-
nars, conferences, and workshops at many great institutions, including

the Indiana University Law School; the American Political Development Seminar at the Miller Center of Public Affairs, University of Virginia; the Center for the Study of Law and Society Seminar at the University of California-Berkeley; the Legal Studies Seminar at Brown University; the Program in Law and Public Affairs at Princeton University; the Department of Political Science at Yale University; the Russell Sage Foundation; the Economic Sociology Workshop at Harvard University; the Stanford Workshop on Migration, Ethnicity, Race and Nation; the Conference on "Racing the Republic: Ethnicity and Inequality in France, in American and World Perspective" at the University of California-Berkeley; the Conference on "Fractures: Defining and Redefining the Twentieth-Century United States" at the University of Pennsylvania; and the "Borders and Boundaries Conference" at the Interdisciplinary Research Institute for Social Sciences, École des hautes études en sciences sociales in Paris.

I also benefited from conversations with such a great number of people that I am afraid I cannot list all of them. Several commented on the entire manuscript. They include Erik Bleich, Frank Dobbin, Tristin Green, and Deborah Malamud. I am grateful for countless long conversations about the issues discussed in this book with Paul Frymer, Tomás R. Jiménez, and Tom Sugrue. I also had helpful conversations with colleagues at UCSD, including Amy Binder, Kevin Lewis, Isaac Martin, Tom Medvetz, and Kwai Ng, and with the members of what we then called the Race Reading Group—Marisa Abrajano, Amy Bridges, and Zoltan Hajnal. Other colleagues at other institutions patiently answered questions, shared their work, or offered their constructive reactions. Among them, I wish particularly to thank Bruce Ackerman, Frank Bean, Chris Bonastia, Emilio Castilla, Ming Hsu Chen, Roger Clegg, Robert Cole, N. Jeremi Duru, Amin Ghaziani, Michael Jones-Correa, Rodney Hero, Jacques Ho, Milo Ho, Thanh Ho, Mohan Kanungo, Rick Karr, Lee Ann Kim, Desmond King, David Kirp, Jennifer Lee, Glenn Loury, Philip Martin, Cristina Mora, Orlando Patterson, Efrén O. Pérez, Brian Powell, Russell K. Robinson, Wendy Roth, Susan Silbey, Audrey Singer, David Sklansky, Marie Skrentny, Stanley Skrentny, Robin Stryker, Steve Teles, Dorian Warren, Mary Waters, David Wilkins, William Julius Wilson, and Ezra Zuckerman. I apologize for any omissions in this list. Despite this great volume of wise counsel, I of course could not follow all of it, and the faults in the manuscript are fully my responsibility.

This book also benefited from the efforts of many research assistants. Several graduate students were instrumental in the writing of the book, including Melody Chiong, Emma Greeson, David Keyes, Jack Jin Gary

Lee, Jane Lilly Lopez, Shehzad Nadeem, and Sabrina Strings. UCSD un-
dergraduates Hilda Chan, Kellie Egan, Stella Kim, Samira Motaghedi,
Diane Truong, John Whittemore, and Joe Woodring also helped.

This research was made possible by generous grants from the Gug-
genheim Foundation and University of California Institute for Labor and
Employment. Eric Schwartz at Princeton University Press was incredibly
helpful and patient in offering guidance on editorial questions both big
and small. Sara Lerner and Eva Jaunzems offered expert and detailed
editing.

In the early stages of my research, Minh Phan-Ho offered many insights regarding employment practices in the hiring of teachers in school
districts. Later, after doing years of research, I found myself totally and
utterly stuck, still lacking not only an argument, but also any reasonable
plan for how the book should be written. Over dinner at a restaurant,
she helped me to shape the vision, structure, and goals that guided the
writing until the very end. I could not have finished this book without
her contributions. To Minh, my wife and intellectual partner, this book
is dedicated.

AFTER
CIVIL
RIGHTS

1

Managing Race in the American Workplace

What role should racial differences play in American life? Americans have debated this question for decades. In fact, if the question is understood broadly, they have been debating it for centuries. Yet the America of the 2000s is very different from the nation at its founding. It is quite different also from the America that existed, now a half-century in the past, when our civil rights laws first took shape. Civil rights law is, of course, the primary tool we use to authorize and enact our visions and plans for how race should or should not matter. Can civil rights laws made a half-century ago still adequately govern race relations in today's America? Do they reflect our current practices and goals?

There are several civil rights laws, but my focus is on the venerable, celebrated Civil Rights Act of 1964. Could it be that *this* law—which legal scholars have called a "superstatute"[1] or "landmark statute"[2] because of its constitution-like importance in American law—is in some ways out of sync or anachronistic in today's America? The point here is not that the Civil Rights Act may out of sync because it has failed to stop discrimination, which studies show is still common.[3] That only suggests that (as with almost all laws) the job of the Civil Rights Act is not yet done. The point is, rather, that the assumptions and the world that created the Civil Rights Act may no longer be true or exist, and that it may well be time to rethink the law and what we as Americans want it to do. Put another way, we may have entered a period *after civil rights*—a stage in American history when we can constructively and productively manage racial differences with a focus that goes beyond the protection of rights.

Consider that American racial demography has changed greatly from the period when our current civil rights laws were born. In place of the focus on the black/white divide that dominated congressional debates in 1964, controversies about immigration and the growing Latino population have taken center stage in American racial politics. Meanwhile, as I describe below, the economy has been transformed by globalization and technological changes, remaking the workplaces that the Civil Rights Act was intended to regulate.

The way Americans talk about race and what pragmatic and progressive voices say that they want has changed as well. Never before has such a wide variety of employers, advocates, activists, and government leaders in American society discussed the benefits of racial diversity and the utility of racial difference in such a broad range of contexts.[4] Having employees of different races, we are told by these elites, is good for businesses, the government, schools, police departments, marketers, medical practitioners, and many other institutions. When managed properly, racial differences make organizations work better, or make Americans feel better, or both. In short, race can be a qualification for employment.

It is less discussed, but we see an analogous dynamic at the low end of the job market as well, where employers of low-skilled workers also consider the race, as well as immigrant status, of potential employees. These employers, the most willing to talk, tell both journalists and social scientists that they prefer Latinos and Asians as workers, and especially immigrant Latinos and Asians, because they work harder, better, and longer than others, including white and black Americans. These perceptions have helped to fuel the great waves of migration that have transformed America since the 1980s.

What we have not come to terms with, however, is that the lauding of racial differences as beneficial for organizations suggests a new strategy for thinking about and managing race in America. It does not fit (certainly not in any obvious way), with traditional conceptions of equal rights and citizenship. It is an issue quite apart from, and perhaps beyond, civil rights. And yet the country is mostly flying blind. We put into practice our new conceptions of race in ever wider realms and contexts, while holding on to more traditional ways of thinking about race and civil rights, and we do this with little awareness of what is going on. Our laws and conversations enact multiple strategies and multiple goals in an incoherent jumble. Significant opportunities and values are lost in the shuffle.

The purpose of this book is to provide a picture of the racial dynamics of the American workplace. I aim to show how race matters, the perceptions employers and others openly express when they talk about race, and especially how current practices fit with the Civil Rights Act. I argue that since 1964, there have been three main strategies for managing race in employment. These vary greatly both in how they conceive of race, and also in how much support they have in law. The most important point is this: the strategy of using membership in a racial group as a qualification, what I will call *racial realism*, has prominent support in society but surprisingly little in law.

Another purpose of this book is to call for debate. Legal scholar Bruce Ackerman has emphasized that the civil rights era, the "Second Reconstruction," was a great constitutional moment and an elaborately deliberated creation of "We the People."[5] But the current era is evolving with little awareness let alone debate in Congress, the courts, or the public sphere. My point is not to criticize any particular strategy, but to argue that we should be mindful of the gap between everyday practice and the law, and that we should consider reforming the law to bring the two into sync, so as to ensure that we act in accordance with our most fundamental values. The task is complex: we must balance or manage employment opportunities and restrictions to Americans of all racial affiliations, as well as to immigrants. Given this country's violent history, we should keep our eyes wide open when institutionalizing practices on matters of race.

If we do not know what we are doing, we are likely to do it badly. If we tacitly allow racial meanings to figure in the workplace, without thinking through how this should be done, we will—and already have, as I will show—sacrifice the consensus goal of equal opportunity. Moreover, too great of a disjuncture between law and everyday practice diminishes respect for the law and invites arbitrariness in its enforcement.

Strategies for Managing Race in Employment, Law, and Politics

Since 1964, there have been three dominant strategies, or cultural models,[6] for managing how race matters in the workplace, all variously supported by employers, politicians, civil rights groups, workers and judges. Current employment practices and employment civil rights laws are a mixed bag of these three competing strategies: classical liberalism, affirmative-action liberalism, and racial realism. The key point here are that these strategies vary in both the significance as well as utility or usefulness that they attribute to racial distinctions, and in their organizational goals (these are summarized in table 1). They also vary in their political support and in their degree of legal authorization.

TABLE I
Strategies for Managing Race in the Workplace

	Classical liberalism	Affirmative-action liberalism	Racial realism
Significance of race	No	Yes	Yes
Usefulness of race	No	No	Yes
Strategic goal	Justice	Justice	Organizational effectiveness

Before discussing their differences, it is important to acknowledge that these strategies do have one thing in common: they are not based on rigorous thinking about what "race" is, but rather on cultural or folk understandings that are usually quite intuitive to Americans but can be utterly inscrutable to outsiders. We can see this in the attitudes of employers, who may discriminate against or prefer certain people based on perceptions of physical differences in skin color, hair or facial features, and on their beliefs about traits associated with regional or national origin. Notably, none of the statutes governing employment discrimination *define* race, an issue I discuss below.

The Classical Liberal Strategy: A Color-Blind Workplace

The classical liberal strategy of how race should factor in employment can be stated simply: in order to achieve justice, race should have no significance and thus no utility, or usefulness, in the workplace. This strategy is rooted in the Enlightenment view of individuals as rights-bearing entities of equal dignity. Opportunities should be allocated based on ability and actions. In the classical liberal view, which has intellectual roots perhaps most prominently in John Locke's political philosophy, immutable differences such as race or ancestry should not determine opportunities or outcomes.

The classical liberal strategy for managing race is solidly institutionalized in American civil rights law. It is the guiding vision behind the primary statute regulating the meaning of race in the workplace: Title VII of the Civil Rights Act of 1964. Title VII states:

It shall be an unlawful employment practice for an employer -
(1) to fail or refuse to hire or to discharge any individual, or otherwise to discriminate against any individual with respect to

his compensation, terms, conditions, or privileges of employment, because of such individual's race, color, religion, sex, or national origin; or

(2) to limit, segregate, or classify his employees or applicants for employment in any way which would deprive or tend to deprive any individual of employment opportunities or otherwise adversely affect his status as an employee, because of such individual's race, color, religion, sex, or national origin.[7]

The message here on the relevance of race to employment seems clear: there isn't any. When employers do any of the things that employers normally do—when they make everyday decisions regarding whom to hire, fire, or promote; what their workers should be doing; with whom they should be working; and how much they should be earning—they must not have race (or any of the various other qualities mentioned in Title VII, or identified in other laws, including immigration status and disability) in their minds at all.

Congress founded the law on this vision in part as a response to the reality of race in America, and in particular in the Deep South, where the brutal caste system known as "Jim Crow" held sway. Through both law and norms, life in the Southern states was thoroughly and openly based on a hierarchy in which whites were the dominant race. At work, this meant that employers typically excluded African-Americans from the better jobs, that they did so openly, and that, typically, workplaces were segregated.[8] Though discrimination was rampant in the North as well,[9] civil rights leaders fought against these Southern practices in particular. Congress therefore designed Title VII with a classical liberal vision: Jim Crow–style intentional discrimination was finally made illegal.[10]

Title VII was not the first classical liberal intervention in federal law that governed employment. In a similar response to racial discrimination in the South, Congress passed Section 1981 of the Civil Rights Act of 1866. It states "all persons . . . shall have the same right . . . to make and enforce contracts . . . as is enjoyed by white citizens. . . ."[11] Though it remained dormant for decades after the failure of Reconstruction, Section 1981 today is often a part of court decisions on employment discrimination because it allows plaintiffs to sue for compensatory and punitive damages. The Fourteenth Amendment's guarantee of "equal protection of the laws" can also justify classically liberal nondiscrimination in the specific context of government employment.

· Considerable evidence indicates that Title VII and these other laws have contributed much to the goal of equal opportunity. Most obviously, the kind of open exclusion of African-Americans and preference for whites that was common in 1964 is no more. Many scholars focus now on more subtle but nevertheless powerful kinds of discrimination that are deeply, almost invisibly institutionalized in employment practices or the result of unconscious bias.[12]

Given its successes, and its fit with foundational documents in American history such as the Declaration of Independence, the Constitution, and specifically the equal-protection clause of the Fourteenth Amendment, the classical liberal strategy for managing race remains dominant in American politics. Its basic premise—that race should have no meaning or significance in employment—is the official view of the mainstream of the Republican Party.[13] Republicans tend to emphasize that discrimination is wrong and should be prohibited by law no matter whom it benefits. For example, the Republican platform in 2012 stated, "We consider discrimination based on sex, race, age, religion, creed, disability, or national origin unacceptable and immoral," and added, "We will strongly enforce anti-discrimination statutes." At the same time, social policies that target racial minorities in order to boost their opportunities, in the Republican view, violated the principle of merit: "We reject preferences, quotas, and set-asides as the best or sole methods through which fairness can be achieved, whether in government, education, or corporate boardrooms. . . . Merit, ability, aptitude, and results should be the factors that determine advancement in our society." In the GOP view, race should have no bearing on law or life chances, and the elimination of racial discrimination requires a commitment to colorblindness.[14] Legal scholars often call the Republicans' strict interpretation of classical liberalism the "anticlassification" view of race and law.[15]

Affirmative-Action Liberalism: Seeing Race to Get beyond Race

An alternative strategy for managing race in employment, what I will call here "affirmative-action liberalism," grants significance to race, but asserts that it should not have usefulness for an organization. That is, race has meaning for employers, but only to ensure the goal of justice (and specifically, equal opportunity). It should not carry any messages about a given worker's usefulness to the day-to-day functioning or effectiveness of a business or government employer.

This strategy has coexisted with the classical liberal vision, though it is always subordinate in political discourse and in the way employers talk about their hiring. It is also less prominent in law, as it is not enshrined in a statute, let alone a landmark or superstatute. Yet affirmative-action liberalism is certainly institutionalized in the federal regulations and guidelines that implement Title VII,[16] as well as in a presidential order, Labor Department regulations,[17] and several Supreme Court rulings.

What is affirmative-action liberalism? While activists at the grass roots fought for jobs across America in the 1960s, Washington policy elites—civil rights administrators, judges, and White House officials—gave legal shape to this new vision of race in employment.[18] Shortly after Title VII went into effect, administrators at the new Equal Employment Opportunity Commission (EEOC), the agency created by Title VII to enforce the law, concluded that race should have some significance. In their view, it was important to monitor the hiring of different racial groups to learn whether or not employers were using race in their decision-making. They began to require large employers (those with at least one hundred workers) to count the number of workers on their payroll, categorize them by the nature of work they performed and their race and sex, and report that those data annually to the agency. This meant that every year, employers looked over their entire workforce and categorized all workers according to their race. It marked the rise of affirmative-action liberalism: The administrators made counting race a tool for measuring equal opportunity.

There followed other developments in civil rights law that infused racial differences with significance. In 1971, the Supreme Court created a new understanding of discrimination in *Griggs v. Duke Power*.[19] The court declared, "If an employment practice which operates to exclude Negroes cannot be shown to be related to job performance, the practice is prohibited"[20] and "good intent or absence of discriminatory intent does not redeem employment procedures or testing mechanisms that operate as 'built-in headwinds' for minority groups and are unrelated to measuring job capability."[21] This meant that employers had to pay attention to the racial impact of whatever means they used to select and place employees. Those that had a "disparate impact" on minorities and women would be illegal unless they could be justified by business necessity.

Another important factor was the Labor Department's development of affirmative-action regulations to implement Lyndon Johnson's Executive Order 11246. This 1965 order had stated only that government contractors needed to promise not to discriminate in employment, and also to take some undefined "affirmative action" to ensure equal opportunity. It took several years, but by 1970, Labor Department regulations explained that "affirmative action" meant that the contractors must promise to hire certain percentage ranges of racial minority workers at various job levels by specified time periods.[22]

Firms that did not have government contracts also began to implement their own affirmative-action employment programs, either voluntarily or in agreement with labor unions or civil rights groups. They typically used the same racial hiring goals and timetables as were set out in the federal affirmative-action regulations. In two key decisions in the 1980s, the Supreme Court created the legal rules for these voluntary efforts. An employer's plan was in compliance with Title VII only if certain conditions were met: 1) it had the goal of remedying an imbalance in the organization's workforce; 2) there were no unnecessary limits on opportunities for whites/males (in practice, this meant there should be no outright bans on the hiring of whites or males, and that whites or males should not be terminated to achieve the plan's goals); and 3) the plan was a temporary fix and could not be used to maintain the desired racial proportions.[23]

These developments infused race with significance, but not usefulness, in the minds of conscientious employers. Race would communicate nothing about an employee's ability, suitability for a particular job, or about the kind of person they would be in offices, meeting rooms, or on the assembly line. Employers were to pay attention to nonwhite races *only* because of their importance for legal compliance and equal opportunity. Employers also learned that a good way to avoid a lawsuit was to make sure that the percentages of different races in their workforces roughly approximated the percentages of qualified workers in their applicant pools. Getting racial proportions reasonably right was to have utility only insofar as it was an indicator that the largest racial group—white Euro-Americans—was not abusing its economic and political power.

Affirmative-action liberalism found most of its defenders on the American Left, especially in the Democratic Party, though their support for the strategy was far more muted than the Republicans' embrace of classical liberalism.[24] For Democrats, affirmative action was an addition to classical liberalism, and not a replacement—or a contradiction. The 2012 Democratic Party platform declared a commitment to antidiscrimination laws and affirmed the classical liberal vision, but also added: "To enhance access and equity in employment, education, and business opportunities, we encourage initiatives to remove barriers to equal opportunity that still exist in America."[25] This was a muting of more explicit language in the 2008 platform, which stated emphatically: "We support affirmative action, including in federal contracting and higher education, to make sure that those locked out of the doors of opportunity will be able to walk through those doors in the future."[26]

In most defenses of affirmative-action liberalism, advocates send the message that while classical liberalism is best for America, practical considerations coupled with a commitment to justice point to the need for affirmative-action liberalism. Due mainly to a past history of racial discrimination and the difficulties of enforcing classical liberalism, race must be acknowledged and affirmative action institutionalized in law so that equality and justice can be achieved.

Perhaps the most eloquent political statement of affirmative-action liberalism and the way it may work in concert with classical liberalism, came not from a Democratic political leader, but from Supreme Court Justice (and appointee of Republican president Richard Nixon) Harry Blackmun. Defending a minority preference program for admission at the University of California at Davis Medical School from a legal challenge, Blackmun wrote, "In order to get beyond racism, we must first take account of race. There is no other way. And in order to treat some persons equally, we must treat them differently."[27]

Other Supreme Court opinions show varying justifications for affirmative-action liberalism. In the early years, Justices William Brennan and Thurgood Marshall saw racial preferences as justified to compensate for past discrimination anywhere in society.[28] Since the late 1980s, however, the Supreme Court has stressed that discrimination must be identifiable in the past practices of the specific organization using the affirmative-action preferences.[29]

The basic concept of what I am calling "affirmative-action liberalism" has a long pedigree in legal scholarship, and it has been called by many names. Perhaps most prominent in recent years is the term "antisubordination principle," but Owen Fiss described what he called the "group-disadvantaging principle,"[30] Laurence Tribe spoke of an "antisubjugation" principle,[31] Cass Sunstein titled an article "The Anticaste Principle,"[32] Derrick Bell provocatively used imaginary narratives to explore the same idea regarding racial inequality,[33] and Catharine MacKinnon made analogous points regarding gender equality.[34]

The common notion in all of these discussions is that true equality is about more than treating individuals equally. It is about attending to the fact that individuals are members of groups, that these groups vary in power and wealth, and that an honest appraisal of the state of American society reveals hierarchies (many scholars tend to focus on race and sex, but there are others).[35] In this view, institutional structures in society often work to maintain or worsen the subordinated positions of individuals in nonwhite groups. Moreover, just and responsible lawmaking and judging interprets the Fourteenth Amendment's guarantee of the "equal protection of the laws" as requiring that these institutional hierarchies be recognized and that attempts to break them up be undertaken.

Not surprisingly, judges appointed by Democrats tend to favor the antisubordination principle and judges appointed by Republicans the anticlassification principle. Given that a Republican has occupied the White House for twenty-eight of the fifty years since the Civil Rights Act, that presidents tend to appoint judges who fit the ideological profile of their party, and that five of the nine current Supreme Court justices were appointed by Republicans, it is not surprising that the anticlassification principle has been in ascendance.[36] Chief Justice John Roberts has even offered his own pithy rebuttal to Justice Blackmun's claim about the need for affirmative-action liberalism: "The way to stop discrimination on the basis of race is to stop discriminating on the basis of race."[37]

Yet legal scholars Jack Balkin and Reva Siegel persuasively argue that, though analytically distinct, both principles continue to coexist in American law. Which principle is dominant at any particular time depends upon political pressures, and both may shape the same judicial opinion.[38]

Racial Realism: Race Has Significance and It Has Usefulness

There is yet another strategy for managing race in employment that has attracted pragmatic thinkers of both major parties, as well as leaders in business, science, government, and the arts. In the "racial-realist" strategy, race has both significance and usefulness in the workplace—and this is true irrespective of government policy or lofty concerns about equality and justice.[39] Unlike the affirmative-action liberals' hopes and dreams for a future of fairness, or for compensations to remedy past injustice, the racial-realism strategy makes a frank assessment of the utility of race for organizational goals. For racial realists, race is a key part of worker identity, and businesses and government institutions can and should use racial differences to their advantage. Given its emphasis on instrumental market logics and employer discretion, along with its downplaying of rights and justice, racial realism is an apt strategy for managing race in the "neoliberal" era.[40]

TABLE 2
Racial Realism in Employer Perceptions

Racial abilities	Racial signaling
Special ability in dealing with same-race clients or citizens	Convey openness, care, or legitimacy to specific racial audiences
Diverse employees will bring new ideas/better functionality to an organization in any job Attitude/work ethic in low-skill jobs	Convey openness, "modernity," lack of racism to wide audience

In racial realism, race has two different types of usefulness for employers (see table 2).[41] The first is what I will call "racial abilities." This refers to perceptions that employees of some races are better able to perform some tasks than employees of other races due to their aptitude or know-how. Racial abilities come in a variety of forms. Sometimes employers link them to specific jobs. In the more high-skilled and professional jobs, there is a common pattern of racial matching based on employers' convictions that employees of particular races have superior abilities, mainly through superior understanding, when it comes to dealing with clients or citizens of the concordant race. In occupations as diverse as advertising/marketing, medicine, teaching, journalism, and policing, employers see value in matching the race of the employee to the race of the clients or citizens he or she serves. Employers at the high end of the labor market are sometimes supported or encouraged in such perceptions by government commissions, task force reports, official statements, advocacy bodies, and civil rights groups.

Employers seeking to fill high-skilled jobs also sometimes evince a desire for racial abilities that are not linked to specific jobs. As I show in Chapter 2, employers may perceive racial diversity as a benefit for the *overall* performance of their organization, linking it to no particular job or client or citizen base. In this view, a racially diverse workforce will generate more ideas and thus more innovation, more productivity, and better overall performance. Employees of difference races (or sexes, or other bases of difference) bring new ideas into the mix because people of different backgrounds, including racial backgrounds, tend to think differently; these new ideas in turn force everyone to be more creative and to move their thinking "outside the box." If an organization has become too dominated by a particular race (usually whites), then the employer may perceive utility in an applicant who brings to the table experience or credentials—*and* a different race. In short, race becomes a qualification for the job.

When it comes to skilled jobs, there is sometimes an effort to understand the basis of racial abilities. Employers may understand that there is no genetic key to racial abilities, and that performance differences simply reflect the influences of the environment and of socialization processes. They will, consequently, acknowledge that members of one race can be taught what amount to the "racial abilities" of other groups, particularly the ability to understand or be sensitive to the needs and preferences of particular populations. At the same time, they may find it far more efficient simply to use race to get the ability benefits and ensuing boosts in performance that they desire.

Racial abilities take on a different look in the low-skilled sector. In basic manufacturing and services, employers want workers who can perform uncomplicated, repetitious tasks for long periods of time without complaining. In short, they require a good attitude or "work ethic." As I will show in Chapter 5, employers across the country frequently identify Latino and Asian workers, and especially Latino and Asian *immigrant* workers, as possessing these traits that fit them for otherwise low-skilled jobs. Here, a kind of "immigrant realism" strategy also comes into play, as employers seek to utilize the special abilities of persons born abroad in ways that classical liberalism and affirmative-action liberalism would ignore. There may even be an "undocumented-immigrant realism" in play when employers perceive that they are leveraging the abilities (especially work ethic) of workers who are not authorized to be in the U.S.

Typically, employers of low-skilled workers do not think often or deeply about what their strategy means; they just "know" that Latinos and Asians are members of groups that are at least on average better workers than both white and black Americans. They may prefer foreign-born workers over native-born workers, but they usually do so in racialized terms, counterposing immigrants with "blacks" and "whites." They also may link the immigrants' race with ability to perform specific jobs or even specific tasks—for example, a particular action on a meatpacking processing line. While the current racial hierarchy of desirability is new, this kind of racial-abilities hiring has existed in America for more than a hundred years—and perhaps it has always existed.

At first glance, it may appear that employer perceptions of racial abilities in low-skilled jobs are so different from their perceptions of abilities in high-skilled jobs as to warrant a completely separate categorization.

After all, the kinds of preferences that employers show for low-skilled workers of particular backgrounds appear to be very similar to the kinds of practices that Title VII was designed to prevent: stereotypes that deem some workers as undesirable, with African-Americans once again at the bottom.[42] But I group low- and high-skilled racial realism together in this book—and I do so for three reasons. First, in many of these cases, there is the common perception that the ability to do a specific job or at least a specific class of jobs varies, at least to some extent, by race. Second, at all skill levels, these perceptions shaping hiring and placement are based on stereotypes or what we might more generously call oversimplified predictions of race-patterned behavior.[43] Third, unlike discrimination in the American South in 1964, both the low- and high-skilled racial realism of the 2000s benefits nonwhites in many circumstances.

The other strand of racial realism in employment is "racial signaling."[44] Racial signaling refers to situations where employers seek to gain a favorable response from an audience through the strategic deployment of an employee's race. There is no assumption here that the employee possesses any special aptitude; the idea is rather to cater to the tastes of a group of clients or citizens. Employers use the racial signaling strategy almost exclusively in the context of skilled jobs, because the majority of low-skilled workers toil behind the scenes (the exception being those employed in retail or food service customer relations).

It is racial signaling when the owner of a drugstore hires a black manager for a store in a black neighborhood because he or she believes the community prefers it, or when a mayor appoints a Latino police chief because there is evidence that the Latino community does not trust the current white leadership of the police, or when a company installs some white employees in fundraising jobs because the company believes that white venture capitalists might feel more comfortable dealing with companies run by whites. In education, when a school hires a nonwhite teacher to serve as a role model for students of the same race, this too constitutes racial signaling.

In most cases of racial signaling, there is a pattern of matching employee race with that of the customers or public, and an assumption by employers that those customers or members of the public will respond more favorably to a person of their own race than to a similar person of a different race. At other times, employers mean to send the racial signal to everyone. Private or government employers, for example, sometimes use racial signaling to encourage all clients or citizens to perceive their organizations as diverse, modern, and open to all. Like the value of racial diversity in organizations, this kind of racial signaling is a phenomenon of recent vintage: a mono-racial workforce now looks old-fashioned.

This is especially true in politics—the racial signaling strategy has made "lily-white" a pejorative in many contexts and produces presidential administrations composed of different colors as well as different genders. Thus, Democrats may make appointments of African-Americans, Latinos, or Asian-Americans as part of a targeted racial signaling strategy because they want to appeal to specific groups of nonwhites, for example, and to reward them for their support at the ballot box. Republicans, meanwhile, concerned about charges of racism or of being behind-the-times, may appoint nonwhites in order to let everyone know that their opposition to certain policies favored by nonwhites does not mean that they are racist.

Racial signaling is absolutely crucial in the entertainment industry, as well as in advertising. No one seems to seriously believe that different races have different abilities when it comes to acting, but it is a wide-spread belief in the industry that audiences will respond differently to different races. In Hollywood films, television shows, advertisements, and even professional sports, decisions regarding whom to place in front of the "eyeballs" of audiences (as marketers sometime put it), or how to at-tract those eyeballs, regularly take into account the economic impact of racial signaling.

Unlike classical liberalism and affirmative-action liberalism, racial re-alism has very little authorization in law.[45] As I show throughout this book, Title VII appears flatly to forbid it, it is difficult to find EEOC regulations that support it, and court opinions authorizing it are rare (the same can be said of immigrant realism). Political elites, especially presidents, seem to support racial realism (as I describe in Chapter 3), and one might argue that this is a sort of quasi-legal endorsement of the strategy. But racial-realist political appointments, while important, are not covered by statutes or the Constitution, and have no explicitly legal authorization.[46]

Instead, racial realism's primary legal peg is a series of court cases that rely on the Fourteenth Amendment. The precedents are thus limited to government hiring, though courts have restricted this potentially expan-sive opening for racial realism specifically to the hiring and placement of police officers and other law enforcement officials. Several legal scholars argue that the courts could and/or should apply to employment a key 2003 Supreme Court decision, *Grutter v. Bollinger*, that used the Four-teenth Amendment to authorize the use, in some circumstances, of racial preferences to achieve diversity in university admissions.[47] As I show in Chapters 2 and 3, except for a case regarding police officers, this did not happen, and the Supreme Court's 2013 ruling in *Fisher v. University of Texas* has made this even less likely.

The primary legal problem for racial realism is that Title VII so strictly limits the usefulness that race can have for employers. Where it permits group differences to have some usefulness for the operation of a firm, it does not do so for race, and where it allows for the consideration of race, it does not do so in a racial-realist way.

Title VII, as described above, would seem to make all uses of race for an organization illegal: its goal is to prevent discrimination and thus create equal opportunities for employment and for participation in workplaces. Classical liberalism speaks most directly to the first half of this, while affirmative-action liberalism speaks to the second half. But there is one provision of the law that takes a very different view of group differences. It states that various characteristics that the law otherwise bans from employer consideration when hiring, placing, promoting, or firing workers *can* be taken into account in some employment decisions. Specifically, employers can consider national origin, sex, or religion when, for a particular job, they are a "bona fide occupational qualification reasonably necessary to the normal operation of that particular business or enterprise."[48] This has come to be known as the "BFOQ" exception.

This sounds like obscure legalese, but Senators Joseph S. Clark (D-PA) and Clifford P. Case (R-NJ) together authored an "interpretive memorandum" explaining how the BFOQ provision was to be put into practice. Their reasoning sounds a lot like the employer logic analyzed throughout this book. "Examples of such legitimate discrimination," Clark and Case wrote, "would be the preference of a French restaurant for a French cook, the preference of a professional baseball team for male players, and the preference of a business which seeks the patronage of members of particular religious groups for a salesman of that religion."[49]

However, there are two problems with the BFOQ as a statutory basis for racial realism. The most critical is that Congress explicitly did not allow a BFOQ defense for racial discrimination.[50] The law allowed it for everything *but* racial discrimination. Why that exclusion? The fact that white, Southern members of Congress—opponents of the entire law— suggested the creation of a race BFOQ provides a clue. Imagine these supporters of Jim Crow segregation and discrimination in the House of Representatives explaining, as they in fact did, their concern for the rights and freedoms of black-owned businesses to hire unhindered by anti-discrimination regulations. They argued that these businesses should be able to maintain a black identity. Some sold products used only by persons of African ancestry, they maintained, such as "hair straightener" and "skin whitener." One brought up the Harlem Globetrotters basketball team. Could Congress force a team from Harlem to hire white people? Another mentioned the need for someone of African ancestry to perform in Shakespeare's *Othello*.[51]

Without debate, the pro-Title VII majority defeated the race BFOQ amendment offered by these enemies of any civil rights legislation. They did not explain their reasoning (though they did point out that the Harlem Globetrotters had too few employees to be covered by the bill). Emmanuel Celler (D-NY) explained simply: "We did not include the word 'race' because we felt that race or color would not be a bona fide qualification, as would be 'national origin'. That was left out. It should be left out."[52]

It appears the defenders of Title VII feared that *any* loophole in a blanket prohibition on race discrimination would be stretched and expanded until the law was rendered meaningless, as happened with Reconstruction-era laws, such as that guaranteeing equal rights to vote. A white restaurant employer, for instance, might claim that his white customers do not like being waited on by a black person, and that being white was therefore a qualification for working in that particular restaurant.[53]

The second problem is that even if Congress were to amend Title VII to include a race BFOQ, it would not likely cover the racial realism described in this book. Despite the early discussions by Senators Case and Clark that suggested the BFOQ exceptions for sex, national origin, and religion could be quite expansive and used to defend discrimination catering to customer preferences, courts have since greatly narrowed the use of the BFOQ to defend sex, religion and national origin discrimination. The statute required that the defense be accepted only when discrimination was reasonably necessary to the normal operation of the enterprise in question—but the courts interpreted "reasonably" very strictly, and created a rule stipulating that a valid business necessity was one that related to the "essence of the business" in question.

For example, consider the attempts by airlines to make female sex a qualification for the position of flight attendant.[54] Airlines claimed that female flight attendants (then called "stewardesses") were more skilled than men at comforting anxious passengers,[55] or that they had the desired sexy image to appeal to a mostly-male business clientele.[56] The federal courts rejected these arguments on grounds that the essence of an airline was to transport passengers safely and not to cater to presumed customer preferences about what would feel comforting (or titillating). The only area where courts have allowed customer preferences to justify discrimination is in sex discrimination cases based on concerns for privacy or, to be more precise, sexual modesty (see Chapter 4).

This means that even if there were a race BFOQ in Title VII—which there isn't—it would be very difficult to use it to defend hiring decisions based on perceived racial abilities and racial signaling. It would be difficult to show that the racial background of employees is critical to the essence of any business. An employer wishing to use a BFOQ for national origin to defend a practice (specifying, for example, people of Mexican ancestry for a particular job) would also find great difficulty doing so within the current legal rules.

The lack of a race BFOQ is not, however, the only legal problem for racial realism. An additional obstacle is that where Title VII does allow race to be taken into account—in applying affirmative action—courts have not allowed race to have any usefulness for employers. The current set of rules for affirmative action requires that race have almost no meaning, relevance, or consequences for the functioning of the organization itself. Intention is everything. Firms need to show that they are only taking an affirmative action in order to repair some imbalance, and included in the notion of race-consciousness-as-repair is the idea that the racial consideration is only temporary. The legal rationale for taking account of race disappears when the imbalance is repaired. This is not the logic of racial realism. As one authoritative essay sums up the trend in employment discrimination, "Under current legal doctrine, judges and other legal actors often treat actions that seem to be race- or gender-neutral as evidence of a lack of discrimination. Likewise, they consider conscious treatment of race in decision making to be evidence of discrimination."[57]

Open support for racial realism in the treatment of nonwhites began at different times in different contexts.[58] Throughout American history, it was not uncommon to find employers professing a belief that racial and immigrant identity was related to aptitude for low-skilled jobs. Political leaders making appointments have considered racial signaling in a taken-for-granted way for whites since the founding of the republic, and for nonwhites at least since African-Americans began to migrate north in the early part of the twentieth century. Racially matching African-American sales and marketing professionals with African-American customers became established practice in the 1930s and 1940s. The sociologist and civil rights leader W.E.B. DuBois argued for the racial abilities and signaling of African-American teachers in the 1930s, and while racial realism was eclipsed by classical liberalism in the 1950s and 1960s, strong advocates for racially matched teaching for Latino and African-American

teachers and students emerged again in the late 1960s. The racial violence of the late 60s gave racial realism a significant boost in a variety of
sectors, especially when the influential report of the National Advisory
Commission on Civil Disorders (the Kerner Report) strongly advocated
for the racial abilities and signaling of African-American police officers
and journalists. Hollywood and advertisers moved to use racial signaling
for nonwhites around this time as well. In the 1980s, racial "diversity"
came to the fore as a corporate value. A desire for the racial abilities and
signaling for nonwhite medical doctors became a priority in the 1990s. In
that decade, the Clinton administration helped set the tone by boasting
that Clinton's government "looked like America." What is "new" about
the American workplace of today is that these forces have all come together at the same time and in a context of unprecedented diversity. In
the early twenty-first century, racial realism is now either entrenched or
strongly supported in all of these spheres, though it awaits explicit legal
authorization in almost all of them.

When We Talk about "Law," What Do We Mean?

A major focus of this book is the gap or disjuncture between employment
civil rights law as it is written and the management strategy many employers and advocates want. The notion of a separation between written
law and lived reality is one of the oldest ideas in the study of law as an
institution.[59] Its pedigree reaches back more than one hundred years to
pioneering analyses by legal theorists on both sides of the Atlantic.

In the U.S., scholars identify the idea with Roscoe Pound, especially
with his essay "Law in Books and Law in Action." For Pound, the law
in books is what the legislators write. The law in action refers to what
enforcers of the law actually do. The law in books is relatively straightforward: it is what the words say. Pound was much more interested in law
as the enforcers enforced it, and in the size of the gap between the two.[60]

The Austrian legal theorist Eugen Ehrlich also made an influential
distinction, though somewhat different from Pound's. Ehrlich noted that
there was a set of norms that guided both the law-writing of legislators
and the law-interpreting of judges. Ehrlich distinguished this from "living
law," which was "the law that dominates life itself, even though it has not
been posited in legal propositions."[61] More than Pound, Ehrlich was interested in social customs and how regular, everyday citizens treated the

law. Thus, while Pound concentrated on the distinction between those who wrote law and those who enforced it, Ehrlich was concerned with the distinction between legal elites and regular folks.[62]

Social scientists in the later decades of the twentieth century moved away from the hoary law-on-books vs. law-in-practice dichotomy, focusing instead either on law as a system of behavior or a set of institutions with no reality outside of the social, for example, or examining variations in "legal consciousness."[63] As legal scholar Susan Silbey has put it, "For most of the twentieth century, legal scholars had treated law and society as if they were two empirically distinct spheres, as if the two were conceptually as well as materially separate and singular. They are not. The law is a construct of human ingenuity; laws are material phenomena."[64] In this view, Title VII is constituted by social relations. It has no reality in itself, and thus it makes little sense to say that Title VII exists as ink on paper—or pixels arranged on an electronic screen. The ink or pixels, the "law in books," must be interpreted for it to have any reality.[65]

The members of Congress who wrote Title VII may have had their own ideas of what their words meant, but judges' fiction of a "legislative intent" does not get us very far in understanding the purpose of a law, because (even if we have a record of the authors' thoughts on a particular bill) different legislators had different ideas in mind when the law passed.[66] Indeed, some may have had nothing in mind—they may have voted for a statute because a president or party leader or some interest group asked them to do so.[67] In the case of Title VII, some legislators were most focused on the persistently high black unemployment rate.[68] Others sought means to achieve equal opportunity and or to avoid burdening employers or limiting the rights of white workers.[69] Still others were more focused not on black workers, or Latinos or Asians, but women of all races, national origins and creeds.[70]

Administrators at the EEOC then interpreted the law, looking for a way to enforce it with demonstrable success and in an efficient manner.[71] Business owners, human resources professionals, and employees—black, white, Asian, Latino, male, female, etc.—also had different senses of what the words of Title VII meant (if they knew about the law at all).[72] The notion that we can determine whether or not an organization is complying with a statute "suggests that the statute has a single, clear, and unimpeachable meaning, so that we can easily judge compliant and noncompliant behavior," when in fact, "legal texts are notoriously indeterminate."[73]

Thus, the closer we look, the more the distinction between law on the books and law in action or "living law" seems to break down, because there is no one "law on the books"—for Title VII or any other law. Different people see different meanings in the law due to their institutional position (e.g., as administrators of the law), but even similarly situated people will see different meanings (consider the views of liberal legislators and judges vs. conservative legislators and judges). Moreover, individuals and organized groups actively contest established meanings of Title VII and seek to establish new meanings—as is the case with the meaning of most statutes and regulations, and indeed of the Constitution itself. This is made clear by the regularity of split decisions when a panel of judges—the supposed experts on the meaning of law on the books—interpret legislation.[74]

While all of this may be true, it does not mean that anything goes. Actors in positions of authority, whether judges or employers, can't do whatever they wish.[75] While judges and administrators have a great deal of freedom, they must operate within boundaries of legitimacy, and they typically agree on most of these boundaries.[76]

In many instances, these shared legal understandings can be quite at variance with everyday practices. The social scientist Kitty Calavita, for example, has highlighted many of these persistent gaps between common legal understandings and everyday practices in a wide variety of areas.[77] She argues that we should seek to explain the gaps between law as it is understood by legal elites and the practical application of law in everyday life, because this can "provide us with clues not just about the workings of law but about the workings of society itself."[78] I would add that understanding and reducing the gap between civil rights law and employment practices is important to prevent arbitrary enforcement of the law (which is an injustice in itself, and at best confusing to employers and employees) and to ensure that racial realism is not practiced in a way that denies basic equal opportunities (more on this below).

Moreover, the widespread advocacy of racial realism suggests a dynamic different from that identified in most research on the relationship between law and society. Regarding today's workplace, employers and policy elites regularly advocate for racial realism, while the courts and the EEOC promote classical liberalism and affirmative-action liberalism (see table 3). This is quite different from what we see in many law/practice gaps, where elites are not involved in advocacy (for example, mainstream elites do not promote the widespread use of officially illegal

TABLE 3
Society, Elites, and Law

	Is the practice common?	Do elites promote it?	Do courts/ agencies affirm?
"Victimless crime" (drugs, prostitution)	Yes	No	No
Organizations' symbolic civil rights compliance measures	Yes	Yes	Yes
Racial realism in employment	Yes	Yes	No or rarely

prostitution or recreational drugs). In other cases, nonlegal actors make *de facto* law, establishing new norms that fill in spaces of ambiguity, and then (eventually) law as written in statues, regulations, or court decisions catches up.[79] For instance, a vision of law may emerge in corporate practices—and then the EEOC or the courts or both affirm that practice, giving it the imprimatur of "the law." We can see this in the ways that organizations have developed symbolic forms of compliance with classical liberalism or affirmative-action liberalism.[80]

By contrast, when it comes to racial realism, employers are not making *de facto* law. They may be constructing "legality,"[81] and establishing practices that many believe are legal, but these practices do not fit with the law as the legal establishment defines it, and in some cases, they flatly contradict recent court decisions, including those by the Supreme Court. What's more, this is occurring not in the shadows, but often openly and loudly, in broad daylight. It may be that the courts will get around to affirming racial realism in employment, but that has not happened yet.

What's at Stake? Why Should We Care?

Should we care about how well law fits the racial realism of American workplaces? I think so. I believe this is an important matter for several reasons.

First, we should care because the greatest conflicts in American history have been, in fundamental ways, about race.[82] The nation's founding documents expressed aspirations for equal opportunity and equal rights, but at the same time the brutal domination and genocide of the indigenous population of North America and the early introduction of slavery were realities.[83] The French social theorist Alexis de Tocqueville predicted as far back as the early 1800s that white Americans would struggle violently with racial difference, and that they would likely seek to exterminate the indigenous population (he was right about that) and would one day replace slavery with another system of racial domination (right again).[84] We now seem far from the days of mass racial bloodshed, but the past serves as a warning of the high stakes involved when race is at issue. The country almost fell apart over the question of slavery in the Civil War, which takes second place to World War II in the number of American war dead, but in terms of percentage of the population killed was more than five times as devastating.[85] The civil rights movement and the racial violence of the late 1960s brought another period of bloodshed and national soul-searching. As recently as 1992, the city of Los Angeles burned for four days in another round of racial violence.[86] The U.S. recently has enjoyed a few decades of racial calm, but a growing body of comparative research shows that while racial or ethnic diversity does not invariably lead to conflict, the ways that governments manage this diversity can mean the difference between cooperation and civil war.[87] Put simply and perhaps somewhat dramatically, rule of law on racial issues is a matter of life and death.

Also at stake is the proper role of government regarding its citizens, an issue that is anything but straightforward. Economists and demographers regularly show that mass immigration is a net positive for the nation, though the benefits may be small, and both benefits and costs fall unevenly on different groups.[88] In an era of economic restructuring and mass immigration, there are many potential goals for policy, many possible ways to benefit the country, and as these ideas are put into practice there may be winners and losers. The clearest example is in the widespread preferences that employers show for hiring immigrants over American workers for low-skilled jobs. As I show in Chapter 5, there is considerable evidence that America now has a declining supply of capable low-skilled workers in a variety of occupations: agriculture, food service, cleaning, and manufacturing. Yet it is also true that millions of Americans are unemployed or underemployed. Should policymakers be helping citizens and ensuring everyone has the right or opportunity for a job, or should they focus on increasing economic growth—and expect those who lose out to simply find their own way?

A third issue at stake is more abstract: respect for the rule of law. It is common for there to be a great discrepancy between the law on the books and what is practiced, but that does not mean we should not be worried about it. The Supreme Court has, in fact, evinced concern regarding a comparable gap between law and practice in another context. When the Court struck down laws banning sodomy in 2003, it cited the argument of the American Law Institute that having laws on the books that forbid practices that were actually quite common undermines respect for law and leads to arbitrary enforcement.[89] The widespread practice of racial realism may similarly undermine respect for the law, lead to arbitrary enforcement, and create an unpredictable litigation environment.

Finally, America's commitment to equal opportunity is at stake. It may seem to be a win-win situation when employers utilize the racial abilities and signaling of employees, as it provides opportunities for nonwhites that may not otherwise exist and may benefit clients and citizens. The problem is that racial realism can also limit an employee's opportunities for transfer or promotion: Why move a nonwhite employee to a position where race provides no extra benefits? In effect, racial realism can provide both a "golden door" of opportunity and a "glass ceiling" limiting mobility.[90]

Thus, how policymakers respond to racial realism will determine whether it is possible for employment regulations to recognize race in a nonhierarchical way that still provides for equal opportunity. Legal and political theorists have debated this issue intensely. For example, Deborah Malamud has noted that equality problems can even arise when employers pursue racial diversity for overall organizational dynamism, which is probably the most benign form of racial realism because it does not pigeonhole or ghettoize nonwhites. But, Malamud points out, nonwhites will often be expected to do the jobs that whites do while *also* contributing their racial abilities, with the result that they do more work than whites.[91] Martha Minow critiques what I am calling here racial realism from an equality perspective when she describes the "dilemma of difference": "When does treating people differently emphasize their differences and stigmatize or hinder them on that basis? And when does treating people the same become insensitive to their difference and likely to stigmatize or hinder them on *that* basis?"[92] Peter Schuck emphasizes the importance of finding the right balance: law should protect existing diversities from discrimination, but should not compel diversity, because when it does so, it renders diversity "illegitimate" and "inauthentic."[93] There are no easy answers to these questions, and this is why it is essential that we have a clear and comprehensive picture of how employers manage racial difference in the twenty-first century.

Why Is There Racial Realism? A Brief Look at Causes

The purpose of this book is to show that there are advocates for a racial-realist strategy of employment, to identify racial-realist employment practices, to identify the relationship of that vision to law, and to suggest possibilities for reform. Though the purpose here is not to explain the factors that brought about the rise of racial realism, a summary of that story will help to frame the empirical and legal chapters that follow. Race has mattered to American employers since the beginning of the Republic, but some recent and very big changes have added new complexity.

The first causal factor is *demographic*. Simply put, America is more racially diverse than ever before. By the late twentieth century, America was beginning to receive immigrants not just from a variety of countries, but from different *continents*. Today America is more Asian than ever before, and it is also more African, Caribbean, and Latin American. A few years after the Civil Rights Act passed, African-Americans made up about 11 percent of the U.S. population, while Latinos were only 5 percent and Asians 1 percent. By 2010, the percentage of black Americans had increased slightly to 13 percent, but the percentage of Latinos had more than tripled, to 16 percent, and Asians numbered 5 percent of the population.[94] Moreover, the geography of immigration has changed, transforming nearly all parts of the country in the last few decades rather than just a few states.[95]

These demographic changes were themselves the result of several forces. Perhaps the most obvious force was the Immigration and Nationality Act of 1965, which ended national origin discrimination in American immigration law and made family reunification the largest visa category.[96] This ended the almost total exclusion of Asians from the U.S. Though the act put quotas on each country's number of immigrants and also established overall quotas for immigration, it allowed American citizens and permanent residents to sponsor family members for visas—and immediate family members were exempt from quotas. Moreover, the law gave some preference to immigrants with skills, a provision that benefited Asians, many of whom had education but no family connections in America. These provisions set off vigorous chain migrations, as green-card holders could sponsor spouses and unmarried children under twenty-one, while naturalized citizens could also sponsor parents and siblings. Even this was not enough to satisfy labor demand, however, and millions of immigrants crossed the border without authorization. Eventually, about eleven million immigrants, or one-third of America's total immigrant population, were undocumented.[97] Whatever their legal status, these new immigrants created new markets for firms to exploit and new populations for governments to service.

The movement toward immigrant-dominated sectors of the low-skilled workforce on a national scale came about as a result of another kind of demographic change. As I show in Chapter 2, many unskilled jobs, especially outside of urban areas, used to attract young people. Today, however, families have fewer children, and so there are simply fewer nonimmigrant white bodies for many of these jobs. For example, jobs on dairy farms, large and small, now sometimes rely heavily on immigrant labor rather than on the local workers who supplied the needed hands for generations.[98] There is nothing particularly surprising about this pattern, which can be seen all over the world. As women become more educated and develop careers, the desire for large families declines.[99] The American fertility rate declined from a high of almost 3.8 children per mother in the 1950s to 1.7 in the 1970s, though it has now rebounded to 1.9.[100]

What is more, all Americans (not just women) are on average better educated than they used to be, which further drains the pool of workers available for dirty, boring and/or difficult jobs. The percentage of Americans with the educational profile to match these jobs has shrunk quite dramatically.[101] Demographer Frank Bean and his colleagues have shown that the percentage of Americans over the age of twenty-five (that is, of prime working age) with a bachelor's degree was only about 5 percent in 1950. By 2010, it was closer to 30 percent. Looked at another way, Bean and his colleagues show that in 1950, nearly 80 percent of the U.S. workforce over 25 had less than a high school education. By 2010, that percentage had fallen to about 10 percent.[102] These demographic changes created a demand for low-skilled immigrant labor, creating the conditions where employers would valorize the abilities of Latino and Asian immigrants especially. By 2000, immigrants were already filling a significant part of the secondary labor market workforce: one in five low-wage workers was foreign born, and two in five workers with less than a high school degree was foreign born.[103]

The second causal force for the rise of racial (and immigrant) realism was *economic*. Though scholars and other observers debate the origins of the trend, it is clear that by the latter half of twentieth century, a "deindustrialization of America" was underway. As the economists Barry Bluestone and Bennett Harrison described this process, profits in the formerly stable and unionized manufacturing sector of the economy began to shrink in the late 1960s and worsened in the 1970s as the nation faced unprecedented international competition in the manufacture of electronics, automobiles, and other durable goods. To maintain profits, American firms turned on their unionized workers, threatening to move their operations in search of cheaper labor unless the unions agreed to limits on wages. Developments in the 1980s in technology, especially in the use of computers, allowed operations to be spread out over the country, which gave firms more leverage to say "take it or leave it" to their workers. They could also play different struggling localities against one another, as suitors for new plants offered tax breaks or help with infrastructure development in order to attract a new plant. The most attractive locations were typically in low-wage, nonunionized sections of the South. If conditions could not be found in the U.S., firms simply moved production offshore.[104]

As sociologist William Julius Wilson has noted, these developments decimated the manufacturing base of the U.S. Between 1967 and 1987, Philadelphia, Chicago, Detroit, and New York City all lost between 51 and 64 percent of their manufacturing jobs. There were new jobs for those without a college education, but they were mostly in the "secondary labor market"—in small, seasonal manufacturing jobs, or in the growing service and retail sectors—and these were far less likely to pay a living wage.[105] Consider the explosive growth in the low-wage restaurant sector: the National Restaurant Association projected 2010 sales at $580 billion—about 13 times greater than 1970's $43 billion. Restaurants now employ 9 percent of the U.S. workforce.[106]

These economic changes contributed to a voracious demand for low-skilled immigrant labor, and immigrants, some legal and some illegal, arrived ready to fill this demand. They found employers who were happy to hire them—as was also the case in the previous wave of immigration, a century earlier. In diverse manufacturing and service sectors, employers perceived Latinos and Asians as the best low-skilled workers. Sociologists and economists, as I show in Chapter 5, have amply documented the racial hierarchy that governed employers' preferences for filling dirty, difficult, and dangerous jobs. Employers ranked Latinos (from Central and

South America rather than Puerto Rico or the Dominican Republic) and Asians above American blacks, and often above whites as well. Increasingly, employers behave according to market principles: they find the best worker for the cheapest price, and endlessly repeat whatever hiring strategy they think works best.

Like the ripples made by a stone thrown into a pond, the demographic and economic changes at the low end of the job market then impacted the more skilled jobs. The explosive growth in the numbers of nonwhites created new consumer markets for countless firms, and also created new populations to be policed, schooled, cared for, entertained, informed, and courted for votes.

In high-skilled and many professional jobs, a third contributing factor was *organizational*. Part of this story relates to a change that occurred in corporate America. As sociologists such as Frank Dobbin, Erin Kelly, and Lauren Edelman and her colleagues have shown, big businesses across America began to comply with the new civil rights and affirmative-action legal regimes in the 1970s. However, following the Reagan administration's relaxing of the enforcement of Title VII and affirmative-action regulations, personnel and human resources professionals in large companies—many of whom worked in "equal employment opportunity" (EEO) offices created to coordinate legal compliance—developed a rationale for their role that no longer hinged on federal enforcement efforts. By the late 1980s, along with consultants and academics, they developed the theory of "diversity management," which held that racial, gender, and other forms of diversity could be a net positive for an organization if correctly managed.[107] What was significant about this development for racial realism, as I show in Chapter 2, is that these efforts infused race with usefulness: diversity management was now important in part because different races brought productivity-enhancing new ideas and new perspectives to organizations.

A fourth factor in the creation of modern racial realism was *political*. As I show in Chapters 2 to 4, in a variety highly skilled employment sectors, change came about as a result of political pressure. Civil rights groups were active in the fields of medicine, education, policing, and media and entertainment. A tremendously powerful motive force was the threat of increasing racial violence in the wake of the widespread racial riots and rebellions of the 1960s. In some specialized occupations, such as medicine, advocates and activists used evidence culled from the social sciences to encourage efforts to match professionals with the clients (or patients) they served.

Also, as I show in Chapter 3, leaders of both political parties—though slow to catch on—ultimately saw that strategically managing the race of their appointments and party spokespersons was in their electoral interests. They set a tone at the top, proudly proclaiming that racial diversity was a good thing for America as they showed off the different racial backgrounds of their various appointees.

Other factors in the political story relate to strategic decisions *not* to act. First, despite past conflict on immigration issues and some evidence that many African-Americans believe immigration limits black opportunity,[108] civil rights organizations, as Rodney Hero and Robert Preuhs have shown, have largely supported the immigration priorities of Latino organizations in recent years.[109] The other key example of political non-action is conservative organizations' decision not to target racial realism in employment in their litigation strategies (more on this below).

A final set of factors is *legal*, stemming from actions in the federal courts, which are of course closely bound to the political factors. The courts' role in the rise of racial realism is complex, and in some ways quite subtle, because there is no evidence of a fully developed legal doctrine for racial realism behind the courts' rulings.

We should first recognize that a key reason why the courts played a role in racial realism was that, while both parties talked about the benefits of racial diversity and made racially strategic appointments, neither political party offered *policy* leadership on the issue, in effect ceding the whole issue to the courts.[110] Since the mid-1970s, Democrats have avoided progressive stands on civil rights issues for fear of losing working-class white votes.[111] Republicans welcomed the white Southern and working-class voters, but other than practicing a rhetorical politics of racial resentment, they have taken little action to retrench civil rights policies, primarily due to a fear of appearing racist and alienating moderate voters. Instead, Republicans have appointed conservatives to the federal courts, most prominently the Supreme Court, so that judges can do the retrenching while the national party itself avoids blame.[112]

So what did the Supreme Court do in its role as civil rights policymaker? First, in a series of cases over the past few decades (all 5-to-4 decisions), the Supreme Court has, as Republican presidents intended, slowly curtailed the use of affirmative-action liberalism in a variety of contexts. Two key rulings focused on government contracting preferences for firms owned by minorities. The Court ruled that governments wishing to use affirmative action in this way had to pass "strict scrutiny" in order to do so—that is, they had to demonstrate that the preferences were necessary to achieve a compelling purpose. For the Court, that compelling purpose had to be compensating for past discrimination by the specific government institution practicing the affirmative action.[113] While the aforementioned *Grutter v. Bollinger* decision, stating that some types of racial preferences were constitutional in university admissions when implemented to achieve a diverse student body, would seem to stand as an important counter-example, the Court has applied strict scrutiny to limit affirmative-action liberalism in other education cases, and therefore limited the impact of *Grutter*. For example, in a 2007 case regarding disputes in Seattle and Louisville school districts, the Court's majority ruled that the school districts did not demonstrate that their methods of assigning students to schools on the basis of their race was necessary to achieve a compelling interest.[114] In the words of one legal scholar, the ruling "stifled" the expansive possibilities of the Court's decision in *Grutter* by likely confining it to the higher education context.[115] More recently, the Supreme Court ruled on another admissions case, and appeared to limit the use of race even in the context of higher education admissions. This time a seven-justice majority insisted that universities using racial preferences must be able to demonstrate to courts not only that their goal is diversity, but that there are no workable race-neutral policies that would lead to the same educational benefits.[116]

Another case, this one focused on employment, was significant because it also limited affirmative-action liberalism. More specifically, it narrowed the use of disparate impact law to justify considering race in employment. The case involved the New Haven, Connecticut fire department, which, fearing a lawsuit from African-Americans, sought to throw out the results of an ability test when no African-Americans scored high enough for promotion. The Court ruled that the fire department lacked a strong basis in evidence for fearing a legal challenge, and therefore its "express, race-based decisionmaking violates Title VII's command that employers cannot take adverse employment actions because of an individual's race."[117]

There is reason to think that the Supreme Court's increasing constraints on the use of affirmative action actually encourage racial-realist strategies in the nation's workplaces.[118] However, in its only ruling on racial realism in employment, the Supreme Court was also mostly negative. That case, *Wygant v. Jackson Board of Education*,[119] discussed in detail in Chapter 3, focused on racial signaling in the employment of teachers. It stated unequivocally that teachers cannot be hired to be racial role models. There remains some amount of ambiguity for racial realism, however, because of the narrow focus of that ruling on teaching.

Why is there so much ruling on education, and so little guidance from the Supreme Court on racial realism in employment, and especially private employment? There are, I believe, two main reasons. First, the Court can only rule on the cases that come to it, and there have been relatively few challenges to employment racial realism. Though I explore the legal rules derived from a great many lower-court cases in the pages that follow, these cases are close to the entire universe of court rulings on employment racial realism, and there are no obvious disputes between circuits that cry out for Supreme Court adjudication. Thus, though there are countless employment rulings on various technical issues related to the use of evidence, who has standing to litigate, what counts as an adverse employment action, etc.,[120] the prominence in the national discourse and the nation's workplaces of racial realism has not translated into a flurry of grass roots, individual legal challenges. The result is that both the practice of racial realism and its advocacy have space to continue—even in teaching, where the Supreme Court has said they must stop.

The second reason for the lack of Supreme Court action on racial realism in employment is that conservative legal organizations have not made it a target in their litigation strategy similar to what they have done with university admissions. This inaction itself stems from two main causes. The first is ideological. Two of the key organizations fighting race preferences in the courts, the Center for Individual Rights (CIR) and the Cato Institute, have (unlike the Republican Party) a libertarian focus and so have concentrated on discrimination by public institutions. For example, CIR, which describes its mission as "the defense of individual liberties against the increasingly aggressive and unchecked authority of federal and state governments,"[121] has litigated against preferences in twenty-four cases, but only four were specifically about employment, all targeting the government and none of them involving racial realism. They have supported litigation challenging racial realism in university admissions instead. Cato is similarly uninterested in challenging private employment practices, believing instead that employers should have discretion to do what they please.[122]

The other factor preventing conservative legal organizations from taking on employment racial realism is practical. CIR was originally focused on constitutional law, because, in the words of CIR founder, Michael Greve, "On any other issue, the regulatory state will eat you alive."[123] CIR instead used its limited resources to go after universities on free speech issues and affirmative action. The difficulty and expense of litigation involving the Civil Rights Act of 1964 was just too daunting.[124]

Roger Clegg, president and general counsel of the Center for Equal Opportunity, an organization opposed to affirmative action, has provided more insight into the difficulties of civil rights litigation strategies focused on employment. He argues that employment preferences are "less overt" than those practiced in university admissions, which enables employers to deny that they are actually using any racial preference when they hire, fire, or place an employee. They may claim that they stress race only in the recruitment phase of employment. In other words, "that it's harder to bring these cases helps explain why there are not more of them."[125]

Besides Supreme Court inaction on racial realism, a second legal factor that has allowed racial realism and its advocacy to flourish is more obvious: there are those rare instances when lower courts have acted to *authorize* racial realism. In a handful of cases, courts made law in creative new ways in this highly controversial area. As I note in the chapters that follow, while restriction of affirmative action has been mostly the work of judges appointed by Republicans, case law specifically enabling racial realism has been a bipartisan undertaking: judges appointed by both Democratic and Republican presidents have played roles. There are no partisan fingerprints on this judicial enabling, nor does there seem to be a pattern on the cases that specifically deny it.

How did judges create new law? They could do this for several reasons. Judges have considerable freedom to interpret statutes, and they may do so as urged by litigants or activists, or as directed by their own ideology. In legal scholars' strongest arguments on this point, judges simply choose precedents to fit the argument they want to make rather than making decisions based on precedents.[126] Political scientist Shep Melnick argues that shifts in legal interpretation occur particularly when the statutes are vaguely written.[127] This was certainly the case in the early years of Title VII, which did not even define the term "discrimination." In addition, as legal scholar William Eskridge has noted, statutes are based on assumptions that may "unravel over time" because culture, institutions, and expert opinion may change; courts therefore interpret them dynamically.[128] This point would seem to fit well with Title VII, written fifty years ago for a far less diverse population.

What is odd in the case of racial realism is that many of the arguments regarding judicial creativity stress *statutory* interpretation, but for racial realism, the clearest enabling decisions have been *constitutional*. This may be surprising because courts are less likely to engage in adventurous interpretation of the Constitution than of statutes.[129] In Chapter 3, I describe a series of Fourteenth Amendment cases that allow an "operational needs" defense to law-enforcement institutions (and only law-enforcement institutions) to hire and place nonwhites—even if those nonwhites resist. In Chapter 4, I describe one federal district court case establishing a precedent that the First Amendment's free expression protection allows racial realism in casting. Title VII's lack of a BFOQ defense for race has proven to be too limiting on statutory interpretation. The two Title VII cases that have enabled racial realism did so only indirectly, by allowing a particular worker recruitment method. As I discuss in Chapter 5, these cases appeared to go against Title VII precedent and EEOC guidelines to allow greater employer discretion to use word-of-mouth hiring to remake their workforces with Latino and Asian low-skilled immigrants.[130]

All of these various factors—demographic, economic, organizational, political and legal—combined to slowly enable or encourage the advocacy and practice of racial realism described in the next four chapters. The complexity of their possible combinations also helps explain why this strategy for managing race arose without debate, direction, or analysis.

Some Notes on a Conceptual Framework and Methods

This book is about the meaning of "race"—a term that for decades has been controversial in the social sciences. The thrust of much recent theorizing has been to deny the existence of "race" or "racial groups" as such, or at least to emphasize their cultural nature. Race, in this view, is something that needs to be explained, not something that explains other things.[131]

I share with these scholars the notion that there is nothing necessary or natural about race, and that racial categories change over time and vary in different places. My interest in this book, however, is not in the origins of the racial understandings of employers (though that would make for an interesting project). I want to show that for many employers, as well as for various other interests concerned, for whatever reason, race matters in racial-realist ways, and that this has complex and important implications for civil rights law. In the sections of the book where I describe racial realism advocacy and practices, therefore, "race" connotes the largely ascriptive and incoherent collection of folk understandings that employers mean by their use of the word—what David Hollinger has called the "ethno-racial pentagon" of American Indian, Asian, black, Latino, and white.[132] Though increasing immigration and intermarriage are blurring America's color lines and destabilizing America's "racial order," there is not yet much evidence that employers care about whether employees are mixed-race or how races are arranged in any power hierarchy outside of their own workplace.[133]

The concept of race is hardly more developed in employment discrimination law. Title VII does not define race. The EEOC says what race is not ("Race and ethnic designations as used by the Equal Employment Opportunity Commission do not denote scientific definitions of anthropological origins"), and then outlines how various regional ancestries fit into each category ("White" means "having origins in any of the original peoples of Europe, the Middle East, or North Africa").[134] Employers are told that in addition to not discriminating on the basis of race, they must not discriminate on the basis of an employee's partner's race, or on the basis of "cultural practices or characteristics often linked to race or ethnicity," such as dress or speech, and that "discrimination on the basis of an immutable characteristic associated with race, such as skin color, hair texture, or certain facial features violates Title VII, even though not all members of the race share the same characteristic."[135]

There is a related issue here regarding Latinos and national-origin discrimination. Is an employer who leverages the utility of Latino identities practicing *racial* realism, or something else? In official government statistics, Latinos are an ethnicity and not a race.[136] However, EEOC instructions for classifying employees long treated "Hispanic" as a category identical to "black" or "white," and only since the late 2007 did they begin to require that employers treat "Hispanic or Latino" background as an ethnicity.[137] Even now this category has a racial character because employees who select "Hispanic" or "Latino" are counted separately from whites, blacks, and Asians.[138] Moreover, the EEOC *Compliance Manual* discusses discrimination against Latinos in both its race and national origin discussions, noting that "discrimination based on physical traits or ancestry may be both national origin and racial discrimination."[139] In addition, some researchers argue that for many Latinos in America, "Latino" is effectively a racial identity, because various micro-processes involved in the daily life of living in the United States have helped create the notion of "Latino" or "Hispanic" as a discrete race, separate from "black" and "white."[140] Larger forces, including the media, contributed as well to the view of Latinos as a discrete, racial category.[141] Regardless of how Latinos see themselves, the issue in discrimination law is how *employers* see them, and throughout this book, the discourse surrounding Latinos, Hispanics, and even more specific groupings (e.g., Mexicans or Puerto Ricans) is a racial discourse that typically counterposes them with whites and blacks.[142]

Related to the conceptual issues regarding race is the issue of employers perceiving that some workers have special abilities to work in low-skilled jobs by virtue of their foreign-born status. As described briefly above, there is little doubt that employers do sometimes perceive immigrant status as a qualification for some jobs, and that it is this status rather than race that suggests the special abilities. There is thus an "immigrant realism" apart from and in addition to a racial realism. As I show in Chapter 5, this approach to hiring and placement is, like racial realism, not authorized by any statute or court ruling, and therefore appears also to be a legal violation. However, while analytically distinct from race, immigrant realism often has a racial component. Employers sometimes show slippage and inconsistent language when talking about immigrant or nonimmigrant employees: they may speak in terms of national origin groups (e.g., "Chinese") or they may use pan-ethnic or racial terms (e.g., "Asian"). Even when valorizing immigrant abilities, they may be perceiving the workers through a racial lens when, for example, they compare "Mexicans" or "immigrants" to "blacks" and "whites."[143]

An important caveat or explanation is in order in this discussion of race. I focus on racial realism that lauds the abilities or signaling of *non*whites. This focus is not meant to deny that *whiteness* continues to matter most in employment. In fact, overwhelming evidence shows that discrimination against people of color is still an enormous problem, as I have discussed above. I focus on nonwhite racial realism for the important reason that it is nonwhite races that are explicitly a part of the racial-realist strategy. Employers, advocates, experts, political leaders all openly discuss the benefits flowing from the employment of nonwhites. They say little about whiteness. No mainstream advocates are (yet) discussing seriously strategies of managing race that place importance on the abilities or signaling of whites. I do discuss white racial abilities and white signaling when it is especially salient (such as in entertainment, and in a few contexts in business employment), but since it is not a part of the racial-realist vision that many people normatively want for the country, it is not a focus of analysis here.

A final note on race: I use the terms "black" and "African-American" interchangeably. I use "Latino" to describe persons with ancestry from

Latin America, though some of the speakers or other sources that I quote use the term "Hispanic."

In designing this study, I have aimed for a policy-oriented, "big picture" synthesis of findings in social science and legal scholarship. Researching employment practices that may be beyond the law is not easy. Employers are not always willing to talk, and their approach to questions varies from uninhibited to evasive.[144] Fortunately, there is a vast amount of excellent social science scholarship on employment, and much of it has not up to now been connected to the work on employment law in a comprehensive way. Still, in many cases, we have only the words of employers and various advocates regarding their intentions in hiring, and some data on the employment picture for different races. Though I present what data are available, it is not possible to offer a solid estimate of the extent to which certain employment practices are widespread, institutionalized, or even supported. I do believe, however, that the following chapters will make clear that support for racial realism is significant, and that it comes from employers and advocates with a variety of interests and from a diverse array of sectors. These practices are considered normal by mainstream and often elite voices throughout American society, despite their limited legal authorization, and that is a key point of the book.

The choice of cases analyzed here is based on a mix of factors: their intrinsic importance either in daily life or because of the functions they perform for government or industry; the amount of existing social science evidence and analysis; the amount and urgency of advocacy for racial realism; and the distinctiveness of the legal context. These are not the only cases where racial realism plays a role in employment. There are others with potentially interesting racial-realist dynamics that I could not include—for example, the military, bureaucrats and administrators in government, attorneys, and people involved in workforce recruiting.

The Plan of the Book

The next four chapters are empirical and have a similar organization. They are based on the specific legal regime that governs the employment sectors in question: high-skilled and professional employment; government employment; entertainment and media; and low-skilled employment. In each, I mostly stick to a common format. First, I describe the employment practices and/or advocacy in the relevant sectors of employment, showing the various ways that a strategy of racial realism motivates or would motivate hiring, worker placement, and firing. I then review whether or not social science evidence supports the assumptions motivating this hiring: does race really provide the benefits that employers believe it does? In every case, there is mixed but still not insignificant evidence that employers do achieve their goals by hiring with race as a job qualification. I conclude by exploring the court decisions and EEOC guidelines regulating the relevant sectors of employment, showing the limited extent to which law can authorize or support racial realism.

Chapter 2 examines racial realism in white-collar and professional employment. I focus on medicine, journalism, and marketing, providing evidence of the strong support for hiring on the basis of racial abilities and signaling in these jobs. I also show the support for the racial abilities and signaling that make racial "diversity" attractive to corporate employers. When it comes to legal authorization for racial realism, there is surprisingly little in this sector, as the courts have refused to allow a race BFOQ, and they have not modified rulings that prohibit customer tastes as a justification for racial discrimination. Another key legal obstacle here is that courts have not allowed voluntary affirmative action to be motivated by racial-realist goals.

Chapter 3 focuses on government employment. I begin at the top, because political elites set the tone for America. I show that politicians do not practice what they preach: they may give rhetorical support to classical liberalism, but both parties commonly follow racial-realist logics when appointing government officials, including judges. I then show the long and prominent support given to racial realism in policing and education. The chapter concludes with an analysis of the constitutional jurisprudence that has authorized racial realism in law enforcement but barred it in other sectors, including education.

Chapter 4 explores racial realism in the advertising and entertainment industries (movies, TV, and professional sports). These cases are distinctive because they are almost totally focused on racial signaling—the image of the worker is very much the product that the employers are selling. Racial signaling is thus common in all of them, though rarer in sports than the other sectors, especially in the last few decades. In film, television, and advertising, racial preferences in hiring are widespread and blatant, including in casting calls. I show that Title VII law does not authorize these practices. I also examine the possibility that television shows' dependence on use of federally-regulated airwaves, and sports teams' dependence on the public financing of stadiums might provide legal openings for racial realism in these sectors. Since this employment sector is about expression, I explore possible First Amendment defenses for these employers, and show that at least one court has found a constitutionally-protected freedom to discriminate.

Chapter 5 focuses on low-skilled employment. I show that employers have a racial hierarchy of preference and that they rely on word-of-mouth hiring to attract Latino and Asian workers with the racial and/or immigrant abilities they prize. I give special attention to meatpacking, a sector that has been racially remade in the past few decades. I then explore the ways Title VII should prevent this kind of hiring, which is more clearly based on crude racial stereotypes than the preferential hiring in skilled sectors, and I point out that it has for the most part been ineffective despite some recent EEOC victories. I show how judges have in fact created new opportunities for employers to use word-of-mouth hiring to build and maintain their Latino and Asian workforces without running afoul of the law. This chapter also shows how two other laws, the Immigration Reform and Control Act and the Racketeer Influenced and Corrupt Organizations Act, would seem to prohibit immigrant realism but have nonetheless failed.

The concluding Chapter 6 suggests several possible principles for reform that could guide attempts to bring law and practice closer together in a way that accepts at least some racial realism but is also in line with American values. These emphasize efforts to keep jobs open to all, encouraging employers and the government to have awareness of and take responsibility for the negative impacts of racial-realist management strategies, and efforts to shape the regulatory incentive structure so as to encourage movement toward these goals.

Leverage: Racial Realism in the Professions and Business

Racial realism looks different in different employment sectors, but if there is a purest or most typical sector, it would be in skilled private employment—the professions and business. All of the most basic dynamics and dilemmas can be found here.

Here we see both types of racial realism, and different approaches to racial abilities specifically. Most commonly employers perceive that workers have specific racial abilities that help them excel in the provision of services to those of their own race. We therefore see a matching dynamic—African-Americans performing services for African-Americans, Asians for Asians, and so on. In some cases, employers and other advocates do not link racial abilities to particular jobs or particular customer bases but instead believe that racial diversity benefits a firm because it fosters new ideas and dynamism.

The role of race in this process is not theorized deeply, and it sometimes appears to be a proxy for culture or experience, but race nevertheless becomes a kind of job qualification. Employers believe that some races can do things that other races cannot, and that their strategic management of race can therefore affect performance and profits. This is what employers mean when, as I show below, they talk about "leveraging" diversity.

In the professions and business, we also see (though to a lesser extent) the other major mode of racial realism: racial signaling. Employers may have no opinion on the actual abilities of employees of one race or another, but they may be concerned that customers are more responsive to professionals of their own race because they are more at ease with them or trust them more. Concerns regarding racial signaling to *other employees* can also affect who gets hired or placed: if a firm wants to send a signal to the workforce that racial diversity is valued, for example, who better to do that than workers of racially diverse origins placed in high visibility positions? As with racial abilities, here again the race of job applicants and employees becomes a qualification in ways that do not fit with classical liberalism or affirmative-action liberalism. The bottom line is that the strategic management of race can affect performance and profit.

Other themes that appear in other chapters are also apparent here. One is the nature of the social science evidence on whether or not employers are right in thinking that racial realism is good strategy. In all cases, the evidence is mixed, varying somewhat from context to context, as different tendencies and patterns emerge, but still showing considerable support for the strategy.

Another pattern here, as elsewhere, is that the stakes are high for those concerned with providing equal opportunities for minorities. Racial realism can provide minority applicants with chances they might not otherwise have, if nonwhites have an advantage in getting hired. But if an employer prefers them for a specific job because of their race, that employer may also limit them to that specific job. As we will see, this can lead to segregation, stunted careers, and serious resentments.

In this chapter, I analyze the rise of racial realism in three key areas where it is especially prominent—medicine, journalism, and marketing—and also as a general organizational strategy. In each section, I also look at the evidence regarding the usefulness of racial realism. Finally, I assess the gap between practice and law in these sectors, showing that existing case law does not offer much support for racial realism. Its most obvious legal authorization would come from the BFOQ defense in Title VII, and affirmative-action law. The problems here are straightforward. First, even if racial abilities and racial signaling *could* be considered to be BFOQs, there is no BFOQ for race. Second, the legal rules governing affirmative action demand that all affirmative-action programs use race only for remedial purposes. When the situation is viewed with a skeptical eye and from the perspective of classical liberalism, it appears that when employers seek out particular races for the benefits of "diversity" or when they racially match employees with clients, they often are hiring or placing employees based on stereotypes. Moreover, when it comes to racial signaling, employers may be violating Title VII because they are catering to discriminatory customer preferences.

Racial Abilities and Signaling for Better Health

Because there is a long and tragic history of racial discrimination in the provision of health care, a lot of money and time has been spent researching racial realism in medicine. Much of that research has been on the potential benefits of racial abilities and signaling in the physician-patient relationship. The primary question is simple: are nonwhite patients better served by physicians of their own race? Researchers refer to this kind of matching as "racial concordance," and advocacy for it is so strong as to be conventional wisdom in the medical field.

The Late Twentieth-Century Discovery of Racial Inequality in Health Care

One impetus to racial realism in medicine is the persistence of racial inequality in health indicators. Civil rights groups battled in this arena for years and finally found support from the federal government in 1985, when the Department of Health and Human Services (HHS) issued its *Report of the Secretary's Task Force on Black and Minority Health*.[1] This report put the issue in stark and memorable terms: each year 60,000 minority deaths occur that would not have occurred if the deceased had been white. This bold claim was derived from differences in mortality rates from a variety of killers, including cancer, cardiovascular disease, stroke, cirrhosis, diabetes, homicides, and accidents. The report spurred the creation, in 1986, of HHS's Office of Minority Health. In 1990, the National Institutes of Health (NIH) founded its own Office of Minority Programs, and the Health Revitalization Act of 1993 established, within NIH, the Office of Research on Minority Health.[2] Several states followed suit, setting up their own infrastructures to deal with minority health issues.[3]

Despite this progress, studies indicate that discrimination, substandard treatment, and unequal access to care continue to be serious problems. A study of California, for example, has shown that even after controlling for income, the numbers of doctors in a community is inversely related to the number of blacks and Latinos who live there.[4] Black patients are likely to face discrimination in such areas as admission to hospitals and bed assignments.[5] Minorities are less likely than whites to receive heart bypass surgery when conditions would call for it, less likely to receive pain management commensurate with symptoms, and more likely to undergo amputation.[6]

There are numerous other statistics that document inequalities in the health of nonwhites and add to the sense of urgency. Blacks continue to have a lower life expectancy than whites, and they are more likely to die from stroke, cancer, asthma complications, and diabetes. Both blacks and Native Americans have higher infant mortality rates. Blacks have higher rates of hypertension and heart disease, and black women are twice as likely as white women to die from cervical cancer.[7] Mexican Americans are more likely than white Americans to have uncontrolled hypertension; tuberculosis is more common among Asian-Americans, Latinos, and African-Americans than among whites; and African-Americans and Latinos are more likely than whites to report that they are in only fair or poor health.[8]

While these numbers seem clear enough, their relationship to the employment of white or nonwhite physicians is not. The first major issue is the small number of physicians who are not white or Asian. The paucity of black physicians is in part a legacy of deliberate discrimination by the medical establishment. The American Medical Association (AMA) unofficially excluded blacks until the civil rights era.[9] Medical schools limited admission of black students and most hospitals forced black doctors to work in segregated and substandard units. When trying to limit the numbers of doctors in order to raise their status in the early 1900s, the AMA targeted for closure most of the existing all-black medical schools.[10] Not until the 1960s did things change, and change came only after black physicians picketed AMA meetings.[11]

Growth in the number of black physicians was therefore very slow. In 1938, only 1.6 percent of all medical students were black (while blacks made up 10 percent of the overall population) and 87 percent of these attended a black medical school. While the numbers increased over the next few decades, the percentage of medical students who were black stayed below 3 percent until 1968, when the American Association of Medical Colleges began to encourage member schools to seek a target of 12 percent black students by the 1975–76 school year. The goal was not met. Blacks comprised only 6 percent of enrollments in 1977 and not quite 8 percent in 1997.[12]

Moreover, being a medical school student does not guarantee a career as a physician, and the most recent numbers reflecting racial diversity in the medical profession are not impressive. At the end of the first decade of the twenty-first century, African-Americans made up only 3.5 percent of the nearly one million physicians in the U.S. Latinos were at 4.9 percent, American or Alaskan Natives at 0.16 percent. Asians were at 12.2 percent, though their actual numbers may be different, as 23.4 percent of America's physicians are of "unknown race" (and 1.3 percent are "other").[13]

Support for Racial Realism in Medicine

Since the 1990s, there have been many elite and mainstream voices promoting the use of nonwhite physicians' racial abilities and (to a much lesser extent) racial signaling. Physicians, policymakers, healthcare administrators, and other high-profile advocates have united behind this strategy of managing race in the medical workplace. The urgency and common-sense quality of this advocacy can be seen in the views of Barbara Stern, a vice president at Harvard Pilgrim Health Care, a Boston-area HMO. She explained to *Fortune* magazine in 1996 that her company had a "diversity imperative" because "many of these customers demand health-care workers who aren't judgmental—and we have to make sure we provide them."[14]

Congress acted a few years later, adding further momentum to racial realism in medicine. There was no partisan or ideological resistance in response, nor did any controversy arise. The Minority Health and Health Disparities Research and Education Act of 2000, sponsored by Senator Edward Kennedy (D-MA), passed Congress with virtually no opposition.[15] On the Senate floor, Kennedy supported his call for the Act by citing the results of a study published in the *New England Journal of Medicine* that showed that white physicians were less likely to recommend certain medical procedures for African-Americans than they were for white Americans (see below).[16] The act contained two provisions premised on the notion that racial realism could help reduce disparities: grants were available only to institutions that had a "significant number" of minority students, and grant winners had to "train members of minority health disparity populations or other health disparity populations as professionals in the area of biomedical or behavioral research or both."[17]

The new legislation seemed to catalyze advocacy for racial realism in health care. The next decade saw several major foundations and other elite groups arguing for more nonwhite physicians for nonwhite patients. In 2002, for example, the Commonwealth Fund, a Washington, DC-based foundation pursuing better health care for disadvantaged people, published a report that concluded that health care needed "cultural competence" on the organizational, systemic, and clinical levels—and that this could be achieved through training, the provision of language interpreters, and of course, hiring more nonwhites to treat nonwhites.[18]

But probably the most forceful advocacy for racial realism in medicine, and particularly for the racial abilities of some physicians, came in 2004 from the high-profile Sullivan Commission on Diversity in the Healthcare Workforce, chaired by President George H. W. Bush's former Secretary of Health and Human Services, Louis W. Sullivan. Funded by the W. K. Kellogg Foundation, staffed by leaders in the fields of medicine, law, and medical insurance, and featuring another Republican, former Senate Majority Leader Bob Dole (R-KS) as an honorary cochair, the Sullivan Commission issued a report that made the case for racial realism at multiple parts of the medical education process.

Specifically, the commission argued that minority students in medicine "benefit greatly from mentoring by minority faculty," that minority health professionals keep health equity on the policy agenda, and that these professionals are also essential for health-care provision that is responsive to minority patients. The commission explained that nonwhites would also promote cultural competence at multiple levels. At the level of treatment, it was important to respond to cultural variations among patients and to nonwhites' distrust of the health-care system. After reviewing this evidence, the report stated: "The Commission believes that a unique level of connection is achieved when a provider has an inherent cultural affinity, shared social experiences, and perceived trustworthiness with a patient. Minority providers may identify with the understandings, experiences, and perceived barriers of patients of the same race or ethnicity."[19]

The Sullivan Commission expanded these arguments for racial abilities to include nonwhite medical professionals at the level of the health-care system: "When a health care organization is not racially and ethnically diverse, the cultural competence of its policies, programs, and processes are inherently and systematically compromised." This was because "minority health professionals" are able to bring "a unique sense of community-based cultural affinity and shared social experience to the organizational processes of system design, policy and procedure development, research, and other activities that support the effective cross-cultural operation of a health care system."[20] According to the commission, racial minorities aided the cause of "cultural competence" not only when interfacing with patients, but also in shaping the overall policy and strategy of health-care organizations: "Underrepresented minority health care professionals can enhance an organization's efforts to ensure staff and other service providers have the requisite attitudes, knowledge, and skills for delivering culturally competent care" and "can enhance the organization's goal-setting, policymaking, and other oversight vehicles in ways that promote cultural competence."[21]

Finally, in the view of this elite, high-profile commission, racial realism was not only a matter of better health. It was good business. The commission presented approvingly the view of Mark Jaffe, director of the Greater New York Chamber of Commerce, who reported that hospitals and health networks with more minority doctors were better able capture the minority market.[22]

Other voices and organizations have promoted physicians' racial abilities. Also in 2004, Dr. Lauren Oshman, president of the American Medical Student Association, an advocacy group, stated: "Diversifying the physician work force is a priority. . . . Minority patients are more likely to be satisfied with their care when treated by a physician of the same racial or ethnic background," because "physicians are more likely to understand patients who look and talk like them."[23] In that same year, in a report entitled *In the Nation's Compelling Interest*, the Institute of Medicine (a part of the National Academy of Sciences) pressed for more minorities in health because their increased inclusion would improve health care (specifically, by improving minority access, satisfaction, and educational experiences).[24] The following year, the American Hospital Association, a lobbying group representing five thousand hospitals, cited health disparities and called for increased minority employment in health care.[25]

In 2006, HHS issued a report examining evidence regarding racial realism in health care. It found (among other things) that minorities were more likely to serve in minority areas, and that physicians had racial abilities to deliver better care to patients who shared their race. Stating the matter most plainly, it concluded: "These findings indicate that greater health professions diversity will likely lead to improved public health by increasing access to care for underserved populations, and by increasing opportunities for minority patients to see practitioners with whom they share a common race, ethnicity or language. Race, ethnicity, and language concordance, which is associated with better patient-practitioner relationships and communication, may increase patients' likelihood of receiving and accepting appropriate medical care."[26]

Though emphasizing that all physicians should possess the necessary cultural competence to treat any patient, the American College of Physicians has also endorsed the importance of racial abilities in medicine. In 2010 its "Position Paper" on "Racial and Ethnic Disparities in Health Care" declared, "A diverse health care workforce that is more representative of the patients it serves is crucial to promote understanding among physicians and other health care professionals and patients, facilitate quality care, and promote equity in the health care system."[27]

How Common Is Racial Realism in Medicine?

There is little research on how many hospitals and medical groups recruit their staff or whether they see race as a qualification, but there are other ways to assess the sincerity of this advocacy. What evidence is available suggests that medical advocacy groups really do believe in the value of racial abilities and/or racial signaling, though they are not excelling at implementing these strategies.

The best indicator that these groups believe in racial realism is that they fight for it. Major medical associations have pressed their commitment to racial realism in amicus briefs to courts reviewing affirmative action in university and professional school admissions.[28] For example, several groups banded together to defend racial preferences in university admissions in the 2003 *Grutter v. Bollinger* case. A total of thirty groups signed on to the document, arguing for the necessity of a racially diverse medical corps. They included the American Medical Association, the Association of American Medical Colleges, several associations representing various medical specialties, as well as the American Dental Association, the American Association of Colleges of Pharmacy, and the American Association of Colleges of Nursing. The crux of their argument was that minority doctors are more likely to practice in geographic areas with more minorities, which "fills a real and pressing need within our health care system."[29] Regarding patient care, the brief stated that it was not necessary for minority physicians to treat minority patients, but nevertheless summarized the results of studies showing the benefits of racial concordance (see below), and concluded, "responding to consumer choice, particularly when it helps to increase patient satisfaction among those with the greatest need for improved health care, constitutes another significant justification for the consideration of race and ethnicity in the admissions process."[30] Finally, citing support from the National Institutes of Health and the Minority Health and Health Disparities Research Act (see below), the brief argued that the presence of minority researchers in the medical field will lead to the inclusion of minority health issues on to the national agenda.[31]

Major medical associations teamed up again in 2012 for the *Fisher v. University of Texas* case, and again defended the use of race in university admissions. In this case, however, while not denying the racial abilities or signaling of physicians, these organizations emphasized much more strongly the point most germane to this case—namely, the utility of race in the classroom, rather than for doctors. The brief argued that racial diversity in the classroom made all students more effective as physicians, explaining that one goal of valuing diversity in medical education was to change the reality that nonwhite physicians have a superior ability to treat nonwhite patients.[32]

Another indirect indicator of the practice of racial realism in medicine is the degree to which patients and physicians are matched by race. Different studies have yielded different conclusions. On the racial-realist side, for example, one study found that after controlling for socio-demographic factors such as education level and urban origins, nonwhites were two and a half times more likely than whites to have minority physicians.[33] Other studies have shown similar results for both blacks and Latinos. Specifically, black physicians had patients who were on average 56 percent black and Latino physicians had patients who were 30 percent Latino, while nonblack physicians had patients who were only 8 to 14 percent black and non-Latinos had patients who were only 6 to 9 percent Latino.[34] On the other hand, a more recent study of four thousand patients nationwide found that 82 percent of whites but only about a quarter of blacks and Latinos have racially concordant physicians.[35] While this may be an indicator of the general shortage of black and Latino physicians, another study suggests that this is not the case. After controlling for physician specialty, practice setting, and location, evidence of racial matching shrinks, sometimes to the point of statistical insignificance.[36] It appears, then, that racial realism in medicine is still the object of aspiration, rather than a description of reality—though race *and* class do come together in complex ways in the physician-patient relationship: according to one study of more than thirteen thousand physicians, minority physicians were twice as likely as nonminorities to practice in medically underserved areas.[37]

Does Physician Race Really Matter in Medicine?

Given the high stakes, it is not surprising that social scientists have given a lot of attention to the role of a physician's race in health outcomes. While not overwhelming, there is much evidence supporting the wisdom of racial realism in this context, and the federal government gives most weight to this evidence.

First, some research shows that race and ethnicity may matter in the doctor-patient encounter due to cultural differences in the ways different groups communicate about physical symptoms. For example, blacks and Latinos tend to express pain differently than whites, while some ethnic groups tend not to manifest pain at all, and these divergences may have negative impacts on physicians' confidence in their interpretation of clinical symptoms.[38] Blacks and whites also tend to show different understandings of the causes of mental illness. Blacks indicate less support than whites for genetic and family-based explanations, and more support for "chemical imbalances" and explanations based on life stresses. Given these differences in perceptions, African-Americans also tend to seek treatment for symptoms of mental illness less often than white Americans.[39]

Cultural variations also appear to contribute to one of the most consistent findings in the research on race and medical care: communication problems between racially different physicians and patients. For instance, a study of white and black patients matched with racially concordant physicians found they were more likely to say that they felt able to participate in decisions about their health care.[40] The race effect remained even after controlling for age, gender, marital status, education, health, and length of the relationship with the physician. Physician-patient gender pairings made no difference.[41] Other research has found that blacks and Latinos, who are less likely overall to have same-race doctors than whites or Asians, were also less likely to say that their physician explained things clearly or listened to their concerns.[42]

Not surprisingly, a comparison of black, white, and Latino patients also found greater levels of *satisfaction* when patients were racially matched with physicians, though there were subtle variations between groups. Blacks were most likely to be satisfied with the care that they received if they had a racially matched physician. Whites with white physicians were only more likely to say that their doctor listened to their concerns. Latinos with Latino physicians were more likely than other Latinos to report that they were satisfied with their overall health care, though they did not indicate greater satisfaction with their physicians specifically.[43] Another study found that visits with same-race physicians were longer than with physicians of a different race, and patients were more satisfied with them.[44] A study of black, Latino, and Asian patients found that respondents with a same-race physician were more likely to report satisfaction with the care they received, and also found that those who could choose the race of their physician were more likely to choose one of the same race.[45]

Researchers have found it difficult to identify objective differences in the interactions to explain the different patient ratings. Analysis of audiotapes of physician-patient encounters did not reveal significant differences in participatory decision-making in racially concordant or discordant encounters. This suggests the impact of racial signaling or, in the words of the researchers, that "race concordance has an independent effect on patients' judgment of the visit regardless of the verbal nature of the medical dialogue."[46]

More disturbing evidence includes findings of prejudice and racial bias among physicians. Experimental techniques have shown unconscious physician preferences for patients of particular races. Senator Edward Kennedy argued that part of the justification for his health disparities legislation was a 1999 experimental study of 720 physicians that analyzed physician recommendations to manage chest pain. The researchers varied the race and gender of actors playing the part of patients, and found that blacks were less likely to be referred for a procedure called cardiac catheterization than similar whites (and women were less likely to be recommended for the procedure than men).[47] Racial bias may also shape the diagnoses that psychiatrists provide when different races (black or white) as well as genders are in question. For instance, one experimental study found that when given two mental illness scenarios (schizophrenia and dependent personality disorder) without information on a patient's race or gender, 290 randomly-selected psychiatrists, guided by the criteria in the *Diagnostic and Statistical Manual for Mental Disorders*, typically agreed on the correct diagnosis. However, when the researchers added race and gender information to the scenarios, the psychiatrists tended to make the same determination only when they shared the same race and gender of the patient in the scenarios. Psychiatrists were more likely to diagnose black patients as having paranoid schizophrenia, which is a more violent disorder. That is, they saw black patients in the study as being more violent than they did whites or patients with exactly the same symptoms about whom no racial information was included. Black psychiatrists were more accurate than whites, though they also exhibited the same bias, though to a lesser degree.[48]

Other research has shown bias against African-Americans. A study of internal medicine and emergency medicine physicians found that physicians were more likely to consider black patients "less cooperative" and thus were less likely to treat black patients with thrombolysis for acute coronary symptoms than similar white patients.[49] Another study found that physicians of all races were not different from the general public in both their stated and unconscious racial preferences for whites, though black physicians showed on average no unconscious racial preference for whites or blacks.[50]

Opinion polls show great variation among physicians regarding whether they believe patients are treated unfairly due to race. Thirty-nine percent of female physicians think this occurs "very or somewhat often" while only 26 percent of male physicians think so, and the results vary even more by race. Only 25 percent of white physicians and 33 percent of Asian physicians believe patients are treated unfairly due to race or ethnicity "very or somewhat often," while 52 percent of Latino physicians and 77 percent of black physicians agreed with that assessment.[51] This finding may help explain the results of a focus group study showing that black physicians were more comfortable than white physicians when discussing race and links between race and health outcomes with their patients.[52]

The biggest concerns leading to support for racial realism in medicine regard not physicians' mental states as revealed by experiments, but actual differences in treatment or outcomes. In the mental health context, for example, though some studies find no influence from racial matching,[53] there are some robust findings of real differences. For instance, in the context of health care for mental illness, African-Americans stick with treatment longer when with African-American doctors of the same gender.[54] Kennedy also reported on the floor of the Senate the findings of a study regarding which patients received a surgical procedure found to be helpful to persons suffering from a particular kind of lung cancer—a cancer that had a lower survival rate among African-Americans than among whites. After controlling for a variety of factors, the researchers found that nearly 13 percent fewer African-Americans received the surgery than whites. Since both races had similar survival rates following surgery, the authors concluded that the discrepancy in surgery rates explained the discrepancy in death rates (the authors were noncommittal regarding whether the different surgery rates were the result of patient or physician choices).[55] A study of black and white patients with HIV, a disease that is more likely to kill blacks than whites, focused on when doctors initiated antiretroviral treatments, which do not cure the disease but can slow its progression. White doctors waited considerably longer before prescribing the treatment for black patients than white patients. Even after controlling for various factors, such as disease symptoms, patient insurance, type of HIV exposure risk, and use of drugs and alcohol, significant variation remained: African-American patients with white doctors received the treatment after a median 461 days, while African-Americans with

African-American doctors waited a median 342 days. By contrast, there
was no difference in the timing of treatment between racially matched
black patients and racially matched whites.[56] Similarly, another study of
2,200 whites, blacks, and Latinos with regular physicians found that even
after controlling for various demographic factors such as health status,
income, and insurance status, blacks were more likely to report receiving
preventive and necessary medical care if they had a black physician.[57]

Yet there is also solid research that has identified no effects traceable
to racial factors. For example, a study of 116 cocaine-dependent African-
Americans found no difference in outcomes whether they had black or
white therapists.[58] And a study of thousands of elderly black and white
patients in North Carolina found that physician race made no difference
for black patients in diagnoses of hypertension, the prescription of medicine, or the likelihood that they would take the medicine prescribed.[59]

Despite the mixed evidence, as mentioned above, when HHS issued
a report on the relevance of race to medicine, it concluded that "minority patients tend to receive better interpersonal care from practitioners of
their own race or ethnicity, particularly in primary care and mental health
settings." It called for more research, but not on physicians' racial abilities.
Instead, the report cited a need for further information on whether the racial abilities of other health professionals might matter, especially nurses.[60]

Racial Realism and the Finding
and Reporting of Information

Advocates, experts, and employers argue that different races vary in their
ability to find and report information. This view is not uncommon in the
fields of social science, but it is most prominent and prevalent in journalism. However, in their quest to raise the numbers of nonwhite journalists,
civil rights and advocacy groups have faced an uphill battle.

Race and the Pursuit of Truth in
Qualitative Social Science Research

In social science, racial-realist principles have long been debated in the
context of qualitative studies that involve interviews or ethnography. Sociologists sometimes refer to the issue as the distinction between "insiders"

and "outsiders."[61] Especially in the late 1960s and early 1970s, scholars wrote about the unique insights that people of color would have in understanding their own ethno-racial groups.[62] For example, an African-American social scientist interviewing an African-American subject would, many believe, conceive of questions that a nonblack interviewer could not, and would ask those questions in a manner that would put the black respondent in a frame of mind to share more information. As scholar Maxine Baca Zinn has put it, "The unique methodological advantage of insider field research is that it is less apt to encourage distrust and hostility, and the experience of being excluded (e.g., as a white researcher) from communities, or of being allowed to 'see' only what people of color want them to see."[63]

While more recent discussions of the issue have pointed out that any researcher studying a nonresearcher will typically be an outsider to some extent, most scholars do accept the notion that race, gender, age, and other factors of a researcher's identity can shape the data studies yield.[64] For example, a study of African-American women's experiences with racism during Hurrican Katrina varied the race of the interviewer, using both black and white women. It found that though the likelihood of respondents' saying they experienced racism did not vary, the descriptions of experiences varied in other ways depending on whether the interviewer was white or black.[65] In a recent study of the meaning of race for Latinos, Wendy Roth concluded that if she (a non-Latina woman) brought a cultural insider to her interviews with Latinos, the quality of the data obtained would improve. "The crux of bicultural interviewing," she maintained, "is that the insider and the outsider both attend an interview and compare perspectives and insights."[66]

"If the media are to report with understanding . . .": Racial Realism in Journalism

The same racial-realist ideas identified as affecting social-science studies are found in the much larger field of journalism. Here the basic notions at work are in part an outgrowth of the long tradition of black and immigrant newspapers in the U.S. The tradition of black newspapers extends at least as far back as the early 1800s, though the better-known papers, such as the *Chicago Defender* and the *Amsterdam News*, were launched in the early 1900s. Immigrants also established their own newspapers shortly after arriving. The tendency of the mainstream press to ignore the lives and issues of black Americans accounts in part for this diversity of journalism. Immigrants were also outside the mainstream, but in their case language differences were of course an additional spur to the development of their own journalistic institutions.[67]

The role and meaning of race in journalism changed following the racial violence of the 1960s. As in other employment sectors examined in this book, the National Advisory Commission on Civil Disorders was a significant force for racial realism as it sought to explain the violence and identify preventative measures. Often called simply the Kerner Commission, after its chairman, Illinois governor Otto Kerner, it issued a report in 1967 that became a national sensation. The Kerner report is today best remembered for the powerful phrase that summarized its findings. "This is our basic conclusion: Our nation is moving toward two societies, one black, one white—separate and unequal."[68] But the report also made several, specific, racial-realist recommendations. It blamed newspapers for marginalizing or ignoring black city residents, noting the serious underrepresentation of blacks on newspaper staffs, and stated bluntly, "The media report and write from the standpoint of a white man's world."[69] The remedy was to utilize the racial abilities of African-American journalists: "We believe that the news media themselves, their audiences and the country will profit from these undertakings" to recruit more blacks, the Commission explained, adding, "If the media are to report with understanding, wisdom and sympathy on the problems of the cities and the problems of the black man . . . they must employ, promote and listen to Negro journalists."[70]

The 1960s violence and the Kerner Commission's analysis of it put race and journalism on the national agenda—and there it has remained. The federal government then acted, but it came at the issue from the standpoint of affirmative-action liberalism rather than racial realism. In 1969, the Federal Communications Commission issued a regulation prohibiting discrimination by broadcasters and requiring affirmative action.[71] In 1972, the Radio and Television News Directors Association got into the act when it decided to monitor the hiring of minorities at local stations.[72] The U.S. Commission on Civil Rights added momentum when it released reports in 1977 and 1979 decrying the lack of representation of minorities and women in television news.[73] In these cases, race had significance but not usefulness: there was no explicit expectation that minority journalists would report or broadcast news differently, and the concern was for justice and equal opportunity, not about the quality of news.

A bigger move for racial realism came in 1977, when the American Society of News Editors (ASNE) created a Minorities Committee. That body, under the leadership of a white Tennessean, Richard Smyser, acted emphatically, declaring in 1978 that "the commitment to recruit, train and hire minorities" was not only "the right thing to do" but also "in the newspaper industry's economic self-interest." Leaders representing minority journalists successfully urged Smyser to adopt a goal of making American newsrooms mirror the racial diversity of the national population by the year 2000.[74]

Despite the bold claims and the high stakes (at least as viewed by the Kerner Commission), the diversification of journalism started at a glacial pace and did not pick up momentum until the late 1980s. Part of the reason for the upsurge was pressure from civil rights groups, such as Operation PUSH, headed by the Reverend Jesse Jackson. After the CBS affiliate in Chicago demoted an African-American anchorman in 1985, Jackson called for a nationwide boycott of CBS stations, demanding that CBS hire more black and Latino station managers, news directors, program directors, executive producers, and newscasters.[75] In 1988, a body made up of representatives from newspapers across the country, the Task Force on Minorities in the Newspaper Business, chaired by *Detroit Free Press* publisher David Lawrence, issued a report calling for more minority inclusion to improve both reporting and profits, stating over and over that race had significance and utility for news organizations. It called the shortage of minorities a "serious tactical error," and argued: "A staff with awareness and sensitivity about issues important to minority readers can establish minority sources and can contribute to increasing newspaper circulation among minority households."[76] Nonwhites could bring both abilities and signaling: "The impression as well as the quality of the coverage is critical. Minorities who feel they are unrepresented have little incentive to subscribe or advertise."[77] The signaling power of race extended up to newspaper management: "Minority executives and managers in the business office, as well as in the newsroom and on the editorial page, can send significant signals to readers and advertisers that the newspaper cares about representing all segments of it market."[78] A diverse workforce would signal that the newspaper was a "full participant in the economic, political and cultural life of the community."[79]

By the 1990s, the news media's effort to become more diverse itself became the subject of media reports. At the center of some controversy was the *Washington Post*, which in 1970 was an almost totally white operation in a majority-black city. Following an EEOC charge of racial discrimination in 1972, the *Post* began an effort to diversify.[80] A lack of progress led the paper to decide in 1986 on a hiring goal: One in four new employees would be nonwhite.[81]

In 1995, a caustic exposé in the *New Republic* sought to discredit the *Post*'s initiative, but the effort backfired when the author of the article, a twenty-four-year old named Ruth Shalit, was caught plagiarizing and making many false statements in her story.[82] Shalit left journalism in disgrace, but not before her story had upset many, particularly her fabrications related to her intended message that journalistic standards were brought down by diversity efforts. In a scathing letter to the editors at the *New Republic*, *Post* executive editor Leonard Downie, Jr. pointed out factual errors in the piece, but reiterated his support for the racial abilities of his staff: "Shalit's racial McCarthyism will not deter our efforts to diversify the staff of the *Washington Post* so that we can report intelligently on an increasingly diverse community and nation."[83]

Shalit's *New Republic* report sought to scandalize news organizations that equated race with reporting skill, arguing that the connection was facile and unfair to whites. Throughout the 1990s, however, the notion of racial abilities in journalism became increasingly established. While the numbers of nonwhite journalists actually hired continued to lag, the link between the diversity of a news organization's staff and the success of that organization became only more entrenched in the discourse of foundations, publishers, and advocacy groups—which continually highlighted the gap between rhetoric and the hiring reality.

A 1996 report from Harvard University's Shorenstein Center on the Press, Politics and Public Policy offered an especially thoughtful analysis. The report noted the continuing underrepresentation of minorities on newspaper staffs, as well as bias in the portrayal of minorities.[84] News organizations, the report alleged, tended to comment on minority races in stories, but not on whites, notably in descriptions of those accused of crimes. Latino and Asian gang affiliations were mentioned, for example, but not white gang membership. News stories also tended to present stereotyped portrayals of nonwhites. Blacks were lazy, American Indians were drinkers, Latinos were lazy, Asian-Americans were passive or inscrutable, Middle Easterners were terrorists, and Japanese business initiatives were "invasions."[85] Though acknowledging the possibility that such biased coverage was just the result of bad journalistic training, a chapter entitled "Race and the Question of Qualifications" emphasized that race would impact what journalists could do on the job. This was in part because of how readers would respond to a journalist's race: "If success in journalism is defined in part by the ability to produce understanding for readers, then readers who are more trusting of the reporting of members of their own race have some control over what it is that makes a successful report."[86] In an argument similar to that made about social scientists conducting interviews, the report also contended that sources might be more trusting of journalists who shared their background.[87] Though admitting the validity of the "frequent complaint of minority journalists" that they were "channeled almost exclusively into race-specific stories,"[88] the Shorenstein Center report still came down on the side of journalists having racial abilities: "We believe that it is unrealistic to suppose that race and ethnic affinity are irrelevant in today's world in determining, in part, who trusts whom, who talks to whom, who understands what, and how people see the world around them. As long as race and ethnic background remain salient in just this way, then there will be many tasks within journalism in which the race or ethnicity of the journalist is as relevant as his or her ability to write well, to locate sources, and to test assertions for accuracy."[89]

In 1998, after realizing they would fall short of their racial diversification goal (by a lot), ASNE decided to keep the same goal but extend the deadline for achieving it—to 2025.[90] Perceptions of racial abilities continued to justify the effort: "ASNE believes that diverse newsrooms better cover America's communities." The ASNE mission statement connected racial realism both to profits and political values: "To cover communities fully, to carry out their role in a democracy, and to succeed in the marketplace, the nation's newsrooms must reflect the racial diversity of American society by 2025 or sooner. At a minimum, all newspapers should employ journalists of color and every newspaper should reflect the diversity of its community."[91]

Major newspapers have appeared to be on board with racial realism in journalism. William E. Schmidt, associate managing editor at the *New York Times*, in 1999 stated that diversity was a goal because "we need people with a lot of talents, a lot of voices, a lot of languages, a lot of perspectives. And to me, that's the bottom line."[92] Managing editor for the *Baltimore Sun*, Jean Thompson, rejected a "homogenized perspective on the news" and said, "We have to recognize that every single person—male or female, gay or straight, black or white—is going to bring something different to a story that makes us a healthier, stronger newspaper, and that also makes for an article that rings true. . . . Our goals at the *Sun* are to better reflect our readership. . . ." Charlotte Hall, managing editor at Long Island, New York's *Newsday* and also chair of the ASNE's diversity

committee, added, "You can't do the kind of journalism that's relevant to
an increasingly diverse population unless you have a diversity of backgrounds and cultures in the newsroom."[93] Veronica Jennings, *Newsday*
project manager, stated, "America is changing . . . and if we're going to attract young people coming up in this multicultural world—as readers, as
advertisers, as potential newspaper professionals—they must see themselves reflected in the newspaper."[94] Critics from the field have also been
outspoken, arguing that these efforts were actually hurting journalism.[95]

News organizations have given voice to their belief in racial abilities
and racial signaling more publicly as well—on their websites. The Tribune Company, owner of a nationwide newspaper and broadcasting empire, has a diversity statement that links racial background with company
performance: "[The] Tribune focuses on recruiting, developing, retaining
and advancing employees of diverse backgrounds to enhance our market performance and remain competitive."[96] In this company's view, "a
diverse workforce (including women and people of color) increases opportunities to reach new markets, improves recruitment and retention,
deepens customer loyalty and strengthens employee commitment and
morale. It is no longer just the right way to do business, it is a business imperative."[97] The New York Times Company similarly declares that
"in a rapidly changing world, our diverse workforce will strengthen our
competitive position in the global marketplace"[98] and sees urgency in the
diversity imperative: "There is a committed effort to make greater, faster,
measurable strides towards creating the diverse and inclusive workforce
that is so crucial to our continued success."[99] The Gannett Company, a
publisher of *USA Today*, as well as several city papers, has stated simply
that "diversity drives innovation,"[100] and has used on their website al-
ternating images of Asian, black, Latino, and white employees to signal
openness to different backgrounds.[101]

All Words and No Action on Racial Realism in Journalism?

Despite strong advocacy by some of the larger news organizations, racial
realism has not resulted in the hiring of large numbers of nonwhite journalists. An extensive report for the Knight Foundation, which promotes
innovation and democratic values in journalism, media, and the arts,
found that by 2004 (the last year of the study, which was begun in 1990),
only 27 percent of 1,410 newsrooms were at peak diversity, meaning that

most were backsliding.[102] The news was somewhat better regarding television news anchors and reporters, as broadcast media have traditionally done better at attracting nonwhites.[103] One study found that while newspapers have had about 13 percent nonwhite employees, nonwhites make up about 22 percent of broadcast journalism staffs.[104] An analysis of 125 stations in a sample of forty television markets found that stations employed black and white news anchors in percentages that reflected the population of their marketing area, though Latinos and Asians were less well represented.[105] In short, progress has been unsteady and uneven.

Given the lack of progress, it is not surprising that advocacy groups have continued to push news organizations on diversity, sometimes employing the same racial-realist rationales as the news organizations themselves used. Latino groups have been especially active. The National Association of Hispanic Journalists issued a report, *Network Brownout 2003*, that documented a shortfall in the coverage of Latinos and Latino issues, as well as negative and stereotypical coverage, and concluded: "We believe the lack of Latinos working in network newsrooms and in broadcast management is a major reason for the poor coverage of the Latino community."[106] Juan González, then president of the National Association of Hispanic Journalists, and Joseph Torres, the organization's deputy director of policy and programs, issued a report in 2004 that argued that the low numbers of minorities in journalism "assured that the press would routinely misrepresent, distort and stereotype the role played by people of color in U.S. society," and that diversity of race was required for a diversity of viewpoints.[107]

UNITY, a group representing all journalists of color, along with the Walter Cronkite School of Journalism and Mass Communication at Arizona State University, added a strong voice in 2008, criticizing the lack of diversity in the Washington press corps. They took a census of minority journalists at major newspapers and different news services, counting both total staff numbers and the numbers of their Washington staffs. They found that 13.1 percent of the 495 reporters, correspondents, columnists, editors, and bureau chiefs in the Washington press corps were minorities (about the same as the percentage as for all journalists, but far below the roughly 25 percent of the U.S. population that is made up of minorities), and that only three of thirty-six bureau chiefs (about 8 percent) representing major daily newspapers and newspaper groups were minorities.[108] African-Americans made up 7 percent of the Washington press corps, Latinos only 3 percent, Asian-Americans 3 percent, and

Native Americans 0.2 percent. News bureaus varied widely, with New-house News Service (which closed in late 2008) in the lead with 30 per-cent minorities on its Washington staff; among the daily paper bureaus, *USA Today* and the *Chicago Tribune* led with both at 20 percent.[109]

Despite the underrepresentation of minorities, the survey found evi-dence that the news bureaus did act on their professed beliefs in the util-ity of race in journalism. When asked to "describe the impact your race had on your ascension to Washington," 7 percent of minority journal-ists said that it "strongly helped" and 47 percent reported that it "helped somewhat." None believed it "strongly hurt" and only 3 percent said that it "hurt somewhat." Thirty-seven percent reported that their race had no impact.[110] In response to a similar question that asked, "What impact does your race have on your ability to continue to move upward in your news organization," 38 percent reported that it "somewhat helps," while 7 percent said it "somewhat hurts" and 3 percent said it "strongly hurts." Fifty-three percent reported that it had no impact.[111]

In my interviews with journalists in an early stage of this project, the issue of racial realism limiting opportunities for nonwhites came up, sometimes poignantly. One Latina journalist ultimately decided to leave the field—but not because she was unable to find a job. She could find jobs. The problem was that she could not move out of the pigeonholed jobs she was offered covering the Latino community. Though she enjoyed this "taco beat," as it was sometimes called, eventually she wanted to cover new issues—such as religion, or Mexico itself, as a foreign cor-respondent. Yet she was denied such assignments. In a telling remark, her editor told her that she should "do what you do"—which was to write about her own community.[112]

When I described this story to a senior African-American journalist, that journalist sighed and told me, "That's not an unusual story." Though young journalists of color often relish the opportunity to cover their own community, this enthusiasm does not last: "As they mature, they want to try different things. . . . I know of quite of few reporters who resent being pigeonholed as the 'ethnic reporter,' who always has to write about his or her race." In this journalist's view, this was a consequence not of the editors' belief in superior abilities, but of signaling: "Very often a reporter from a given background is an ambassador" and using minority journalists "gives the appearance of awareness" and "makes public rela-tions sense," which is helpful for marketing purposes.[113]

In short, while many news organizations fail to achieve their diversity goals, this does not mean they are not trying. News organizations say they manage race following the principles of racial realism, advocacy organizations push them to do so, and surveys of nonwhite journalists indicate that race creates opportunities more often than it limits them.

Is There Evidence to Support Racial Realism in Finding and Reporting Information?

That there is a difference between insider and outsider perspectives, and the value of these differences, has long been established in the social sciences, but there is little social-science research regarding whether racial realism in journalism is justified, especially when compared to the amount of research on racial realism in medicine. The few published studies on racial abilities (there are none on racial signaling) do, however, indicate that race may have some effects on journalism, but not unanimously.

On the negative side of the ledger there are the findings from the authors of a study of stereotyped portrayals of blacks in the television news media, which showed that "structural forces," rather than the race of journalists, led to stereotyped portrayals, and that the reporting of black anchors on television news was indistinguishable from that of whites.[114] However, there is other evidence of racial differences in journalism. An analysis of print and broadcast journalism in Boston found that the black-owned media gave more attention to education, city government, community cultural and arts stories, as well as profiles of educators and entrepreneurs than did the white-owned media. In addition, the black media's stories on black neighborhoods were far more likely to challenge stereotypes, focusing on black educational achievements and neighborhood improvements, with these positive stories representing 57 percent of coverage, while the white-owned media presented negative stereotypes 85 percent of the time; only 22 percent of its stories on blacks were positive.[115]

In addition, studies of political coverage may confirm the conventional wisdom of both publishers and advocacy groups regarding racial realism. A study of race and gender in the coverage of a 1992 House of Representatives banking scandal and an analysis of the coverage of black and white members of Congress indicate that mainstream press outlets tend to give unfavorable treatment to minority legislators.[116] An analysis of black, Latino, and Asian newspaper coverage of minority members of the 2001–02 Congress also found differences: these papers gave more coverage to same-race legislators and also to other minority legislators than did the mainstream press.[117]

Less direct evidence also indicates support for the racial-realist strategy. First, there are some data about the public's views on racial realism in journalism. A 1994 USA Today/CNN/Gallup poll of American attitudes toward journalism found that 74 percent of blacks, 68 percent of Latinos, 63 percent of Asians, and 43 percent of whites believed it made "a great deal" or "a moderate amount" of improvement when a reporter of their own race covered a story related to their race or ethnic group. In this survey, African-Americans showed the most discontent with the majority-white journalism in their communities, with 47 percent indicating that their local newspaper papers' reporting on race "worsens relations," while only 14 percent said it "improves relations."[118]

Second, there are the views of journalists themselves. UNITY and the Cronkite School's survey of minority journalists in Washington found strong support for the idea that considerations of race are critical to good journalism: 80 percent of the minority journalists believed that a more diverse Washington press corps would have "some" or a "significant" impact on coverage of the news. Similarly, nearly 75 percent believed that the race of a journalist has "some" or a "significant" impact on her/his coverage of our nation's government.[119] As for the impact of a respondent's race on her or his ability to cover race-related issues, 20 percent said it "strongly helps" and 70 percent said it "somewhat helps" (none believed that it hurt in any way).[120] Finally, 60 percent of minority respondents reported that colleagues "regularly" or "occasionally" looked to them for expertise on race-related stories, and 67 percent felt "significant" or "some" responsibility for suggesting stories related to race.[121] A 2007 survey of Asian-American journalists also found belief in the impact of race: 53 percent said that they had been able to make a "substantial" or a "modest" impact on how their news organization covered racial and ethnic minorities. When asked, "How frequently do others in your newsroom seek your help or participation in coverage of racial/ethnic minorities?" 39 percent said that it happened once every couple of months, 10 percent that it happened at least once a month, and seven percent replied "constantly—such coverage is my job or beat."[122]

Interviews I conducted in the early stages of this project add some insights on how race can be a factor in journalists' abilities. A Latina journalist's anecdote illustrates the value of the minority perspective. Selena, a music artist very popular with young people, especially Mexican-American women, had passed away suddenly in 1995 while this journalist was on vacation. "No one in the bureau knew who she was except me," she told me, "and I was gone. So it took them a while to get who she was and how important she was to young Texas Latinas and others across the United States. It surprised many reporters how many people showed up at a memorial for her."[123]

An African-American editor echoed this viewpoint: "I can't tell you how many times I've been in a meeting that would have to do with an ethnic community, and I would make a point and everyone would look at me as if I were speaking Martian." He told me that though white reporters "can do extremely valuable work," they "can't ever be as good" as a minority reporter covering a minority community. He believed white reporters tend to have an "arrogance" when covering minority communities that leads them to look down on those communities, and he admitted, "I just don't think they will achieve the intimacy they need to be able to do that job as well as someone who is steeped in it." However, these racial abilities were not a genetic endowment: "There's also a chance that a black reporter won't be able to do that either; it depends on where they are raised." Moreover, he complained that newspapers tended to train minority reporters to report "in the traditional way" and to report "like white people." This effectively stripped minority reporters of their racial abilities. The result was that "you are not going to be successful because the [minority] readers will say there is nothing in this for me."[124]

Marketing to a Diverse America

Business employers have used racial-realist strategies for filling skilled white-collar positions for generations. This has been especially apparent in sales. Many in corporate America believe that more and better sales will result if they deploy what they perceive as racial abilities to sell to racially concordant markets. Despite little scientific support, this has become so commonly accepted as to be considered "common sense."

Discovering Diverse Markets, and How to Sell to Them

Segregation created both oppression and opportunity for African-Americans interested in business. Books published in the 1940s showed that African-Americans were unable to break into the mainstream market in a variety of industries, but that the neglect of the segregated black market also gave them a field of limited but still valuable opportunity.[125] An example of this dynamic at work is provided by one of the first black advertising agencies, Claude A. Barnett Advertising, which had a simple but compelling slogan: "I reach the Negro."[126]

In the 1930s, Claude Barnett teamed up with the Rumford Baking Company and Paul K. Edwards, a white professor at Fisk University, to experiment with using black sales professionals to sell products to the African-American market. The experiment, which also made use of the black press, was successful enough that the company hired blacks for its permanent marketing staff; a competitor soon followed suit.[127] Edwards also convinced the L.C. Smith & Corona Typewriter Company to add a black sales representative.[128] A handful of other companies, including Esso Oil, the American Tobacco Company, and Pabst Brewing Company, hired black "goodwill ambassadors" to encourage sales in black communities.[129]

By the 1940s, more companies were beginning to hire African-American marketing consultants and sales professionals specifically to market to blacks.[130] Of these, it was the soft drink company Pepsi that became best known for using employees' race to actually develop an African-American market. Perhaps most notable in this regard is the fact that Pepsi's practices already had the hallmarks—both positive and negative—of the current strategies used in racial-matching marketing: Pepsi gave opportunities to nonwhites where none had existed before, but also kept these workers isolated and limited to racialized jobs.

Pepsi's most significant move came in 1947, when it hired Edward F. Boyd to lead the sales effort. Boyd was not a marketer at all but an activist working for the National Urban League to stop discrimination against blacks in housing. It was his knowledge of the foreign land that was the nascent African-American market that qualified him as a marketer of soft drinks. Boyd would go on to create a pioneering national team of black sales specialists at Pepsi.

The goal of Pepsi's president, Walter S. Mack, was not social progress but cash. As business reporter Stephanie Capparell has written, "Mr. Mack had long believed that being different could sometimes provide an advantage."[131] The black sales team worked exclusively in the black community, and they developed innovations that were radical at the time but now seem commonplace, such as using black models in advertisements (see Chapter 4).[132]

In 1953, there were enough black marketing professionals to sustain the creation of a national organization: the National Association of Market

Developers.[133] This organization, as well as articles in the trade press, advocated the use of black professionals to help tap the African-American market. One article stated: "Do not invest one dime in a marketing program for Negroes without first securing proper guidance. This may take the form of a sales promotion and marketing member on your staff, or the services of a private organization. *But do it* (original emphasis) or, with the best intention in the world, you may not get your product off the ground."[134] The definition of "proper guidance" was left to the reader.

By the 1990s, as Asian-Americans and Latinos became significant new sectors of the market, the utilization of racial abilities in targeted marketing was commonplace and, for some, it was taken for granted as rational. The basic idea in a variety of industries was that a firm needs its marketing staff to match the race of those it wishes to market to. As *Fortune* magazine explained matter-of-factly, "A company with a diverse work force will have an easier time serving markets that themselves are becoming more multicultural."[135]

It was not surprising that a consumer products firm like Procter & Gamble would utilize racial abilities in the 1990s. As Senior Vice President for Advertising Robert Wehling stated succinctly, "When we started getting more diverse . . . we started getting richer marketing plans, because they came up with things that white males were simply not going to come up with. . . ."[136] Yet there does not seem to be any logic that links racial marketing abilities to any particular products or services, and firms that have no obvious connection to ethno-racial cultures or lifestyles may value racial abilities in marketing. For example, William Orton, a marketing director for MetLife, declared in the early 1990s that in the insurance industry, "You can't have an all-white male filled force and expect to be successful marketing to Asians, or Hispanics, or African-Americans, or women. . . . That may seem obvious."[137] Metlife appears to still use racial realism; today, the company's website describes how the company "leverages diversity" for profits as it helps "better serve our customers" and builds "relationships in the communities we serve."[138]

Racial abilities in marketing are valued in pharmaceutical and chemical companies as well. Chair and CEO of Dupont, Jack Krol, recounted an incident in which a Latino manager suggested selling a drug with both English and Spanish instructions—a simple move he credited for creating millions of dollars in sales. Afterward, Krol stated, "We have proof diversity improves our business performance."[139] *Fortune* magazine reported in the 1990s how DuPont benefited from black employees who developed new marketing plans focusing on black farmers, and from a multicultural team that earned $45 million in new sales by finding new color patterns for its Corian synthetic countertops that were attractive to overseas homeowners.[140]

By the 1990s, technology companies were also managing racial abilities for marketing. Lou Gerstner, as chairman and CEO of IBM, has explained that his company's commitment to diversity arose because "we made diversity a market-based issue. . . . It's about understanding our markets, which are diverse and multicultural."[141] IBM thus included members of the target group on every team that was designing a marketing plan. Today, the IBM website describes their commitment to "Diversity 3.0" which means "leveraging our differences for innovation, collaboration and client success."[142] Matching is important because diversity "is the bridge between the workplace and the marketplace, and as such, victory with the customer begins with winning in the workplace."[143]

Not surprisingly, we find this same lauding of targeted racial marketing abilities where racial phenotypes actually matter, such as in the sales of cosmetics or other personal products. Avon CEO James E. Preston (later succeeded by Chinese-Canadian Andrea Jung) stated matter-of-factly that the U.S. has an "increasingly diverse marketplace," and asked, "Who can best understand and serve this changed and changing market? Certainly not the 'old boy network'. It takes a diverse work force at all levels of the company, including senior management."[144] Avon's website today also uses the language of "leveraging diversity."[145]

And on and on. There may be no major firm in any industry that does not believe that racial abilities help marketing. There are even incidences of firms professing a value in racial abilities when it is not entirely clear what they think the payoff is. The Enterprise car rental company, for example, has shown great concern for diversity and has sent out recruitment teams made up of different minority groups. Enterprise also offers rewards to managers who hire and develop workers who reflect local markets. As Ed Adams, the VP of human resources explains, "We want people who speak the same language, literally and figuratively, as our customers. . . . We don't set quotas. We say, 'Reflect your local market'."[146] It is not clear what it means to "figuratively" speak the same language as African-Americans, Latinos, and Asians, but it is clear that Enterprise has confidence that this will increase profits.

While there is belief in racial abilities across industries, it is also found in companies of different sizes. Business administration scholars Robin J. Ely and David A. Thomas have identified (what I am calling) the racial-realism strategy for understanding customers in their study of diversity in small service firms. For example, a retail operations manager at an inner city bank, catering primarily to black customers, stated that having people of color on the staff meant having workers "who actually know how to relate to . . . the people that are in the neighborhood, and what they actually *feel*, and, you know, how they actually communicate with one another, and those kinds of things" (original emphasis). This manager felt that an all-white bank would be limited by "the discomfort with the community, or not being able to relate to the borrowers or stand in their shoes so to speak."[147]

As with other jobs discussed in this book, being hired or placed on the basis of perceived racial abilities or signaling is not entirely a plus for the nonwhite marketer. In a roundtable discussion in *Advertising Age*, a trade magazine, Eliot Kang, then president of Kang and Lee Advertising, said that "being an ethnic person within the corporation" is "not a plus" when trying to win a budget battle. The problem, he said to some agreement, was that such an employee could be perceived as a racial advocate. Whites in the corporation may say, "You're just saying it of course because you're Asian, because you're African-American, and so you're going to push that."[148] In such a case, coworkers may perceive not just racial abilities, but racial interests, creating divisions and limitations.

Still, at least one major civil rights group, the Urban League, sees racial realism in marketing as in the interests of nonwhites. A 2005 study (funded by Enterprise Rent-A-Car) surveyed more than five thousand workers regarding diversity practices at their companies. Among the various diversity initiatives studied, the most popular was "marketing to diverse customers and consumers," with 63 percent of surveyed workers reporting that it is very important or extremely important. The report said this practice resulted in "increased customer satisfaction" and "increased customer diversity." While there were several suggested ways to "make it work," including analyzing demographic shifts and group-specific testing, the Urban League also counseled that firms should "recruit associates to mirror the demographics of consumers."[149]

The Selling of Racial Abilities for Marketing:
Multicultural Marketing Texts,
Diversity Consultants, and Ethnic Marketers

It is not only the case that large or small firms dominated by whites are "leveraging" the racial abilities of nonwhite employees to increase sales. There are also many independent professionals, typically nonwhite

themselves, working as writers, consultants, or in advertising, who make
a living based on the notion that racial abilities are helpful if not essential
for selling to diverse markets.

First, there are textbooks that teach the "how to" of selling to diverse
markets. These texts exoticize these markets but then show how even
clueless whites can tap into them.[150] "Understanding and thinking in a
different culture is a challenge," counsel M. Isabel Valdés and Marta H.
Sedane, "but it is not impossible."[151] Still, the easier route to sales is to
leverage racial abilities of employees rather than to learn them. In his
textbook on *Multicultural Marketing*, Alfred L. Schreiber, a marketing
veteran and former president of a firm called Diversity Imperatives, is
especially direct in his advocacy of racial abilities. For example, he argues
that a minority marketing executive "likely possesses outlooks, attitudes,
and abilities that will equip a company to market more effectively than
before to members of that executive's constituency" and "will often add
a greater depth."[152] Moreover, diversity is "cost-effective," because "a diverse company doesn't need to go to outside consultants and agencies to
understand the fundamentals of what ethnic and minority consumers are
thinking and buying. That expertise is already resident in the house."[153]

Also promoting racial abilities in marketing are the diversity consultants. Though these professionals more typically advise on how firms
can manage and leverage diversity to take advantage of racial abilities
throughout the organization (see below), they also link race specifically to
marketing. As Taylor Cox, Jr., a leading African-American diversity consultant, explained in his textbook on diversity management, "Firms may
gain competitive advantage from the insights of employees from various
cultural backgrounds who can assist organizations in understanding culture effects on buying decisions and in mapping strategies to respond to
them."[154] Cox illustrated his point by describing how nonwhite employees
helped in the marketing of the *USA Today* newspaper to diverse communities, and how Avon struggled with its inner-city marketing until it
turned to black and Latino managers for help in devising strategies.[155]

There are also marketing firms with business models predicated on the
concept of racial marketing abilities. Though mainstream firms started
to hire nonwhite marketers in the 1940s, as described above, the niche
for race-specific marketing firms continued to develop in parallel, though
they were fighting over a limited fraction of the American consumer dollar. They had to sell their racial abilities to win accounts, because their
racial background disqualified them from competing for the more general
market.[156]

These dilemmas came to a head in 1972 when a major agency, Young and Rubicam, created a specialized unit inside the larger company to focus on marketing campaigns designed to sell to blacks and Latinos. Some welcomed the move as a way to bring the nonwhite market more into the mainstream, while some owners of minority-owned agencies thought that if the idea caught on, it would put them out of business. At the same time, it would channel black and Latino marketing professionals into segregated cells within the larger companies, and it would be hard for them to move outward and upward. As historian Jason Chambers explained, "The agency drew the ire of the black advertising community as both an affront to black agency ownership as well as a potential limitation of blacks' roles in mainstream firms."[157]

Yet multicultural marketing continued to grow in the 1970s, and with the changing American demography, firms found solid success targeting either the black or the growing Latino markets. The Burrell McBain Advertising Agency, for instance, scored a major account when it began to develop commercials aimed at the black market for the McDonalds fast-food chain.[158] By the 1990s, it was becoming standard practice for firms to develop one campaign for the mainstream market and then use specialized, multicultural firms to develop parallel marketing directed at blacks, Latinos, and Asians.[159] Mainstream firms, meanwhile, often continued to have divisions of targeted marketers, typically drawn from the target demographic. As Dolores Kunda, then a vice president of the Hispanic unit at Leo Burnett, proudly told *Advertising Age*, "There's this group called the Hispanic Group inside of Leo Burnett, and we do Hispanic marketing. And you know what? We're all Hispanic, and we speak Spanish in the elevators."[160]

As before, firms that specialize in ethnic or multicultural marketing continue to advertise their own racial diversity as a qualification for designing marketing strategies. In her study of marketing to Latinos, anthropologist Arlene Dávila wrote, "The first generation of ad executives I talked to recalled corporate clients expecting them to just know about the market—after all, they too were Hispanics—rarely investing for research, as would be customary in the general market."[161] Though firms now do research, she notes, they are still typically run by Latino marketing professionals.[162] She noted that the Association of Hispanic Advertising Agencies required members to have at least 65 percent Latino staff, and sought to defend its turf with a mission to "grow, strengthen, and protect the Hispanic marketing and advertising industry by providing leadership in raising awareness of the value of the Hispanic market opportunities. . . ."[163] Historian Marilyn Halter similarly has argued, "Among multicultural marketing firms, the diversity of in-house staff is often crucial to the company's success" because "having a workforce that is representative of the ethnicities of the primary target audiences not only helps to ensure that cross-cultural marketing campaigns succeed, but also adds greater credibility to the business, particularly concerning issues of authenticity."[164]

A tour of the multicultural marketing firms advertising themselves on the web quickly reveals strategies of racial signaling and the touting of racial abilities. For example, EMG, a creator of "culturally relevant advertising campaigns . . . based on a deep understanding of the Hispanic consumer behavior across all acculturation levels and channels," boasts that its team has years of experience in bilingual and multicultural marketing to the U.S. Latino market and in Latin America, and, in addition, "Our diverse ethnic backgrounds give us the sensibility and the insights to really understand and connect with the Hispanic consumer."[165] Similarly, Améredia describes itself as "a full-service multicultural advertising, marketing and public relations firm specializing in reaching diverse ethnic groups nationwide."[166] Part of their marketing *is* their diversity: "Our team consists of experienced professionals of different ethnicities who have worked with various media and advertising organizations in the U.S., Asia and other global markets."[167] Aiming for a more specific racial market is a specific racial group: the punnily named adCREASIANS bills itself as a "professional yet passionate group of Asian-Americans with curious ideas for creative advertising targeted towards the Asian-American market."[168] There are, in fact, so many of these niche marketing agencies that a firm called Multicultural Marketing Resources, Inc. has created a website with a directory that helpfully provides the percentage of minority ownership of each firm.[169]

How Common Is Racial Realism in Marketing?

As we have seen, there is ample evidence that some firms use racial realism to manage race in marketing positions. But exactly how common is it? One indirect indicator comes from a study of racial inequality in wages that showed blacks earning on average lower wages in jobs, such as financial services, real estate, insurance sales, actuarial work, and as lawyers and physicians, where monetary success depends on the wealth of the clientele. Sociologists Eric Grodsky and Devah Pager suggest that lower earnings in these occupations result from a racial-matching effect: blacks find most opportunities in these occupations when their clients are also black. Because black clients are, on average, poorer than nonblack clients, this depresses the income of the racially-matched employees. This point is underscored by data showing that there are fewer racial disparities in earnings when customer relations are not a measure of productivity, as in the case of bus drivers.[170]

Another indirect indicator of the spread of racial realism in marketing is the rate of growth in targeted advertising strategies, which often are vehicles for racial realism, particularly when the advertising agency is a boutique firm specializing in multicultural campaigns. While less than one percent of total marketing dollars are spent on targeted efforts to reach nonwhites, already by the 1990s more than half of Fortune 500 companies were making targeted efforts, including customized product lines, advertising, packaging, and promotional activities.[171] In 2010, the top ten agencies marketing to African-Americans took in nearly $163 million, and the top ten agencies marketing to Latinos took in almost $241 million.[172] Most of the growth has been in the rapidly expanding Latino sector; between 1990 and 2000, ads aimed at Latinos increased by 487 percent in print media, 463 percent in radio, 251 percent in television, and 269 percent in other media.[173]

Lower on the employment hierarchy are retail sales jobs, but since these positions have a significant customer relations and marketing component, it is not surprising that employers use racial realism here as well. A study of Atlanta, Boston, Detroit, and Los Angeles found that 70 percent of surveyed retailers admitted to race matching their employees to their client base,[174] and a study of 167 businesses in Florida also found a correlation between black employment and percentages of black customers.[175]

As is the case of racial realism in health care, another indicator of the commonality or spread of racial realism in marketing is the willingness of major corporations to argue in legal arenas for its value. Several major corporations have offered arguments for racial marketing abilities in amicus curiae briefs supporting affirmative action in university admissions. In the *Grutter v. Bollinger* case that evoked support from major medical organizations, businesses also took action. MTV Networks, a division of the media giant Viacom, told the Court that "a diverse workforce is critical to the development and marketing of programming targeted at specific racial and cultural communities, as well as to developing a robust environment for other business initiatives."[176] MTV's brief explained:

> An Hispanic director may not be essential to producing successful "Hispanic" programming; an African American talent scout may not have been needed to recognize the artistic value of rap music. But it cannot be doubted that membership in a racial or ethnic minority in this society entails experiences and perspective that would be valuable to the entertainment industry. It seems self-evident that a person from a Puerto Rican community, who speaks Spanish, and grew up listening to Puerto Rican–influenced music likely will add value to the process of developing authentic programming and effective marketing to the "Latin" niche.[177]

A group of sixty-five Fortune 500 companies also submitted a brief in the case making a similar argument. Its wording hinted at the usefulness of racial abilities in marketing more obliquely: a diverse workforce was "better able to develop products and services that appeal to a variety of consumers and to market offerings in ways that appeal to those consumers," and "a racially diverse group of managers with cross-cultural experience is better able to work with business partners, employees, and clientele in the United States and around the world."[178]

It is essential to note, however, that widespread belief in the value of racial abilities or the racial signaling of nonwhites, and the hiring of *some* nonwhites in marketing positions in mainstream advertising firms, does not mean that large numbers of nonwhite marketers are being hired. The New York City Human Rights Commission, for example, has long targeted the advertising industry for special attention due to its poor record of hiring African-Americans. In the early 2000s, only 2.5 percent of more highly paid advertising employees (those making at least $100,000 a year) were black, a percentage that had not changed significantly since the mid-1960s.[179]

Is Racial Realism in Marketing Good Business Strategy?

Evidence for the value of racial realism in marketing is only suggestive at this point. A handful of studies that examined the impact of race on sales at the retail level found little support for racial realism. One examined black and white sales representatives and found that they performed equally well, though the study did find that the race of the sales manager affected the performance of sales representatives.[180] Another found that "contrary to theories of customer discrimination, communities with more Whites, Blacks, Hispanics or Asians did not buy more from stores with similar employees."[181] The author of one review of the literature has argued that firms should pursue diversity in their employees, buyers and suppliers, but that ethnicity "is not a substitute for expertise in understanding and relating to cultural differences."[182]

Supportive evidence for the benefits of racial abilities in marketing is mostly weak or indirect. In the first place, studies do show that different ethnic and racial groups have different buying habits and media usage habits. For example, though some apparent racial differences result from differences in average education levels, blacks are more likely to be high-users of magazines and television rather than newspapers, whereas whites are more evenly distributed in their use to different media sources. Latinos, on the other hand, prefer television and radio over print media.[183] Another study found that African-Americans engage media for longer periods and are more receptive to different sources, while Chinese Americans use media the least and are best reached through community networks.[184] Of course, with immigrant groups, media usage patterns change over time.[185] More broadly, over a range of products, different racial groups show different preferences and attitudes toward different products and toward consumption itself.[186] These findings suggest that savvy, targeted campaigns would be more effective than a one-size-fits-all approach.

Moreover, research indicates that marketing and advertising that is designed to fit the culture of the targeted audience is more effective,[187] especially if the audience members strongly identify with their race,[188] and evidence that using race-matched models or actors in advertisements has an impact on the target audience (as described in Chapter 4).[189] Yet there is little evidence for or against the proposition that trained professionals drawn from the targeted audience are better at designing this marketing than are professionals from other groups.

Racial Diversity as the Key to Innovation and Profit

For race to be useful for a business, many employers and advocates believe racial abilities need not be tied to specific tasks or jobs. Rather, firms can manage race so as to obtain better ideas in any part of a firm's operations.

As far back as the 1950s, some firms professed to see a connection between fair employment practices and profits, but in most cases they meant either to exploit racial marketing abilities, as described above, or to implement classical liberal policies of nondiscrimination—believing that better profits would follow the more immediate goal of fair employment practices.[190] One of the earliest examples of public advocacy of racial abilities for overall organizational effectiveness came in the National Association of Manufacturers' amicus brief in *Local 28 of the Sheet Metal Workers v. EEOC*,[191] where the normally conservative organization extolled the "new ideas, opinions and perspectives generated by greater workforce diversity."[192] In that same year, the Bureau of National Affairs' survey of employment practices quoted a personnel executive for Cummins Engine Company who explained that "cultivating differences" was "a key competitive advantage for our company" because "differences among people of various racial, ethnic, and cultural backgrounds generate creativity and innovation as well as energy in our work force."[193]

These sorts of statements from corporate leaders became commonplace in the 1990s, and they continue to be common today. The CEO of Bell Atlantic, which later became the Verizon telecommunications company, told *Fortune* magazine, "If everybody in the company is the same, you'll have a lot fewer arguments and a lot worse answers."[194] Gail Snowden, an executive with BankBoston (later purchased by Bank of America), similarly explained, "I think we have to be able to show that having a seat at the table has a business payoff, that by bringing a different point of view and a different kind of knowledge, you open things up. I've seen so many times that having people of diverse backgrounds working together makes conversations so much fuller and richer because there are so many more perspectives—there's less groupthink. People challenge assumptions and beliefs, and the company ends up benefiting."[195] This racial-realist strategy extends to the corporate boardroom. According to Sara Lee CEO John Bryan: "Having a diverse board is a strategic imperative at Sara Lee . . . the diversity of our board has been a major source of the confidence we needed to reach beyond our experience for new and potent opportunities. I do not believe a more homogenous board with a narrower range of backgrounds would have been as supportive, or as constructively critical. . . ."[196]

Diversity consultants and academics have strongly promoted racial realism as leading, in the words of consultant Taylor Cox, Jr., to "creativity and innovation."[197] Management scholars David Thomas and Robin Ely argue that racial minorities "bring different, important, and competitively relevant knowledge and perspectives about how to actually do work—how to design processes, reach goals, frame tasks, create effective teams, communicate ideas, and lead. When allowed to, members of these groups can help companies grow and improve by challenging basic assumptions about an organization's functions, strategies, operations, practices, and procedures."[198]

Civil rights groups have also used this language of racial realism in their advocacy. The Urban League produced studies in 2005 and 2009 on the benefits of diversity, for example. The 2009 report urged corporate leaders to "*Take the lead* and act upon a genuine commitment to diversity and inclusion by treating it, not as a program, but as a business strategy complete with required leadership competencies and accountabilities" (original emphasis). Rather than simply focusing on equal opportunity or social justice goals, firms should "develop a diversity and inclusion strategy that is directly tied to . . . corporate business objectives." More concretely, this meant that the corporate leaders should "continue to *foster the recruitment, retention, career development and advancement of emerging minority racial/ethnic groups* in the United States that continue to make a profound impact on the composition of the workforce" (original emphasis).[199]

Perceptions of the benefits of racial realism are not universal, but they appear to be widespread.[200] Thanks to research by Frank Dobbin, Lauren Edelman, and others, we know a lot about the spread of firms' interest in racial diversity. For example, Dobbin and his colleagues found in a survey of 829 employers that none had diversity policies in 1971, but in 1990 10 percent did, and by 2001 the number had increased to about 40 percent. (The percentage with equal employment opportunity policies increased from 20 percent to more than 90 percent between 1971 and 2001.) A survey of 389 employers found a much smaller percentage with a diversity task force in place, but also showed an upward trajectory: from zero in 1971 to about 15 percent in 2001.[201] In an examination of management periodicals, Lauren Edelman and her colleagues found that discussions of the usefulness of diversity started in 1987 and took off in the early 1990s, when they were more prominent than discussions of civil rights. While "diversity" can refer to many bases of difference, 85 percent of the articles discussing diversity did so in terms of race and ethnicity.[202]

Research by the Urban League also suggests that diversity practices are becoming established in the private sector. The organization surveyed about twelve hundred employees in 2009. It found that 44 percent agreed with the statement, "Leadership at my company is committed to diversity," and 42 percent agreed with "My company has an effective diversity initiative." A slight majority (51 percent) agreed with the statement, "My company is committed to developing people who are diverse."[203]

Moreover, not only do business leaders talk about these kinds of organizational racial abilities and hire consultants to help utilize them, but they also continue to mention them when they fight for programs that can deliver a supply of racially diverse workers. MTV Networks's brief in the *Grutter* case emphasized racial abilities when the network argued, "The continual innovation required for success in the industry depends on heterogeneity in MTV's creative work-teams."[204] The brief from the Fortune 500 companies also argued that "a diverse group of individuals educated in a cross-cultural environment has the ability to facilitate unique and creative approaches to problem-solving arising from the integration of different perspectives."[205] It cited a story in *Personnel Today*, a human resources magazine, finding that "four out of five organizations believe there is a direct link between diversity and improved business performance, according to independent research."[206] A brief by Fortune 100 corporations, from Abbott Laboratories to Xerox, made similar arguments in *Fisher v. University of Texas*, stating, "For amici to succeed in their businesses, they must be able to hire highly trained employees of all races, religions, cultures and economic backgrounds."[207]

Does Racial Realism Lead to More Dynamic, Innovative, and Profitable Firms?

When it comes to the use of racial abilities or "diversity" in business organizations, research has begun to catch up with practice. Research results, while they offer qualified support for this kind of racial realism, also highlight some downsides.

On the negative side, for example, there is evidence that diverse organizations have less employee commitment.[208] Research also shows that employee dissatisfaction and higher turnover rates are more common in diverse organizations.[209]

Scott E. Page, an economist who has written perhaps the definitive social science book supporting the notion that diversity of perspectives aids organizations by spurring ideas and innovation, offered qualified support for racial abilities in his review of the literature on what he called "identity diverse groups." His biggest concern regarded the importance of managing the costs that may come with diversity. Page argued that most studies found support for the benefits of diversity, including in the areas of problem-solving, ability to predict, and innovation, but the results varied considerably due to different contexts having different challenges in managing communication problems, cultural styles, and preference conflicts. In Page's view, racially diverse employees will make organizations perform better when several conditions are satisfied, namely, when there is shared engagement in problem solving; when identities are translated into "relevant tools" (meaning that different racial identities correspond to different perspectives and problem-solving styles); when there are shared preferences; and when group activity is sustained (so that employees can work out their differences over time). Also helpful in maximizing benefits and reducing the costs of diversity is a climate of identity validation, contribution verification for individuals, and shared expectations of diversity's benefits.[210]

The leading field-based study in this area—a large analysis of the effects of diversity on business performance—which is cited by Page, can be read as reinforcement of Page's general observation that effective diversity management is not easy. It concluded that the effects of racial and gender diversity were generally positive, but less dramatically so than advocates had long claimed. A large team of experts on organizations and diversity, led by the management scholar Thomas A. Kochan, closely examined four large, respected, and diverse companies. These included two information-processing firms, a financial service firm, and a large retail company.

One of the first findings was that firms willing to be studied were hard to come by, and that "not only had none of the organizations . . . contacted ever conducted a systematic examination [of the impact] of their diversity efforts on bottom-line performance measures, [but] very few were interested in doing so."[211] The study also showed, similar to Page's arguments above, that it was far more difficult to leverage race and gender diversity into productivity gains than first thought. Neither, however, did they find consistent problems created by diversity. Though other research had found that diverse firms tended to have stronger sales, market share, and profits,[212] the main finding of this comprehensive analysis was of a *lack* of effects, either positive or negative, on overall performance. More specifically, the study found that racial diversity created more problems than gender diversity, but where diversity had a negative effect, "it was mitigated by training and development-focused initiatives." A highly competitive context tended to exacerbate the negative effects of diversity, but in firms that promoted learning from diversity, diversity could enhance performance.[213]

Kochan and his colleagues conclude, much as Page does, that what is needed is *better diversity management*. They urged managers to focus on "the conditions that can leverage benefits from diversity or, at the very least, mitigate its negative effects."[214] This required that executives and managers experiment more with different programs and strategies to deploy diversity and collect data on successes and failures. They also suggested firms dial down the claims made for the business benefits of diversity and emphasize instead that it is a "labor-market imperative" (meaning that racial diversity is necessary due to demographic changes) and a "societal expectation and value."[215] With this last suggestion, the authors of the study, unlike Page, appeared to move back toward affirmative-action liberalism, with an emphasis on justice.

Perhaps the most poignant analysis of the risks entailed in leveraging racial abilities, either in marketing or in the larger, organizational sense, comes from sociologist Elijah Anderson's ethnography of a racially integrated business workplace. Anderson said of many black executives:

> [They] often informally see themselves as communication links between people of their own racial background and the predominately white firm. In informal conversations, they sometimes attempt to edify and sensitize their white colleagues about black life. . . . But because of this communication function and because blacks are so poorly represented at the higher reaches of the organization, the black executive runs the further, and often debilitating, risk of becoming all-consumed by this role. Sensitive to the risks involved, many black executives strongly resist this feature of their position. . . . When they feel themselves being used simply as communication links and representatives of blacks, many feel themselves seriously compromised and complain that they are unable to do the work for which they have been trained. . . . For some, this perception leads to demoralization, cynicism, or deeper questions concerning their real value to the organization.[216]

Sending Messages:
Racial Signaling in the Corporate World

A final way that corporate employers use race has nothing at all to do with perceptions of how race is linked to ability. Rather, it involves the value that race has for signaling certain meanings. Firms sometimes will use racial signaling to respond to customer demands. For example, a Merrill Lynch vice president told the *New York Times*, "Our clients, our shareholders are demanding more and more that our employees look like them."[217] *Fortune* magazine similarly noted, "The idea that many minority customers are highly aware of a company's minority friendliness is more important than many executives think," and went on to describe how Union Bank of California benefited from the racial signals projected by a 54 percent nonwhite workforce. Vice Chairman Rick Hartnack told the magazine with evident satisfaction, "Walk into a branch in a Latino area, and you'll see lots of personnel who are Latino."[218]

The intended audience of the signaling could be potential customers, or it could be current or potential employees. Diversity consultant Alfred Schreiber's textbook advocated deployment of targeted racial signaling to appeal to nonwhite current and potential employees. If firms "place minority employees in visible positions," he writes, "the job [of diversity] will be done."[219] Schreiber predicted that "nondiverse companies" would have trouble appealing to diverse professionals because they would look "anachronistic."[220] On the other hand, "a CFO who is a minority sends a message to minority employees throughout the firm and to diverse candidates that that company has a top-level commitment to diversity."[221]

There is evidence that employers perceive racial signaling to be especially important in jobs related to human resources, equal employment opportunity (EEO), and diversity management positions. Companies originally began to hire EEO compliance officers in the 1970s to attend to the burdens of Title VII and affirmative-action regulations.[222] Many companies appeared to believe that if they were going to hire someone to report to the government and to their own employees that the company was fair to all racial groups, then the best person for that job would be a racial minority: A *Conference Board* report noted that when filling this position, corporate employers "tended to look for people who were anything *but* white males" (original emphasis).[223]

This remained unchanged as the position morphed from "EEO specialist" with responsibility for legal compliance to "diversity officer," concerned with leveraging diversity for company profit. Human resources consultant Cornelia Gamlem told *Conference Board*, "Organizations are searching for someone who looks the role." Diversity consultant Mauricio Velásquez echoed that view: "This job was specifically created for anybody but the dominant group."[224]

Mirroring the concerns about nonwhites pigeonholed as marketers to minorities only, sociologist Sharon Collins's study of black executives indicated that racial signaling placements had detrimental effects on the mobility of nonwhites. Collins found that fifty-one of the seventy-six persons she interviewed felt they were stuck in racialized jobs that limited their mobility—a phenomenon Collins called the "African-American mobility trap." One interviewee spoke bitterly of an event in his career where he had to tell a personnel manager, "I don't want a nigger job, and I don't want to be dead-ended." He was referring to jobs that are "pre-identified for blacks only," "have high-ranking titles and are highly visible but do not have any power in a company" and "would not turn into any kind of career with the company." This interviewee avoided companies where blacks are left "to die on the vine."[225] A forty-six-year-old sales vice president worried that if one does these kinds of jobs "too well," then management may believe "this is where you need to be." Many of Collins' respondents insisted on time limits when taking racialized jobs, and they actively sought to be moved from those jobs.[226]

Legal scholar David Wilkins found similar patterns in law firms, where "minority lawyers sometimes find themselves being 'matched' in areas in which they have no interest and with which they have no business being involved."[227] For example, a Puerto Rican associate working in corporate law was suddenly assigned to work with Latin American clients with responsibilities focusing on translation, and black attorneys told Wilkins of situations where they were asked to work on discrimination litigation when their specialties were in other areas, such as mergers and acquisitions.[228]

The *Conference Board* report argued that one of the reasons for the paucity of whites in the role of "diversity director" was that whites, who had many access points to a corporation, avoided diversity jobs because they also saw them as dead ends. As Clayton Osborne, the vice president of Human Resources for Bausch and Lomb, explained, "Diversity, like Communications and HR, is a support role in most companies. . . . Because such roles aren't viewed as valuable to the company and critical to its success, white men don't want the job. It's not perceived as having enough power and influence." Minorities take it, Osborne explained, because "minorities see it as a way of helping other minorities."[229] Others gave different reasons. Management consultant Kenneth Sole argued that minorities accept such positions because they are a quick and familiar way to get in the door.[230] CSX Corporation's assistant vice president of diversity, Susan Hamilton, said the job was "stereotyped" for minorities and because of that, minorities should "think twice about taking this job"—it is more helpful to "break new ground in another area."[231] Diversity consultant Roosevelt Thomas agreed, explaining, "Fifty percent of the time, it's a dead-end job, in that a person becomes fairly disgruntled when diversity isn't valued much at an organization."[232] Osborne from

Bausch and Lomb added, "Some companies put a person in a diversity department to get rid of him."[233]

Besides the possible limits on a nonwhite's mobility that come with the territory of a diversity job, there are racial signaling dilemmas that need to be deftly managed when appointing an EEO or diversity officer. According to diversity consultant Sondra Thiederman, white male employees may see a minority diversity officer as someone with an ax to grind—but if employers target the racial signaling at white male employees and place a white male in that role, "Minorities in the organization might look at him and say, 'He's not one of us.'"[234]

Nevertheless, some firms are making whiteness a qualification for diversity jobs due to its signaling effects. The *Wall Street Journal* noted a trend toward what it called an "unusual tactic"—namely, "enlisting white males to foster diversity efforts." The goal of signaling to whites made whiteness a qualification for the job: "Having a white man champion diversity efforts—particularly one who works in Operations rather than Human Resources—can help bring other white males on board, the theory goes." Chris Simmons, the chief diversity officer for PricewaterhouseCoopers LLP who appointed white male Keith Ruth to oversee diversity efforts in the tax division, told the *Journal*, "A lot of the people we want to hear the message are white males. . . . We really have to get away from this model of it just being white women and minority people. . . . [Appointing a white male] sends the message that we think all kinds of people can be committed to diversity."[235]

Though employers are far less willing to talk about it, some still use the racial signaling of whites in more traditional ways, such as signaling competence or connections with the mainstream of American business. The only real difference between this tactic and the deployment of nonwhite race is that the signaling power of whiteness is almost never discussed openly and is not part of the racial-realist vision. However, Arlene Dávila, in her study of the Latino marketing industry, found that some firms were willing to discuss privately how they reserved key spots for non-Latino whites. For sales staff at a management level in the Latino entertainment industry, including such giant firms as Univision, "a Hispanic's authenticity . . . is a hindrance for entering and successfully operating within the inner circles of corporate America." Instead, it is whites who "have the contacts and command the greatest authority" or who enjoy "legitimacy that is vested in them on the basis of their 'whiteness.'" One salesperson told Dávila that with whites, clients "don't have to worry about saying the wrong or insensitive thing."[236]

There is no research that I am aware of that specifically examines the effectiveness of racial signaling in creating the desired reactions in either employees or potential clients. The research cited above, however, that dramatically demonstrates the unhappiness of some nonwhites who feel they have been "dead-ended," suggests that even when it creates the hoped-for reactions, racial signaling needs to be done with great care to avoid creating blocked opportunities and resentments.

Moreover, even when not limited to particular jobs, racial signaling may fail to create significant opportunity. Legal scholar David B. Wilkins sees this practice in legal firms as a "numbers game" that does little to advance the careers of nonwhites: "My interviews are replete with examples of black lawyers who have been trotted out to impress a black politician or corporate counsel and then trotted back into the oblivion from whence they came, never to see the work that their diversity helped to procure."[237]

Racial Realism in Business and the Professions: When Is It Legal?

Employers are saying that they already hire and place professional and white-collar employees based on perceptions of racial abilities and racial signaling, and foundations, consultants, and advocacy groups argue that more of this should occur. Underscoring the widespread acceptance of this strategy of management is the practice of nonwhites forming businesses and marketing their racial abilities to sell products to their own groups. Assessing the legality of racial realism in professional and white-collar private employment is challenging because there is not a large body of relevant case law. However, what does exist does not appear to provide any legal authorization for these practices. Some courts have said explicitly that race *cannot* be used the ways these employers are using it (or say they are using it). In private employment, where Title VII and Section 1981 are the relevant statutes, only classical liberalism and affirmative-action liberalism have court backing.

When someone sues a racial-realist private employer for taking race into account in hiring and placing workers, that employer has few options to defend this usage. One option is to deny that they are actually using racial realism: they may claim that though they value diversity, they are not, in fact, considering race when they hire, fire, or place employees in particular jobs. This would transfer at least some burden of proof onto the charging party to show that discrimination actually had occurred. No cases have gone to trial where this has happened in white collar or professional jobs, however. Employers who practice racial realism in these sectors have admitted it when challenged, or simply settled with the charging party, as I show below. For this reason, my discussion of the challenges that litigants face in proving discrimination is deferred to Chapter 5 and the context where it matters the most, which is the low-skilled employment sector.

Employers of white-collar workers and professionals who own up to their use of racial realism cannot claim that race is a "bona fide occupational qualification" for their jobs. As described in the introduction, Title VII, which regulates private employers, has no BFOQ defense for race, and the same is true for Section 1981, another statute prohibiting racial discrimination in private employment. Another defense for considering race in hiring and placement is that it fits into the employer's affirmative-action program. The problem for advocates of racial realism here is that there are sharp limits on how race can be used in affirmative action, and legally acceptable affirmative-action programs do not allow for the recognition of racial abilities or for racial signaling.

The key case here was *United Steelworkers of America v. Weber*.[238] This 1979 case dealt with a voluntary affirmative-action plan that Kaiser Aluminum & Chemical Corporation in Gramercy, Louisiana negotiated with its union. Their plan provided rules for the training of unskilled workers to fill skilled jobs. In the early 1970s, less than 2 percent of the skilled craftworkers at Kaiser were black, while the surrounding area's labor force was almost 40 percent black. This was a big discrepancy, and it was the result of discrimination by the labor union. Kaiser and the union agreed to train craftworkers from within, and to promote lower-level workers (who were predominantly black) to the training program (where they were not previously included). Blacks were to make up 50 percent of the trainees until their presence in the craft job reached the level of the surrounding labor force—40 percent. To achieve this goal, blacks would have to be trained before whites who had more seniority at the plant. Brian Weber, who was one such white, sued the union for race discrimination.

In an opinion written by Justice Brennan, the Court acknowledged that these were employment practices that took race into account, but also emphasized that it was a voluntary effort that was consistent with the goals of Title VII. Kaiser and the union had adopted their plan to eliminate patterns of racial segregation, which fit with Title VII because Congress had intended the law to move blacks into employment. Brennan therefore approved, in part because both Title VII and the plan "were designed to break down old patterns of racial segregation and hierarchy," and also because (quoting Minnesota's Democratic Senator Hubert Humphrey) they were designed to "'open employment opportunities for Negroes in occupations which have been traditionally closed to them.'"[239]

Brennan emphasized that employers were not free to do just anything to bring about black opportunity. For example, they could not "unnecessarily trammel the interests of the white employees."[240] This would be the case if Kaiser and the union were firing whites—literally removing them from employment. The affirmative-action plan did not do this, nor did it bar whites as a category in the program (which also would have rendered it unacceptable), since at least half of the trainees were to be white. Finally, the plan was only temporary, and the race preference would end as soon as the racial imbalance was eliminated.[241]

These became the rules for assessing voluntary affirmative action and they were, for the most part, affirmed and clarified in 1987 in another Supreme Court decision, *Johnson v. Transportation Agency of Santa Clara County*.[242] An employer using race for an affirmative-action program was different from an employer practicing intentional "disparate treatment" discrimination, and affirmative action could be a nondiscriminatory rationale to defend an employer from a white male worker's charge of discrimination. But the plan had to have certain characteristics. Courts would ask, first, whether or not there was some imbalance at the firm that the employer was trying to remedy. Second, they would ask whether or not the actions of the employer unnecessarily limited opportunities for whites (or males), which meant that the plans could not result in whites being fired or completely banned from certain opportunities. Last, these plans had to be temporary with the goal of fixing something that had gone awry. That thing "gone awry" was the racial imbalance. For a plan to be legal, it had to pass all three of these tests, not just one of them.

The racial realism discussed in this chapter, whether due to a belief in the value of racial abilities or racial signaling, is rarely if ever linked to the firing of any workers due to their race (but see below), and though race was a qualification for marketing, journalism, and medical jobs, it does not appear to necessarily block certain races from certain jobs. Certain races are better at certain jobs, the logic goes, but that does not mean that other races could never do these jobs. Racial realism would therefore pass that part of the test. What separates it from affirmative action, and thus what creates the legal problem, is that when employers are using racial abilities or signaling, they are thinking about the *future performance* of the firm or organization, or about how *customers will react* to that firm or employee. Though there may actually be some racial imbalances at the firm, the employers are not trying to remedy imbalances by seeking a diverse team of idea generators, a skilled marketing team, the right doctor for a population of patients, or the most sensitive journalist. They are seeing race as useful instead of only significant, and they are linking it to firm performance, not to justice or equality. As in criminal law, motive matters.

What is now called the *Weber* test has left a legacy of failure for racial-realist employment aspirations, particularly in private employment. Judges appointed by Republican presidents have authored several of the key opinions here, though as stated in Chapter 1, this does not appear to be a partisan effort. What is notable is that these presumably conservative judges have not favored an interpretation of conservatism that might prioritize employer discretion. Instead, these judges have favored a strict, classical liberal or affirmative-action liberal reading of Title VII and the *Weber* test, an interpretation that has made it difficult for employers to win cases if their racial-realist goals are challenged.[243] There was some possibility that the 2003 Supreme Court decision that approved of diversity as a goal in admitting students to schools, *Grutter v. Bollinger*,[244] might have some application to employment, but that did not last, and this was only ever a serious possibility in public employment for reasons I will discuss in the next chapter.

The first test of the diversity rationale in employment occurred in a public context, but since it was a Title VII case, courts have cited it in the private employment context. In *Taxman v. Piscataway Board of Education*,[245] the New Jersey Third Circuit Court of Appeals considered the claim of a white school teacher who had been laid off while the school district retained a similarly qualified black teacher because, the school district argued, that black teacher's racial diversity added value to the education process. Theodore Kruse, the school board president, emphasized the racial signaling value of the black teacher and obliquely suggested that black teachers brought something to teaching that white teachers could not. He told the court that because the community was diverse, it was "valuable for the students to see in the various employment roles a wide range of backgrounds, and that it was also valuable to the work force and in particular to the teaching staff that they have— they see that in each other."[246] Kruse's explanation was not clear, but indicated a racial realist rationale. A teacher's race sent signals that the district believed the staff should be diverse not as a matter of justice, but as a means to an educational end. His explanation mentioned a variety of terms related to culture, backgrounds, contact, awareness, and understanding, but there was no emphasis on fairness or remedying imbalances (also see Chapter 3).

In an opinion written by Judge Carol Los Mansmann, a Reagan appointee, the Third Circuit rejected the Board's reasoning, arguing that Congress intended Title VII to stop discrimination or remedy previous discrimination, and only the latter goal justified employers using race in making employment decisions. The court specifically rejected the Board's attempt to use the 1978 Supreme Court decision, *Regents of the University of California v. Bakke*, that upheld "diversity" as a constitutionally permissible goal in university admissions,[247] arguing that the context of university admissions was totally different from and thus not applicable to employment at a high school.[248]

Though dealing with government use of race preferences, the *Taxman* ruling denied that Title VII authorized a racial-realist, strategic management of race by employers, and it thus supplied a negative precedent for racial realism in white-collar or professional private employment. For example, in *Schurr v. Resorts International Hotel*,[249] the Third Circuit (in another opinion by Mansmann) rejected an affirmative-action plan with a diversity component. The court applied the *Weber* test and cited its own opinion in *Taxman*. The case involved a white man, Karl Schurr, who had been an occasional light and sound technician at an Atlantic City casino. The casino passed over Schurr for a full-time job that it eventually gave to a qualified African-American male, Ronald Boykin, also a casual employee.

Resorts International was not pushing its own racial-realist vision—the hotel, as a casino licensee in New Jersey, was following an affirmative-action regulation that a state commission created to implement New Jersey's Casino Control Act. But this was no standard affirmative-action regulation. Though it was not quite racial realist in its vision, its purpose was focused on the future and not on remedying past discrimination. The Casino Control Commission stated, "The Legislature recognized that a once renowned tourist area had become blighted and had been largely abandoned by tourists. The Legislature was also aware Atlantic City had and has a large minority population, and sought to ensure that the job creation which would accompany casino developments would benefit all segments of the population."[250] But the court insisted that any rationale for considering race had to be based on the goal of remedying discrimination. Therefore, the casino had no legal authorization to prefer Boykin, because it was not remedying discrimination. The court stated definitively, "This absence of any reference to or showing of past or present discrimination in the casino industry is fatal."[251] While the goal of improving Atlantic City neighborhoods is different from goals of improved service and legitimacy achieved through racial realism, the logic of this opinion suggests racial realism would similarly fail.

The judge-made law of affirmative action looks unfriendly, then, to a business that wants to hire Asians to help develop marketing plans to sell products to Asians, or a hospital that wants hire black doctors to ensure satisfied black patients and better treatment, a news organization that wants to bring in a Latino to show the Latino community it understands them, or even a Fortune 500 company that wants to hire an American Indian because it does not have many and believes the American Indian's perspective will lead to innovative ideas. The logic of the remedial rationale would not be available as a defense for an employer who was concentrating workers in areas where he or she believed they would have special abilities such as giving services or developing products for persons of the same race or ethnicity, or to an employer moving around people of different races just because of the belief that diversity adds to innovation. Affirmative action is a backward-looking defense, but any racial-realist strategy looks forward.

Are other defenses available? Some employers may think they can do what they almost always do when making a business decision: appeal to the market. If customers want something, the shrewd business owner or operator will try to provide it. Racial signals and some notions of racial-abilities-based employment rely on assumptions about what customers prefer. Yet justifying hiring decisions based on customer preference is problematic from the perspective of discrimination law. If consideration of customer preferences for different races were allowable under Title VII, then store owners (and just about anyone else) would have used this loophole to avoid hiring blacks. Jim Crow employment practices never would have been dismantled.

The law itself says nothing about customers, but the EEOC's guidelines for employers explicitly state that employers cannot use the desires of customers to justify discrimination: "Title VII also does not permit racially motivated decisions driven by business concerns—for example, concerns about the effect on employee relations, or the negative reaction of clients or customers."[252] Moreover, courts have rejected arguments from employers who tried to use their customers to justify discrimination—at least when it was whites' preferences that were at issue. For example, when the EEOC filed suit against the owner of a network of Dairy Queen restaurants in Texas for hiring local teenagers rather than African-Americans who applied but would have to commute to the jobs, the EEOC won the case. The Fifth Circuit showed thinly veiled contempt for the Dairy Queen owner's argument that Dairy Queen's teenaged white customers preferred "to be served by persons of their own 'culture,'" simply announcing that the court was "discarding" the argument and moving on to more serious but equally inadequate "reasons" for not hiring blacks—putting "reasons" in quotes.[253]

Probably the best court test for racial realism in private, white-collar employment came in a 1999 Alabama case in which a court again rejected this strategy of managing race. The Parker Group (TPG) was a business that performed telephone marketing for political campaigns. If a campaign asked for it, TPG assigned callers to voters on the basis of a belief that racial abilities or signaling or both would lead to a more effective campaign. TPG also physically segregated black and white employees to facilitate supervision. The Alabama district court described the practice, and also indicated it was a recurring strategy in campaigns:

> It is undisputed by TPG that a small percentage, approximately 10%, of its "get out the vote" calling—which constituted roughly 60% of its overall business—was so-called "race-matched" calling. Race-matched calling means that black callers call only black voters and white callers call only white voters. The rationale for this practice is that it is more likely to lure these voter groups to the polls on election day. Put another way, the theory behind this race-matched strategy is that black voters will more readily identify with and be sympathetic to "black voices" whereas white voters will more readily identify with and be sympathetic to "white voices." Different "scripts" are also utilized depending on which racial group is being solicited. The voice-matched strategy is also used with regard to regional dialects, i.e., callers with Midwestern accents will be employed to call Midwesterners. Race-matched calling is only employed by TPG when it is specifically requested by a customer. TPG customers who apparently requested this service include, but are not limited to, former Alabama Governor Jim Folsom, U.S. Congressman Earl Hillard and Birmingham Mayor Richard Arrington.[254]

TPG used Shirley Ferrill, an African-American woman assigned to the company by a temporary employment agency, in its racial-matching strategy. When TPG laid her off following the campaign of Alabama governor Jim Folsom in 1994, she sued. Not eligible to use Title VII because she was technically an employee of the temp agency, she sued under the similar law, Section 1981, claiming TPG had discriminated against her based on her race in her assignment and termination.

The district court ruled for TPG on the termination issue, accepting TPG's claim that she was laid off because the campaign was over. But noting that Ferrill's assignment was based on "stereotyped assumptions," the opinion, by Reagan appointee William Acker, Jr., said Ferrill's assignment was an "obvious violation of the law" because "'practicability' . . . is not a defense to racial discrimination"—and because the candidates for office "should have known better."[255]

TPG appealed and fared no better. In assessing her claim, the Eleventh Circuit, in an opinion written by Nixon appointee Judge Anthony Alaimo, stated that the issue in the case was whether an employer "who acts with no racial animus but makes job assignments on the basis of race can be held liable for intentional discrimination under Section 1981" and that the ruling was obvious: "Clearly, the answer is yes."[256] The court noted that allowing TPG's practices would mean that race was a BFOQ and that Section 1981 was similar to Title VII in that there was no statutory basis for a race BFOQ.[257] The court also rejected an affirmative-action defense, arguing that TPG was not taking any affirmative action because it was not trying to correct a racial imbalance. Instead, its employment strategies were "based on a racial stereotype"; namely, the belief that black voters would respond better to marketing pitches if black callers delivered them.[258]

The Walgreens drugstore chain has learned more recently that however useful racial realism is to a company's bottom line, it still does not fit with the law. Similar to some of the businesses discussed above, Walgreens had a practice of matching black managers with black communities. The company's record of hiring African-Americans as store or district managers was excellent. Fully 17 percent of managers were African-American, well above the industry average of 9 percent. Community groups in black neighborhoods, Walgreens said, actually asked for black managers in those stores. The problem was that blacks did not always want to be assigned to these stores. For example, when Johnny Tucker, an African-American man who lived in a mostly white, affluent Kansas City suburb, found himself assigned to manage a store in a grim inner-city neighborhood, the job caused him so much stress he ended up taking a 90-day sick leave. Moreover, these stores generated, on average, less revenue than stores in other neighborhoods. This was a problem because Walgreens tied store revenue to a manager's promotion opportunities.[259] Standard decisions based on employer belief in racial abilities to know a market thus took on an ominous tone. For example, a senior vice president stated that the East St. Louis store managed by another African-American, Angela Miller, was making a mistake by stocking premium ice creams such as Haagen-Dazs rather than "ethnic products" like "cheap hair care and hot or spicy food"—and that this failure to know her market was evidence that Miller was not "black enough."[260]

The EEOC filed a suit in addition to Tucker's. In its press release, the EEOC specifically attacked the consideration of race in placement—something that presumably occurs in medical, journalistic, and marketing jobs all the time. EEOC St. Louis District Director James R. Neely, Jr. charged that Walgreens limited African-Americans' job opportunities because, "Essentially, Walgreens has made store assignments based on race."[261] Robert G. Johnson, the EEOC St. Louis Regional Attorney—with apparent disregard for practices that are celebrated across America as progressive and wise business decisions—said, "It is unthinkable in this day and age that a company of Walgreens' size and reputation would differentiate between its managers based on their race."[262] Rather than go to trial, Walgreens agreed to give $24 million to 10,000 black employees, to use outside consultants to review placement and promotion procedures, and, of course, to stop assigning managers based on race.[263]

It appears that Title VII as written and interpreted by the EEOC and in the existing case law make it very difficult for a firm, news organization, or even a hospital to defend hiring or placement based on racial realism. The lack of a race BFOQ in the law, and the limited rules for the allowance of a BFOQ defense, render this defense unlikely to help an employer wanting to hire based on perceived racial abilities or signaling. Moreover, the rules for a legal affirmative-action plan require the motives for the plan to focus on remedying a racial imbalance, and not on providing better service or making certain customers feel welcome, trusting, or comfortable. Finally, the established interpretation of law as forbidding hiring and placement based on stereotypes also suggests that employers seeking the benefits of racial realism will run into legal trouble when challenged. In short, many advocates, experts, and employers believe racial realism in white-collar employment and the professions is necessary for health and good business, but it is difficult to find any legal authorization for it.

3

We the People: Racial Realism in Politics and Government

One might wonder why government employment should get its own chapter. After all, most government employees are skilled workers and professionals, similar to the skilled and professional workers who were the focus of Chapter 2. It is also the case that since 1972, Title VII has applied to government employment.

Yet government employment is also very different. This is because government employers sometimes have goals that private employers do not. In some cases, government employers may perceive a need to pay back voters with government jobs. Another objective may be to provide role models for young people. For both of these reasons, racial signaling has far more importance in government employment than in private employment, where it matters only sometimes in white-collar employment and hardly matters at all in blue-collar jobs. Yet racial abilities also matter a lot in some government jobs, especially policing and teaching. Thus, the American tradition of racial realism in government jobs is rich and long—and it has become even richer and more elaborate in keeping with the increasing racial diversity of the population.

Yet government employment is also very different, and racial signaling especially important, because it relates to power and nationalism in unique ways. As described in Chapter 1, government jobs are deeply linked to a group's sense of having a say in their destiny—a big factor in the perception of government legitimacy. Denial of representation and influence in government has been a factor in secessionist movements and ethnic nationalism around the world.[1] In some contexts, visible inclusion in the government (what political scientists called "descriptive representation") can lead to better representation of previously excluded interests, allowing a wide and diverse segment of the public to feel included, and thus increasing the stability of the government.[2] Widespread racial unrest and violence are certainly not unknown in the U.S., and the racial violence of the 1960s, as well as the six straight days of fighting that took place in Los Angeles as recently as 1992, reminds us that it *can* happen here.

Another key difference with government employment, and a factor that makes it necessary to treat it separately, is that it involves a different legal regime. Both Title VII as well as the Constitution regulate government employment. The Fourteenth Amendment's guarantee of equal protection of the laws creates, as we shall see, new possibilities. The framers of the Constitution and the Fourteenth Amendment, apparently preoccupied with other concerns, wrote nothing about "BFOQ" employer defenses. There is, consequently, no explicit constitutional statement of an exceptional *lack* of a BFOQ for racial discrimination in government employment as there is in Title VII. This clears the way for a judge-made race BFOQ. The problem for racial realism is that few judges have seized this opportunity: for the most part, courts allow hiring for racial abilities or signaling only in the context of law enforcement.

Nevertheless, racial realism (or its advocacy) is common in the practice of government employment, whether or not it is sanctioned by the law. This chapter focuses on three contexts of government employment. I begin at the top: elected positions and appointments made by elected officials. Technically, these are not "jobs" in the way other positions in this book are jobs. Presidents, members of Congress, mayors and the like are obviously not "hired"; they are chosen by voters. Furthermore, the appointments they make are not subject to Title VII any more than their election is governed by Title VII.[3] At the federal level, for example, appointments are governed by the Constitution, which says little about the process other than that the President is to make the appointments with the advice and consent of the Senate. This constitutional provision was geared not toward equal opportunity, but toward avoiding the appointment of cronies.[4]

Yet these officials do work for us. They have jobs, and they draw paychecks. More importantly, if we are going to assess which strategies of managing race in employment are dominant in America, it is essential to understand how race matters at the top. What messages are our political leaders sending when they make appointments, and what messages are we sending to them when we elect them?

I will argue that our political officials entrusted with enforcing the laws—that is, executive branch officials—commonly make appointments based on interests in racial signaling and that there is a long history of this practice, though it used to be done more narrowly. While the only race that mattered was whiteness for most of the nation's history, racial signaling with nonwhite appointments has occurred at the local level for more than a century, and at the federal level, it began with the Franklin Delano Roosevelt administration. In recent decades, it has expanded beyond black and white to include Asians and Latinos, and it can be seen in White House appointments, positions of party leadership, and appointments to the judiciary. I also review evidence that supports the notion that race has important effects in the highest levels of government.

Next, I show how racial realism has shaped advocacy and employment in two key areas where citizens regularly interact with government: policing and teaching. Here again there is a long history of racial realism in practice, and an even longer history of advocacy, particularly in teaching. The notion that police officers and teachers should be hired and placed with an eye toward their racial abilities and signaling continues to be alive and well, and has changed and expanded as American demography has become more racially diverse. There is evidence to support racial realism in both cases, though as usual, that evidence is mixed.

Finally, I will explore the ways that the courts have treated this issue, highlighting their use of constitutional jurisprudence to get around the problem of a lack of race BFOQ in Title VII, as well as their inconsistency in crafting these legal rules. Courts have been more open to finding a compelling interest to use race in the hiring and placement of police officers than in teaching—even in instances where minority officers have resisted assignments to mostly minority neighborhoods—as they have identified an "operational needs" compelling interest that justified racial realism. On the other hand, racial-realist ideas common in education, such as the notion of racial "role models" for students, have either found no support or have been explicitly prohibited.

I also explore the implications of one of the Supreme Court's most important rulings on race and compelling interests. Though it dealt with racial preferences in university admissions, many hoped the case would act as a catalyst for changes in employment law and increase opportunities for at least government institutions to use race in their hiring. In 2003's *Grutter v. Bollinger*, the Supreme Court articulated a governmental interest in racial diversity due to its civic benefits, which would seem to have relevance to both upper and the lower positions in government employment. However, despite initial speculation, the *Grutter* opinion had only a very limited influence on government employment practices.

In emphasizing non-Title VII "employment" at the outset—that is, the ways that elected officials use race in governing the country—I am very deliberately trying to highlight the inconsistency in our laws and the practices of government officials. There can be little doubt that the leaders of American government regularly practice racial realism, and this makes it all the more remarkable that civil rights law offers so little authorization for what these leaders so clearly believe is the right thing to do.

Racial Realism in Political Appointments: An American Tradition, Now Multiplied

When Americans choose political leaders, they tend to choose those who look like themselves. White Americans have typically supported white leaders, and other races supported leaders of their own race. The dominance of white elected leaders is thus largely the result of the numerical dominance of white voters. The election rates of black and Latino leaders increase when these groups become a majority or near majority in a district.[5] Throughout American history, elected Asians in the Senate have for the most part represented Hawaii, the only state with an Asian plurality.[6] It is not clear why voters tend to vote for their own race, but it would seem likely that many use racial-realist strategies when voting, for example when considering which candidates will have the ability to represent them effectively. Knowing this, elected officials tend toward racial realism when making appointments as well.

Early Racial Realism in Urban Politics

Racial signaling for nonwhites became entrenched in the politics of local appointments by the early 1900s, when nonwhite populations with voting rights became large enough to sway elections. The strategy was to use the racial signaling to show that voter support was appreciated and to suggest that particular races had a voice in the government. As explained by political scientist Harold Gosnell in his 1935 study of the growing importance of African-Americans in Chicago politics, "When the Negroes had developed a small professional and business class, when their importance to a given faction or party was strategic, when they found white politicians who were courageous enough to back them under the fire of hostile sections of the white public, they secured some local and state positions."[7] But a hundred years ago, racial signaling required a delicate balancing act. A mayor wanting to reward blacks for their support had to be careful to avoid angering racist whites, who generally would allow immigrant groups to get their patronage rewards or have their own candidates but resisted sharing power with blacks.

In 1915, Chicago's mayor, "Big Bill" Thompson, who enjoyed great support from the city's African-Americans, was thus forced to defend his appointment of blacks to some quality government jobs:

> My reason for making such appointments were [sic] three fold: First, because the person appointed was qualified for the position. Second, because in the name of humanity it is my duty to do what I can to elevate rather than degrade any class of American citizens. Third, because I am under obligations to this people for their continued friendship and confidence while I have been in this community.[8]

In city politics, the issue was whether city hall could use racial realism in the same ways that it had used ethnic realism to benefit such white groups as the Irish or Italians. As Thompson's defensiveness shows, it was not always an easy sell.

Origins of Racial Realism in the Federal Government: New Deals and Great Societies for African-Americans

Nonwhite voters found the federal government far less welcoming than cities like Chicago. They could find jobs, but opportunity was sharply limited well into the twentieth century. President William Howard Taft's administration was the first to segregate the federal civil service, but Woodrow Wilson did the most to formally institutionalize that policy. It stayed segregated until the end of the Franklin Delano Roosevelt administration, though discrimination against African-Americans remained the rule until Lyndon Johnson took office.[9]

Despite his efforts to segregate, Taft was also a pioneer in that he was the first president to appoint an African-American to a position with policymaking power when he appointed William H. Lewis to be Assistant United States Attorney General.[10] But it was FDR who, late in his first term, established racial realism as a normal management strategy at the federal level. In 1933, black leaders pressured Roosevelt to create a position for someone to oversee the treatment of blacks in his new programs. Clearly attempting a politically sensitive balancing act, the president chose a white Southerner for the position. Roy Wilkins of the NAACP told the administration that blacks "bitterly resent having a white man designated by the government to advise them of their welfare," and the administration responded again, this time by adding Robert Weaver, a Harvard-educated economics Ph.D., to serve alongside the white official.[11]

Despite the inauspicious start, there was progress. By 1935, Roosevelt had appointed more than forty African-Americans to low-level positions in cabinet departments and New Deal agencies. Several of them would meet regularly with the president to advise on racial matters. They were informally dubbed the "Black Cabinet."[12]

Roosevelt's policies helped move African-American support from the Republicans to the Democrats. Truman's support of civil rights helped to consolidate this support. Eisenhower, however, managed to win 40 percent of the black vote and rewarded that support with the high-level appointment of E. Frederic Morrow as a White House adviser.[13] Still, the title of Morrow's memoir, *Black Man in the White House*, trumpeted the exceptional nature of a high-level black appointment in the 1950s.[14]

Lyndon Johnson, who did so much for African-American causes, also appointed the first black cabinet secretary, Robert Weaver, as the head of the new Department of Housing and Urban Development (HUD). The story behind Weaver's rise from a low-level official in the Roosevelt administration to higher level posts under John F. Kennedy and Johnson, explored in rich detail by historian Wendell Pritchett, is useful to recount because it highlights the strategic thinking driving racial signaling in high-level appointments, as well as the meanings of both blackness and whiteness in an era when classically liberal nondiscrimination became the law of the land.

During the hard-fought 1960 campaign, Henry Cabot Lodge, the vice presidential running mate of Republican candidate Richard M. Nixon, announced to an audience in Harlem that Nixon would make history by being the first president to appoint an African-American to a cabinet position. Worried about his standing in the South, Nixon denied Lodge's claim, and then Lodge denied he had ever made it. Kennedy said that making a appointment on the basis of race was "racism in reverse, and it's worse."[15]

Kennedy, however, won three quarters of the black vote, and—reflecting the hypocrisy that is so common in American racial politics—sought to reward blacks with federal appointments. Over the resistance of Southern members of Congress, Kennedy appointed Weaver, who had been a civil rights activist focused on segregation issues in New York City, to run the Housing and Home Finance Agency. One black newspaper, the *Pittsburgh Courier*, said approvingly that the appointment was a strike against housing discrimination, "because the new administrator, not appointed to the job necessarily because of his race, but because of his ability, will serve as a symbol."[16]

Weaver's rise would continue. Congress passed the Department of Housing and Urban Development Act in 1965, creating what came to be known as HUD. Johnson ultimately decided to appoint Weaver to the new cabinet post, but it took several months of analysis, as there were many concerns about his suitability for the job, some of which were related to race. For example, Senator Robert F. Kennedy (D-NY) argued that Weaver's race was a problem in both the North and South, and both Kennedy and Johnson agreed there was "some advantage to having a white man in there."[17] Worrying about relations with Congress, Johnson told Roy Wilkins of the NAACP that "a white man can do a hell of a lot more for the Negro than the Negroes can do for themselves in these cities."[18] Yet Johnson was also very concerned about the racial signaling value of a Weaver appointment to black voters. He worried that appointing a white person would be a letdown to "little Negro boys in Podunk, Mississippi," and that despite Johnson's achievements for civil rights, blacks would see the Weaver snub and conclude that "when you get down to the nut-cutting . . . this Southerner just couldn't quite cut the mustard—he just couldn't name a Negro to the Cabinet."[19]

While Johnson agonized about the decision, the black press urged him to move forward, with the *Baltimore Afro-American* arguing that Weaver would "wipe out big-city racial ghettoes," the *Chicago Defender* maintaining that Weaver was the most qualified candidate, and the *Pittsburgh Courier* again playing up the racial signaling, stating that Weaver's appointment "would mean that a Negro was a full-fledged member of the top power structure and would counteract much of the urban Negro revolt to the Republicans. . . ."[20] Roy Wilkins warned in a public statement that failing to appoint Weaver "might galvanize the Negro community into thinking that in rejecting Mr. Weaver [Johnson] was rejecting them."[21]

Johnson told his attorney general, Nicholas Katzenbach, "I doubt this fellow will make the grade" and predicted he would be "a flop," but at the same time, Johnson could not resist the powerful value of racial signaling. Therefore, "We've got to get a super man for number two place [*sic*], and then send this fellow all around policy touring and let this second fella do the work with the Congress and with the President and with all the other people."[22] Satisfied with this plan, Johnson announced on January 13, 1966, that Weaver would be the secretary of HUD. Civil rights leaders and the black press cheered.[23] Johnson would also ingratiate himself further with civil rights groups when he nominated Thurgood Marshall to be the first African-American on the Supreme Court—a move the NAACP had lobbied for since the Kennedy administration.[24]

As the story of Weaver's appointment makes clear, presidents may make appointment decisions while seriously considering the racial implications of their decisions. It also shows a widespread expectation of racial realism in appointments, and media elites and advocacy groups typically lobby specifically for appointments, emphasizing the importance of racial signaling or racial abilities or both.

Moreover, advocates for African-Americans were far from alone in this kind of lobbying. Latino groups were especially active during the Johnson and Nixon administrations, directing much of their lobbying energy toward securing government representation.[25]

By the late 1970s, presidents did not have to be pushed very hard. Jimmy Carter kept computerized records of the race and gender of his political appointments. During his term, 21 percent of his appointments were nonwhites (and 22 percent were women), including two black cabinet members (Donald F. McHenry was Secretary of the Army; and Patricia Roberts Harris was first Secretary of Housing and Urban Development and later headed Health, Education, and Welfare).[26]

The Republican Move to Anti-Affirmative Action—and Racial Realism

The current period of racial realism in government, in which both Republicans and Democrats know that how they manage racial signaling with their elected leaders and appointed officials is important to party success, began in the 1980s with the Reagan administration. This is also the period when the Republican party moved squarely to define itself as the party of racial conservatism (which by the 1980s meant classical liberalism), and thus to take stands opposed to affirmative action and other policies supported by African-American leaders. Though appointments of nonwhites fell to 9 percent, less than half of Carter's percentage (women were 37 percent of all appointments), Republicans' stated opposition to affirmative-action liberalism did not mean opposition to racial realism, as I show below.[27]

The main Republican strategy is to signal to white voters that they are not doing anything special for blacks—but also that they are not racists. Both parties increasingly appoint Latinos and Asians to top posts, and Republicans especially display their nonwhites as prominently as possible. As Paul Frymer has shown, the challenge for Democrats is to keep black voters loyal while not alienating white voters.[28] Democrats have continued to support both affirmative-action liberalism in policy and racial realism in practice, but by the 1980s, some leaders in the Democratic party were arguing that being too closely identified with the interests of African-Americans was hurting the party's chances at the ballot box.[29]

The primary way that Republicans have managed race has been to find, promote, and display people of color who criticize any or all racially liberal policies. We can see the importance of this racial signaling strategy for the modern Republican party in the meteoric rise of two African-Americans: renowned economist Glenn Loury and future Supreme Court Justice Clarence Thomas.

In the 1980s, Loury was building on his groundbreaking work on "social capital," or how network ties play a key role in social mobility. He had begun to question the role of the government in ameliorating black inequality. If discrimination was not the key factor keeping blacks down, he reasoned, then government attempts to fight it, such as affirmative action, might be misguided.

Loury came to the attention of Republicans after his 1984 speech to a group of civil rights leaders in Washington, DC. To an audience that included Coretta Scott King and John Jacob, the president of the National Urban League, Loury put surprising emphasis on a pillar of conservative thought: that the black poor have a responsibility to help themselves, including in such areas as low educational achievement, high crime rates, and out-of-wedlock births. Many in his audience were appalled.[30]

But conservatives loved it. The *New York Times* noted in a profile, "As a black critic of racial liberalism, Loury rose rapidly in Republican public-policy circles." He sat with Reagan at a White House dinner, and his friend Bill Bennett, then Secretary of Education, offered him a position in his department as undersecretary. Other conservatives embraced Loury, including many identified with the neoconservative movement.[31] Loury would go on to chair the board of a new initiative, the Center for New Black Leadership, organized to constitute a new and different (that is, not liberal) black political voice.

But Loury became disillusioned with conservatism, particularly on matters of race. In his view, the strand of conservative thought with which he identified, neoconservatism, which acknowledged at least some shared responsibility to bring about more racial equality, was losing its distinctiveness.[32] The emerging conservative positions on race in the 1990s, such as the resurgence of biological explanations of poverty rooted in theories of racial differences in intelligence,[33] offended Loury both intellectually and morally. He turned away from conservatism, and conservatives then turned their backs on him.

Loury later authored a very personal and insightful reflection on his relationships with conservatives, focusing on Jewish neoconservatives. Writing in the pages of *CommonQuest*, a short-lived but bold magazine focused on African-American and Jewish relations, Loury wrote of the signaling value of his race:

> That I existed—a black neoconservative with the courage to lend his voice to the chorus, even while being branded a traitor by other blacks—was a certain kind of statement. . . . [M]y "breaking ranks" helped to confirm [the neoconservative positions on race] as valid and non-racist. Interestingly, given the color-blind mantra which animated much neoconservative criticism of affirmative action policies, my color became part of my qualifications as an intellectual warrior. Had I been white, my "brilliant, perceptive, courageous" insights would surely have seemed a lot more like pedestrian, commonplace complaints. . . . How could I insist to my black detractors, who accused me of being disloyal, that they should simply respond to my arguments, when it was not only, or sometimes even mainly, the power of my arguments that mattered?[34]

The racial signaling here was simple: if a black intellectual thought as Republicans did, then these thoughts could not be anti-black.

Supreme Court Justice Clarence Thomas's story is similar to that of Loury—except that Thomas has not offered public reflections on the role of race in his ascendance, and he has stuck with the conservative program. For this, he has been richly rewarded. In his memoirs, Thomas recounts a phone call from the Office of Presidential Personnel in 1981. The caller invited Thomas to take a position as assistant secretary for civil rights in the Department of Education. Thomas was unenthusiastic, in part because he wanted the Department of Education to be abolished. But that was not the only reason for his reluctance: "I had no background in that area, and was sure that I'd been singled out solely because I was black, which I found demeaning."[35] He chose to accept the position anyway, however, because he was interested in racial issues.

Thomas seemed to get over his concern that he was being offered government appointments on racial grounds. His memoirs make no mention at all of the fact that the Reagan administration chose him to be chair of the EEOC—after the Senate had rejected another black conservative candidate, Detroit lawyer William Bell, following criticism from civil rights groups.[36] This is all the more notable given that Thomas recalled that liberals were continually calling the Reagan administration racist. He himself urged more appointments for blacks, but offered no rationale for it, saying only that it was "important."[37]

Thomas's account of his elevation to circuit court judge and later to the Supreme Court also reveals little sense that his race played much of a role in his advancement, even though there is a history of race, ethnicity, and other demographic variables influencing court appointments, and even though President George H. W. Bush chose Thomas to replace Thurgood Marshall, the only other black justice in Supreme Court history. According to his memoirs, Thomas asked White House counsel Boyden Gray whether race was the deciding factor in his nomination. According to Thomas, "Boyden replied that in fact my race had actually worked against me. The initial plan, he said, had been to have me replace Justice (William) Brennan in order to avoid appointing me to what was widely perceived as the court's 'black' seat, thus making the confirmation even more contentious." Brennan had retired earlier than expected, and the Bush administration had felt Thomas, who had been a judge only a few months, needed more seasoning on the circuit court (nevertheless, Bush would wait less than two years before putting Thomas on the Supreme Court).[38]

Thomas's mostly color-blind account of events surrounding his appointment contrasts sharply with the public discourse of the time. Lauding Thomas's self-help ideology, conservative columnist Cal Thomas wrote, "It will be amusing to watch the civil rights establishment trying to oppose him on such a clearly all-American agenda."[39] Pulitzer-Prize-winning political cartoonist Jim Morin drew Bush standing between Marshall and Thomas, pointing to each across his chest with opposite hands, and saying, "What this means is I'm anti-quota, but pro-coincidence!!"[40] The Brookings Institution's Thomas Mann said, "I think that Bush has moved very cleverly," but "it is disingenuous for Bush to argue that race was not a factor in his appointment of Thomas."[41] The U.S. News & World Report wrote, "The president, despite his frequently stated opposition to quotas, was acutely conscious of the need to preserve black representation on the court after Marshall's retirement. Bush also wanted to show sensitivity to black concerns after opposing Democratic civil rights legislation as a 'quota bill' earlier this year." The right-leaning magazine also quoted a Bush adviser, who gloated that after confirmation, "'the two highest senior black officials in the federal government will be Colin Powell [chairman of the Joint Chiefs of Staff] and Clarence Thomas. Both were named by a Republican president, and both cases suggest that the route to success is self-help and black pride, not dependence on white society."[42] Legal scholar Michael J. Gerhardt wrote in 1992 that Thomas "has done little, if any, memorable work" in any area outside of civil rights,[43] and "no one took seriously the President's characterization of Justice Thomas as 'the best person' in the country to serve on the Court."[44] Perhaps the most extreme criticism came from Senator Bill Bradley, who compared Bush's use of race in the Thomas nomination to a campaign ad used against Michael Dukakis that highlighted the saga of murderer Willie Horton, who raped a woman while on a Massachusetts furlough program. Bradley argued that Bush's "tactical use of Clarence Thomas, as with Willie Horton, depends for its effectiveness on the limited ability of all races to see beyond color and, as such, is a stunning example of political opportunism."[45]

A scholarly account of the appointment reveals the predictable considerations of racial signaling. Bush asked staff to concentrate on finding "non-traditional" candidates, and they provided the names of two appeals court judges: a Latino, Emilio M. Garza, and Thomas. Chief of Staff John Sununu supported Garza on the theory that Garza's appointment might help win Latino votes, while appointing Thomas would not entice the overwhelmingly Democratic black voters to cast ballots for Republicans. White House Counsel C. Boyden Gray supported Thomas because of Thomas's solidly conservative views. Bush went with Thomas because of his conservatism, which would satisfy the most conservative Republicans, and also because Bush anticipated that being African-American would ease the path to confirmation of a conservative nominee.[46] It would be hard to oppose Thomas after Scalia and Kennedy had made it through the confirmation process, and African-Americans would have an especially hard time opposing him. Another factor was that the NAACP had privately said they would not oppose Thomas.[47]

By the mid-1990s, Republicans were regularly using racial realism while criticizing affirmative action. Oklahoman J. C. Watts, who in 1994 became the first black Republican member of Congress from a southern

Figure 1. Cartoon by Jim Morin shows George Bush during the nomination process for Justice Designate Thomas. Courtesy Jim Morin / The Miami Herald / Morintoons Syndicate.

state since Reconstruction, experienced a totally unsurprising meteoric rise in the Republican Party. Watts was young, smart, possessed a warm personality, and was a gifted speaker, but he had little experience and no leadership position in the House. Nevertheless, the party gave him opportunities to maximize his visibility to voters. As *USA Today* reported in 1998, "A party seen as hostile to minorities meanwhile basks in a symbol of diversity who is also a bedrock conservative," and "Republicans showcased Watts at their national convention in 1996 and chose him to give their response to the president's State of the Union message in 1997."[48] It was the first time that an African-American gave the response to the State of the Union address. When the new Republican congressional majority made a move to retrench affirmative action, Watts played a key signaling role. He was a coauthor with senate leader and eventual GOP presidential nominee Robert J. Dole (R-KS) of a *Wall Street Journal* op-ed calling for an end to the controversial policy.[49] Like Thomas, Watts hardly reflects in his memoirs on the role of race in gaining him these high-profile opportunities.[50]

Following Clinton's unprecedented efforts at implementing diversity in his administration, which included African-Americans but also multiple Latinos and women, plus one Asian-American (which he called having a cabinet that "looks like America"[51]), the administration of George W. Bush went even further. He appointed consecutively two African-Americans to one of the most prestigious jobs in the administration, Secretary of State, with Condoleezza Rice, Bush's National Security Advisor, succeeding Colin Powell (who had been Reagan's National Security Advisor and also Chairman of the Joint Chiefs of Staff under George H. W. Bush and Clinton). Bush also appointed African-Americans as secretaries of Housing and Urban Development (Alphonso Jackson) and Education (Rod Paige). Latinos ran the Commerce Department (Carlos Gutierrez) and the Department of Housing and Urban Development after Jackson (Mel Martinez), and Asian-Americans oversaw Labor (Elaine Chao) and Transportation (Norman Mineta, who had been Secretary of Commerce in the last year of the Clinton administration).

The Impacts of President Obama and the Growing Latino Vote on GOP Racial Signaling Strategy

Two circumstances—the election of America's first president with (known) African ancestry, and the rapid growth of Latino and Asian populations— have appeared to increase pressure on Republicans to signal openness to nonwhites.[52] The Republicans installed the African-American former Lieutenant Governor of Maryland, Michael Steele, as Chair of the RNC. Steele bested another African-American, Ken Blackwell, the former Secretary of State of Ohio, as well as four white candidates. Though most party leaders (typically) downplayed the role of race in the process, some in the party openly celebrated the benefits of having Steele at the helm. Jim Greer, the chair of the Florida party, told the *New York Times*, "There certainly is an advantage of a credible message of inclusion if you have a minority as chairman."[53] Andy McKenna, chair of the Illinois Republican Party, declared that Steele would "show our ideas are good for people across the economic spectrum, across the ethnic spectrum," and Kevin DeWine of the Ohio party predicted Republicans would see Steele's election "as a significant sign of change."[54] Joanne Young, a member of an advisory committee for the Washington, DC Republican Party, told the *Washington Post*, "He is very truly the representation of the party of Lincoln. . . . He will reach out to women and moderates. It's a very positive message for the country to have an African-American who is at the helm of the Republican Party." Upon election, Steele himself admitted: "We have an image problem," because "We've been misidentified as a party that is insensitive, a party unconcerned about the lives of minorities. . . . That day is over."[55]

Steele's rise coincided with that of another nonwhite Republican, Louisiana Governor Piyush "Bobby" Jindal. Like J. C. Watts, Jindal was smart, young, and a gifted speaker when Republicans tapped him to represent the party following a Democratic president's State of the Union address. Choosing a white Republican (which, not counting four Cuban-Americans, was the only option if they were to choose a speaker from Congress) would, it was apparently believed, have made for an unpleasant contrast to Obama. Much of the enthusiasm for Jindal's role was, accordingly, due to his Asian immigrant roots. A GOP strategist ticked off Jindal's positive attributes—and then added, "The Republican Party very strongly wants to have a new look. . . . They're saying, 'We're not just a party of old white guys,' and he's part of that appeal."[56] Republican consultant Alex Castellanos told *New York* magazine that Jindal and Steele "look like the future."[57]

Latinos became the largest minority in 2009, and this, too, had impacts in American politics and racial signaling strategies. In a replay of the strategy of finding African-Americans to take stands against policies typically identified as benefiting that group, in 2010 the GOP was showcasing Latino candidates to counteract the party's strong anti-illegal immigration stance. Republican leaders have gone out of their way to recruit Latino candidates to represent conservative white districts around the country, including Georgia and North Carolina.[58] The 2010 Republican candidate for the governorship of New Mexico, Susana Martinez, was an outspoken opponent of illegal immigration, arguing that undocumented immigrants should be prohibited from getting driver's licenses, and she also defended a controversial Arizona law that required local police to detain suspected illegal aliens. She explained to the *Wall Street Journal*, "There is a stereotype that Hispanics must be in favor of different policies than I am expressing, and that's not what I'm finding at all."[59]

The Latino backgrounds of even a few candidates were a plus for the national party as well. Whit Ayres, a Republican pollster, told the *Washington Post*, "Republicans need to be clear that they not only want but welcome Hispanics into the Republican Party, and having . . . prominent, successful Hispanic Republicans sends that message loud and clear."[60] Similarly, Ayres told the *Wall Street Journal*: "Having Hispanic candidates be successful on the Republican ticket and visible nationally will go a long way toward rectifying . . . [the] damage" caused by the party's restrictionist stance on immigration.[61] Immigration restrictionist Congressman Lamar Smith (R-TX) penned a *Washington Post* op-ed in which he argued that opposing the legalization of undocumented immigrants was not hurting the GOP with Latino voters, while at the same time he emphasized the signaling power of the election of anti-legalization Latino governors, congressmembers, and a senator.[62] In the run-up to the 2012 election, some conservatives openly discussed the strategy of using Cuban-American Marco Rubio as a running mate to lure Latino voters.[63]

Following the 2012 election, where Republicans held their majority in the House but failed to take the Senate or unseat Barack Obama, Republican leaders began a period of analysis of the failure of their presidential candidate, Mitt Romney, to attract more than 27 percent of the Latino vote and 26 percent of the Asian vote. Reince Priebus, the replacement of Michael Steele as head of the Republican National Committee, created a "Growth and Opportunity Project" to research plans for the future of the party. Much of its report focused heavily on demographics and strategies to reach nonwhites, women and youth. Despite the new tone of urgency, the report called for more of the same racial realism strategies the party had used for decades. It recommended the creation of a Growth and Opportunity Inclusion Council, which would (among other things) "train and prepare ethnic conservatives for media presentations nationally and locally. . . . This new organization should encourage governors to embrace diversity in hiring and appointments to the judiciary, boards and commissions."[64] The report also recommended that the RNC "hire Hispanic communications directors and political directors for key states and communities across the country" and "improve on promoting Hispanic staff and candidates within the Party," using them in the media, and showing them "involved in political and budget decisions."[65] The report recommended similar actions for Asian-Americans and African-Americans. A section on "candidate recruitment" was heavily focused on finding nonwhite Republicans, as well as women.[66] The party quickly began implementation of the report's recommendations, hiring, for example, two Asian-Americans, Jason Chung and Stephen Fong, to focus on communications and grass roots campaigns aimed at Asian-Americans.[67]

The Latino ascendance has impacted Democrats as well. The Democrats' use of racial signaling in political appointments remains conventional, following the logic of patronage politics similar to that exemplified by Big Bill Thompson at the start of this chapter or Johnson's appointment of Weaver. Because Democrats receive the majority of Latino votes (as well as the majority of black and Asian votes, though there are ethnic variations within the Latino and Asian blocs), they continue to offer appointments to members of these groups either to reward them for their support or because organizations acting on behalf of these groups pressure the Democrats to make these appointments. For example, the Congressional Hispanic Caucus lobbied Obama to choose a Latino to replace Supreme Court Justice David Souter when he announced his retirement. The Caucus explained, "appointing our nation's first Hispanic justice would undoubtedly be welcomed by our community and bring greater diversity of thought, perspective and experience to the nation's legal system."[68] Other groups lobbying Obama for a Latino Justice were the National Hispanic Leadership Agenda, the Hispanic National Bar Association, and a group calling itself Hispanics for a Fair Judiciary.[69] After Obama chose Sonia Sotomayor for the Supreme Court, the *New York Times* was able to report on the wide ripple effect in a satisfied Latino community, though there was also skepticism that one high-profile appointment was enough to earn votes.[70] Obama allegedly sought diversity on the Court and especially a Latino justice well before the appointment, and he did appear to get a slight bump in support.[71]

Racial realism showed itself in the Sotomayor nomination in yet another way, when it became known that she had touted her own racial (and gender) abilities relative to a white male judge in a 2001 speech. She declared, "I would hope that a wise Latina woman with the richness of her experiences would more often than not reach a better conclusion than a white male who hasn't lived that life."[72] Critics pounced on the statement, and it became an issue in the confirmation process. Perhaps most prominently, conservative commentator Rush Limbaugh and former Republican Speaker of the House (and 2009 Republican candidate for president) Newt Gingrich called Sotomayor's comments racist. Gingrich wrote, "A white man racist nominee would be forced to withdraw," and "a Latina woman racist should also withdraw."[73] Meanwhile, Latino support for congressional Republicans after the nomination fell from an already dismal 11 percent approval to 8 percent.[74]

Is Racial Realism Prevalent in Federal Appointments?

The foregoing should suggest that political elites regularly consider the race of their appointees and that they strategically manage racial signaling to achieve their electoral goals. Political scientists have only begun to study this phenomenon, however, so it is difficult to make broad, verifiable statements about how common this kind of racial realism is in appointments. The one area where it has been studied is in judicial appointments, and here most scholars are in agreement that appointments are made following racial-realist principles. Research has shown that presidents making appointments to the federal bench regularly consider race, as well as religion and gender.[75] While Johnson was the first to appoint an African-American to the Supreme Court, it was Jimmy Carter who made racial as well as gender diversity a major goal of his overall judicial appointment strategy, and established the strategy as normal in presidential politics.[76] Moreover, senators appear to believe that a Supreme Court Justice's race matters to their electoral fortunes: Democrats were more likely to support the Clarence Thomas nomination if they had sizable black constituencies, and this was especially true if they were facing a reelection campaign.[77]

More recently, studies have shown that appointments of minorities to district courts correlate with the percentage of minorities in the voting age population of a district, as well as with the numbers of potential minority campaign donors.[78] At the circuit court level, one study found that presidents' decisions to appoint a minority judge correlates with ideology (conservatives being less likely to appoint minorities at this level) and whether a state in the circuit has a minority representative in Congress,[79] but it is important to note that there are fewer minorities who share a conservative than a liberal ideology (and Republicans will rarely appoint liberals in order to pursue racial signaling goals). An analysis of George W. Bush's appointment record not surprisingly found that he pursued racial and gender diversity goals when they fit with his ideological commitments.[80]

Does the Race of Government Officials Matter?

One important caveat must be kept in mind as we assess the effectiveness of racial realism in the top echelons of government: namely, that comprehensive evidence is difficult to obtain, and this for the simple reason that despite their growing presence in the electorate, there are still few nonwhite leaders in government, especially Asian-American leaders.[81] Nevertheless, social scientists have studied this subject extensively, so much, in fact, that it is very difficult to summarize the massive number of findings on different racial groups and their impact on different aspects of government and politics.

The field can be divided into research on elected officials and research on appointees or bureaucrats. While my main interest is how political elites strategically use race when they "hire" and place different people through the appointment process, it is important to note that a very large body of research has also explored the ways in which the racial identities of elected officials themselves have effects on and importance to voters. The focus of this research has been on what political scientists call "descriptive representation" (when minority groups are represented by members of their own groups) and "substantive representation" (when those who represent minorities actually vote or take other actions that are in the minorities' interests). This latter concept roughly conforms to what I have called throughout this study "racial abilities."

Regarding this research on race and elected officials, it presents us first with evidence on the ways race matters to voters. One review of the literature found most evidence that whites and blacks both tend to prefer candidates of their own race, that whites tend to prefer lighter blacks over darker blacks, and that they say that they vote for African-Americans more than they actually do. Experimental study designs also show that race matters to voters. One experiment gave white subjects identical descriptions of political candidates, varying only the race of one of the candidates, and found that whites were more likely to vote for candidates when they were white rather than black. For these reasons, it is not surprising that only four blacks have ever served in the U.S. Senate, and only two since Reconstruction.[82]

Then there is evidence regarding how the race of elected leaders affects the attitudes or behavior of the public. One study has shown that blacks living in regions where the mayor of the largest city is black are more politically informed: they are more likely to be able to name their local school board president, their representative in Congress, and their state governor. Moreover, those blacks who are more informed tend to be more active. Participation in voting, campaigning, civic associations, and contacting government officials goes up when there is a black mayor. Having blacks in office also leads black citizens to be more trusting of government. Black mayors have some opposite effects on whites: they are less likely to know their school board president or representative in Congress than they would be if the mayor were white.[83]

Researchers have found racial signaling effects at varying levels of government. Blacks are more likely to approve of the job their member of Congress is doing if that member is black, and blacks represented by blacks tend to know more about their representative than when they are represented by other races.[84] Other evidence shows that black citizens are more likely to contact their legislative representative when that representative is black rather than white. White citizens are more likely to give favorable assessments to white representatives than nonwhite, and also are more likely to contact same-race representatives.[85]

Research on the 2008 election of Barack Obama has found that the election was the most racially polarizing in American history, as he especially attracted racial liberals and repelled racial conservatives.[86] Black approval of Obama's performance in office seems to be linked to his race, as blacks, regardless of their party and of their opinions on his policies, show more approval of Obama than do whites and more than blacks showed for President Clinton.[87]

There is also growing literature on what has become known as the "Obama Effect," which essentially refers to the power of Obama's racial signaling to change attitudes or other social dynamics. This research has identified a variety of effects linked to Obama, his race, and the context of presidential power, expertise, leadership, and family in which he is continually portrayed. For instance, there is evidence that Obama's election has had positive effects on racial attitudes. One study found that exposure to Obama via television led to reductions in anti-black prejudice among conservatives, who had the most prejudice to begin with. This was true even when the exposure came via conservative television programs critical of Obama.[88] On the other hand, an experimental study found that priming subjects to think about Obama was associated with no change in some measures of bias and actually seemed to produce increases in others associated with resentment of African-Americans.[89] Along these lines, an analysis of discrimination law cases found that Obama's election had no reduction in filings, and in fact charges of racial harassment discrimination began to identify individuals who "made references to Obama in ways that demonstrate racial animus against blacks."[90] One study found that black students improved their performance on standardized tests in periods right after extensive media coverage of Obama (specifically, his convention speech and his election), though a study using an experimental method found no difference in test performance between black students prompted to think about Obama before taking the test and those who were not so prompted.[91]

A more established line of research indicates that black legislators have racial abilities, showing more responsiveness to black interests than do white legislators. Though there are some prominent exceptions in the scholarly literature,[92] one review concluded that much evidence indicates that black lawmakers are "far more likely than white Democrats to reflect the interests of their black constituencies" and are "also more likely to propose legislation consistent with African-American policy preferences."[93] Black legislators also more often locate their offices near the African-American community and staff these offices with African-Americans who have ties to the community, and they prove more successful in delivering federal funding for local projects that benefit blacks, including funding for historically black colleges and universities.[94] Black and Latino members of Congress are also more likely than whites to exercise oversight of federal agencies in congressional hearings that deal with race or social welfare issues.[95] Another racial effect relates to employment: a study of Southern communities found a correlation between the numbers of blacks on the city council and blacks in local government jobs.[96]

The evidence on Latino racial signaling and abilities is more mixed because of the heterogeneity of Latinos. Experts, activists, and Latinos themselves disagree on the meanings of the "Latino" or "Hispanic" categories, as both are made up of complex groupings of persons from Mexico, the Caribbean, Central America, and South America.[97] Here is how one leading expert on Latino politics summed up the state of knowledge in the early 2000s: "As was true in 1990, in 2004 Latinos do not behave as a political group united by ethnicity. Latinos do not see themselves as united politically and they report that they will not vote for a candidate because of shared ethnicity."[98] One study has found that a candidate's Latino identity has only an indirect impact on Latino voters.[99] Moreover, a study of California and Texas found that having Latino legislators in the state legislature or the House of Representatives was associated with only a modest decrease in Latino political alienation.[100]

However, there are many recent studies showing that Latino identities do matter when it comes to filling upper-level federal positions and positions in more local governments. Districts with Latino populations, for example, are more likely to elect Latino candidates for state and congressional offices.[101] A survey that asked respondents how they would vote in an election between Latino and non-Latino candidates (including scenarios where the Latino was of the opposite party of the respondent) found that Latinos with high degrees of ethnic attachment were more likely to support the Latino candidate when no party label was included, and somewhat more likely to vote for the Latino of the opposite party.[102] This study also analyzed voting data in five mayoral elections in Los Angeles, Houston, New York, San Francisco, and Denver, as well as state legislative and congressional elections, and found that areas "with larger proportions of Latino registrants are more likely both to evidence high turnout rates when a Latino candidate is running for office and to vote for that candidate."[103] The reason for the higher turnouts may be not only a response to candidate race; Latino candidates in this study were found to make greater efforts to mobilize Latino voters than other candidates.[104] While having a Latino representative or executive in office may have positive effects on voters (and an interview study found that Latinos in office tend to believe they have racial abilities to better represent Latinos[105]), there is little evidence that Latinos in office represent Latinos differently than non-Latinos.[106]

Studies of racial signaling or racial abilities on the part of appointees are far fewer, but they tend to show impacts. A survey experiment examined how same-race appointees affected three different measures of African-American and Asian-American racial identity: perceptions of shared racial fate, closeness to members of their own race, and a racialized political identity among blacks and Asian-Americans. Researchers showed half the respondents pictures of Democratic and Republican cabinet officials of their own race and included text highlighting their racial background (Ron Brown and Rod Paige to African-Americans; Norman Mineta and Elaine Chao to Asian-Americans), while the control group saw no pictures. For both African- and Asian-Americans, the individuals who viewed the same-race cabinet members were more likely to respond affirmatively on all of the three measures of racial identity.[107]

Data on the racial signaling effects of nonwhite judges, a group of appointees with high status but low visibility, are mixed. For example, a study of the effects of black judges in Mississippi on black Mississippians' attitudes of the fairness of the state courts showed little impact.[108] However, a study using an experimental survey technique has shown blacks to be more likely to view judiciaries as legitimate when they have black judges; this was true of even conservative blacks. Whites, including liberal whites, showed less support for a judiciary where blacks were well represented.[109] A study of Texas Latinos' attitudes toward the U.S. Supreme Court before and after the appointment of Latina Sonia

Sotomayor showed an increase in approval of the Court as well as better-than-expected knowledge of the appointment, but showed Sotomayor's appointment having little effect on the attitudes of non-Latino whites.[110]

Nonwhites may support appointments of nonwhite judges for a variety of reasons, but the jury is still out on whether nonwhite judges have racial abilities that white judges lack (e.g., the "wise Latina" that Justice Sotomayor had celebrated, discussed above). Evidence exists both for and against the existence of racial abilities in judging. Supporting the view that there are no racial abilities in judging, a comparison of sentencing in trials presided over by a black judge with those where a white judge presided found no significant differences, as both black and white judges tended to impose harsher sentences on black defendants than on whites.[111] Other studies have found no differences in sentencing, though the race of attorneys may be an intervening variable.[112] A study of Clinton appointees also found no difference between black and white judges' rulings in cases involving black issues.[113]

But other studies show that the race of the judge can matter in the administration of justice. A study of Carter's black appointees found that they cast 79 percent of their votes in favor of the criminally accused, while Carter's white appointees voted similarly only 53 percent of the time (oddly, however, this same study found almost no difference between the rulings of black and white judges in race discrimination cases).[114] An analysis of black and white judges' decisions on criminal search and seizure—a potentially better measure of racial abilities because judges have more discretion on these cases—found that black judges were more receptive to allegations of misconduct by law enforcement officials than were white judges.[115] Another study of black and white judges' decisions to incarcerate in a large American city found, after controlling for factors such as a defendant's prior criminal record, that white judges were less likely than black judges to send white defendants to prison, though black and white judges treated black defendants with equal severity. On the other hand, black judges tended to be more lenient to black defendants on other measures of sentence severity, such as duration of jail time and opportunities for probation.[116]

In short, though the results are not consistent and there are likely differences between groups, there is considerable evidence that party leaders are wise to manage the racial signaling of elected officials and appointees. The race of government officials does often impact the public's attitudes. There is also considerable evidence that the race of government officials

matters in how they do their jobs. In other words, voters have good reason to care about the race of government officials, and party leaders have
good reason to use the racial-realist strategy extensively.

Policing While Black: Racial Realism
and the Enforcement of Law

Could the government's most basic duty—the provision of law enforcement, public safety, and justice—require attention to the race of law enforcement officers? The belief that good police work requires racial realism has a long history in the U.S. and may be more entrenched now than
ever. Advocates speak from positions of authority, such as federal commissions or government positions, and also come from grass roots nonwhite communities. They argue that officers vary by race in their ability
to police a neighborhood, or that the race of an officer can communicate
a powerful signal of self-sovereignty because when the police look like the
policed, there is at least an appearance of fair law enforcement.

Race Matching of Police: An American Tradition

Though current practices and advocacy reflect a departure in terms of
scale and diversity, police departments in America have long hired and
placed officers on the basis of race. Early moves in this direction were intended to produce effective policing, but they were more about managing
racial signaling to whites than to nonwhites. In the nineteenth century,
city governments doled out police jobs as rewards for political loyalty,
and blacks received these patronage rewards on occasion. But they faced
serious problems: some white officers, as well as white citizens, were
so offended by the idea of a black man in a uniform—a black man with
authority—that black officers faced violence, including physical assaults.
Departments therefore segregated black officers and sent them to police black neighborhoods, because it was only there that they could work
without disruption.[117] As late as the 1950s, the two African-Americans on
the police force in New Orleans could only patrol black neighborhoods,
could not wear uniforms, and could not arrest whites.[118]
    Yet even in these early years there were some who believed being
black made some officers better qualified to enforce the law in black

neighborhoods. This perception of racial abilities would become more prevalent among government officials and scholars over the next few decades.[119] For example, as early as 1931, a report by the National Commission on Law Observance and Enforcement stressed the benefits of recruiting diverse police officers familiar with the language, habits, and cultures of ethnic groups.[120]

It was the racial violence of the 1960s, however, that boosted racial realism in policing to the national agenda. Studies of the violence almost always found that even in the best of times, there was a disconnect between white police forces and black neighborhoods, with blacks often feeling that they were under foreign and hostile occupation. At worst there was brutality and other abuses of power by police.

It was often a rumor of police brutality that set off the 1960s megariots (many called them rebellions) in the urban North, including the riots in Harlem and Rochester in 1964, in the Watts section of Los Angeles in 1965, and in Detroit and Newark in 1967. There were also hundreds of other riots/rebellions in cities big and small. Some caused tens of millions of dollars in property damage, almost all of it in predominately black neighborhoods. Thousands were injured and/or arrested.[121]

Observers increasingly saw racial mismatches between police and neighborhoods as a major part of the problem. Lyndon Johnson's aides communicated from the front lines that the whiteness of the police and the resulting lack of racial understanding were creating tensions in black communities and called urgently for more black faces on the police and National Guard forces trying to maintain order.[122] Whether the strategy was racial signaling, racial abilities, or both was unclear, but it was certainly more an instance of racial realism than affirmative action when New York installed an African-American to head the Harlem precinct after the riot there, and created a new post of "Community Relations Coordinator" in Harlem. The African-American officer appointed to that post was asked by the *New York Times* if race was a factor in his appointment, and he replied, "Candidly, I suppose it was. And that's all right with me. The important thing is I think I can improve the situation there."[123]

Similarly, in 1966, New York City used a $2.9 million federal grant to recruit one thousand disadvantaged blacks and Puerto Ricans to the police force. According to the *New York Times*, this effort aimed to "lessen the odds of race rioting."[124] A New York police chief explained, "The recruitment of Negroes into the department is not simply opening up jobs to all members of the community, but also a political necessity for pacifying the Negro community and winning the support of its members."[125]

A year later, Lyndon Johnson's President's Commission on Law Enforcement and the Administration of Justice extolled the value of racial signaling in the police force. Calling for "a sufficient number of minority-group officers at all levels of activity and authority," the report stated that "a department can show convincingly that it does not practice racial discrimination by recruiting minority-group officers, by assigning them fairly to duties of all sorts in all kinds of neighborhoods, and by pursuing promotion policies that are scrupulously fair to such officers. If there is not a substantial percentage of Negro officers among the policemen in a Negro neighborhood, many residents will reach the conclusion that the neighborhood is being policed, not for the purpose of maintaining law and order, but for the purpose of maintaining the ghetto's status quo." Moreover, if this effort was to show an advance over the old policy of a segregated police force, it would need to be balanced by a strategy of placing black officers in white neighborhoods as well.[126]

This report also cited a need for the racial abilities of black officers, explaining that a "lack of understanding of the problems and behaviors of minority groups is common to most police departments" and is a "serious deterrent" to effective policing. The report concluded that "a major, and most urgent, step in the direction of improving police-community relations is recruiting more, many more, policemen from minority groups."[127]

A better-known federal government report, though one that came to similar racial-realist conclusions, was that of the National Advisory Commission on Civil Disorders, more popularly known as the Kerner Commission. As it did for journalism, the report also gave prominent support to racial realism in policing. Black officers have special abilities, the report argued, because they "can increase departmental insight into ghetto problems, and provide information necessary for early anticipation of the tensions and grievances that can lead to disorders." In addition, "There is evidence that Negro officers also can be particularly effective in controlling any disorders that do break out."[128]

Other official bodies have fostered the notion that effective policing requires racial realism in hiring and placement. A 1973 report by the National Advisory Commission on Criminal Justice Standards and Goals, for example, added its voice to previous commission findings, stating that "minority officers are better able to police a minority community because of their familiarity with the culture."[129]

At around the same time, Congress was debating amendments to Title VII that would expand its coverage to government employment. While Senate and House reports noted the value of having nonwhites in a variety of government positions, law enforcement received special attention. Though the bill supported a classically liberal approach, the Senate Report stated in 1971, "The exclusion of minorities from effective participation in the bureaucracy not only promotes ignorance of minority problems in that particular community, but also creates mistrust, alienation, and all too often hostility towards the entire process of government."[130] The House echoed this theme: "The problem of employment discrimination is particularly acute and has the most deleterious effect in these governmental activities which are most visible to the minority communities (notably education, law enforcement, and the administration of justice) with the result that the credibility of the government's claim to represent all the people is negated."[131]

Nearly twenty years later, the message was the same following some incidents of police brutality in Los Angeles, most notably the beating of Rodney King, which was caught on grainy, graphic video. A report on the Los Angeles County Sheriff's Department called for better nonwhite representation on the force and better utilization of the racial abilities of nonwhite officers. It argued, "These officers have important knowledge, experience and insights regarding effective and sensitive community-based policing. . . . Their cultural knowledge and communication skills could be invaluable in defusing tensions on a street corner or in a jail cell. . . . Many minority officers have a broad historical and societal perspective that is most useful in the Department's efforts to increase the sophistication and effectiveness of its community-policing efforts."[132]

Though conservatives can be suspicious of racial realism in policing,[133] George W. Bush's Justice Department declared in 2001: "A diverse law enforcement agency can better develop relationships with the community it serves, promote trust in the fairness of law enforcement, and facilitate effective policing by encouraging citizen support and cooperation." More practically, it advised: "Law enforcement agencies should seek to hire and retain a diverse workforce that can bring an array of backgrounds and perspectives to bear on the issues the agencies confront and the choices they must make in enforcing the law."[134]

While many advocates speaking on behalf of the government have long supported racial realism in policing, local groups advocating on behalf of nonwhites have done so as well.[135] In Brooklyn in 1964, the head of a group called the African Nationalist Pioneer Movement stated: "The assignment of more Negro patrolmen to the Bedford-Stuyvesant area will go a long way to improve community relations with police."[136] When the city put a black officer in charge of its largest station in Harlem, one civil rights leader remarked in 1966 that the effort "has made a dramatic difference. It's more difficult for the inhabitants of Harlem to look upon the police as their enemy when he's the same color as they are."[137] The most common pattern for advocacy of this kind would be an egregious incident of police brutality spurring calls from local civil rights leaders and African-American ministers for an increased black presence on the ground and in the police administration. For example, after the NYPD's 1997 beating and torture of Haitian immigrant Abner Louima, the Giuliani administration worked with civil rights groups on a plan to move more black police officers to the Brooklyn precinct where the torture occurred (see below).

Some government officials have discussed the racial abilities and signaling benefits of African-American cops in African-American neighborhoods in interview studies. An analysis of black economic equality in the South found this perspective to be common. One white police chief explained, "We need to understand all citizens and can't understand blacks without having blacks on the force. . . . It helps us deal with a culture we [whites] don't understand. Blacks can be loud, boisterous, and in your face—most white officers don't understand this."[138] A black officer in Quincy, Florida, explained, "When it gets 'hot' in black areas, they [blacks] want and need black officers. . . . Blacks frown on white police . . . they're a symbol of white control and power. Black police are trusted more and have an attachment to blacks."[139]

It should be noted that some police departments have sought to take advantage of racial abilities and signaling by means that stop short of hiring actual police officers. One strategy is to set up a "multicultural storefront" police station, staffed at least in part with "community service officers" who share the race and ethnicity of the community. This strategy allows for closer day-to-day contact and better relations, and arose partly in response from public pressure to "do something visibly special" for minorities.[140] It also avoids the problem of finding minorities who can pass the various background and aptitude tests required for all police officers. Though not actually police officers, community service officers can act as cultural emissaries for the police department as well as signal some degree of self-sovereignty.

Another strategy is to institute advisory boards or appoint special assistants to the chief representing different ethnic and racial groups (as well as women, gays, and lesbians). These representatives are intended to serve as conduits of racial and ethnic culture and knowledge.[141] Though citizen advisory boards were first set up in the late 1970s, and nearly 90 percent of departments in big cities have some citizen oversight for complaints, there is very little evidence as to whether or not the boards have an impact.[142]

The Evidence: Do Cops Have Racial Abilities?
Does Racial Signaling Work?

Racial meanings are deeply woven into the interface between the police and the American public. Opinion polls reveal that blacks, whites, and Latinos have very different attitudes toward the police. These divergent opinions are especially apparent when the local headlines are dominated by an incident of police brutality. Shortly after the February 1999 police killing of Amadou Diallo, for example, a *New York Times* poll found that 72 percent of blacks and 62 percent of Hispanics, but only 33 percent of whites thought most officers use excessive force. Similarly, a June 1999 Quinnipiac College poll found that while only 25 percent of whites thought police brutality was "very serious," 81 percent of blacks and 59 percent of Hispanics thought so.[143]

For some, this is already ample grounds to justify racial realism, but there is more direct evidence that specifically supports the strategy of racial signaling. Large numbers of blacks and Latinos appear to believe that a police officer's race matters. A comprehensive survey study of attitudes toward race and policing conducted in 2002 found that nearly 70 percent of blacks thought there were differences between black and white police officers, while about 45 percent of Latinos saw differences, and about 38 percent of whites did. Almost half of blacks thought that Latino officers were different. About 30 percent of Latinos saw a difference between Latino and white officers, slightly more than whites did.[144] This study also found that all three groups tended to see white cops as "tough/arrogant/insensitive" and black cops as "courteous/respectful/understanding," though this pattern was most evident among black respondents.[145] As one black respondent explained, "Black officers are more empathetic toward citizens. Black officers are taught, by virtue of their racial background, not to have bias or prejudice, whereas their white counterparts are not. Black officers are taught . . . not to lump everyone into one category. . . . White officers are taught that certain people *always* behave a certain way" (original emphasis).[146] Though only 5 percent of blacks and 4 percent of Latinos wanted exclusively black and Latino officers, respectively, majorities of blacks and Latinos perceived race to matter enough that they preferred a racial mix of officers in their neighborhoods.[147] These respondents lauded racially mixed policing teams as a means whereby nonwhites could educate whites on the job, and associated them with "impartiality," "fairness," and "checks and balances."[148] Given these attitudes, it is not surprising that one study found that Latinos in Houston would sometimes wait days until they thought they saw a Latino officer before they were willing to report a crime.[149]

There is also evidence that police officers themselves, as well as representatives of the nation's police departments, believe racial realism is sound strategy in policing. For example, one interview study of fifty black police officers in the South found that the officers were "nearly unanimous" in believing they had special insights into problems.[150] As one stated:

> I really believe that African Americans, because we have always been on the receiving end of a lot of that stuff, that we really have a deeper level of understanding and compassion for other people. I really think it's difficult for whites today to really see even the subtle vestiges of discrimination and prejudices. . . . I'm just saying that I think whites by and large have real difficulty, really being able to perceive and understand people who have to walk through that stuff, day after day after day.[151]

The argument that nonwhite officers can better understand nonwhite citizens also came up repeatedly in my research assistants' interviews with police officials from around the country. Representatives from eight of the nine large city departments with whom we spoke cited a goal of racial balance in the police force, and four of the nine described the racial ability of understanding of people and neighborhoods as one of the reasons. The liaison to Asian police officers in a major West Coast city, for example, told us that his department tried to employ the same percentage of minorities as lived in the city, explaining that a major challenge for police in his city was "the trust factor," and that a way to gain minority residents' trust was to employ officers who "resemble them or understand their cultures and traditions." He explained, "I think if we have a specific Latino officer in a Latino community that'll actually go a longer way. The reason why is tradition, cultural, history, language. Those are just barriers that officer will not have to deal with."[152]

We can see, then, that the public and many officers and their leadership seem to care a lot about race and offer support for at least some hiring and placing based on racial-realist principles. Are they right to do so?

Despite the claims of government bodies, civil rights leaders, city residents, and some police officers themselves that nonwhite officers have special racial abilities of understanding, social scientists have had trouble demonstrating that the phenomenon is real and has significant effects on policing. Here we have the benefit of two especially comprehensive, authoritative reviews of an extensive literature. First, legal scholar David Sklansky's analysis of the research on police officer race shows, first, that there was an impressive increase in the percentage of nonwhite officers in major cities across the U.S. between 1967 and 2000. For example, New York City's police force increased from about 5 percent to 35 percent minority; Chicago and Philadelphia both increased from around 20 percent to 40 percent; Detroit went from 5 percent to 65 percent minority; and San Francisco from 5 percent to 40. But when it came to the effects of this diversification, Sklansky found contradictory conclusions in the literature. He noted, on the one hand: "There are studies finding that black officers shoot just as often as white officers; that black officers arrest just as often as white officers; that black officers are often prejudiced against black citizens; that black officers get less cooperation than white officers from black citizens; and that black officers are just as likely, or even more likely, to elicit citizen complaints and to be the subject of disciplinary actions." On the other hand, "there are also studies concluding that black officers get more cooperation than white officers from black citizens; that black officers are less prejudiced against blacks and know more about the black community; and that black officers are more likely to arrest white suspects and less likely to arrest black suspects."[153] Despite the mixed findings, the weight of scholarly opinion, Sklansky concluded, is currently on the side of race *not* impacting the performance of police officers.

The prestigious National Research Council has also assessed the evidence and pronounced authoritatively that while there is much evidence that officers of different races tend to have different occupational outlooks and different knowledge about neighborhoods, these factors do not seem to translate into differences in behavior. For example, there is little evidence that race affects the use of coercion or deadly force, whether an officer acts with respect toward citizens, comforts a citizen, or grants a citizen's request to control someone. Noting a study that found that whites were more likely to arrest nonwhites and that nonwhites were more likely to arrest whites, especially for minor crimes such as drunk driving, prostitution, and public disorderliness, and that a move to same-race policing would lead to a decline in arrests of 15 percent, the National Research Council argued that these results could reflect differences in beat and shift assignments and expressed other doubts about the study's methodology as well.

Even the skeptical Council researchers were not yet willing to walk away from racial realism, however. The Council's assessment ended with the suggestions that race might affect the officers themselves, that researchers should compare departments where minorities are in the majority with those where they are in the minority, and that the effects of the race of the officer might still depend on the race of those with whom they interact.[154]

It should also be noted that whatever their beliefs about their own racial abilities, nonwhite police officers themselves have not been unanimous in wanting assignment to racially concordant neighborhoods. The interview study of black police officers found that though civil rights organizations pushed for more black officers in black neighborhoods and black officers said they encountered less hostility there than white officers, some black officers nevertheless saw their race as a liability in black neighborhoods. One explained, "Even to this day a lot of blacks still accuse police officers, black police officers of being programmed, instruments of white authority."[155] Another complained, "You've got to work three times as hard to convince the African-American community that you're not a sellout and you're truly there to do a job and to do the best that you can to help them." This was true, he explained, "because the distrust of police officers has been there so long."[156] Another negative for police departments' deployment of racial signaling is the pressure put on the small numbers of black officers. Departments typically put them in high visibility positions to signal that the department is progressive and fair. As one black female officer explained, "Everything fell on my shoulders. And they used me royally."[157]

"From Their Own Point of View": Does Equal Education Require Racial Realism in the Management of Teachers?

Perhaps the most dramatic case for racial realism in government employment can be made in the field of education. The progressive argument for having students taught by teachers of their own race is far less known than the progressive argument for integrated schools. Yet when the Supreme Court issued its historic ruling in *Brown v. Board of Education* that declared segregation illegal, there was already a long tradition of advocacy for the notion that black teachers were best for black children. Viewed with a wide-angle lens and a over a long sweep of American history, the drive to racially integrate American schools looks anomalous, and racial-realist arguments for the management of teachers appear to be the norm. What is new is that these arguments have become even more pronounced and nuanced as the U.S. Latino population has grown.

The Tradition of Black Teachers for Black Students

It was an argument that came from experience rather than principle. In the nineteenth century, many northern states maintained integrated schools, a practice that was frequently disastrous for black children. As early as the 1830s, black parents and progressive Northerners were urging that schools be segregated and teachers racially matched to students. For many black parents, then, it was *integrated* schools that were the problem.

A major stressor was the racist attitude of many teachers. Some openly referred to black students as "niggers," and in schools in Boston and Cleveland in the mid-1850s, white teachers punished misbehaving white students by making them sit in the "nigger seat"—a seat next to a black student.[158] A white principal in Chicago in the 1930s called black students "niggers" and warned them that if they caused trouble he would send them "back to the jungle where you belong." In 1940s Portland, Oregon, a white teacher said that academic achievement was not to be expected of blacks as they were really only good at dancing and sports.[159]

White teachers also tolerated (and probably encouraged, if only indirectly) white students' tormenting of blacks. A school committee report from Providence, Rhode Island stated, "It is deeply to be regretted that one of the most popular amusements for the young at the present day, consists in caricaturing and holding up to ridicule, the peculiarities and eccentricities of a long-neglected and downtrodden race. Our children are taught to be merry and indulge in hilarity over the weaknesses and follies of a people that have the strongest claim for sympathy."[160]

Starting nearly 200 years ago, then, many black leaders were joining black parents in questioning the value of integrated schools. Progressive black intellectuals made the move to racial realism when they argued that whites could not effectively teach black kids and would make unequal demands of white and black students. An attendee at a Pennsylvania State

Equal Rights League meeting said in 1865 that "experimental knowledge" showed that "colored children make greater advancement under the charge of colored teachers than they do under white teachers," and that "therefore we consider it to be our incumbent duty, as lovers of the advancement of our race, to see to it, that our schools are under the charge of colored teachers."[161] A movement in the 1880s, strongest among black Baptists, maintained that whites who taught blacks were prejudiced, incompetent or both. For example, Rev. E. K. Love, the pastor of Savannah's First African Baptist Church, said that white teachers could not know black students on a social basis, and were therefore "incompetent to teach the Negroes civil rights, equity and justice," that they taught that "all the heroes and heroines were white," and that they took blacks away from their cultural roots. "Our race battles must be fought by Negroes alone," he argued. "Negroes must lead and teach Negroes."[162] Similarly, William Kelley of the Milwaukee Urban League argued in 1939 that when black students had black teachers they learned to value hard work and good jobs became possible for them.[163]

W.E.B. DuBois, the black scholar and activist, was also a prominent and forceful advocate of racial realism in the management of education. In an essay entitled "Does the Negro Need Separate Schools?", he argued that the answer was yes as long as whites lacked the skills or judgment to treat black students equally. The "proper education of the Negro race" required a "sympathetic touch between teacher and pupil; knowledge on the part of the teacher, not simply of the individual taught, but of his surroundings and background, and the history of his class and group; such contact between pupils, and between teacher and pupil, on the basis of perfect social equality, as will increase this sympathy and knowledge; facilities for education in equipment and housing, and the promotion of such extra-curricular activities as will tend to induct the child into life." Issuing an early call for what later would be called Black Studies and Afrocentric education,[164] DuBois urged blacks to study such topics as slavery, emancipation, Reconstruction, and the current situation "from their own point of view." He claimed this "separate negro school, where children are treated like human beings, trained by teachers of their own race, who know what it means to be black in the year of salvation 1935, is infinitely better than making our boys and girls doormats to be spit and trampled upon and lied to by ignorant social climbers, whose sole claim to superiority is ability to kick 'niggers' when they are down."[165]

DuBois was sometimes explicit that blacks and whites saw the world differently and thus taught differently—even suggesting these racial abilities were not only real but permanent. When a majority of black students at Lincoln University, a black college in Pennsylvania, opposed having black professors, DuBois blamed it on the white professors, who "certainly have not actively and conscientiously instilled in their students a knowledge of what the Negro has done in the past, or what he is doing now, and of what he is capable of doing. Indeed, this sort of thing is just what white men in the very nature of the case cannot teach even if they tried, just as Negro professors alone cannot wholly and completely present the case and attitude of the white world."[166]

Despite these concerns, the major civil rights organizations, supported by black newspapers in the North, continued to call for an end to mandatory school segregation.[167] By the 1950s, the Supreme Court was moving to strike down its legal basis. Given the abusive treatment that black students were receiving in so many integrated schools in the North, it is ironic that the crux of the Court's argument was that segregation hurt black students' self-esteem and thus their ability to learn.

In 1954's *Brown v. Board of Education of Topeka*, the Court dealt with elementary school children who were forced to attend segregated schools. The NAACP lawyers representing the children convinced a unanimous Court that schools segregated by law could never offer equal protection of the laws. Pointing out that education was "perhaps the most important function of state and local governments" due to its key role in making citizens, "awakening the child to cultural values," and preparing him or her for professional life,[168] the Court said that a child deprived of education was deprived of a chance to succeed in life. The decision drew heavily on the U.S. Supreme Court's own precedents in previous segregation cases, as well as on a Kansas court decision that ruled against the black children but also stated that segregation gave students a sense of inferiority that weakened their motivation to learn.[169] Controversially, the Court also cited social science evidence that seemed to show that black students received negative messages when the state mandated segregation and it made them perform less well.[170] This, the Court said, was a violation of the Fourteenth Amendment's guarantee of equal protection of the laws.[171]

Southern schools dragged their feet and managed to avoid doing much of anything to integrate schools for the next ten years. Real desegregation did not occur until the mid-sixties, when the Civil Rights Act of 1964's Title VI declared that school districts receiving federal funds could not discriminate on the basis of race, national origin, or religion. It was only then that southern schools began to respond.[172] It was also then that people began to notice what many black parents and intellectuals had noticed more than a hundred years earlier: white teachers for black students might not be such a good thing. Desegregation would be followed by fond memories of the virtues of segregated schools, especially of the caring and sense of community they provided.[173]

Advocates for the racial abilities of black and Latino teachers were heard from soon after the historic *Brown v. Board* decision, and by the late 1950s schools in Detroit and Milwaukee practiced racial realism in the hiring and placement of teachers. In New York City, school reformers argued that black and Puerto Rican teachers "had something to give" to minority students that white teachers could not or would not provide. Nonwhite teachers, these reformers insisted, better understood the cultural backgrounds of nonwhite students, and the failure of many minority students in city schools was the result of racist white teachers' incompetence or lack of commitment. Though the NAACP resisted these reforms for fear that they would limit the opportunities of blacks to teach whites, by 1966 the New York school district's director of personnel agreed that "because of the kind of society we have had, unfortunately, it may be that a Negro teacher, generally, may have a greater likelihood of developing rapport, and if this is an important characteristic, then we ought to try to tap it to the extent possible in getting this characteristic into our schools."[174]

Though many of these concerns were first voiced on behalf of African-Americans, they had parallels for Latino students. In New York, ASPIRA (not an acronym), an organization devoted to helping Puerto Rican youth, issued a report stating that in the growing number of classrooms filled with Spanish-speaking students in New York and other cities, "the sense of estrangement that often baffles both the teacher and her students would be relieved by the presence of a Puerto Rican teacher." "The sooner we get Puerto Rican teachers into our schools," it concluded, "the sooner we will make headway" in improving Puerto Rican students' academic success.[175]

Meanwhile, on the other side of the country, there were similar demands, but from a different Latino group. Mexican-American parents were complaining that white teachers treated their children as "third-class citizens." In their view, their children were better off working in the fields than in schools staffed with white teachers.[176]

The call for racial realism in teaching expanded not only to minorities besides blacks, but also up to higher levels of education. Protests swept college campuses across the country, as black, Latino, Asian-American and Native American students made demands for their own recognition on campus. Student protesters often used separatist arguments and demanded specialized courses taught by and for nonwhites. But at the higher education level there was more second-guessing of this strategy. Many felt that separating the new "ethnic studies" departments off racially from the rest of campus would make them more vulnerable to critics intent on rolling back their gains. However, the architects of ethnic studies typically argued that the departments had to get beyond a "white mind-set" and put in place an overt agenda of helping ethnic communities that would encourage a large representation of nonwhite faculty in ethnic studies departments.[177]

In more recent decades, calls for racial realism in teaching continue to be made, though the tone is more professional and less passionate. In the 1980s and 1990s, the rapidly growing presence of minority students in the nation's schools added new urgency to the demands for more minority teachers. Foundations, research organizations, and academics became the most consistent advocates. In 1986, the Carnegie Forum on Education and the Economy declared: "The race and background of their teachers tell [students] something about authority and power in contemporary America. These messages influence children's attitudes towards school, their academic accomplishments and their views of their own and others' intrinsic worth. The views they form in school about justice and fairness also influence their future citizenship."[178] In 1987, Patricia Albjerg Graham, then Dean of the Harvard Graduate School of Education, advocated a massive effort to produce large numbers of black teachers, explaining, "It is important for black children to have at least some black teachers to provide valuable role models of successful black people who are contributing members of society. Black teachers are also vital role models for non-black students who need to learn the same lesson. . . ."[179] Historian John Hope Franklin had a similar view, as he called the need for black teachers "desperate," predicting that if a decline in the numbers of black teachers continued, it would "mean not only that blacks will drop out of one of the oldest and most honored professions, but also that young blacks will be deprived of the role models and a special kind of caring that are essentially irreplaceable. And the drop-out rate among them will continue."[180]

A 1989 National Education Association report emphasized demographics and teaching efficacy as drivers of a racial-realist strategy. "With the percentage of minority students rising," it warned, "the need for minority teachers is becoming increasingly urgent. If school systems across the country that serve large numbers of minority students are to remain viable, they must increase the number of minority teachers, and they must do it quickly." The report cited research identifying differences in black cognitive styles, which were said to be more universalistic, intuitive, and person-oriented than what was required by schools (which tended to be a more analytical, sequential, and object-oriented cognitive style). Other benefits to follow from hiring more minority teachers were said to include a more stimulating pedagogy and a blending of community and school curriculum.[181] Also in 1989, a Stanford University Committee on Minority Issues argued that creating a multiracial campus was more important than ever because "More minority faculty members are needed as role models and mentors for undergraduate and graduate students."[182]

Despite a 1987 Supreme Court opinion ruling out some racial-realist hiring (see below), urgency on the issue continued into the 1990s. In 1996, the National Commission on Teaching and America's Future, a research advocacy organization, published a report that stated "across the nation there is a critical need for many more teachers who reflect the racial and cultural mix of students in schools."[183] The Education Commission of the States, a clearinghouse of education research and policy advice run by and for state policy elites, also issued warnings about the shortage of minority teachers.[184] Its Director of Policy Studies, Barbara J. Holmes, argued that the shortage would dampen the aspirations of nonwhite students and limit their cultural knowledge of America and of their own heritage, and noted that more than half of all states were seeking to address this problem.[185]

The states of California and Texas, both facing large and rapidly growing Mexican American populations, made perhaps the strongest effort in this direction. California's Education Code 44100 justified efforts to hire more minority teachers by emphasizing their racial signaling and racial abilities. The law states: "It is educationally sound for the minority student attending a racially impacted school to have available to him or her the positive image provided by minority classified and certificated employees. It is likewise educationally sound for the child from the majority group to have positive experiences with minority people, that can be provided, in part, by having minority classified and certificated employees at schools where the enrollment is largely made up of majority group students." Moreover, "Lessons concerning democratic principles and the richness that racial diversity brings to our national heritage can be best taught by staffs composed of mixed races and ethnic groups working toward a common goal."[186]

Similarly, in 1994, the Texas Education Agency issued a report that expressed alarm at the fact that 77 percent of all teachers in the state were white, while the student body was 50 percent nonwhite. The report explained that diversity was important for three reasons that touched on both racial signaling and racial abilities. First, nonwhite teachers were needed "because students need role models of like characteristics in professional positions, and all students need exposure to professionals who reflect the diversity of the state." A lack of minorities in the teaching corps sends a "negative message that opportunities are unavailable to persons from their backgrounds." The second reason was that "teachers may interact more successfully with students who have culturally similar backgrounds to their own." Racially matching teachers with students, the report claimed, results in higher academic achievement by minorities. The third reason related to the ability of nonwhite teachers to improve the skills of white teachers: "Diversity within a school's teaching force may increase knowledge and understanding of different cultural groups for all the teachers, thereby enhancing the ability of all teachers to interact successfully in diverse classrooms."[187]

The federal government also added its voice to the call for racial realism in teaching in the 1990s. A U.S. Department of Education report stated in 1990 that "Minority teachers serve as important role models for minority youngsters and provide evidence that America's heritage and opportunities are intended to benefit all citizens." It quoted Mary Hatwood Futrell, a past president of the NEA, who warned, "We're cheating minority students of the positive role models they need, role models who can bolster their pride and self-esteem."[188] Seven years later, the Department noted, "Many educators believe it is important for both minority and nonminority children to be taught by minority teachers, arguing that minority teachers are better equipped to motivate and work with minority students and that both minority and nonminority children benefit from having successful minority professionals as role models."[189] In 1998, Secretary of Education Richard W. Riley justified a call for more diverse teachers by appealing to both racial abilities and racial signaling, explaining, "We need teachers who can relate to the lives of diverse students, and who can connect those students to larger worlds and greater possibilities. . . . Children need role models—they need to see themselves in the faces of their teachers." "By their shining example," he added, "teachers of color help fight the tyranny of low expectations—the pernicious voices that whisper into young ears, 'You can't do it. Don't even try.'"[190]

Professional schools have also called for racial diversity in their faculties as part of a racial-realist strategy. The American College of Physicians justified this position by stating, "Evidence shows that racial and ethnic minority faculty can have a profound impact on minority students, acting as mentors and providing new scholastic challenges and insights."[191] The KPMG Foundation started its "Ph.D. Project" by partnering with major universities to increase the racial diversity of business school faculties based on the racial-realist premise that having more nonwhite professors would increase racial diversity in corporate America. According to the Project's mission, "As faculty, [African-Americans, Latinos, and Native Americans] serve as role models, attracting and mentoring minority students while improving the preparation of all students for our diverse workplace and society."[192]

While most universities have focused their diversity efforts on their student bodies, some have also made the obvious link to faculties, using racial-realist strategies along with arguments based on affirmative-action liberalism. The University of California's diversity statement, for example, advocated a diversity of both students and employees to send the signal of openness to all people, and thus "sustain the social fabric of the State." The statement also touted racial abilities: "Ideas, and practices based on those ideas, can be made richer by the process of being born and nurtured in a diverse community."[193] Similarly, a group of elite liberal arts colleges submitted an amicus brief to the Supreme Court in *Fisher v. Texas* linking diversity of students to diversity of faculty, and pointing to the racial abilities of diverse faculty members. Different races, the brief argued, would ensure that classrooms were places of "dialogue, not monologue," and would aid education "because teaching and learning at their best are conversations with persons other than ourselves about ideas other than our own."[194]

Finally, given the rise of charter schools and other forms of educational institutions, it is worth noting that both establishment and alternative educational organizations appear to advocate the racial-realist strategy for managing race in the classroom. A coalition of education groups (including the National Education Association and the American Council on Education) calling itself the National Collaborative on Diversity in the Teaching Force, issued a report in 2004 stating boldly, "Policymakers, teacher educators, members of ethnic communities, and school leaders agree that the education profession needs more teachers of color." The reasons for this advocacy, the group stated, was the ability of nonwhite teachers to provide role models for nonwhite students, their ability to teach all students about ethnic, racial, and cultural diversity, and their abilities as "cultural brokers" who would aid students in the school environment and encourage parents' involvement. Ultimately, these benefits would lead to heightened achievement, because "students of color tend to have higher academic, personal, and social performance when taught by teachers from their own ethnic groups."[195]

Teach for America (TFA), the influential nonprofit organization that places top college graduates in the nation's most disadvantaged school districts, lauded by both Presidents George W. Bush[196] and Barack Obama,[197] also places a strong value on diversity in the teacher corps. The TFA website explains that the "power of diversity" is that "each corps member's unique background and life experiences add tremendous value to our work." The benefits of racial diversity in a teaching staff include idea generation to help improve education strategy, but the ultimate advantage lies in the racial signaling that teachers with racial abilities can provide their students: "While we value all forms of diversity, we place particular emphasis on recruiting individuals who share the racial or socioeconomic backgrounds of the students we teach, 90 percent of whom are African-American or Latino. Corps members who share their students' backgrounds serve as powerful role models and have potential for a profound additional impact based on their personal experiences."[198] The view from the inside of TFA is basically the same. The TFA recruitment manual has stated, "While everyone in the organization must operate with knowledge and understanding of the communities in which we work, we move further faster when decision-making groups and discussion groups are inclusive of people who have a shared experience and/or identity with the diverse individuals we serve."[199]

Are Teachers Being Hired Following the Racial-Realist Strategy?

While advocacy for racial realism is common, is hiring actually occurring along racial-realist lines? Given the low numbers of minority teachers, it is impossible for the majority of students of any group (other than whites) to have a teacher of their own race. For example, in California in the 2009–10 school year, 5.2 percent of the kindergarten through grade 12 public school teachers were Asian, 17.4 percent were Latino, and 4.2 percent were African-American, while 69.2 percent were white (the remainder were American Indian, Native Hawaiian or Pacific Islander, Filipino, had multiple races, or did not report a race).[200] The kindergarten through grade 12 public school students, on the other hand, were 8.5 percent Asian, 50.4 percent Latino, 6.9 percent African-American, and 27.0 percent white.[201] National figures show a similar mismatch. In 2007–08, though 34 percent of the U.S. population and 41 percent of elementary and secondary students were minorities, only 16.5 percent of elementary and secondary school teachers were minorities.[202]

However, though there are not nearly enough of them, there is evidence that nonwhite teachers do tend to teach nonwhite students. Specifically, in 2003–04, 63 percent of minority teachers taught in schools that researchers classified as "high minority," while 53 percent taught in "high poverty areas," and 50 percent taught in urban school districts.[203] Despite this concentration, even high minority schools employed mostly white teachers—only 42 percent were nonwhite. This was, of course, a far cry from the situation in low-minority schools, where nonwhites made up only 2 percent of the faculty.[204] Gary Orfield's Civil Rights Project found similar numbers: though the average white teacher teaches in a school that is only 12 percent Latino, 10 percent black, and 4 percent Asian, the average Latino teacher's school is 37 percent Latino, 13 percent black, and 9 percent Asian. Black teachers teach in schools that are 10 percent Latino, 54 percent black, and 2 percent Asian. Asian teachers also show a racial matching pattern; the average Asian teacher is in a school that is 32 percent Latino, 14 percent black, and 22 percent Asian.[205]

These patterns, of course, may not be evidence of racial-realist hiring and placement strategies. It is unknown to what extent racial matching results from the preferences of teachers, or is driven by discrimination against nonwhites in mostly white school districts.

Does the Evidence Support Racial Realism in Teaching?

There is a massive amount of social science research on the effects of teacher race on the educational process, and, as in other areas of employment, the results are mixed, but with considerable evidence suggesting racial abilities and signaling should not be ignored. Much of the research has been on whether bias on the part of white teachers harms student performance. Scholars have also debated whether or not stereotypes of minority students, even if they exist, could be sustained in the context of repeated interactions with the same student or students (a pattern of interaction that contrasts with those of police, who typically do not interact with the same person or persons every day).[206]

Much evidence indicates that white teachers are indeed biased—though nonwhite teachers are not necessarily much more fair-minded. Researchers since at least the 1970s have found evidence of whites lacking racial abilities for equal teaching and counseling. One early study that examined the impact of ethnicity as well as racial groupings used films and videotape to document the gatekeeping function of counselors, and found that when counselors and students were racially matched, their interactions had a better emotional tone and students were offered more special help.[207] Early research into schools in the Southwest backed up complaints from Mexican American parents that white teachers tended to think of Mexican-ancestry students as unintelligent and not destined for leadership positions, and that they often simply ignored these students.[208] For example, a 1970–71 U.S. Commission on Civil Rights study of 430 schools in California, Texas, and New Mexico found that teachers praised or encouraged whites 36 percent more often than Mexican students, and used or built upon the comments of whites 40 percent more often. When all types of approving and accepting comments were combined, the results showed that 40 percent more positive attention was given to white students. The report blamed teachers' neglect of Mexican culture for the reluctance of these children to contribute.[209]

More recent reviews of the literature have varied in their assessments of the state of white teacher bias against nonwhite students. Supporting the notion of white bias, one review of the literature found that white teachers tend to ignore black children more than white children, praise them less even when they give the same answers as white children, but reprimand them more.[210] For example, an experimental study had sixty-eight white female elementary school teachers listen to recordings of fifth-grade boys talking about their favorite TV show. The recordings were paired with photos of black or white kids, and researchers asked the teachers to rate the responses for personality, quality, and current and future academic ability. Race proved a significant factor for all of these assessments.[211] But another a review of sixteen studies of teacher expectations for black vs. white students yielded only nine studies that showed white teachers having lower expectations for black students, and in only five of those were the results statistically significant.[212] A study of more than seven thousand teachers in a school district in the American Southwest found that a teacher's race had no impact on course grades, though students had lower absentee rates when their teachers shared their race.[213]

What about the racial abilities of nonwhite teachers—do they show less bias than whites? Results are again mixed. The early U.S. Commission

on Civil Rights study cited above found no evidence that Latino teachers differed from white teachers in their treatment of white students; in
fact they actually tended to praise white students more than did white
teachers.[214] On the other hand, a study of "paraeducators" (assistants
who typically come from the community and help the licensed teachers)
showed them to have racial abilities. When paired with Latino students,
Latino paraeducators could talk to students about many topics, including things outside the classroom, and demonstrated *cariño* (a kind of
affection expressed in words that non-Latinos would probably not use,
such as *mi amor* and *mijo/mija*, as well as in touch, proximity, and facial
expressions). Their cultural style minimized the negative effect of correcting behavior and created a more relaxed instructional style: "being
Latino and speaking the same language helped them foster a sense of
confianza."[215] In addition, a nation-wide, longitudinal study of twenty-
five thousand students found that while teacher race did not impact how
much students learned, it did correlate with teachers' subjective evaluations of their students. In some circumstances, black teachers gave significantly higher evaluations of black students than did white teachers,
and the same was true of Latino teachers with Latino students.[216]

Other scholars have argued that racial abilities matter in ways not
directly related to the race of students. For example, research has found
that teachers of different races vary in how they choose materials to use
in the classroom, in the instructional activities they favor, in the kinds of
examples they use to illustrate a new concept, and in how they manage
a classroom.[217]

Reviews of the literature on the actual effects of teacher race on students, rather than just on their biases or behavior, have sometimes found
no or only weak support for racial realism, but other studies have found
some robust effects. In the 1980s, for example, many scholars argued
for the importance of racial signaling, maintaining that schools without
minority teachers were sending the message that only whites belong in
positions of authority—a message that would lower career goals for nonwhite students.[218] However, many empirical studies of this kind of racial
signaling—the "role model" theory—in fact found little effect. A 1992
study of gender and race role models, using a sample of nearly 2,500 students who had taken an economics course, found that a teacher's gender
did not matter at all in the amount of economics learned and that the
benefit for black students of having black teachers as role models, though
statistically significant, was very small.[219] A study of almost eight thousand college students from thirty-four colleges and universities found

that although students, and especially African-American students, tend to seek same-race role models,[220] whether or not they have such a model has no effect on their choice of a career in academia, except in the case of African-American males, who were 3 percent more likely to choose an academic career if they had a same-race role model.[221]

Perhaps because it seems so commonsensical, social scientists have nevertheless continued to emphasize the positive evidence, and to assert that same-race teacher role models are crucial for successful learning.[222] Moreover, there *are* studies that show student performance varying with teacher race. One review of the literature found studies showing that minority students taught by a teacher of the same race had fewer behavior problems, lower dropout rates, and better attendance than students whose teachers were of a race other than their own.[223] A study of twelve thousand black and white students in Tennessee found that each year of exposure to a same-race teacher was associated with an increase of between 2 and 4 percentile points in reading and math.[224] A study of school districts in Texas in the 1998–99 school year found that having Latino teachers positively impacted Latino students' test scores, attendance, dropout rates, and the rates at which they took advanced and AP classes.[225] The same effect has been found at the college level. For example, a 2011 study found that the gap between white students' and black and Latino students' drop-out rates and AP exam pass rates falls by half when the latter are taught by a same-race professor.[226]

In sum, there is evidence that white teachers are biased against at least some nonwhite students, and there is evidence that teacher behavior to some degree varies with race and also that, to varying degrees, teacher effects on student outcomes varies by race. While certainly not overwhelming, in the education context there is, as with policing, enough social science evidence to make it difficult to deny there is at least some value in racial-realist management.

Law and Racial Realism in Government Employment: Contradictory Messages

Since 1972, Title VII has covered government employers, but this does not mean that government employment is legally identical to private employment. First of all, there are a large number of positions that are "jobs" in the sense of being paid positions, and even having benefits attached, that are not "employment" within the rules of Title VII. Section 2000e of the law states: "The term 'employee' means an individual employed by an employer, except that the term 'employee' shall not include any person elected to public office in any State or political subdivision of any State by the qualified voters thereof, or any person chosen by such officer to be on such officer's personal staff, or an appointee on the policy making level or an immediate adviser with respect to the exercise of the constitutional or legal powers of the office."[227] So voters are not employers in the meaning of the law (which is not very shocking), and neither elected officials nor their staffs can be sued for discrimination. They are not employers or employees as those words are defined by the statute.

Therefore, government officials can legally appoint persons to jobs explicitly because of their perceived racial signaling or abilities with complete impunity—and voters can be entirely motivated by whatever racial chauvinism, goodwill, or animus they may have in their hearts when they cast their votes. American law gives free rein to racial realism in filling what are arguably the country's most important and most visible jobs—and there can be no doubt that elected officials and voters both take advantage of this freedom.

Placement in "civil service" and professional jobs, those not filled by appointment, is to be done according to legal rules, however. Yet this form of government employment also differs from private employment, though in another way. Depending on the claim of the litigants and the judge's discretion, it is regulated not only by Title VII, but also by the Equal Protection Clause of the Fourteenth Amendment to the Constitution. Crucially, unbound by any rules about race and BFOQs in hiring and placement, the Constitution can allow racial realism in government employment in ways that may for now be blocked under Title VII in other employment categories.

In current constitutional jurisprudence, racial classifications are acceptable in law as long as they are narrowly tailored and designed to achieve a compelling purpose. So the question before courts in government employment cases may be: are there any purposes in government hiring that are compelling or substantial enough to justify racial realism?

Some courts in the past few decades have asserted that there are. The courts are willing, however to see a compelling interest in race-based hiring in one area only; namely, law enforcement. In one case, a court approved of the racial-realist placement of nonwhite officers, not withstanding the fact that those officers litigated to stop the placement. Even here, there is evidence of judges struggling with racial realism, with some early opinions seeing it as discrimination, or catering to discriminatory tastes of citizens. One judge went so far as to compare the limitations of African-American officers to African-American neighborhoods to slavery. Yet a clear pattern has now taken shape of a judge-made opening for racial-realist management of law enforcement. Throughout, I note which president appointed the writers of these opinions to highlight the nonpartisan nature of the court rulings.

On the other hand, the long history of advocacy and the research record purporting to show that a teacher's race is critical to the education process—which if anything is actually a bit stronger than for law enforcement—has simply not persuaded American judges. It is difficult to discern why judges would treat the employment of educators differently, though the history of violence spurred by incidents of white-on-black police brutality appear to be what makes racial realism "compelling" in law enforcement.

Authorizing Racial Realism in Policing

In no other area of public or private employment have the courts made more effort to authorize racial realism as they have in policing and law enforcement. Even in this field, however, it took several years for racial-realist legal doctrine to develop, and, especially in the early years after Title VII went into effect, some courts ruled that race had no place in policing. The more recent trend has been for courts to find a compelling interest in using race for the "operational needs" of the department, even though some nonwhite officers, like the African-American managers who sued the Walgreens drugstore chain (see Chapter 2), have litigated to prevent being placed in nonwhite neighborhoods.

One can trace the transition in court rulings by beginning with a 1968 case that considered the constitutionality of the St. Petersburg, Florida police department's practice of assigning black officers to police black neighborhoods. The city actually drew up a zone to encompass both the black residential and black business areas and then assigned black officers to patrol that zone and a black sergeant to oversee those officers. The police chief's testimony lauding the racial abilities of black officers was a factor in persuading a district court to accept the practice. The Fifth Circuit Court also noted Chief Harold C. Smith's view that black officers "are better able to cope with the inhabitants of that zone, who on occasion become abusive and aggressive toward police officers during a

disturbance; and, further, that they are able to communicate with the inhabitants of the Negro area better than white officers and are better able
to identify Negroes and investigate criminal activities in that zone more
effectively than white officers."[228] But in an opinion by the Judge John
Minor Wisdom (an Eisenhower appointee with a strong liberal record on
civil rights), the court overruled the district court, holding that the practice violated the equal protection guarantees of the Fourteenth Amendment. Going further, the court argued that racial matching (at least in
this case) was analogous to slavery and thus would violate the Thirteenth
Amendment if considered as a slavery case: "What the St. Petersburg
Police Department did was to superimpose on natural geographic zones
an artificial zone that rests on the department's judgment of Negroes as
a class. The Department concluded that Negroes as a class are suitable
only for the zone appropriately numbered 13. This is the kind of badge
of slavery the thirteenth amendment condemns."[229] Though noting in a
footnote that racial assignments may be justified for undercover infiltra-
tions of black crime organizations, or during periods of racial tension or
unrest, the court held that the racial abilities argument that "Negro officers are better able to police Negro citizens cannot justify the blanket
assignment of *all* Negroes, and *only* Negroes to patrol Zone 13."[230] Citing
the Kerner Commission report for support, the court instead suggested
that "Negro officers should be rotated among the various patrol zones of
the city, in the same manner as white officers insofar as ability, available
work force, and other variables permit."[231]

A district court also rejected racial realism for policing in a 1994 Title
VII case involving a single white officer on the police force of a predominately black university, though here the issue was not officer abilities
but the public's discriminatory preference for black police officers. This
white officer believed that the department subjected him to more disciplinary actions than the black officers and that this constituted racial
discrimination against him. The court ruled in favor of the white officer,
citing the black police chief's racial-realist view that the white officer's
race was as "a negative factor" when he "had to confront certain black
persons, mostly students, in the discharge of his official duties" because
"a white officer would be perceived negatively by a portion of his constit-
uent community which, in turn, could lead to racial responses and con-
frontations." The opinion, written by Nixon appointee Garnett Thomas
Eisele, noted that considering customer preferences this way would be
tantamount to ruling that race could be a BFOQ—a ruling that Title VII
clearly forbade.[232]

However, other courts have been more sympathetic to racial-realist arguments in hiring police officers or other law enforcement officials.[233] In 1973, a Second Circuit Court ruled on a case brought by black and Puerto Rican applicants for the Bridgeport, Connecticut police force, who had found their opportunities blocked by an examination procedure they believed to be discriminatory. The court sided with the litigants, and using the Fourteenth Amendment for authority, approved hiring quotas for minority police officers to compensate for past discrimination. But this opinion, written by Nixon appointee William Hughes Mulligan, moved beyond traditional affirmative-action principles to justify its decision: "The most crucial consideration in our view is that this is not a private employer and not simply an exercise in providing minorities with equal opportunity employment. This is a police department and the visibility of the Black patrolman in the community is a decided advantage for all segments of the public at a time when racial divisiveness is plaguing law enforcement."[234]

A year later, in a case involving the Alabama Department of Public Safety, a Fifth Circuit Court cited as precedents the Bridgeport case and also school desegregation cases that relied on the Fourteenth Amendment, and also ordered racial hiring quotas to make up for past discrimination. Nixon appointee Charles Clark's opinion approvingly quoted the above passage on the strategy of deploying the racial signaling of black officers.[235]

More explicit and forceful support for racial signaling came in a Detroit case that was notable for a circuit court's overruling of a very strongly worded district court opinion. Following the disastrous 1967 riots, the city government decided that black officers were better for black neighborhoods and instituted an affirmative-action plan that was motivated not just by a desire to compensate for past discrimination, but also by the belief that African-American officers could do a better job of policing the city. In the 1970s, several white officers sued the city, claiming they had been passed over for promotions. In a Michigan district court, the city defended itself with a variety of arguments, including the claim that black officers are better at communicating and gaining cooperation than white officers when dealing with black citizens. Detroit also argued that the crime rate and citizen complaints both went down after its affirmative-action plan went into effect and that a racial-realist management strategy was therefore an "operational need" of the police department. The district court's Eisenhower appointee, Frederick Kaess, soundly rejected this defense on the grounds that effectiveness is dependent upon skill, training, and attitude, and that race preferences hurt department morale and thus police work as well.[236] Moreover, approving this legal logic would lead to the perverse result of justifying racial preferences for whites as well: "If better public communication would exist by hiring more blacks and promoting more blacks to supervisory positions then the problem lies in a racially motivated populace. In the eyes of this Court catering to such racial prejudice cannot be said to be 'compelling'. On the contrary, the Court would consider it to be pandering. If the defendants' claim of 'operational need' can be considered as compelling then apparently any all white community, via the police department, could lay claim to such a 'compelling interest' in forming a basis to reject all non-whites."[237]

On appeal, the Sixth Circuit reversed, arguing that perceptions of the value of racial qualifications were not based on "provincial beliefs" but on law enforcement experience. The circuit court opinion, written by Nixon appointee Pierce Lively, cited four different federal studies[238] and noted that they all "recommended the recruitment of additional numbers of minority police officers as a means of improving community support and law enforcement effectiveness."[239] Having African-American officers would give the community confidence in the police and make them feel that they were not being policed entirely by whites, and this would in turn lessen the risk of violence. Supporting the national studies were the local voices of Chief William H. Hart, Executive Deputy Chief James Bannon, and former Police Commissioner John F. Nichols. Given this evidence, the appeals court argued there was a substantial interest that justified the race categorizations because of signaling:

> The argument that police need more minority officers is not simply that blacks communicate better with blacks or that a police department should cater to the public's desires. Rather, it is that effective crime prevention and solution depend heavily on the public support and cooperation which result only from public respect and confidence in the police. In short, the focus is not on the superior performance of minority officers, but on the public's perception of law enforcement officials and institutions . . . the justification offered by defendants is a substantial one.[240]

A Fourth Circuit Court issued a similar correction to a wayward district court that had mistakenly denied the constitutionality of racial realism in policing. The circuit court's opinion in *Talbert v. City of Richmond*[241] is distinctive because it is one of the few cases to apply to employment the "diversity" rationale for race preferences in university admissions that the Supreme Court had articulated in the famous *Bakke* decision. Richmond,

Virginia, sought to use race as a factor in promoting minorities to the top ranks of the police department in order to (in the words of the court's John D. Butzner, a Johnson appointee) "advance the operational needs of the police department by achieving diversity. . . . It viewed such diversity as important to effective law enforcement in a city whose population was approximately 50% black."[242] The court agreed that "the city's claim that diversity is beneficial to operation of the department is akin to the claim accepted by Justice Powell in *Bakke* that a school has a legitimate interest in obtaining a diverse student population."[243]

More recent cases strengthened the argument for a racial-realist strategy in policing or, more broadly, law enforcement. A 1996 case involved employment practices in a Greene County, Illinois boot camp, where young criminals would be given regimens of extreme military-style discipline in the hopes of encouraging them to become constructive citizens. At the camp, 68 percent of the two hundred inmates were black, but only two of the forty-eight correctional officers were. There were also three white captains and of the ten lieutenants, only two were black. Three white applicants for the lieutenant position sued, claiming they were discriminated against on the basis of their race when one of the black lieutenants was hired. The Seventh Circuit opinion, written by Reagan appointee Richard Posner, sided with the boot camp. Posner noted that the Supreme Court had held against "role model" theories of discrimination (see below) because there is little evidence supporting racial role models and the theory has nearly boundless reach. But the boot camp's desire for a black lieutenant was different, he claimed—and justified:

> The black lieutenant is needed because inmates are believed unlikely to play the correctional game of brutal drill sergeant and brutalized recruit unless there are some blacks in authority in the camp. This is not just speculation, but is backed up by expert evidence that the plaintiffs did not rebut. The defendants' experts—recognized experts in the field of prison administration—did not rely on generalities about racial balance or diversity; did not, for that matter, defend a goal of racial balance. They opined that the boot camp in Greene County would not succeed in its mission of pacification and reformation with as white a staff as it would have had if a black male had not been appointed to one of the lieutenant slots.[244]

Here the court was very cautious. The ruling emphasized that the boot camp was not authorized to engage in race-based hiring in response to "extortionate demands" from same-race prisoners and was not authorized to make the racial mix of its staff mirror that of its inmates. Moreover, the racial realism was based here not on principle but on empirical evidence, and if other evidence was forthcoming that would successfully countered the claims of the boot camp experts in Greene County, then the practice might have to stop.[245]

Six years later, in 2002, the Seventh Circuit and Judge Posner had a chance to revisit this thinking, this time in a case involving Latinos and Chicago's police department. White male police sergeants and lieutenants challenged the promotions of black, Latino, and female officers. Past discrimination against these groups justified Chicago's affirmative-action plan, but, they argued, the city could not use affirmative action to justify promoting Latino officers because there had been no evidence of discrimination against Latinos. There were only a few Latino lieutenants in the city despite a population that included half a million Latinos, but this discrepancy was due mostly to the rapid growth in this population.[246] Chicago therefore defended the Latino preference by arguing that Latinos could sensitize the department to the specific problems of the Latino community and serve as trusted "ambassadors."[247] Posner agreed, noting that "many courts . . . have at least left open a small window for forms of discrimination that are supported by compelling public safety concerns." "Especially in a period of heightened public concern with the dangers posed by international terrorism," he argued, "effective police work must be reckoned a national priority that justifies some sacrifice of competing interests." If "promoting one Hispanic police sergeant out of order is important to the effectiveness of the Chicago police in protecting the people of the city from crime," then this was acceptable, even if it was racial discrimination.[248]

Finally, in another Chicago case, a Seventh Circuit Court ruled that the operational needs of the city's police department formed a compelling interest in a racially diverse department.[249] The case was especially significant for using the *Grutter v. Bollinger* opinion to justify a practice in policing (see below).

Even in a legal environment where courts are authorizing police departments to use racial realism in their hiring and placement of officers, the practice is subject to some limits. Two cases show nonwhite officers challenging racial realism (with some degree of success) for the negative impacts it can have on their work experiences.

First, a district court in 1982 ruled on a charge made by an organization of police officers in Bridgeport, Connecticut. As described above,

Bridgeport had been the site of an early case where a court noted approvingly the racial signaling impact of nonwhite officers to justify racial preferences in hiring. Ten years later, those black and Latino officers were challenging in court their disproportionate concentration in high-crime areas, where violent, physical assaults were most common and police work was at its most challenging and stressful. The city did not squarely attempt to defend this policy as one of operational needs, however. Superintendent of Police Joseph Walsh said obliquely that officers' assignments are based on "the relative importance that they may have in different types of neighborhoods."[250] The judge in the case, Carter appointee T. F. Gilroy Daly, took his statement to be an admission that officers are matched to neighborhoods that correspond to their race, and rejected it as a justification for policy, arguing that it was based on the stereotype that black officers work better with black citizens. This was an impermissible "racially-based motive."[251]

The most prominent challenge to racial realism in policing followed a particularly shocking case of police brutality involving torture. New York City officers beat and sodomized a black Haitian immigrant, Abner Louima, with a toilet plunger, sending Louima into the hospital for months of surgeries to repair serious injuries. Two days after the torture of Louima, Mayor Rudolph Giuliani met with police officials, community leaders, religious leaders, and Una S. T. Clarke, the councilwoman who represented Brooklyn's 40th District, where the violence had occurred. After the meeting, Police Commissioner Howard Safir decided to assign twenty-seven black police officers to the precinct. Safir later explained, "We discussed the issue that this was an emergency situation, that we believed and I believed that there was great potential for civil disturbance and we needed to very quickly and very expeditiously calm the community and make sure that the community understood that we took this incident very seriously, that we were not going to cover it up, that we were not going to let it go unnoticed and we were going to take very firm and decisive action."[252]

Twenty-two of the twenty-seven officers, who self-identified variously as African-American, Black-Hispanic, Jamaican, West Indian, Trinidadian, or Guyanese, sued the city, charging racial discrimination in their deployment to this problem precinct. They argued that their status was lowered, that they lost promotion opportunities, and that their new precinct was "hostile and difficult," leading some of the officers to fear "for the safety of themselves and their families."[253] The city responded that "the minority community's distrust of the NYPD was heightened by the Abner Louima incident and could have resulted in a collapse of the social order,"[254] and that the *Bakke* decision had established that the city did not have to demonstrate past discrimination against blacks to use race for hiring and placement.[255] Judge Shira A. Scheindlin, a Clinton appointee, agreed with the city: "In order to carry out its mission effectively, a police force must appear to be unbiased, must be respected by the community it serves, and must be able to communicate with the public. Thus, a police department's 'operational needs' can be a compelling state interest which might justify race-based decision making."[256] The court took a balanced approach however: the city's placements had to be temporary and officers would be able to request transfer.[257]

The Supreme Court has not ruled on racial realism in policing.[258] The trend in the circuit courts, however, appears strongly supportive of the practice in this specific employment sector. Numerous precedents allow law enforcement agencies of various types to consider the strategy of nonwhite racial signaling and racial abilities. This is, however, the only avenue where multiple courts have given legal authorization for the strategic deployment of racial realism in employment.

Blocking Racial Realism in Teaching

The story of racial realism in teaching is in some ways the opposite of that in policing. Rather than failing at first and then becoming more established later, in education it began more positively in the lower courts, but the Supreme Court emphatically ruled out at least the racial signaling strategy in the 1980s. Subsequent lower court decisions reinforced the legal prohibition on other racial-realist management strategies in education. Whether that will change again remains to be seen.

The *Brown v. Board of Education* Supreme Court decision, as well as some earlier rulings, had shown concern that segregated blacks could never learn when they were educationally isolated, while evincing no concern about the potential abuse of minority children in majority schools.[259] By the 1960s, courts were beginning to order school districts to integrate their faculties as well as their students. In these cases, courts did not say that teacher or administrator race had any particular correlation with ability or signaling. Rather, a racially balanced faculty was important mainly as an indicator that schools were no longer segregated.[260]

In the riot-torn late 1960s, however, at least one federal court began to see great value in racial realism. *Porcelli v. Titus*[261] involved the school system in the city of Newark, New Jersey, which had been the site of some of 1967's worst rioting.[262] Superintendent of Schools Franklyn Titus had urged the school board to suspend the normal, examination-based procedure of promoting teachers to administrative jobs. The school board accepted the move, allowing more blacks to move into these administrative positions. Titus explained that in the more than two decades since the old promotion procedure was developed, "the conditions in the City had changed, educational philosophy had changed. There was a high[er] premium on sensitivity than had existed hitherto."[263] Titus continued: "Sensitivity, as I see it, is that element of a person's personality which makes him aware of the problems of the ghetto, unique to the circumstances surrounding being a member of a minority group, sensitive to the educational needs that go out of the deprived conditions in many of our— most of our neighborhoods. . . . As I see it, and I see it very clearly in my own mind, anybody who is in a position of leadership today in a city like Newark has to be able to identify, has to be able to understand."[264] Other witnesses supported Titus's argument that suspension of the promotion lists was the right move because the lists "didn't represent the kinds of racial mix that I feel is most important in accomplishing an educational program in the City of Newark."[265]

Various educational experts also testified in the case, arguing that poor reading levels showed that an "educational crisis" existed in Newark, and that hiring nonwhites was the way to turn things around. An urban education professor at Brooklyn College, Dr. Robert Trent, testified, "If you want significant change in the school performance of the ghetto population, it is highly advisable to involve as much as you can competent black professionals." Trent argued that blacks could inspire students as role models, blacks would be better at disciplining black children, and blacks would be better at bringing black parents into the educational process— though in some circumstances a white person could also do the job.[266]

In supporting Titus, Judge Anthony Augelli, a Kennedy appointee, emphasized that the record showed there was no intention to discriminate against whites or to exclude them from consideration. Blackness in Newark's educational system was simply a qualification: "Despite a desire to provide an avenue for the appointment of more Negro administrators, the ultimate objective of the Board was to promote those persons most qualified to suit the needs of the Newark school system."[267]

Other lower courts also affirmed racial realism. The decision in a case involving the Kalamazoo, Michigan school district amounted to an endorsement of the racial signaling role model theory in education. The district had been under a 1973 court order to desegregate, and faced a challenge several years later when a fiscal crisis forced the district to lay off more than one hundred teachers. The district sought legal authorization to avoid having to lay off the most recently hired teachers, who were predominately black. The court sided with the district, citing approvingly the testimony of Dr. Robert Green, a court-appointed expert who had written a study of the Kalamazoo school district. Green argued that desegregation required a "critical mass" of black teachers and administrators so that the students could have role models. Judge Noel Fox, appointed by Kennedy, agreed with Green that "the need for role models is important because they can encourage minority students to higher aspirations and at the same time work to dispel myths and stereotypes about their race."[268] Laying off black teachers, as the court paraphrased Green, would "take away badly needed student role models and would have a psychological impact on the students and the general community who could perceive the District's actions as being inequitable and a disavowal of its promises to desegregate."[269] Fox's opinion noted that in assessing a Title VII case, the court only had to consider possible injuries to employees, but in a constitutional case focused on equal protection, possible injuries to students also must be considered—and these students needed to have same-race role models.[270]

But after two more lower courts affirmed the idea, the Supreme Court explicitly rejected the idea of the hiring teachers to provide racial role models. In *Wygant et al. v. Jackson Board of Education* (1986), the Court considered a situation, also in Michigan, that was similar to that in Kalamazoo. The Jackson, Michigan school board had a plan that protected some teachers from being laid off, with some consideration for race or national origin. The district had lagged in the hiring of black teachers for decades, hiring its first black teacher in 1953. By 1969, African-Americans were only 3.9 percent of the teaching staff, while the student body was 15.2 percent African-American. In 1972, the schools in the district saw considerable racial tension, and violence broke out in Jackson High School.[271] The school district responded by changing its collective bargaining agreement with the union so as to offer protection for minorities from being laid off in tough times.[272] It was this rule that became the center of litigation.

In the federal district court, the Jackson school district defended its hiring plan with arguments emphasizing the need to remedy societal discrimination and the importance of racial signaling. This line of reasoning persuaded this lower court, which issued a ruling that the legality of the plan required comparing the percentage of black teachers with the percentage of black students (rather than the percentage of black teachers in the local labor market).[273] This was because "teaching is more than just a job. Teachers are role-models for their students. More specifically, minority teachers are role-models for minority students. This is vitally important because societal discrimination has often deprived minority children of other role-models."[274] A Sixth Circuit Court agreed, stating, "The school board's interests in eliminating historic discrimination, promoting racial harmony in the community and providing role models for minority students are among the justifications available to support the layoff provisions."[275]

But the Supreme Court was not convinced. Writing for the majority, Justice Powell—author of the "diversity" constitutional rationale for race-conscious admissions in universities—rejected the notion of "societal discrimination" as a justification for considering race when laying off teachers, on grounds that it was "too amorphous."[276] But he also ruled that hiring for racial role models was unacceptable. Powell maintained that "the role model theory employed by the District Court has no logical stopping point. The role model theory allows the Board to engage in discriminatory hiring and layoff practices long past the point required by any legitimate remedial purpose." Powell expressed concern that relying on racial signaling could in fact *limit* opportunities for minority teachers in schools with few minority students. Most devastatingly, he compared it to Jim Crow discrimination: "Carried to its logical extreme, the idea that black students are better off with black teachers could lead to the very system the Court rejected in *Brown v. Board of Education*."[277]

Justice O'Connor concurred with Powell's view but added that she believed school districts were not barred from considering race for its other organizational or educational benefits, opening the door to some racial-realist hiring or placement. She argued, "Although its precise contours are uncertain, a state interest in the promotion of racial diversity has been found sufficiently 'compelling', at least in the context of higher education, to support the use of racial considerations in furthering that interest. . . . And certainly nothing the Court has said today necessarily forecloses the possibility that the Court will find other governmental interests which have been relied upon in the lower courts but which have not been passed on here to be sufficiently 'important' or 'compelling' to sustain the use of affirmative-action policies."[278] The goal of providing role models "should not be confused with the very different goal of promoting racial diversity among the faculty."[279] By emphasizing the possible constitutionality of hiring teachers for their contributions to diversity,

O'Connor appeared to be trying to give authorization for racial abilities, even if the Court found the racial signaling implied by the role model theory to be unconstitutional.

At least one circuit court did not take the bait. Another blow to racial realism in teaching came in a highly controversial appeals court decision arising out of a case in Piscataway Township in New Jersey, discussed briefly in Chapter 2. This decision specifically rejected O'Connor's suggestion that a goal of teacher diversity would justify considering race when managing a district's teachers. The specific situation once again involved the consideration of race when laying off teachers. The education board had laid off a white teacher, Sharon Taxman, while retaining a similarly qualified black teacher, Debra Williams, because its affirmative-action plan directed the board to consider the value that the black teacher's racial diversity could add to the education process. Williams was the only black teacher in the Business Education Department. The board sought to use the diversity rationale as articulated by Powell in the *Bakke* decision, as well as O'Connor's concurring opinion in *Wygant,* to justify its affirmative-action plan and the retention of Williams, though in their understanding diversity was useful for *both* the racial signaling and the racial abilities that nonwhite teachers could provide. Theodore Kruse, the school board's president, told the court that because the community was so diverse, it would be "valuable for the students to see in the various employment roles a wide range of background," and that "it was also valuable to the work force and in particular to the teaching staff that they have—they see that in each other." In his view, keeping the black teacher "was sending a very clear message that we feel that our staff should be culturally diverse, our student population is culturally diverse and there is a distinct advantage to students, to all students, to be made—come into contact with people of different cultures, different background, so that they are more aware, more tolerant, more accepting, more understanding of people of all backgrounds."[280]

The district court rejected the board's argument, stating that affirmative action in employment must be justified by a rationale specifically focused on remedying past discrimination in the school district.[281] The Third Circuit's *en banc* decision (written by Reagan appointee Carol Los Mansmann, but supported by future Supreme Court Justice Samuel Alito in the majority) also rejected the board's reasoning. Mansmann argued that Congress intended Title VII to stop discrimination or remedy previous discrimination, and only the latter goal justified employers using race in making employment decisions: "there is no congressional recognition of diversity as a Title VII objective."[282] The court specifically rejected the board's attempt to use the *Bakke* decision's approval of "diversity" as a constitutionally permissible goal, as well as a decision relating to the Federal Communications Commission's connection of racial diversity and broadcasting,[283] because these contexts were totally different from employment at a high school.[284] It considered the case as a standard affirmative-action case, and failing to find the proper legal arguments to defend affirmative action (remedying a racially imbalanced workforce with a temporary measure that would not trammel the interests of whites), ruled against the school board.[285]

Racial realism for teachers no longer fares well under the Constitution either. The Texas Education Agency's goal of having a staff that matched the racial and ethnic demographics of Texas students was challenged in federal court by Karen Hansen Messer, a white female administrator who believe that she was denied promotions and higher pay because the agency needed more nonwhites and males to "produce a workforce that reflects the ethnic and gender diversity of the state's population."[286] While not strictly a racial-realism case (the hiring and promotion plan did not say what the diversity was intended to accomplish), it likely would have failed if there were racial ability or signaling components, because this court, in an opinion written by Reagan appointee Edith Jones, ruled the racial preferences were not constitutional "in the absence of remedial action to counteract past provable discrimination."[287]

Court Rejection of Government Racial Realism outside of Policing and Teaching

Racial realism in other areas of government employment has also failed to receive judicial authorization. There have been few challenges, and the contexts have not involved such pressing and ongoing concerns as can be found in policing. As with Piscataway's *Taxman* case, the courts have treated the challenges as basic Title VII cases, refusing to bring in the constitutional doctrine from the law enforcement cases or non-employment contexts. This means that the lack of a race BFOQ has led these courts to disallow racial realism, just as they have in private, skilled employment.

A 1981 New York case involved what is likely a common practice of employers in many contexts who are interested in a diverse workforce: the use of nonwhite recruiters to attract nonwhites. The case involved a challenge from an African-American man, James Knight, who worked for the Test Development Division of the Nassau County Civil Service Commission. Knight was hoping for a promotion, but the Commission assigned him instead to a minority recruiting position. Knight claimed that the failure to promote him and the recruiting assignment were prompted by considerations of his race. A Second Circuit Court ruled that there was no discrimination in his failure to be promoted, but that his transfer "was clearly based in significant part on his race. The Commission apparently thought that Knight would develop a better rapport than would a white person with the members of minority groups whom the Commission was trying to recruit. Although his salary and benefits remained unchanged, Knight claims that the assignment was racist and demeaning."[288] In an opinion written by James Oakes, who was appointed by Nixon but was a prominent liberal, the court ruled in a way similar to the anti-racial-realist position taken by the court in the Piscataway school case. In other words, given the lack of a BFOQ for race, race could be a factor in such government placements and not violate Title VII or the Constitution *only* in affirmative-action contexts, and this was not an instance of affirmative action—it was discrimination. Knight's transfer was not acceptable because it "was based on a racial stereotype that blacks work better with blacks and on the premise that Knight's race was directly related to his ability to do the job."[289]

Another case involved an African-American worker, Carl Rucker, who worked for a state agency in Wisconsin, the Higher Educational Aids Board, that provided counseling services to disadvantaged kids, most of them black.[290] Rucker was under pressure from his boss (also African-American) and local African-American preachers not to grant permanent-employment status to a white counselor; they believed that disadvantaged black youths should be counseled by members of their own race. The preacher even told Rucker, "You're going to have to get a black woman and put her on that job. It's as simple as that."[291] Rucker resisted and was eventually fired.

The court, in an opinion written by Richard Posner, who had accepted racial realism in policing, rejected the board's racial realism, first on grounds that courts have rejected customer discrimination as a justification for preferences in cases dealing with employer preferences for women in some jobs.[292] Second, the court noted that the board's view was even less warranted than in a gender case because considering customer preference would in this case be the same as saying there was a race BFOQ. Therefore, no racial realism was allowed: "Title VII is a blanket prohibition of racial discrimination," and even though it is "not irrational" to "refuse on racial grounds to hire someone because your customers or clientele do not like his race," it is nevertheless "clearly forbidden by Title VII."[293]

These cases suggest that it is not education that presents an exception in disallowing racial realism in government employment. Rather, law enforcement is the exception in that it is only in this arena that the courts have opened space for management strategy utilizing racial abilities and signaling.

The Failure of the Grutter Decision to Change the Game in Government Employment

The year 2003 brought one of the most significant Supreme Court decisions on race in years, and one with special application to government employment because it dealt with constitutional limits on racial classifications. Like the *Bakke* decision, it focused not on employment but on racial preferences in university admissions. A white female applicant, Barbara Grutter, was denied admission and sued the University of Michigan Law School, arguing that the school's use of racial preferences in its admissions policy violated both the Constitution and the Civil Rights Act of 1964's Title VI. Specifically, she argued that the school violated the Fourteenth Amendment's guarantee of equal protection of the laws and Title VI's prohibition against discrimination in programs receiving federal assistance.

By a 5 to 4 decision, the Court upheld the University of Michigan Law School's admissions plan. In the majority opinion, Justice Sandra Day O'Connor largely supported several arguments made by the Law School. She noted that the Law School gave a preference to African-Americans, Latinos, and Native Americans in order to achieve a "critical mass" of these groups (that is, a large enough number that students in these groups would not feel isolated or that they had to be spokespersons for their race). The Court's majority was persuaded that the goal of admitting a critical mass of minority students, and the resulting diverse student body, was a compelling interest that justified otherwise suspect racial classifications because it promotes "cross-racial understanding," breaks down stereotypes, and produces livelier, more interesting and spirited classroom discussions.[294] In other words, the nonwhite students had the ability to produce particular effects that would be missing without their presence—and this was especially true, apparently, of those students who did not fit stereotypes. Though there was no "characteristic minority viewpoint on any issue," nevertheless growing up as a minority would lead to viewpoints different from those of the majority.[295]

Though the case dealt with school admissions policies, and O'Connor emphasized that her reasoning was shaped by the educational context,[296] there were reasons to expect that the decision would have impacts in employment law. First, the opinion contained some connections to employment. Amicus briefs convinced the Court that a diverse student body leads to better learning and better preparation for an increasingly diverse workforce. The majority appeared impressed with the brief from the Fortune 500 companies, discussed in Chapter 2, and cited it for the point it made that being among diverse students developed skills "needed in today's increasingly global marketplace."[297] In another important potential link to employment, and in particular to government employment, the majority admitted to being impressed by an amicus brief from retired military officers, who had argued that "a highly qualified, racially diverse officer corps . . . is essential to the military's ability to fulfill its principle mission to provide national security."[298] In order to ensure they had a diverse officer corps, the military needed educational institutions that could use race preferences at least to some degree. In the most direct acknowledgement of the value of racial signaling in government employment, the majority wrote of the value of racial signaling: "In order to cultivate a set of leaders with legitimacy in the eyes of the citizenry, it is necessary that the path to leadership be visibly open to talented and qualified individuals of every race and ethnicity. All members of our heterogeneous society must have confidence in the openness and integrity of the educational institutions that provide this training."[299]

Second, courts ruling on employment discrimination routinely cite as precedents cases that regard vastly different contexts, spreading their influence far and wide.[300] As discussed above, at least one court cited *Bakke*, which is also about university admissions, to allow the utilization of racial realism in the employment of police officers.

Some legal scholars expected, therefore, that *Grutter* would migrate to employment.[301] Virtually all of the arguments for the notion that racial diversity of student bodies aided the educational mission of universities would, it was believed, also apply, at the least, to professors and teachers and to secondary and primary schools as well as to universities.[302]

No court, however, has relied on *Grutter* to allow racial realism as a strategy for hiring educators at any level.[303] The reliance on the

Constitution to justify the racial utility, as well as the emphasis on the civic benefits of racial diversity, made it even less likely that *Grutter* could migrate to private employment and Title VII jurisprudence.[304]

Grutter's only influence in employment was on the path of least resistance: policing. The case, once again, involved the city of Chicago. This time the issue was an examination the city used in the mid-1980s to promote black and Latino officers to the rank of sergeant. After years of procedural battles, the Seventh Circuit issued a ruling that was based closely on the ruling in *Grutter*. Judge Terence Evans, a Carter appointee, cited a criminologist, Samuel Walker, whose research showed that minorities tended to distrust the Chicago police and tended not to cooperate with them, and that if officers were supervised by minorities this would mitigate the problem. Police officials also supported this argument, and added that minority cops helped defuse "potentially explosive situations."[305] Citing other policing precedents, Evans summed up by referring to *Grutter*: "All in all, we find that, as did the University of Michigan, the Chicago Police Department had a compelling interest in diversity. Specifically, the [Chicago Police Department] had a compelling interest in a diverse population at the rank of sergeant in order to set the proper tone in the department and to earn the trust of the community, which in turn increases police effectiveness in protecting the city."[306]

The diversity argument and the *Grutter* precedent were less successful in a more challenging context—racial diversity in Newark's fire department. Racial realism had already failed in a fire department context in Chicago.[307] Even armed with the *Grutter* opinion, Newark would fare no better. In 2002, Newark's mayor, Sharpe James, issued a "diversification order" requiring that all fire houses in the city be integrated. The stated purpose was "to improve morale" and also to respond to an old consent decree regarding racial discrimination by the fire department.[308] Thirty-four firefighters who had been forced to transfer or not allowed to transfer due to the policy joined with the union to bring a Title VII and Fourteenth Amendment discrimination suit against the city and fire department. The city defended its action, saying it was trying to eliminate *de facto* segregation in the fire houses, that it needed to act because of the old consent decree, and that (citing *Grutter*) it had a compelling interest in racially diverse fire companies because of the "educational, sociological and job performance" benefits that diversification would bring about.[309]

The Third Circuit Court, in an opinion written by Maryanne Trump Barry (sister to the real estate developer Donald Trump, and originally appointed by Reagan but elevated to the circuit by Clinton), rejected Newark's argument that seeking diversity was a compelling reason for considering race when staffing fire departments. It chose to read *Grutter* as a decision about law school education. Fire departments were different because they are not meant to educate. Their mission is to put out fires. There was in this case no compelling interest in the educational benefits of diversity, and the city had neither made a claim nor provided evidence that racial diversity helped to put out fires and was therefore one of the "operational needs" of the fire department.[310]

What, then, do we know about racial realism in government employment? We know that leaders of both parties appoint advisers, aides, administrators, and judges based in part or entirely on strategic considerations of racial signaling. Moreover, they sometimes do this while declaring that racial discrimination is wrong and in fact *always* wrong. Voters are right there with them, as they often support candidates based on racial considerations, and studies show they commonly respond differently to political leaders of different racial backgrounds—and also that they have reason to do so, as white and nonwhite official do behave differently in some circumstances. Police departments and schools also consider racial signaling as well as racial abilities in making hires and appointments, though social science evidence does not consistently support the benefits of these efforts. Neither civil rights law nor the Constitution constrain the use of racial realism by elected officials (or by voters) but both have much to say about law enforcement and teaching. Courts have thus far granted legal authorization for racial realism only to law enforcement institutions. The varying authorizations in law appear to bear little relationship to everyday practice.

4

Displaying Race for Dollars: Racial Realism in Media and Entertainment

Employment in media and entertainment is both similar to and different from the other sectors considered in this book. As in the case of the high- and low-skilled employment covered in Chapters 2 and 5, at stake in the hiring of advertising models, actors, and athletes are potentially huge profits for employers and job opportunities for a diverse pool of workers. And not surprisingly, employers perceive the benefits of racial realism in the media and entertainment industries, just as they do in other business sectors.

Yet media and entertainment employment is also different. To make money, these businesses display workers before the eyes and brains of thousands, or even millions, of customers or potential customers, and their business model is centered on audience response to a visual product. To be sure, there are many other kinds of jobs where the image of a worker is very important to the employer. Salespeople, waiters and waitresses, and flight attendants come to mind. But "merit" for each of these employees consists in the efficient performance of a service. The employee's image is not the essence of the job: salespeople move inventory, "close the deal," and win contracts; food servers remember orders and bring the food in a timely fashion; flight attendants perform countless tasks related to the safe and comfortable transportation of customers. By contrast, merit for actors, models, and athletes depends on the reactions of those who simply view these employees, typically without interacting with them, and most critically on whether they respond by spending money to see more of them. For employers, this is the main measure of a job well done. In this context, therefore, racial signaling plays a key role.

There are other factors as well that set some entertainment employers off from the employers discussed in other chapters. In moviemaking, for example, the financial stakes are very high. Films are often highly risky investments, costing hundreds of millions of dollars to bring to market. (When the Motion Picture Association of America stopped releasing data in 2007, the average production and marketing cost of a movie was $106.6 million.[1]) This leads to aggressive, demography-based marketing to recoup investments. However, though profit motives often dominate, some employers in the film and television industries are motivated by an *artistic* vision of how their employees should look; this may conform to audience expectations or it may go radically against them. These factors have combined to make entertainment employers especially prone to stereotyping, resistant to classical liberal antidiscrimination principles, and also resistant to affirmative-action liberalism.[2]

Some entertainers are linked to public investments in ways that other private employers are not. Producers of television shows, for instance, are dependent on licensed access to publicly-owned broadcasting bandwidth. Owners of professional sports teams are linked to the public in a different way: they play a quasi-civic function in their cities (think of the parades for league champions), and often enjoy the wild devotion of fan bases.

A final set of differences between entertainment and media employment and other private employment categories regards the relationship between this sector of employment and its legal regulation. First, the distance between what the law says these employers can do and what they actually do is wider here than any other sector. Only in advertising, film, and television employment is it commonplace to *openly* discriminate— both in print and in pixels: help-wanted ads regularly specify the desired race of the applicants. Second, only in this sector of employment are First Amendment concerns relevant to the hiring and placing of employees. Thus, the familiar problem of the lack of a BFOQ for race may have a solution here: employers in this sector may claim that their freedom of expression justifies a racial realism that benefits both whites and nonwhites. Third, legal regulation of broadcasting bandwidth may play a role in legalizing racial realism, if it can benefit the public good.

In this chapter, I first explore racial realism in advertising, showing that advertisers have long preferred whites in mainstream advertising, but have, after pressure from civil rights groups, moved toward the view that hiring models and actors of diverse races can win appeal for their products in more markets. Some nonwhite groups are now over-represented in ads relative to their numbers in the population. Second (after a brief visit to Broadway, which was the site of the most significant race and casting controversy in American history), I examine racial realism in the employment of actors, showing the rampant deployment of racial signaling in film and television. Third, I analyze the role of race in professional sports. Here, employers typically resisted hiring nonwhites until the middle of the twentieth century, when teams in a variety of sports began to choose players on the basis of ability rather than race. There have been some holdouts, however, in markets where teams used racial signaling to appeal to the discriminatory tastes of white fans or, more recently, the discriminatory tastes of Latinos. In each of these sectors, I also review the social science evidence that tends to offer at least qualified support for racial-realist strategies of employment.

Finally, I explore the current state of civil rights law, which, despite the greater possibilities afforded by constitutional jurisprudence and even cultural expectations, offers little authorization for the commonplace use of racial realism in entertainment and media. Much of this is driven by stereotypes and beliefs about customers' preferences for seeing entertainers or models of their own race. Hiring with a view toward customer discrimination is typically prohibited in American law, but here more than in any other sector, victims of discrimination and the EEOC are very timid and litigation is almost unknown. Activists have produced some change, but for the most part this sector operated without any legal authorization—until a single 2012 district court case. The decision in that case protected racial signaling in a casting decision as free speech, but one Tennessee district court decision is a very tenuous support for multi-billion-dollar racial-realist enterprises. I explore this and other possible ways of closing the gap between law and employment practice in this sector that so dominates the cultural life of the nation.

Advertising: Using Racial Images to Sell Products

Given that whites have long been the majority race in the U.S. and the holders of the preponderance of the nation's wealth, it is not surprising that advertisers have typically used white models to sell products. What may be surprising is that nonwhites were mostly kept out of advertisements until the 1980s. Their exclusion was troubling to civil rights groups, because advertising images were displayed to the entire nation and purported to show "normal" life in America.

The advertising sector is significant for other reasons as well: a *lot* of money is involved. Barclays Capital estimated that in 2011, for instance, various industries spent $60.3 billion for television ads, $15.7 billion for magazine ads, $22.6 billion for newspaper ads, and $30.0 billion for on-line ads.[3]

The Early Years in Advertising: A Struggle for Equal Rights and Fair Representation

In the early years of advertising, and even as black purchasing power grew, advertisers seemingly had no strategy for pursuing the dollars of nonwhites. Depictions of nonwhites in mainstream ads ranged from the unflattering to the deeply offensive. Cartoon-like images that exaggerated the features of African-Americans, depictions of them as cannibals, and the use of racial slurs were common in the early years of the twentieth century.[4] The most positive black images in mainstream advertising were still quite negative, often showing happy African-Americans serving whites, such as "Rastus," who represented Cream of Wheat breakfast cereal, and "Aunt Jemima," a black domestic worker who became the public face of a pancake mix.[5]

As described in Chapter 2, separate marketing industries gradually developed for whites and blacks. Especially in the 1940s, African-American marketing professionals leveraged their racial abilities to sell themselves as experts on the African-American market. In doing so, they created opportunities for black models—but only for these limited markets. Few nonblacks saw the ads.

In 1946, an African-American commercial artist, Edward Brandford, created the first modeling agency designed to provide female black models to advertisers. Firms targeting the African-American market would hire the models, particularly when selling beauty products. Brandford tried to expand the agency into a full marketing firm, but failed for reasons that highlight the faith that many firms had in the power of racial signaling. Historian Jason Chambers's explains: "Unfortunately for Brandford, while executives were willing to use his models for campaigns to black consumers, he found that they were less eager to hire his advertising agency. At this time clients active in the black consumer market thought that simply changing the race of the models was enough for racially specific targeting."[6]

By the late 1960s, blacks made up about 11 percent of the U.S. population and spent about $30 billion a year, but advertisers continued to resist using nonwhites in ads aimed at the American mainstream, or if they did use them, they stuck to the old, stereotyped depictions of nonwhites as subservient. Civil rights groups, concerned that the advertisers' distorted image of American life was being broadcast around the nation, began to pressure advertisers to create opportunities for nonwhites in ads and to improve the image of the nonwhites that they did use.

The Congress of Racial Equality (CORE) and the NAACP met with the American Association of Advertising Agencies to urge them to expand marketing to blacks and develop accurate views of black consumers.[7] In 1963, CORE and the Urban League successfully pressured forty advertisers to agree to integrate their advertisements.[8] Household products manufacturer Lever Brothers, for example, responded to the call for more blacks in ads, and framed their new thinking in racial-realist terms: "A broader cross-sectional representation of Americans in advertising today is good business."[9] Lever, a major television advertiser, ran 167 commercials with mixed-race casts over the next four years.[10]

Early successes did not create a trend, however. In 1970, the NAACP went so far as to appeal to the Federal Communications Commission to use its authority to ensure that advertisements used blacks for more than very minor roles, arguing that stations needed to review commercials for racial content just as they did for good taste.[11] Advertisers finally began to cast nonwhites, especially blacks, in ads in the 1970s. Comedian and actor Bill Cosby became the most favored pitchman: he promoted Del Monte foods, Jell-O pudding, Ford automobiles, Ideal Toys, Texas Instruments, Coca-Cola, and Kodak.[12] In the 1980s, other celebrity endorsers followed—Michael Jackson and Lionel Ritchie worked for Pepsi, and a variety of athletes (with basketball superstar Michael Jordan most prominent) sold shoes, toothpaste, fast food, cameras, and several other products.[13]

Activists continued to focus on particularly recalcitrant industry sectors. In Washington, DC, they turned their attention to the almost complete absence of black models in advertisements for real estate developments. How bad was it? Consider that a tally of *Washington Post* ads over a sixteen-month period in the mid-1980s found that only 2 percent of the 5,300 models in the paper's real estate ads were nonwhite (in a city that was 75 percent black). Taking advantage of a provision in 1968's Fair Housing Act that prohibits real estate ads that indicate racial and other preferences (see below), the activists secured a promise from the *Post* to ensure that 25 percent of real estate ads would contain African-American models. Activists in other cities, including New York, Los Angeles and Richmond, Virginia, secured similar agreements.[14]

Advertisers Discover the Value of Racial Signaling

Content analyses confirm the glacial pace of change. For example, one study of blacks in advertisements in large-circulation magazines found little change in their overall representation over the twenty years between 1946 and 1965. Less than one percent of ads contained the image of a black person. There were changes, however, in the roles of blacks. In 1946, 78 percent of the blacks in ads were depicted in the low-status roles of maids, waiters, slaves, personal servants, or other domestics, such as "Aunt Jemima." Only 3 percent showed blacks in high-status professional, managerial, or clerical jobs, or in public-service roles, such as police officers or firefighters, and of these 15 percent were entertainers or sports figures. By 1965, however, blacks in high-status jobs had increased to 9 percent of all black ad images, and their sports and entertainment depictions had exploded to nearly 60 percent, while ads showing African-Americans in menial jobs fell to 13 percent.[15]

Civil rights group pressures paid more dividends in the late twentieth century, as advertisers began to see racial signaling as good business. By the early 1980s, magazine ads regularly showed blacks in work settings as equal in status to whites, though ads were slower to depict cross-racial socializing.[16] A study of magazine ad portrayals in the early 1990s found blacks represented in numbers nearly proportionate to their share of the population, while Latinos continued to be underrepresented, at half of their proportion of the population. Depictions of racial groups varied considerably. Ads tended to show Latinos in family settings. Asians were depicted using complex or technical products, while ads were notably less likely to show blacks using technology.[17]

However, another study of mainstream magazines that compared ads in 1994 with those in 2004 found blacks, Latinos, and Asians to be over-represented in both years, while whites were underrepresented. Moreover, nonwhites were actually *more* likely to be favorably portrayed than whites.[18] An analysis of business magazine ads from 1957 to 2005 found that by the late 1970s blacks were overrepresented in terms of the numbers of ads in which they appeared (about 15 percent), whereas by 2005 they were overrepresented in terms of the numbers of people appearing in ads—and most frequently they were by now portrayed in managerial, professional, and clerical jobs rather than in the blue-collar roles that they played in 1950s and 1960s advertising.[19]

Studies of minorities in television commercials have also showed improvement. As early as 1984, a study of all commercials during primetime in a seven-day period found that 26 percent featured black actors—a respectable figure given that blacks were only about 11 percent of the population at the time. Latinos appeared in numbers closer to their share of the U.S. population; they were featured in 6 percent of primetime television commercials.[20]

Despite the progress, there are two important qualifications to note here. First, not every advertiser has made the move to racial signaling in ads. For example, though represented well overall, African-Americans in television commercials are not equally represented across product lines. They are less likely to be cast in commercials for luxury goods such as watches, perfumes, and vacations.[21]

Second, there is still evidence of inequality in terms of the roles that different races have played. One study of Asian-Americans on network television ads in 1994 found that Asian-Americans were overrepresented, but tended to be shown in stereotypical background roles in business rather than home settings.[22] A massive study of morning and daytime commercials on six different networks in 1997 yielded 813 commercials that featured actors. Of these, 99 percent of the commercials featured Caucasians. Blacks appeared in 50.9 percent of the ads, Asian-Americans in 9.2 percent, and Latinos in 8.7 percent. Advertisers appeared to be adding nonwhites to cover their commercial bases, but they rarely risked alienating white customers with minority-only ads. Specifically, Caucasians were the only group in 47.5 percent of the ads, blacks were the only group in 1 percent, and Latinos and Asian-Americans never appeared as the only group. Whites were also more likely to be in major roles in ads and less likely to be in minor roles than other groups.[23]

Does Racial Signaling in Advertising Work?

If advertisers are now hiring models and actors and deploying their races strategically (as indeed they appear to be doing), are they wise to do so? Can the race of models or actors in advertisements affect viewer responses—and, presumably, sales? Much of the evidence suggests that racial signaling does matter, at least under some conditions, providing support for this strategy of managing racial difference.

For several decades, studies have shown that blacks tend to evaluate products and advertisements more positively when black spokespersons are used, while whites show a similar response to same-race spokespersons, though to a lesser extent. One 1979 study examined the reactions of black and white women to black models in ads. The results showed strong racial effects, particularly with regards to facial features: black respondents rated a product highest when models had black features, while whites preferred more Caucasian features.[24] A 1991 study similarly found that whites were less likely to have positive attitudes toward a product and less likely to buy it when advertisements used black actors.[25]

Other studies found similar racial signaling effects in the 2000s. For example, using same-race spokespersons increased not just the viewers' liking for the ad, but also their memory of the ad and of the brand, as well as their intentions to purchase the product.[26] A comparison of "Q scores," a marketing industry metric for measuring the consumer appeal of personalities and brands, showed that though many black celebrities were very highly ranked, their scores varied widely based on the race of the assessor—blacks gave much higher scores than whites to black celebrities. Perhaps not surprisingly, evidence also showed that use of African-American celebrities was more effective at stimulating attention to and recall of ads for African-American audiences.[27]

One particularly creative experiment compared consumer responses to online ads for Apple's iPod music player that varied the race of the hand holding the iPod. Variations included a white hand, a black hand, and a white hand with a wrist tattoo, with the hand representing the seller of the iPod. The black seller received 13 percent fewer responses and 17 percent fewer offers than the white seller—about the same as number as the seller with the wrist tattoo. In addition, those making buy offers bid 2–4 percent less, and showed signs of less trust when the seller was black: they were 17 percent less likely to put their name in their email, and 56 percent more likely to show concern about making a long-distance payment. Black sellers did worst in the Northeast and in areas with high property crime rates.[28]

Nonwhites are typically more likely to respond to nonwhites in ads than whites are to respond to whites. This was shown in a study that aimed to answer the question whether the ubiquitous practice of using racial diversity in corporate recruitment advertisements actually impacted potential recruits. When researchers showed respondents ads that varied the positions of black and white workers at a corporation, black respondents were most positive about ads that showed blacks in both entry-level positions and positions of power, while ads showing whites in positions of power had no effect on whites.[29] Other studies support the conclusion that picturing whites in ads has little or no impact on whites, and have also shown that blacks and Latinos respond positively to ads featuring minorities, whether it is blacks or Latinos who are featured in the ads, and that blacks' positive responses increase as the number of blacks in ads increases.[30]

There is also research on which respondents within racial groupings are more likely to respond to racial signaling. Some cohort effects have been noted, as older subjects were more likely to be influenced by a spokesperson's race than younger subjects.[31] Whites who scored low on assessments of prejudice were (perhaps not surprisingly) more likely to respond favorably to black actors.[32]

But one key finding may help explain why racial signaling typically works better with black audiences than white audiences: the extent to which research subjects give importance to their own racial identity impacts their responses to race in ads. For example, one research team compared Latino and white responses to same-ethnicity spokespersons in a city where Latinos were the minority with responses in a city where Latinos were a majority and whites a minority. Results showed that groups in the minority saw same-ethnicity spokespersons as more trustworthy and the product as more appealing.[33] Similarly, research also indicates that blacks who strongly identify with black culture respond more favorably to black models in ads; blacks with only a weak identification with black culture respond similarly to black and white spokespersons.[34] A study of African-Americans' responses to real estate ads found that they were more likely to say they liked the models in the ads when they included African-Americans, and the more they identified with their race the more likely they were to say that they identified with same-race models, though the presence of those models did not affect their intentions to make purchases.[35]

Advertisers appear to believe in the power of racial signaling. Social science evidence suggests that racial signaling is highly variable in its effects, but mostly supports the use of the practice. Put simply, racial signaling in ads is good business strategy.

How They Cast It: Racial Realism in Film and Television

Creators of entertainment media, such as movies and television shows, have long been conscious of actors' race in their casting decisions, and understandably so. In these cases, racial phenotypes are part of the product itself, so that the stakes in this context are far higher than in a magazine, an online ad, or a 30-second television commercial.

The process of casting a film or show is complex, involving many steps and many players: studio executives, producers, directors, casting directors, writers, and others. The writer, of course, can specify the race of all of the actors in a screenplay, and these specifications are usually followed. But in fact the writers—94 percent of whom are white in film, and 91 percent in television[36]—have no power in the process unless they double as producers or directors. It is studio executives who make the final decisions, and they most often focus on profits rather than artistic merit or equal opportunity issues. In short, racial signaling in the movies and television is largely driven by beliefs about profit maximization.

When Only Whiteness Mattered

Hollywood studios have always used nonwhite actors; the problem was that in the early decades of film, they used them only rarely and almost always in marginal and demeaning roles. The struggle for nonwhites centered therefore on winning meaningful roles, and it was long and hard-fought. Protests against racist depictions in film are almost as old as the commercial film industry—the NAACP picketed the opening of the racist film, *The Birth of a Nation*, in 1915, and through protests at the opening and other showings, convinced five states and nineteen cities to ban the film.[37] In the 1920s, as the commercial film industry grew, nonwhites continued to appear rarely and usually in low-status positions. The most typical black role, in the words of historian Thomas Cripps, was "one that confirmed the enduring system and the place of white people in it, so that any deviant black role leached through to the surface only as a sort of Freudian slip."[38] Asians, Latinos, and Native Americans also suffered demeaning portrayals.[39] Since the majority of the audience was white, studios either gave no thought to their portrayal of race or actively resisted civil rights groups' calls for equality for reasons of dollars and cents: they kept their sights set on the mainstream American white audience and its presumed racist sensibilities.

As in so many other areas of civil rights, however, America's battle with a racist dictator in World War II gave new leverage to black leaders. Walter White, the head of the NAACP, seized the opportunity and was able to make studio heads promise to cast blacks in more diverse roles and to match in films their numbers in society. At the urging of White, the Office of War Information took a new interest in images that portrayed America as a land of racial equality.[40] White and other advocates were vigilant in promoting parts for African-Americans that showed them in a positive light.[41] For the studios, racial signaling was now not so much about fairness, or profits, but about national security. Even with this effort, however, blacks found themselves passed over for lead roles throughout the 1950s and 1960s. One notable exception was Sidney Poitier, who was typically cast as an especially dignified (and unthreatening) man whose race was relevant to the plot.[42]

Casting decisions were less anti-black than they were pro-white. Nonwhite actors, no matter how talented, had to struggle for roles. There were, for example, few roles written for Asians, and even these were often taken by white actors in "yellowface" (makeup designed to make them look Asian) because producers felt that white audiences would not accept Asian actors.[43] This pattern extended to other entertainment media as well, and seemingly obvious acting opportunities were thus taken from minorities. In the early 1960s, for example, producers put together a stage version of Japanese filmmaker Akira Kurosawa's celebrated film, *Rashomon*. Though the story was set in medieval Japan, the parts did not go to Asians. When the accomplished actor Makato "Mako" Iwamatsu auditioned for a part, the casting director allegedly told him, "You gave a great reading, but as a real Japanese, you'd be too conspicuous. All of the other actors are white made up to look Japanese."[44]

The Miss Saigon Controversy: Race, Opportunity, and Artistic Vision

The historical background above will help us understand what was perhaps the greatest racial controversy in American entertainment: the fight over who should play the role of "the Engineer," the half-Vietnamese, half-French character in the musical *Miss Saigon*. While my focus here is on film and television, the high-profile casting struggle in this Broadway musical is significant because its implications extended to all entertainment media, and it highlights so well the major issues surrounding racial realism and acting: opportunity, racial qualification, artistic integrity, and, of course, money.

Two French citizens, Alain Boublil and Claude-Michel Schönberg, wrote the musical as an updated version of Puccini's opera, *Madam Butterfly*. Instead of Japan, however, they set *Miss Saigon* in Vietnam at the end of the American war. The musical retained *Madame Butterfly*'s basic plot of an Asian woman, now called Kim, who was spurned by but nevertheless in love with a white American, now called Chris, and who loved selflessly the child she had with the American. This plot, which was dated and insulting to many Asian-Americans, might have produced controversy on its own, aside from the bitter struggle over casting.

Miss Saigon opened in London with acclaimed British actor Jonathan Pryce in the role of the Engineer. The Engineer played a key role in the story as a pimp who sells Kim to Chris. Pryce helped develop this role for the London production, was the only person that producer Cameron Mackintosh considered for the part, and won an award for his performance, the Olivier, given to the best performer in the London theatre season. Asians played all of the other Asian parts, including the part of Kim, played by Filipina Lea Salonga, who went on to stardom. The critics and the public loved it, and it played to sell-out crowds for six months following its September 1989 opening.[45] Given this success and the common practice of retaining the original casts when plays went overseas, Mackintosh wanted Pryce to reprise his role in the U.S. production, set to begin in 1991.

It was then that the conflict developed. The Actors' Equity Association (AEA), a union of American actors that has veto power over casting choices, initially insisted only that *Miss Saigon* feature more blacks as soldiers, because many American soldiers in the war were in fact African-American. Mackintosh agreed, casting an African-American for the role of "John," who buys Kim for Chris.[46]

But by June 1990, some activists began to resist the casting of a white man to play the Engineer. American actor B. D. Wong and producers Tisa Chang and Dominick Balletta fired off a letter to the AEA executive director on June 6 that compared the casting of Pryce to having a white actor appear in blackface. They argued that in standing up only for minor roles for blacks, the AEA was sending a message to its minority members: "We will support your right to work as long as your role is not central to the play."[47]

Of course, the female lead in *Miss Saigon* was Asian, but the larger point was entirely valid: in 1990 there was no way that even a mixed-race

African-American character would be played by a white actor in a dramatic production. Moreover, given the history of major Asian roles, especially male roles, going to white actors, and the vanishingly small number of parts for Asian actors in general, the casting of Pryce in yellowface makeup to play a half-Asian character was to many in the American entertainment business nothing less than an outrage. A national movement sprang up quickly, and a new group formed—the Asian Pacific Alliance for Creative Equality (APACE).

APACE was willing to play hardball to stop the yellowface casting. On June 21, Wong and APACE members sent multiple copies of the same letter to the AEA, demanding that the AEA use its authority to deny Pryce's visa to come to the U.S. to perform the role. The letter demanded that the AEA also "force Cameron Mackintosh and future producers to cast their productions with racial authenticity."[48]

After two months of struggle that attracted national media attention, the AEA agreed on August 7 to deny Pryce his opportunity to reprise his role, explaining in its announcement that Mackintosh had not even tried to find an Asian actor for the role. The war was on, and Mackintosh went nuclear: he cancelled the entire production.

On August 9, 1990, he took out an ad in the *New York Times* in which he announced the cancellation of the much-anticipated show, and called the AEA position "irresponsible" and "a disturbing violation of the principles of artistic integrity and freedom." He denied any racist intent, explaining that he agreed with the Asian actors on the fundamental issues, including their disapproval of "stereotype casting," explaining that it was just this disapproval that lay behind his defense of "freedom of artistic choice." With Mackintosh's decision, the thirty-four Asian-American actors already cast in the musical lost their jobs—and $25 million worth of advance tickets had to be refunded.

The money at stake was simply too much for the AEA, however, and the organization caved. On August 16, the AEA allowed Pryce to obtain his visa, and the show had its U.S. premier in 1991.

Though the Asian actors may have lost the battle, it seems that they won the war. The battle served to educate the entertainment industry and the public about the complexity of racial signaling in the late twentieth century. Though the controversy took place on Broadway, it affected casting in Hollywood as well. Henceforth, neither artistic vision nor any other motivation would justify casting whites for nonwhite parts. Nonwhites should be cast for all parts that were written as nonwhite. At the same time, parts where race was not germane to the story were henceforth to be open to actors of all races. This came to be known as "non-traditional casting."[49] In the years since the *Miss Saigon* controversy, whites have only rarely played nonwhites—and then typically for parody.

Racial Realism at the Movies: Racial Signaling, Defaulting to Whiteness, and the Importance of the Bottom Line

Though some forward-looking film writers, directors, and producers have made casting decisions with an eye toward creating equal opportunities (that is, with an affirmative-action liberalism strategy), getting nonwhites cast in major roles continues to be a challenge, whatever the motivation. In contrast to advertising, there are many obstacles that prevent Hollywood from using a racial-realist strategy in such a way as to boost profits through the increased use of nonwhite actors. Chief among them is the fear of a catastrophic economic loss: In any Hollywood or television undertaking the stakes are high, the economic footprint is enormous, and no one really knows how to predict what will make money.

How much money is at stake with casting decisions? Even if we restrict our focus to movies, we are dealing with a huge industry. According to the Motion Picture Association (MPAA) of America, movies made $10.6 billion in box office revenues in the U.S. and Canada in 2010 (up from $8.1 billion in 2001).[50] Racial groups vary in their movie-going habits; the average Latino sees nearly seven films per year, while whites, blacks, and (MPAA's residual category of) "others" all see on average only four.[51] Given the ubiquity of cinemas and their relatively cheap admission prices, it comes as no surprise that movie attendance dwarfs other forms of paid entertainment. In 2010, 1.3 billion movie tickets were sold in the U.S. and Canada, while theme parks sold 339 million tickets, and combined sales for professional baseball, football, basketball, and hockey leagues totaled 132 million tickets.[52]

Box office sales are only one source of the movie industry's revenues, however. Video sales can amount to triple the revenue from box office sales, and television licensing revenue (which is almost pure profit) can more than double box office take.[53] And then there is merchandise. Films, including those that were not very successful, can recoup production costs by licensing a variety of products that feature the film logo and characters. For example, the film "Cars," an animated movie from Pixar Studios about talking automobiles, generated $10 billion in sales of licensed products (such as toys, bedding, clothes, and even food) in the five years after its 2006 release.[54] In 2009, the MPAA estimated that the movie and television industries combined generated 272,000 jobs in the U.S. in producing, marketing, manufacturing, and distributing, and paid $40.5 billion in wages.[55] In short, a lot of dollars and a lot of effort go into the American film industry.

Nonwhite casting presents a particular economic challenge to the movie industry. Making movies is not for the faint of heart. There is fierce competition, and up-front investments in entertainment products that may fail disastrously commonly run in the tens or even hundreds of millions of dollars. Each year, only a handful of films earn almost all of the revenue in the industry, and most films lose money.[56]

Which films will succeed? Which ideas should studios "green light"— that is, allow to move into production? Hollywood observers and insiders alike are fond of quoting screenwriter William Goldman's answer to this question: "Nobody knows anything."[57]

The high stakes and the extreme uncertainties of movie making discourage studios from adventure-seeking. Instead, they are tremendously risk averse. Rather than looking toward innovation, they (for the most part) stick to what has worked in the past. That is why America's multiplexes are awash in sequels and prequels, film adaptations of successful TV shows, novels, and comic books, and remakes of movies that proved successful in the past or in other countries. The studios love special effects, because special-effects blockbusters have worked in the past. And of course they love casting big stars.

Risk aversion extends to thinking about race, and contributes to the movies' tendency to fall back on traditional stereotypes, more so than is common in advertising. The stakes are simply higher in the movies. Moreover, race is part of the product itself,[58] and the modal movie ticket buyer is still white. Hence risk aversion limits opportunities for nonwhites. Studios seek proven, winning formulas to convert to box office profits, and if they find a proven winner in another context that features nonwhite characters, there is a good chance they will convert those nonwhite characters into whites to hedge their bets. For example, the producers of the hit movie *21*, which detailed the exploits of MIT students using mathematical strategies to win big money in Las Vegas, made the principle characters white when in reality several of them were Asian-American.[59] More recently, Hollywood has based films on Japanese *anime* hits, transforming the main characters from Asians to whites (and creating some grassroots pushback; see below).

Studios do sometimes take a risk and discover a winning formula that relies on nonwhite actors. This happened in the 1970s with the advent

of the so-called "blaxploitation" films. Beginning with Melvin Van Peebles's 1971 independent film *Sweet Sweetback's Baadasssss Song*, these
films used sex, violence, and racial realism—mostly black casts in tales
about blacks coming out ahead of whites—to appeal to black audiences.
Though Van Peebles was an African-American, most of the films came
from white-owned studios. Because the principal subject matter was
crime, especially the exploits of urban black gangsters, the films angered
some African-Americans. The NAACP formed a group, the Committee
Against Blaxploitation, to stop the films, but gave up when black filmmakers objected. Though the films ghettoized blacks, boxing them into
a narrow niche where they occupied low-status roles and appeared in a
negative light, the filmmakers correctly pointed out that the films generated a lot of employment for African-American actors in Hollywood.[60]

Hollywood's risk aversion can benefit nonwhites in the comparatively
rare instances when a nonwhite actor gets a break and becomes known
as a "bankable" star (meaning studios perceive that casting him or her
guarantees big revenues). Studios cast bankable stars without auditions
or open competitions. There are many ways of assessing which stars have
this power, and thus many lists of varying racial diversity, but only a few
nonwhite actors have successfully established themselves as bankable,
according to various rankings over the past several years. Eddie Murphy and Will Smith have made several lists, and a loose interpretation
of "nonwhite" would add half-Cuban Cameron Diaz and half-Mexican
Jessica Alba.[61]

Casting even proven nonwhite stars can appear risky to many executives, however, especially if there are multiple nonwhite stars in a film.
This accounts for the genre of the "black and white buddy film." In these
films, studios use white racial signaling to let white audiences know the
film is not aimed only at blacks. As one analysis of the situation notes:
"Hollywood producers don't want to finance an expensive 'black' film unless they are sure it will also appeal to white audiences, which usually
means the casting of a white star alongside a black one."[62] Similarly, the
Los Angeles Times has reported, "Studios are more comfortable casting
actors of color, such as Jennifer Lopez and Will Smith, despite their popularity, when they include a white star to ensure 'mainstream' appeal."
Regarding *The Mighty Quinn*, a film featuring African-American star
Denzel Washington, one MGM executive stated, "It was clear to us that
with two leading characters being black it would be hard for us to make
this a broad-based picture. . . . Our previews told us it was much easier to

attract a black audience than a non-black one—though once we got them into the theaters, they all enjoyed the film."[63]

If high financial stakes make Hollywood reluctant to take risks with nonwhite stars, what about the lesser parts? Potential jobs for nonwhite actors abound outside of the starring roles, but even here they encounter difficulties being cast. The problem is that decisions that turn on race are part of the entire casting process. It is hard to generalize about the intentions behind these decisions; some appear to be based on an artistic vision, others on stereotypes, and still others on affirmative-action liberalism (which seeks diversity and opportunity without racial signaling intentions), or on a combination of these. In some cases, for example, using a stereotype helps to tell a story. It constitutes a kind of broadly-targeted racial signaling that has no counterpart in other employment sectors.

While studio executives will veto casting decisions based on calculations about how a star's race will affect profits, the typical studio executive will not bother to micromanage the countless supporting roles in a film. That task goes to the casting director. But the process is even more complex than this, because casting directors work through middlemen to reach actors. The major player here is Breakdown Services, Ltd., which "breaks down" the script into character descriptions. The company transmits these breakdowns to yet another set of players in the game, the agents, who decide which actors to push for a particular part. Agents can, of course, promote any actor, but their chances for success will be based on finding the actor who fits the creative vision of the casting director (and the agent's own skill in selling a part).[64]

Breakdowns are essentially "help wanted" ads, but they have one unique feature: unlike any other ad in American advertising, they sometimes specify a race qualification. In fact, legal scholar Russell K. Robinson, in a study of breakdowns, found that about 43 percent specified some race. Specifically, 22.5 specified white actors, while 8.1 percent specified blacks, 5.2 percent Latinos, 4.3 percent Asian-Americans, and 0.5 percent Native American.[65] Sometimes breakdowns use terms that are not explicitly race-based; Robinson's numbers above included oblique terms that nevertheless clearly communicate racial preferences, such as "Waspy" or "pale-skinned." Race is sometimes also communicated without explicit mention by citing prototype actors: a breakdown might mention a sought-after look—"Gina Gershon" or "Mickey Rourke," for example—which effectively communicates a racial preference.[66] Moreover, when race is unspecified, most agents understand that the preference is for a white actor. As René Balcer, executive producer of the TV show *Law and Order* explained, "There is a phenomenon that if you don't specify race in a script, nine times out of ten a white person will be cast—that if you want a person of color you write it down, and if you want a white person you don't write it."[67] Actors themselves try to read between the lines, wondering if "sassy" means "ethnic" or "tough" means "black."[68]

Reading breakdowns and their analysis, especially with Breakdown Services' sponsored book, *How They Cast It: An Insider's Look at Film and Television Casting*, provides more insights into how race matters. The book uses actual breakdowns for well-known movies and television shows as illustrations. Several themes stand out. First, the analyses of how each show or movie was cast give the overall impression that casting directors prefer white actors. As noted by Robinson, some breakdowns in the book explicitly call for white or "Caucasian" actors. For example, the breakdown for character "Will Herman" in the show *Will and Grace* specified "**Caucasian 27–34**, he's an accessibly handsome, masculine, witty and devilishly charming gay man" (original emphasis).[69] More common is the use of national origin or white-linked physical traits. When searching for actors to play Italian-American comedian Ray Romano's family in the hit show *Everybody Loves Raymond*, casting directors believed they had to find an actor to play Romano's brother with "that same kind of olive coloring."[70] The breakdown for the part of "Summer" in the film *School of Rock* described the character as "blonde, privileged, precocious and bossy."[71] Other parts specified European national origins or predominately white regions of the U.S. The breakdowns for *The Princess Diaries* described one role as "the Prince of Genovia (a European principality)," while "Lana Weinburger" was to be "beautiful, blonde, great figure . . . most popular girl in high school"; while "Boris Pelkowski" would be an "Eastern European, always happy, brainy nerd who dressed the part. . . ."[72]

Perhaps most important, there is a whiteness-as-default message created by the fact that sometimes the writer of the breakdown specifies that a part may be for a nonwhite or for actors of "any race." To illustrate, the breakdowns for "Chandler" and "Phoebe" (but not the other characters) in the hit sitcom *Friends* contained the phrase "any ethnicity." Breakdowns for the pilot of the show *The West Wing* listed nineteen different roles, yet only two concluded by adding, "PLEASE SUBMIT ACTORS OF ALL RACES AND ETHNICITIES" (original emphasis).[73]

This pressure to cast a white actor is even greater when breakdowns come with a message to agents along the lines of these words, included in the late December breakdown for Will in *Will and Grace*: "Please submit the **_ONE_** actor who is perfect for this role but you couldn't get him to the audition. All submissions containing your **_ONE_** favorite perfect suggestion will be seriously considered. . . . Your submission is your opportunity. We can be naughty or nice depending on your submission. Ho! Ho! Ho!" These words were followed by the breakdown that contained the "**Caucasian 27–34**" specification cited above. What agent would send an Asian or an African-American actor after reading those words?

A second theme that runs through Breakdown Service's guide is that race preferences may be based on unconscious stereotypes (the assumption, for example, that someone "blonde" would also be "popular"), but they can also be part of a more conscious vision, either artistic and intentionally designed to go *against* stereotypes in order to send some particular message, or they may be motivated by affirmative-action liberalism and simply intended to create more opportunities. These casting decisions may close or open opportunities for nonwhites. For instance, stereotypes seemed to shape many of the casting decisions for the HBO series *Girls*. Critics complained that all of the main characters in this New York-based drama were white, while breakdowns, later discussed in the media, clearly channeled nonwhites into minor roles: the breakdowns for a group of nannies included "[JAMAICAN NANNY] Female, African-American, overweight, 40s, good sense of humor. MUST DO A JAMAICAN ACCENT" and "[20 YEAR OLD NANNY] Female, sexy, 18–20 years old, from El Salvador. MUST DO A SOUTH AMERICAN/CENTRAL AMERICAN ACCENT."[74] The artistic vision was more developed in the film adaptation of J.R.R. Tolkien's *The Lord of the Rings* trilogy. According to John Hubbard, the casting director for the films, director Peter Jackson specifically requested English actors for the films. As Hubbard explains it, "Peter was very respectful to the fact that Tolkien was British" and "was just being very sensitive—to the family, to the fact that it was very much an English classic. And the fact that the book, though it's in a strange land, had a sort of very specific, unique British medieval feel about it, especially the opening scenes in the Shire, and the [Bilbo Baggins] character."[75] With an artistic vision like that, an agent proposing an Asian or African-American was going to be in for a very tough sell.

However, explicit or implicit racial preferences can of course work to the favor of nonwhites as well.[76] The *West Wing* breakdowns contained one part for "Cathy," a secretary, who was to be a "pretty Asian-American woman."[77] A Japanese-American actress, Suzy Nakamura, got the part. African-American actor Gary Dourdan got a job because the breakdown for *CSI*, the crime drama, specified that his character "Warrick Brown" would be "an African-American degenerate sports bettor who lives to be in the action."[78] Breakdowns for the movie *School of Rock* made a special point that most parts offered "equal opportunity" (specifying that agents should "submit all ethnicities"), but sought to go against stereotype by looking for an "Asian to play Japanese" to be "Yuki," a "stunning classical guitar prodigy."[79] (When the search for an Asian guitar prodigy turned up only Asian piano and string instrumentalists, including the perfect-for-the-film Robert Tsai, the script was changed to accommodate an Asian keyboard player, and the guitar player became white.[80]) The breakdowns for the film *Real Women Have Curves*, about immigrant workers in a Los Angeles sweatshop, proved to be a boon for Latino actors, as nearly every character listed was described as either "Mexican-American" or "Mexican," and Spanish language skills were a must. (Ana, the main character, was to have a love interest who was "Jewish-American," and for another character, "Mrs. Glitz," a "European-American" was wanted).[81] While nine separate breakdowns for the spy thriller *Alias* said nothing about race, one part, the "funny and sincere" character of "Francie" was to be "any ethnicity except Caucasian."[82]

The final salient racial dynamic in the casting process is that "artistic visions" are not inscribed in stone. They can change, sometimes considerably, and sometimes due to political pressure. Despite his vision of all-English actors, Peter Jackson ended up casting an American, Viggo Mortensen, in the key role of Aragorn in *The Lord of the Rings*, and several other Americans were also cast in key roles.[83] *School of Rock* started with the vision of an Asian guitarist but ended with an Asian keyboardist. The Eastern European Boris Pelkowski in *The Princess Diaries* somehow morphed into a farm boy. Most significantly, the threat of an NAACP boycott over a shortfall of minority characters in the networks' 1999 fall line-up led them, in Kendt's words, to begin "hastily retooling their ensembles."[84]

The result was the creation of some minority characters—though not without a degree of artistic pushback. John Frank Levey, casting director for *The West Wing*, later recalled, "The network was under pressure, and put us under some pressure to add an African-American character."[85] The initial effort did not work out well: "I remember when they first asked Aaron (Sorkin) to write a strong and important African-American part, he made the president's doctor African-American—and then killed him off in a plane crash in the next episode. . . . It was kind of like 'Don't tell me what to do.'"[86] Kevin Scott, another casting director working on the show (and an African-American), then found another black actor to star in the show—who proved a great success.[87] In short, artists may cherish creative control, but their considerations regarding the race or national origin of roles commonly undergo change, sometimes due to outside pressure.

Battling in the Trenches for Opportunity in Hollywood

Kept out of most starring roles by risk-averse studio executives, and frozen out of many smaller roles by artistic visions or stereotyped thinking, nonwhite actors are only too aware that their exclusion is based on race. "I know that I don't get jobs by auditioning. I'm not blonde," explained Asian-American actress Sandra Oh to the *New York Times*. "It's very difficult for my agents. They say to me 'I have a hard time getting you in,' and all I want is a shot." She noted that Asian-*American* actors fall behind both whites and Asian stars from Hong Kong or elsewhere with proven worldwide appeal, and that she got a role (originally written for a "pert little blonde") in the television show *Grey's Anatomy* because "the woman who runs the show, Shonda Rhimes, is a black woman, which makes a big [expletive] difference."[88] Eva Mendes acknowledged that "there are many times that being Latin has actually helped me, being a Cuban-American has helped me," but she had a similar complaint when she noted that she does not get the same parts as her blonde friend Drew Barrymore. "But it's like, 'No we want more of an American type of girl,'" she explains. "And it's like, America has opened up. I'm an American girl, born and raised. I mean, I was into New Kids on the Block, just like Drew!"[89]

Smaller minority groups, such as Native Americans and Asian-Americans, have the greatest challenge because they cannot rely on their groups' box office dollars to justify being cast. Taiwanese-American actor Roger Fan described a discussion he had with a studio executive about the dearth of Asian-American-themed movies. The executive explained that blacks are getting more parts because blacks make up 26 percent of the movie-making dollar. The rest comes from whites and Latinos. Fan asked whether the executive meant to suggest that Asians never went to the movies. The executive explained that Asian-Americans were identical to whites in what they watched, and so marketers simply lumped them together. Surprisingly, the growing overseas Asian market did not provide opportunities for Asian-American actors, either. If Asians in Asia "are seeing a movie in English, they want Brad Pitt," Fan explained.[90] Korean-American Aaron Yu, who won a part in the film *Disturbia* because the screenwriter (whose best friend growing up was a Korean) wrote the part for an Asian-American, noted: "Movies are an artistic medium run by MBAs."[91]

Nonwhite actors can find that their first battle is with their own agents. Agents continually face a choice when trying to get nonwhite actors cast. They can either fit the racial preference or expectation as they interpret it, or they can take a risk and put forward a nontraditional actor—one who is not white.[92] They also must consider whether stereotyped parts are good for an actor's future opportunities. Korean-Australian actor Leonardo Nam found that his agents typically cast him as "the takeaway dude" (referring to a worker at a Chinese restaurant). Nam finally pointed out that some breakdowns do state that ethnicity for the part is "open," and he persuaded one to put him up for these parts: "I fall under 'open ethnicity! I'm *sure* I do!"[93] Filipino-American Jelynn Rodriguez's agent was more resourceful, and able to get her an audition for a part as a Latina based on her surname—and she won the part.[94]

With perceptions of customer preferences, stereotypes, and artistic visions so often working against them, nonwhites in Hollywood often find their opportunities coming about from sustained pressure. Sometimes this pressure originates at the grass roots. A group calling itself Racebending.com has worked against the studio habit of converting successful Asian novels and anime stories into live-action films with whites in the main roles, thus "white"-washing the storylines. The catalyst for the group's formation was the Hollywood adaptation of a Nickelodeon animated series, *Avatar: The Last Airbender*, which featured Asian and Inuit characters. The film's Indian-American writer and director, M. Night Shyamalan, named the movie simply *The Last Airbender* and cast whites in the leading roles, relegating Asians and other nonwhites to supporting parts. The Racebending group has since organized letterwriting campaigns, with some successes, around similar casting decisions in film adaptations of novels and comics from Asia and elsewhere.[95]

Even better opportunities for many nonwhite actors come from persons in positions of power motivated by classical liberalism, affirmative-action liberalism, or a racial-realist artistic vision (aimed at producing a reaction in the audience) that—for whatever reason—calls for casting nonwhites. This is more common in independent films, where budgets are smaller, risks lower, and the target audience is smaller and more cosmopolitan. Even independent productions need money, however, and audience tastes are a factor. For example, Justin Lin, director of *Better Luck Tomorrow*, an independent film featuring Asian-American actors in every major role, was pressured by (Asian-American) financiers to replace his cast with white actors, and to feature former child star Macaulay Culkin.[96] Lin fought and won the opportunity to cast Asian-American actors.

The stakes were higher for Andy and Lana (formerly Larry) Wachowski's *Matrix* film trilogy, which cost more than $320 million to make and earned about $1.4 billion.[97] The story takes place in a dystopian future, which arguably reduced audience expectations as to the proper races for certain roles (a phenomenon similar to what happened in the original *Star Trek* television show, which was able to make prominent use of Asian-American and African-American actors due to its setting in a distant future). Though the Wachowskis cast whites in three of the films' key roles—the villain and the love interest are both white, and the hero, Keanu Reeves, is mostly white with some Asian ancestry—the writers originally sought African-American actor (and bankable star) Will Smith for the hero role,[98] and people of color are ubiquitous in the Wachowski films. African-American and Asian-American actors in particular fill crucial supporting roles and as well as many "bit" parts.

The racial diversity in their films was apparently motivated by the Wachowskis' affirmative-action liberalism. Philosopher Cornel West, author of the book *Race Matters*[99] and himself an African-American, had deeply influenced Lana Wachowski. His writings on race, identity politics, and religion had in fact such an impact that the Wachowskis even created a role for the philosopher in their films, *The Matrix Reloaded* and *The Matrix Revolutions*.[100] West has maintained that both his work and the movies share a commitment to and recognition of the power of diversity. The trilogy features a city, called Zion, where the last humans live, and most of them are people of color. "It's not just the representation in numbers but the humanity displayed. . . . The acknowledgment of the full-fledged and complex humanity of black people is a new idea in Hollywood, given all the stereotypes and distortions," West told the *Los Angeles Times*.[101]

Some of the hiring of nonwhites was motivated by artistic vision and a focus on a particular actor or actors. The Wachowskis had to fight the studio, Warner Brothers, in order to cast African-American actor Lawrence Fishburne in one of the key roles, that of Morpheus. Warner Brothers resisted Fishburne even though that character—the hero's spiritual guide and a figure of power, strength, and wisdom—is also arguably a stereotype, a "magical negro," albeit a mostly positive one.[102] Warner Brothers asked the Wachowskis to cast a white as Morpheus, but according to Fishburne, "They just said no, it was me or nobody. They wrote the role with me in mind, I wanted to do it, and that was that. . . . Done deal as far as they were concerned."[103]

The director of the 2011 epic *Thor*, Kenneth Branagh, arguably took even more of a risk by casting an actor of African ancestry, Britain's Idris Elba, to play the Nordic god Heimdall. Branagh also made the equally nontraditional choice of casting Japan's Tadanobu Asano—complete with Japanese accent—as another Nordic god, Hogun, though this generated little controversy.[104] But visionary filmmakers with huge budgets and a lot of clout in Hollywood who are *also* committed to casting nonwhite actors are few and far between, and they still meet resistance. Even someone as powerful as George Lucas, creator of the *Star Wars* blockbusters, met resistance when he sought to make a big-budget film focused on African-Americans. Lucas was unable to find financing for a biopic, *Red Tails*, about the Tuskegee Airmen, a regiment of segregated black Air Force pilots during World War II. The problem for studios was the mostly black cast and the absence of a white protagonist. He eventually put up $58 million of his own money to make the movie and also $35 million to distribute it.[105]

Television: Political Pressure and the Discovery of Nonwhite Markets

Television offers more opportunities for racial minorities than film—but not *many* more. African-Americans and other nonwhites have difficulty finding parts, and this was especially true before the 1990s.[106] Television shows, as discusssed above, rely on the same racially exclusionary "breakdowns" that often limit opportunities for nonwhite actors and their agents. The aversion to racial risk-taking that follows from the high stakes and uncertainty that we saw in the film industry also holds in television. Though the investments in each show are not as high as in most films, the sums are still considerable, and network executives tend to play it safe, by imitating success, and, often, by a dreary devotion to formulas and conventions.[107] The goal is to make money, and to do that, networks need viewers—and that is pretty much what they care about. The statement made by a CBS "vice president for television research" back in the 1980s still appears to describe the industry today: "I'm not interested in culture. I'm not interested in pro-social values. I have only one interest. That's whether people watch the program. That's my definition of good, that's my definition of bad."[108]

Serious shows based on nonwhite casts have had an especially tough go of it, even after the unprecedented late-1970s success of the *Roots* miniseries, which focused on the family history of African-American writer Alex Haley.[109] When sociologist Todd Gitlin interviewed studio executives in the 1980s, he got an earful of arguments about the importance of white racial signaling. After the commercial failure of two post-*Roots* black TV dramas, *Roots* producer Stan Margulies told Gitlin, "The word is [that audiences aren't] interested in a black show."[110] ABC executive Stu Samuels put it this way: "It's very hard to find properties about blacks that can also be appreciated by whites," because "it's a white country" and television is "a commercial business."[111]

Risk-averse profit seeking was thus for many years the obdurate practice in commercial television. The opening up of opportunities for nonwhite actors in television came only after protests and other forms of collective action by civil rights groups and a structural change in television broadcasting.

A Civil Rights Struggle for Broadcast Representation

Protests against television portrayals of nonwhites have occurred nearly as long as television broadcasting has existed. One of the earliest and most prominent struggles was the NAACP's fight against the television adaptation of the huge radio hit, *Amos and Andy*. The show was a typical product of the long tradition of depicting nonwhites in low-status roles and as the objects of humor or ridicule.[112] Though the radio show had featured two white actors portraying uneducated African-Americans, the 1951 television adaptation used a mostly black cast. The NAACP and other black leaders nevertheless found the television portrayal of the blacks "stereotypical and derogatory" and organized a letterwriting campaign and a nationwide boycott. They also brought a lawsuit against the show's sponsor. These efforts chased away the original sponsor and the show was soon canceled, but it stayed on the air in syndication for another fifteen years.[113] In the early 1960s, the United Church of Christ, a liberal congregation, complained to the Federal Communications Commission (FCC) about discriminatory practices at WLBT, a television station in Jackson, Mississippi. Taking advantage of laws and court rulings that said broadcasting had to serve the public interest,[114] the Church argued that WLBT's hiring and programming (which included efforts to suppress network news coverage of civil rights demonstrations and the broadcasting of racist editorials) failed to serve the public and that the station therefore should not have its broadcasting license renewed.

Though the FCC denied their claim, the church won in federal court.[115] Congressman Adam Clayton Powell, Jr. (D-NY) held hearings on the entertainment industry in 1962, and similar hearings by the Congressional Black Caucus in 1972 led to the cancellation of a new series about a black congressman that many thought offensive.[116] In 1967, following the final demise of *Amos and Andy*, the NAACP created its annual Image Awards, given to outstanding performances by people of color in the arts, as well as to those promoting equal rights causes through artistic endeavors.[117]

The urban violence of the late 1960s and the Kerner Commission report on how to prevent its recurrence had a critical, legitimating impact on African-Americans' demands relating to race and broadcasting, as they did on some many other areas covered in this book. In the aftermath of the worst race rioting in the nation's history, the Commission found that part of the reason for the violence was that television and the print media had failed to communicate the "degradation, misery and hopelessness of living in the ghetto," leaving whites with no sense of "the difficulties and frustrations of being a Negro in the United States." The media, according to the report, had also failed to communicate "a sense of Negro culture, thought or history."[118]

In that same year, the FCC also acted in the interests of nonwhite opportunity, though weakly: it sought approval of new regulations to require broadcast licensees to stop discriminating. This was partly a call for justice through classical liberalism, but included as well racial-realist hopes for more effective programming and, hence, a reduction in racial violence. In its 1968 petition for the new rules, the FCC declared: "The nation is confronted with a serious racial crisis" and "all sides" have identified the media as having a key role in resolving it. The petition cited the Kerner Commission as its authority, though it also cited "common sense" as a basis for the claim that "there must be greater use of the Negro in journalism, since the Negro journalist is the most effective link with the ghetto: News organizations must employ enough Negroes in positions of significant responsibility to establish an effective link to Negro actions and ideas and to meet legitimate employment expectations." In addition, the FCC argued that "the same considerations are applicable to the case of the Negro in specific programming." However here the FCC, perhaps taking into account the importance of creative control, deferred: "This is not a matter on which this Commission can appropriately intervene. The judgment as to whether to use one performer or another or a particular script approach in a particular program is wisely one beyond the jurisdiction of this Commission. Rather all we do is again raise the question in context of the broadcaster at this juncture of our national affairs."[119] Civil rights groups nevertheless continued to apply pressure, criticizing white-owned stations that sought to serve the black community but mostly failed due to poor quality programming and negative stereotyping.[120]

For decades, protest, pressure, and encouragement were central to the African-American strategy for improving their image and opportunities in television, and by the 1990s, these efforts were beginning to bear fruit. In 1999, for example, a coalition of black, Latino, and Asian groups demanded greater representation in the seasonal programming line-ups, including positions behind and in front of the camera.[121] Their protest led to the strengthening of the NAACP's Hollywood presence as a watchdog and partner for the industry. FOX, CBS, ABC, and NBC agreed to NAACP demands that they hire more nonwhites as actors and to fill other positions in the industry. They also agreed to hire vice presidents of diversity to monitor progress. In addition, FOX and CBS established diversity advisory boards to actively influence casting decisions.[122]

Many of these efforts sought justice, and thus fit classical liberal or affirmative-action strategies for managing race. But they were of vital importance because of the way they upset thinking in this risk-averse industry, and opened the door to more racial-realist strategies for casting aimed at high ratings and profits.

Narrowcasting: Targeted Racial Signaling as a Business Strategy

By the time of the protests in the 1990s, network racial signaling strategies were already creating opportunities for nonwhite (specifically African-American) actors, as new networks were born, including a number that sought to win black viewers. The rise of these new networks, especially FOX, as well as a tidal wave of new competition from cable television shook up the business strategies of the major networks in the 1980s. The major networks shed viewers rapidly. In 1983 they claimed 76 percent of viewers, a number that was down to 60 percent in 1990.[123] Competition was greater and more diverse, and, predictably, the struggle for survival led to specialization.

In broadcast media, the strategy of specialization is called "narrowcasting." The idea was simple: win a consistent audience by targeting a specific, tightly-defined population with shows designed to appeal to that particular population's tastes. You would not of course get the mass audiences of classic programs like the *Ed Sullivan Show* or *60 Minutes*, but those audiences were becoming increasingly rare by the 1980s. The trade-off in the newly dense, competitive environment was a more reliable, better-understood (if smaller) audience—something many advertisers appreciated.[124]

African-Americans were ripe for narrowcasting in the 1980s. They tended to watch TV more than others, and because fewer had cable, they watched 44 percent more network TV than nonblacks.[125] Using a racial signaling strategy centered on the extensive use of African-American actors, the new FOX network aggressively pursued this audience, especially its younger, urban segment. The results were promising: by the 1990s, fully 25 percent of FOX's audience was African-American.[126] FOX's racial signaling strategy also yielded jobs for African-Americans behind the camera. Actresses Queen Latifah and Kim Fields, for instance, who starred in the successful *Living Single* show, both insisted on black writers, a move they and others thought would make black-oriented shows more authentic.[127]

FOX would eventually move away from its narrowcasting strategy. Its successful 1993 bid (of nearly $1.6 billion) for the rights to broadcast NFL football games marked its transition into the mainstream.[128] The UPN and WB networks then took on the narrowcasting/racial signaling strategy in the mid-90s.[129] Cable network TBS is the latest to feature shows targeted at nonwhite audiences. Ice Cube, the former rapper turned actor and television producer, brought the family-oriented comedy *Are We There Yet?* to TBS with success in 2010. Cube told the *New York Times,* "All these other stations, you can't find anybody who will give diverse programming a chance. We had a few other meetings, but I knew if we went to another network, we'd have to teach them. TBS already gets it." The director of the NAACP's Hollywood Bureau, Vic Bulluck, applauded the network's targeted effort to win minority audiences, saying "That's where TBS is really smart." TBS executives characterized their programming decisions as a simple matter of catering to the preferences of their customers. Programming head Michael Wright explained: "The cornerstone of our development is what's already working. . . . We take an audience that's already coming and program to them." TBS president Steve Koonin spoke openly about the racial signaling strategy: "There's a huge audience out there that wants to see people on television that look and live their lives like they do. We're happy to accommodate them."[130]

Narrowcasting through racial signaling appeals to customer tastes for same-race images on the screen. For black actors (or any nonwhite actors) there are opportunities and dangers here. Narrowcasting increases the number of jobs available to nonwhites (especially African-Americans), but it also reproduces on television the same segregation that too often marks daily life in the real world.

Employment of Nonwhites in Television: Reaching Parity?

Despite the history of discrimination and stereotyping, and thanks largely to the efforts of civil rights groups and racial signaling strategies, some nonwhites, particularly African-Americans, are getting television acting opportunities in numbers roughly proportional to their share in the population. A 1973 study of 2,309 characters on television shows and in their accompanying commercials found that only 4.9 percent were nonwhite.[131] By 1996, African-Americans were getting prime-time roles at a rate higher than would be expected based on their population (16 percent of all roles), while Latinos and Asians lagged far behind their population percentages (at 3 percent and 1 percent, respectively).[132] An analysis of 113 prime-time shows in 2004 found that only thirteen had a least one Asian or Pacific Islander actor, and only three had more than one.[133] A study of prime-time programming in the 2000–2008 period also found that African-Americans had achieved parity in terms of numbers (15 percent of roles), but concluded that this was largely the result of a growing number of black-oriented (narrowcasted) situation comedies. Latinos (4 percent of roles) and Asians (2 percent) were underrepresented, but they were cast in a wider variety of genres, including crime, action, and dramatic programs. African-Americans were far more likely to be in programs that had mostly minority casts (37 percent) than were other nonwhites (14 percent).[134]

By the late 2000s, however, black and other nonwhite actors were seeing a general trend toward improvement in television casting, though the numbers went up and down depending on the line-up of shows in a particular year, and other racial minorities—Latinos especially—continue to lag. According to the Screen Actors Guild, African-Americans claimed 13.3 percent of all television roles in 2008, which is roughly at parity with their representation in the population. Asians were somewhat below their representation in the population, but not by much, claiming 3.8 percent of all roles, while Latinos were far below their roughly 15 percent of the population in 2008 with only 6.4 percent of all roles, as were American Indians, who made up 0.7 percent of the overall population but filled only 0.3 percent of all roles. (Actors of unknown/other race had 3.8 percent of all television roles, while whites held 72.5 percent of the total). The percentages for the lead roles in television productions were not greatly different, though African-Americans fell to 11.8 percent, Latinos to 5.2 percent, and Asians to 3.4 percent. All nonwhites did slightly better in supporting roles.[135]

In terms of how they are portrayed, an analysis of prime-time programming in 2007 found that characters portrayed as lazy or aggressive were not disproportionately members of any race, but that black and Latino characters were far more likely to be immoral (9 and 18 percent, respectively) than whites (2 percent). Blacks and Latinos were also more likely to be the least intelligent (15 and 18 percent) than whites (3 percent). On the other hand, 52 percent of black characters were portrayed as the most intelligent on their programs, a far higher percentage than Latinos (27 percent) and even whites (43 percent).[136] Blacks cast in shows with large white audiences tended to be in positions of authority, such as corporate managers and police chiefs.[137]

The early 2000s saw the growth of "reality shows," featuring unscripted dramatic scenarios and talent shows that do not typically use actors, though nonprofessionals are still "casted" by producers. These include such shows as *The Amazing Race*, *Survivor*, *The Biggest Loser*, and *American Idol*. Though no content analyses have confirmed better employment of nonwhites in these shows, journalists, industry professionals, and even the NAACP, have lauded them for their diversity. The motivation for this diversity lies in the forward-looking business rationales of racial signaling and racial abilities. On racial signaling, the executive producer of NBC's *The Biggest Loser*, Dave Broome, explained, "We're looking to create shows that everyday people can relate to, and for that you really need a true representation of the population. . . . A couple of seasons ago, there was an over-the-top character who was white that we could have cast, but we sacrificed that for a Latino. That's how important that is."[138] Another producer emphasized the abilities that racially diverse cast members could bring to his show, since differences in race, as well as gender or sexual orientation, would add the benefits of tension, conflict, and drama to the shows. Jonathan Murray, a creator of MTV's pioneering reality show, *The Real World*, admitted that the diversity preference was not about affirmative-action liberalism: "I don't believe the makers of unscripted programs are necessarily all pro-social. . . . A lot of times it comes down to the fact that diversity just makes those shows better."[139] The reality competition show *Survivor* took this concept the furthest in 2006, when the show was set in the Cook Islands and featured a "race

battle" between four teams—one each for African-Americans, Asians, Latinos and whites.[140]

While expressing regret that the rise of reality shows has put many
actors out of work, especially actors of color, an NAACP report on the
television industry lauded reality shows for their tendency to be more
diverse than other shows. The report also noted that, given the casting
of everyday citizens rather than actors, "Another positive aspect of the
reality show phenomenon has been the opportunity for the world to see
African-Americans, Hispanics and Asian-Americans as professionals,
students, laborers and homemakers."[141] The executive director of the
NAACP's Hollywood office, Vic Bulluck, told the Los Angeles Times that
the move to diversity in reality shows was driven by demographics: "The
marketplace has changed, and the producers of reality shows are obviously more sensitive or conscious of that change than the producers of
scripted shows. It really comes down to relevance."[142]

Does the Race of Cast Members Actually Have an Impact on Audiences?

As in advertising, research regarding audience reactions to race in entertainment indicates that racial realism is indeed good business strategy,
though the data show complex patterns. The great majority of this research has focused on audience reactions to and preferences for different
types of television shows rather than Hollywood films.

To put the research on the impacts of racial realism in context, it is
important to understand that visual media usage patterns vary considerably by race. First, blacks tend to watch more TV than other groups.
The average black household watches about three hours more TV per
day than the average white household, for example. Latinos watch less
than blacks but more than whites.[143] Second, data also show that African-
Americans and whites tend to watch different shows. For example, in
2005 Nielsen Media Research issued a report showing that lists of the
top ten shows watched by whites and the top ten watched by African-
Americans had only three shows in common (in 2004, these were CSI,
Without a Trace, and NFL Monday Night Football). Of the top six shows
in African-American households, five had an average audience that was
at least 75 percent African-American. These shows (Girlfriends, Half &
Half, Second Time Around, One on One, and Eve) all featured casts that
were majority black.[144]

Research findings mostly conform to producers' racial signaling expectations, at least regarding nonwhites: African-Americans tend to report a preference for shows with African-American characters and casts, and this preference spans ages and genders.[145] The same effect has been found among Latinos as well, though some evidence suggests it is weaker.[146] Little is known about Asian or Native American preferences.[147]

Racial attitudes of audiences may affect how they respond to the race of different actors. One experimental study that measured reactions to different movie scenarios found that "contrary to popular wisdom . . . the race of cast members in a film did not influence Whites' desire to see that film in general."[148] However, race and racial attitudes did matter. Some whites were actually more interested in films with black casts than those with white casts. More specifically, whites who scored low on measures of racial prejudice were more likely to identify with black actors and showed more positive attitudes toward black-oriented movies than did more prejudiced whites. The type of movie also seems to matter. Whites indicated more interest in romantic movies where both the male and female leads are white than in movies where there is an interracial romance or both leads are black, regardless of the whites' level of prejudice.[149]

When it comes to reality shows, little data exist. One study of preferences for contestants on the *American Idol* singing talent show found that blacks tended to prefer black contestants on that show, while nonblack households did not exhibit preferences as to the contestants' race.[150]

Though film and television producers typically use racial signaling to win an audience, activists sometimes express the hope that more parts for nonwhites will produce not just equal opportunity (a classical liberal or affirmative-action liberal goal), but also impact and change society by changing stereotypes. To the extent that show producers share this forward-looking rationale, race would thus become a means to an end and a qualification for casting. A comprehensive review of this literature has decried the lack of solid research on whether and how the mass media combine with other social forces to impact commonly held stereotypes.[151] The research that we do have on the effects of racial stereotypes in the mass media often centers on the negative portrayal of race in the news rather than in entertainment.[152]

The early research that did focus on entertainment typically assessed the impacts of racial portrayals on young viewers—and much of this research is now decades old. Data from studies conducted in the 1970s and 1980s showed that casting decisions affected children in various ways.[153] Black children, for example, tended to identify with black characters on

television and rated them higher in positive attributes such as attrac-
tiveness, strength, and friendliness than white characters.[154] Exposure
of black children to negative black stereotypes tended to correlate with
negative self concepts.[155] White children were more likely to learn about
blacks' personal styles and appearance from television than from personal
interaction (40 percent reported that their racial knowledge came from
television), and those with the least real-world interracial experience
were most likely to believe that television portrayals were realistic.[156]

Studies also indicate impacts on adults of media portrayals of race.
In her review of the literature, communication scholar Dana Mastro reported, "In the main, results from such investigations have demonstrated
that even a single exposure to racial/ethnic stereotypes in the media can,
at least in the short term, influence real-world evaluations of minorities."[157] Participants in an experimental study who saw African-American
women in stereotyped portrayals as "mammies," "jezebels," or "welfare
queens" and then saw video of an African-American woman in a job interview more quickly described that woman with adjectives consistent with
the stereotypes they had seen, though only the "welfare queen" impacted
assessments of the woman's suitability for the job.[158] One study asked
white respondents to describe portrayals of African-Americans that they
had recently seen in movies or on television. It found no impact from
recall of positive portrayals, but recall of negative portrayals correlated
with both negative stereotypes of African-Americans and opposition to
affirmative-action policies.[159] A study that had participants watch neutral
and stereotypical portrayals of blacks in comedy skits found that those
who had seen a stereotypical portrayal were more likely to judge a black
accused of a crime in a written vignette to be guilty than if they had seen
a neutral portrayal.[160]

There is also evidence that the tendency to hold ethnic stereotypes
is linked both to how much television participants watched and what
genres they watched. Specifically, heavy television viewers held the most
positive and least negative stereotypes of whites; they held both positive and negative stereotypes of African-Americans and Latinos, but only
negative stereotypes of Asian-Americans and Native Americans. Heavy
viewers of entertainment, sports, and educational programming tended
to hold more negative stereotypes, while viewers of information programming tended to have positive stereotypes.[161]

Finally, there is the anecdotal evidence. Consider the reaction to
an animated children's show, *Doc McStuffins*, that features an African-
American girl who pretends to be a physician while her mother goes to

work as a physician and her father stays home to maintain the house-hold (the black characters are voiced by black actors). The show was a hit for the Disney channel in 2012, and audiences—especially African-Americans—lauded the black characters. One blogger wrote, "It truly warmed my heart and almost brought tears to my eyes when my eight-year-old, Mikaela, saw 'Doc McStuffins' for the first time and said, 'Wow, mommy—she's brown.'" Mark Anthony Neal, a black cultural scholar, commented, "My youngest daughter, who is nine and still has an affinity for stuffed animals, loves the show. . . . Part of the appeal for her is see-ing herself represented in this space of fantasy." The Disney president, Gary Marsh, explained, "What we put on TV can change how kids see the world, and that is a responsibility that I take very seriously," he said. "By showcasing different role models and different kinds of families we can positively influence sociological dynamics for the next 20 years."[162]

Professional Sports: Racial Realism and Our National Pastimes

Putting sports in the same category with film and television may seem odd, but it becomes less so when you consider that professional sports is an entertainment product created by entrepreneurs who are in many respects like film and television producers. That sports programs are (one hopes) unscripted television entertainment suggests that sports might be viewed as the original reality shows, and indeed at their best pro sports have dramatic storylines featuring popular characters who, like bankable film stars, draw large audiences to their every performance. Moreover, athletes vie with film and TV stars for high "Q ratings" (the popularity measurement) that can translate into huge product-endorsement con-tracts. Additionally, like film and television, pro sports are a huge busi-ness. As in film, there are tickets to be sold and television licensing rev-enue is a large and rapidly growing part of the profits in many sports. For example, National Football League licensing rights sold for $1.1 billion per year in the 1994–97 period and $2.2 billion per year from 1998 to 2005.[163] By 2009, that number had increased to $3.7 billion, with programs licensed to five networks (CBS, FOX, ESPN, NBC, and NFL). Other sports are also big moneymakers, though the numbers were smaller. The National Basketball Association (NBA) made $275 million per year in 1995, $365 million in 2005, and $765 million in 2009. In

2009, Major League Baseball received $670 million, and the National Hockey League $72 million.[164]

Broadcast licensing is only the tip of the iceberg, and other numbers, which may include product merchandising, are far higher. One marketing firm estimate puts the annual overall revenue for the "Big Four" sports leagues at about $17 billion.[165] The broadest estimate placed the overall size of the total sports industry in the United States at between $168 billion and $207 billion. This included measures of sports consumption and investment, and government expenditures in leisure, participant, and spectator sports.[166]

Besides performance, popularity, and money, a critical similarity between movies, television, and sports is that all three are visual entertainment, and in America that means that racial signaling matters. The product is a visual image of people, and racial phenotypes and cultural styles are thus part of the product. Sports are, therefore, in the words of sociologist Douglas Hartmann, a "contested racial terrain."[167]

But pro sports also differ from film and television in ways that make them an especially compelling subject from the perspective of racial realism and discrimination law. Economically, professional sports can be perceived to be so important to a city's economic well-being, civic pride, and sense of importance that city governments across the country will use public funds to build stadiums so that for-profit teams can play in them. Despite economic studies that have, with nearly unqualified unanimity, shown that local sports teams do *not* contribute to a city's economic development, $5 billion of the $9 billion used to build twenty-eight stadiums in the early 2000s for NFL, MLB, NBA, and NHL teams came from public sources.[168] Cities commonly compete with each other for the opportunity to attract a major-league franchise. In the early 1980s, for example, Indianapolis financed its $78 million "Hoosier Dome" with $30 million from two local foundations and the rest from a 1 percent sales tax on food and beverages. The city then sought to lure an NFL team to play in it. The mayor contacted the Baltimore Colts franchise and won a bidding war with that city; the "Indianapolis Colts" christened the Hoosier Dome in 1984.[169] City officials across the country use tax money to pay for stadiums because sports teams have powerful lobbyists, because they perceive major-league sports teams as important for the city's national image, and because these for-profit enterprises contribute to civic pride.[170]

Another key difference between sports and other entertainment is that, as legal scholar N. Jeremi Duru has pointed out, professional sports teams, "unlike other employers . . . have fans—avid supporters with no official organizational affiliation—who follow and celebrate the organizations' competitive exploits."[171] This fan dynamic distinguishes these businesses from those discussed in chapters 2 and 5.[172] One study of the public funding of stadiums that sought to take into account the "intangible" benefits of the presence of sports teams argued that these benefits are significant—enough so that stadiums should be financed by taxes on the fans only, since non-fans do not benefit from professional teams.[173] Because these fans *identify* with the organization, there is a unique way in which the races of the players could be especially significant.

As in other realms of entertainment, for much of American history, whites took it for granted that athletes would look like them. It was therefore not surprising that the black American audience gushed with enthusiasm when black athletes began their long record of distinguished achievement in the United States. Sportswriter William C. Rhoden traces the emergence of the black athlete back to July 4, 1910, when Jack Johnson became the first black heavyweight prizefighter—and blacks across America rejoiced.[174]

My focus here is on team sports, rather than on boxing, tennis, or golf, since a team is akin to a workforce and thus comparable to the other sectors analyzed in this book. The owners of teams, because they were mindful of the importance of signaling only whiteness to their fans or because they were themselves racists, resisted employing black players until after World War II. The pioneers among black players are now American legends, with perhaps the most famous being African-American Jackie Robinson, who broke the color barrier in major league baseball in 1947.[175] College sports followed a similar trajectory. In both cases, team managers moved from the exclusion of nonwhite players to a (still racist) valorization of their racial abilities. For example, an athletic director at the University of Texas at El Paso commented in 1968, "In general, the nigger athlete is a little hungrier, and we have been blessed with having some real outstanding ones. We think they've done a lot for us, and we think we've done a lot for them."[176]

Of special interest here, however, is the racial integration of professional football, and especially a particular chapter of this story that highlights the civic role of professional sports, government involvement in stadiums, the notion of sports as entertainment or even art, and even the threat of litigation. The story centers on the Washington Redskins and their owner, George Marshall. The first black players had come into the NFL in 1946, and by 1955, the Washington Redskins were the only team of twelve that had not integrated. In 1961 there were eighty-three black players in the league, but Redskins owner George Marshall still resisted signing even one black player.[177] The racism of Marshall, whose team represented the nation's capital, was intolerable to the Kennedy administration, and in 1961, Secretary of Interior Stewart L. Udall threatened a lawsuit to force Marshall to integrate.

Udall was able to use as leverage a new lease that Marshall had signed to have the Redskins play for the next thirty years in Washington, DC's new stadium. The stadium was financed with public funds and located at Anacosta Flats, part of the National Capital Parks system. The Interior Department was "residential landlord" of the parks, and had final say in what happened there. Udall issued new regulations banning discrimination, explaining in a news conference (that received front-page coverage in the *New York Times* and *Washington Post*), "It is certainly our feeling that here in the Nation's Capital, with the marvelous new facility being built on property owned by all the people of the country, that we ought to set the very highest of standards in terms of adhering to the policies of this administration with regard to treatment of everyone in this country equally."[178]

Marshall argued back that the government's classical liberalism was inappropriate and that he wanted his racial-realist strategy to shape the team. Udall did not have "the right to tell the showman how to cast the play," Marshall said, and claimed that his white team resulted from the fact that the team, which was then the closest in the league to the Deep South states, drafted players from Southern university teams, which were then still all-white. He also argued that his policy was a business decision: he was concerned about the preferences of his southern white audience.[179] The NAACP and Congress of Racial Equality (CORE) picketed Marshall's home and the stadium, and other owners pressured Marshall.[180] Following back-to-back one-win seasons in 1960 and 1961, Marshall changed his ways, and the 1962 team featured four black players, two of whom would become stars on the team (running back Bobby Mitchell led the league in touchdowns). The team won five games.[181]

The integration of the major pro leagues also happened at mid-century, but coaches and general managers remained white for decades longer, as did some of the positions, typically the most important ones on a team, such as the quarterback in football or the pitcher in baseball. This was a result of the owners' own prejudice, but also of racial-realism concerns related to racial signaling and customer preference. Future member of Congress J. C. Watts, a black quarterback in the early 1980s when there were almost none (he ended up starring in the Canadian Football League), expressed his frustration and acknowledged the symbolic freight that race carried in the quarterback position. "NFL coaches and managers had a tough time seeing blacks in leadership positions," he later wrote, "and they worried that fans would react negatively to putting blacks in charge of a team."[182] Black quarterbacks in the NFL and nonwhite coaches in the NFL, MLB, or NBA did not become common until the 2000s.[183]

The Rise of the Nonwhite Player and the Anomaly of Majority-White Teams

In film and television, whites continue to dominate, despite the gains that minorities have made, but by the 1970s, the success of the African-American athlete (and in baseball, Latino athletes) made majority-white teams anomalous and suspect. Yet in the late 1970s and 1980s, the racially polarized city of Boston was host to two of what was by then an increasingly rare phenomena in the NFL, NBA or MLB: teams identified as "white."[184]

One was the Boston Red Sox, the last MLB team to field a black player (fully twelve years after Jackie Robinson broke the color barrier). In 1979, the team began an almost four-year run with only one black player—fewer blacks than any other major league team. That player, Jim Rice, happened to be an All-Star and in 1978, he was not only the best player on the team, but Boston's only African-American was awarded the American League's Most Valuable Player award.[185]

The Boston area was 92 percent white in 1980,[186] and the city had experienced significant racial tension following court-ordered busing to achieve integrated schools.[187] Journalist Howard Bryant wrote of the Red Sox of the early 1980s that "there was a feeling among blacks in the game that the Red Sox were reluctant—in a city that had suffered through busing—to tilt the racial balance of the team toward blacks and Latinos for fear that the city would not in those years embrace a largely minority team."[188]

Unlike the Red Sox, Boston's NBA franchise, the Celtics, had been racial pioneers—the first team to draft a black player (in 1950), the first to play an all-black starting line-up (in 1964), and the first to have a black coach (in 1966).[189] By the mid-1980s, however, the Celtics were again majority white. For two seasons, 1985–86 and 1986–87, they had only four blacks on their twelve-man roster, whereas the average NBA team had nine.[190]

The early years of black Celtics were not without incident. In the 1950s and 60s, Boston racists harassed the team's black stars. Hall of Famer Bill Russell—who led the team to eleven championships in thirteen seasons—felt tension continually during his time in Boston, and at one point arrived at his home to find it vandalized and feces smeared on the walls and furniture. Another black star, K. C. Jones, must have thought he was in the Deep South when he found a cross burning on his lawn in suburban Framingham.[191] Black players in Boston privately complained that the Celtics did not pay them the same as white players of similar ability.[192] Boston fans gave surprisingly tepid support to the Celtics of the Bill Russell championship years, and the team averaged only 10,500 fans per game in Boston Garden, though the stadium had a seating capacity of 15,000 for basketball games.[193] Average attendance in the early 1970s championship years surged to 13,300 when the team's stars were two white players (Hall of Famers Dave Cowens and John Havlicek).[194]

It appeared to be a business decision to use white racial signaling to appeal to white Bostonians. A black player on the Celtics, Jo Jo White, acknowledged this with a shrug, commenting that Boston "wouldn't support a majority-black team, even if it were successful." The Celtics' Hall of Fame general manager, Arnold "Red" Auerbach, in White's view, did not believe that whites had somehow become better players. Instead, he was simply catering to customer preference.[195] White explained, "Management is aware of the city. Red was always smart enough to understand [racism] is there. . . . That's why Red's always tried to keep it even—six whites, six blacks, maybe seven to five."[196] Another, forward Cedric Maxwell, concurred, noting that even the average white players had more endorsement deals than some black stars such as Robert Parish, and that the Celtics were "selling to a particular audience."[197] Part-owner Alan Cohen, nicknamed "Bottom Line" in New York on account of his days as owner of the New York Rangers hockey club, admitted, "I think we recognize that to have some balance on the team, in terms of race, has some possible value."[198]

To be sure, the Celtics majority-white line-up, which won three NBA titles, was nothing like the white Washington Redskins NFL team, which had but a single victory two years in row. Moreover, the 1980s Celtics had Larry Bird and Kevin McHale, both honored at the NBA's 1996 celebration of its 50th anniversary as among the "50 Greatest Players" to ever play the game. The legal scholar N. Jeremi Duru notes that the Celtics' racial-realist strategy was a more pronounced version of practices that were not

uncommon in the NBA. Filling the bench—and especially the last position on the team—with white players was a common NBA practice in the
1990s: though only 27.6 percent of the league's players were white, 52.6
percent of the players who scored the fewest points on each team were
white.[199] The Celtics' racial signaling was most conspicuous in their use of
whites in the lesser positions on the team: with five white guys riding the
pine, the Celtic bench was *especially* well stocked with white guys.

Pro Sports Racial Signaling Changes
with Demographic Changes: The 2000s

The Celtics and Red Sox strategies continue today, but they look different. In the more diverse America of the 2000s, nonwhite races appear to
have more market value than ever before, and some owners and managers may believe that placing nonwhites in visible positions can contribute
to their bottom line. Consider an effort by the New York Mets to appeal to
Latinos in the city, which included hiring more Spanish-speaking ticket
agents and arranging for sponsorship from a bank with a large Latino
client base, Banco Popular.[200] The Mets' market play extended as well
to team dynamics: they signed a Latino pitcher, Pedro Martínez, for the
2005 season. The teams's general manager told a *New York Times* journalist that while Martinez was a star pitcher in his own right, "Pedro was as
much a marketing signing as a baseball signing"—meaning that he hoped
Martínez would attract more Latino fans, especially Dominicans, to the
games. The strategy worked, and average attendance increased by about
five thousand fans when the new pitcher started. Martínez himself was
well aware of his marketing value: "Now the Latin population is coming
in, and you're starting to see some Dominican flags and things like that.
People are going to start following me, and I have a lot of people. And
with the population that we have of Dominicans in New York, I think it's
going to be even greater."[201]
    A parallel effort was taking place with the Washington Nationals base-
ball team in the nation's capital. Here, the team's efforts involved appealing to African-Americans, rather than Latinos, and the effort was a mix
of racial realism and affirmative-action liberalism. The affirmative-action
part of the story came about due to a precipitous decline in the percentage of African-American major league ball players. African-Americans
were 25 percent of the league in the 1970s; by the early 2000s their numbers had shrunk to less than 10 percent.[202] In 2005 the league moved the

struggling Montreal Expos to Washington, DC, bringing baseball back to the city for the first time since 1971, when a previous franchise, the Washington Senators, left the city.

Because Washington was 57 percent African-American in 2005, the move brought attention to that community's interest in baseball, and to the relationship between blacks working in the franchise and blacks in attendance at the games. The Senators had left in part because of a lack interest. Their owner, Calvin Griffith, moved the team to Minnesota, explaining, "Black people don't go to ballgames."[203] According to the *Washington Post*, Major League Baseball, which took control of the team during the move, sought to prove Griffith wrong. It would "reinvigorate" African-American interest in baseball and it would do so in part through racial signaling. The league hired a former African-American star as manager. He was chosen for his managing talents, "but baseball recognizes that it also doesn't hurt to have a prominent minority in a position of authority with the team, according to two sources with intimate knowledge of the league's actions regarding the franchise." Tom Brasuell, MLB's vice president for community affairs, stated, "I think the number of African-Americans playing the game should reflect the population. If the 10 percent we have holds, we'll be okay. If it drops below that, there'll be real concern." The *Post* reported that the team "intentionally and aggressively hired a diverse front office" because, in the words of team president Tony Tavares, "It's our duty to reflect the city we play in."[204]

In contrast, the New York Knicks of the NBA discovered the financial benefits of racial realism by accident. This crucial event was the surprising rise to stardom of Jeremy Lin. The young Taiwanese-American player had been a basketball star at Palo Alto High School in northern California, but major college programs passed on him. He went on to star at Harvard University, but then it was professional teams' turn to pass on him, and he went undrafted. Following a brief but uneventful stint with his hometown team, the Golden State Warriors, and some time spent playing in obscurity in small cities in the NBA's "Developmental League," a wave of injuries on the Knicks gave him playing time. The Knicks were then a losing team and the coach, Mike D'Antoni, was on the verge of being fired. But in a dramatic development that captivated much of the basketball world, Lin responded with all-star caliber play. The team reeled off a string of thrilling victories,[205] and the stock price of the firm that owned the Knicks rose to a record high.[206]

There are a number of elements in his narrative that combined to make Lin a national sensation, in particular the underdog storyline, but there can be no doubt that Lin's race contributed to his appeal and to his market value. Race had been part of his marketing already at Golden State. Sports blogger Jay Caspian Kang described it this way: "Lin's signing was one of the first moves made by the Warriors' new ownership group. The rationale made sense: Bring back the hometown kid and put him in front of the most Asian crowd in the NBA. . . . He was featured during Asian-American appreciation night. Any sportswriter with Asian roots was summoned to Oracle (Arena) for a series of press conferences. (At the time, I had published exactly two pieces for a blog that no longer exists. Even I got a credential for Asian-American Jeremy Lin night)."[207]

Lin's surprising success in New York appealed to fans of all races, but Asian-Americans and fans in Asia responded particularly strongly. Knicks games became "must-see TV in Asia," with stations in China and the Philippines adding them to their broadcast schedules.[208] Asian-Americans gathered in bars to watch the games (and talk to *New York Times* reporters). Commenting on the power of Lin's racial signaling, Korean-American Audrey Kim said, "He's already a success and [has] made so many people proud. . . . He's such an inspiration to young Asian-Americans." Stanley Lee, who shared Lin's Chinese ancestry and also Lin's Christian faith, observed, "He is so much what I am." Another said simply, "An Asian American dunked."[209] A story in *USA Today* quoted Asians of Vietnamese, Korean, and Thai ancestry expressing racial pride in Lin's accomplishments.[210] Peter Kim, a Korean-American actor, told Jesse Washington of the Associated Press that he thought that Lin's success would open up new acting roles for Asians. Noting that a crowd in Toronto had cheered when Lin made a last-second shot giving visiting New York the win, Kim remarked, "That alone should show how significant Jeremy Lin is to the Asian people. . . . He's not just an athlete playing for a team. He's playing for a whole culture and our representation to the rest of the world."[211] So valuable was Lin that the Houston Rockets, a team that had just lost retiring Chinese superstar Yao Ming, lured him away from New York by more than quintupling his Knicks salary. His new contract would pay him more than $25 million over three years.[212]

Beyond the stories of motivations and accusations of motivations behind the use of race in signing and fielding players, there is some small but declining statistical evidence of wage discrimination in the sports world, which is notable because in sports, unlike most jobs, valid measures of ability are readily available.[213] Presumably, if owners thought certain races were more valuable to their profit line, they would pay them more. If that measure is true, it would seem that the value of whiteness has declined. A study of 1989-season player salaries in the NFL (by far the biggest money-maker in sports) found that white players tended to make more, but analyses of the 1994 through 2003 seasons showed that minorities had surged ahead and were being paid more at every position than similarly performing whites except at the quarterback position, where whiteness had a premium value. More recent research has indicated that the quarterback pay gap has decreased, though it has not been completely eliminated.[214] Research on the NBA found that white players had careers that were about two years longer than black players in the 1980–91 period, but a study of the 1989–99 decade did not find evidence of any retention discrimination, and a study of salaries in the 2001–02 season did not show significant discrimination.[215] These studies suggest that racial signaling in pro sports may be pronounced in some markets but is not common.

Does Race Affect the Bottom Line in Pro Sports?

As in so many of the other areas covered in this book, there is evidence to support the belief held by employers in the sports world who believe that racial realism can affect their bottom line. Though there is evidence that whiteness is still important, this appears to be declining, and there is some evidence that nonwhite races can bring greater profits if they are utilized strategically.

Much of the research has focused on the NBA, a league in which about 80 percent of all players are black.[216] These studies have produced mixed results, but typically show positive effects accruing from racial signaling. One study found that viewership of televised NBA games increased when there were more white players on the teams—even if they are sitting on the bench: "The mere presence of white players on team rosters seems to have a more significant effect on Nielsen ratings than the number of minutes white players actually play."[217]

Other scholars have tested the racial signaling strategy that the Celtics, Red Sox, and Mets appeared to be using, as they have examined the link between the race of the players on a team and the racial mix in the team's home city and surrounding area. These studies, focusing on the NBA, have had mixed results, but for most part demonstrate at least some racial effects. In some cases a match between a team's racial demography and that of the local area was found to boost attendance at games; in other cases no such effect was noted.[218] An analysis of NBA

team dynamics in the 1990s found that teams in more white metropolitan areas made revenue gains when they had more white players,
and that white players were worth more when their overall numbers
declined in the league. The highest performing white players tended
to play in the more white metropolitan areas as well.[219] Another study
found that while there was no relationship in mostly white or racially
mixed metropolitan areas between the ratio of white to black players
and home attendance, and there was similarly no relationship between
fan attendance and the ratio of total minutes played by whites compared
to the total minutes played by blacks, race did matter somewhat in areas
where blacks were the predominant race. There, whiter teams had lower
attendance.[220]

Patterns of NBA player trades also seem to have some links to the
racial composition of the local fan base. In general, white players are
traded more often than blacks, and both white and black players tend to
be traded to cities with large white and black populations, respectively;
teams in whiter areas also tend to keep their white players.[221]

In football, the racial signaling patterns seem to be based on a player's
position. A study of the Nielsen ratings of ABC's *Monday Night Football*
found that the level of viewership correlated with whether or not at least
one black quarterback was featured. Specifically, having a black quarterback led to *higher* viewership, at least between 1997 and 2001. Games
featuring black quarterbacks had ratings 13 percent higher than games
with otherwise similar characteristics that featured two white quarterbacks. In 1998, for example, the black quarterback effect led to an increase of more than two million viewers, from 19.28 million to 21.40
million. Noting that higher viewership for NBA games with more white
players occurs in a league dominated by black players, whereas there
seems to be a preference for a black quarterback in populations most
likely to show racial tolerance in a survey, the authors concluded that
viewers do not necessarily have preferences for their own race, but rather
for racial diversity.[222]

While the research for baseball is not as strong or varied as for the
NBA and the NFL, it appears that there has been fan discrimination
in favor of black and Latino players in baseball, at least as measured by
their patterns of voting players for the All-Star game. This research could
not determine, however, whether the voting patterns were driven by the
preferences of all baseball fans or by black and Latino fans preferring
same-race players.[223]

Finally, there is little research on the value of racial signaling in the hiring of coaches, general managers, and other front-office personnel. The *New York Times* found some evidence of discrimination in favor of white coaches in the NBA (at least before the mid-2000s, they were retained 50 percent longer than black coaches).[224] However, another study of the NBA found that there was no relationship between the race of the coach and attendance at games.[225]

The results of studies looking at the impact of a coach's race in the NFL are difficult to interpret, but suggest that discrimination is not a factor or no longer a factor.[226] For example, controlling for player salaries, a study found that black coaches had better records than white coaches in the years between 1990–2002, suggesting that they were held to higher standards than white coaches. However, this effect disappeared after 2002.[227] It was also at this time that the NFL instituted its "Rooney Rule," named after Pittsburgh Steelers owner Dan Rooney, requiring teams to interview at least one black coach when they had an opening.[228] The number of black NFL coaches also increased after 2002, though this may have been because there was now a larger pool of qualified candidates.[229] Still, legal scholar Brian Collins has plausibly speculated that racial signaling will continue to be a factor in teams' choices of their quarterbacks and coaches, since these positions are typically the "face of the franchise," with significance to both investors and fans.[230]

Does the Law Allow Racial Realism in Media and Entertainment?

When employers give significance to race in the media and entertainment sectors, it is sometimes because they practice affirmative-action liberalism, seeing significance in race but only in the pursuit of fair employment opportunities. In other instances, employers practice racial realism. They perceive race as a useful tool to achieve other goals: they select models, actors, and athletes based on a prediction of how audiences will react to employees' racial traits. They may simply seek to increase liking for their media product and thus more money, or they may have an artistic vision that imparts meaning and usefulness to race. This is the only context where employers openly give preferences to whites, particularly in high-profile roles; but employers also increasingly see profits from the racial

signaling provided by nonwhites. What is most distinctive in the media
sectors is how publicly all of this discrimination is practiced: for actors,
job ads often explicitly specify race. Race-based hiring is also candid and
transparent when diversity champions like the Wachowskis take on their
studio or when George Lucas self-finances a film because studios resisted
his reliance on actors of color.

Does any of this square with American discrimination law as written
and as interpreted by judges and administrators? This is not an easy question to answer. Unlike the other employment areas we have considered in
this book, in entertainment and media casting there is almost no relevant
case law.[231] With the exception of a lawsuit filed by two African-American
men—neither of whom was a professional actor—who charged racial discrimination in the casting of a reality show (discussed below),[232] no one
who was not cast has sued an advertising company, film studio, Broadway
production, or TV production company for discriminating on the basis
of race. When it comes to sports, there is discrimination litigation, but it
has not extended to issues related to racial-realism strategies in the hiring of players, coaches, or visible front-office staff. Unlike employment
in low-skilled jobs, in entertainment, the EEOC has not stepped in to
try to prevent discrimination. Given the relative legal vacuum, it may
be unsurprising that entertainment employers appear brazenly to flout
discrimination law.

Are there defenses to justify racial realism in this context—legal fire-
walls to protect racial realism in entertainment and media from the nondiscrimination requirement of Title VII? In an authoritative treatment of
the subject, legal scholar Russell K. Robinson has pointed out that case
law suggests that at least some discriminatory casting decisions violate
Title VII.[233] In this section, I will explore four possible legal defenses that
might protect entertainment and media racial realism: affirmative action,
cultural exemptions, the responsibilities of the entertainment industry
for providing public or civic benefits, and First Amendment protections. I
will argue that while affirmative action cannot protect racial-realist hiring
in this context, the other three defenses are plausible. The first two are
not likely. Though judges sometimes do carve out space for some employment practices with cultural backing but no statutory basis, they have
not done this with race discrimination as they have with sex discrimination. And though there are precedents to see professional sports teams
as quasi-civic institutions, playing in public stadiums, and with a constitutionally permissible option to represent a city's demography, the trend
has been away from these precedents. However, one federal district court

has affirmed the First Amendment defense, and though other courts may or may not follow suit, there are clearly openings for racial realism (and specifically, racial signaling) if more courts frame casting decisions as "expressive conduct."

(Affirmative) Action on the Set—and on the Field?

As discussed in Chapter 2, affirmative-action legal rules do not provide a defense for racial realism, but it is important to point out that in entertainment and media, affirmative-action law does not fit well with race-based hiring in other ways either—and this is true even if the race-based hiring is calculated to further the affirmative-action liberalism goal of justice or opportunity. It is difficult to use affirmative action as a defense for race-based hiring in film, television, ads, and sports due to the structure of employment in this sector where employer-employee relationships are relatively fleeting and project-based.

Recall the rules for legal affirmative-action programs, described in Chapter 2 and given a usefully elaborate description in the EEOC's *Compliance Manual*: voluntary affirmative action is legal, but only if employers demonstrate a clear imbalance in some job categories; the plan does not impose inflexible quotas; candidates compete against other qualified candidates; the interests of non-targeted individuals are not unnecessarily dismissed; and the plan is temporary and designed to end when its goals are met.[234] Even for opportunity champions like the Wachowskis, who appear to be motivated by affirmative-action liberalism (championing diversity as justice and an end in its own right), the affirmative-action defense would likely not apply because each new film project is different from the previous. Job categories lack stability in movies, as well as in commercials and print or online ads. There may even be obstacles to an affirmative-action defense for TV shows, because so many only last a few years. It would be difficult to show that long-standing segregation and discrimination needed to be repaired. There is no statistical imbalance to correct, because there is no history to each new project; and there is no sense of transition, because the actor workforce changes almost completely from film project to film project.

Nor could George Lucas use affirmative action to justify the mostly African-American workforce for his *Red Tails* film, because his motivation in casting was not to rectify a racial imbalance. He sought black actors to conform to his artistic vision, clearly aiming to produce a certain reaction in audiences rather than simply to achieve justice by rectifying racial imbalances.

Affirmative action may be possible when it comes to staffing professional sports teams, but only when the goal is to correct an imbalance that disadvantages nonwhites.[235] Yet it is hard to imagine any coach or general manager using the rectification of past racial imbalance as a strategy for filling the team roster. Given the sometimes-obsessive nature of a team's fan base, it would be difficult to openly employ traditional affirmative-action preferences to justify the hiring of players or coaches. But again, it is important to stress that affirmative action could not be the defense for racial-realist strategies such as the Celtics' desire to appeal to whites, or even the Mets' efforts to appeal to Latinos or the Nationals' to appeal to African-Americans. The primary goal of these strategies is profit, not justice.

Cultural Logics and Acceptable Discrimination

It appears that entertainment and media employment operate in a kind of segmented, cultural bubble, separate from other employment sectors. And all the evidence suggests that even the authors of the law knew this and accepted it. In other words, though there may be a large gap between civil rights law on the books and common practices in this sector, the racial discrimination that does occur so closely conforms to *cultural* expectations of what is legitimate or appropriate that the discrimination gets a pass. In this view, judges may fashion legally incoherent but culturally consonant allowances for racial realism or other forms of race-conscious hiring, even while they are aware at some level that these allowances are not strictly consonant with existing law or legal precedents.

One area where such cultural allowance for discrimination seems to play a role is in the blatant use of racial discrimination in casting breakdowns. The practice of using help-wanted ads that were racially discriminatory was prohibited without controversy immediately after Title VII went into effect. But there were some sectors that clung to the practice of posting discriminatory help-wanted ads. For example, there was some initial ambiguity regarding whether or not *sex* discrimination in newspaper ads was illegal, and defenders of such ads proposed a defense that conceivably could have been extended to race discrimination.

It had long been the practice for news organizations to segregate job ads aimed at men from those aimed at women, and they wished to continue doing so. The practice was in part tradition, based on the sense among many employers that sex discrimination was not pernicious, but the key legal point in defense of these printed ads was that they might be considered speech or expression and thus protected by the First Amendment. The EEOC initially resisted prohibiting job ads that called specifically for male or female applicants, and this became one of the first battles fought by the new agency. After pressure from women in Congress and from the National Organization for Women, the EEOC finally issued a regulation prohibiting sex-segregated want ads in 1968.[236] But this did not settle the issue, and the Supreme Court weighed in on the matter in 1973. It affirmed that the government could ban ads that gave preference or segregated on the basis of sex. In a case involving a Pittsburgh, Pennsylvania ordinance that banned sex-segregated ads, the Court noted that the purpose of the law was not to suppress any messages or speech, and that there was no evidence that the ordinance would cause financial hardship to the plaintiff, the Pittsburgh Press Company. The restriction on ads was thus an acceptable limit on the paper's editorial judgment.[237] The EEOC's current guidelines for employers now flatly state, "It is illegal for an employer to publish a job advertisement that shows a preference for or discourages someone from applying for a job because of his or her race, color, religion, sex (including pregnancy), national origin, age (40 or older), disability or genetic information."[238]

Casting breakdowns, which almost always call for specific sexes and often call for specific races or at least imply a racial preference, would appear to plainly violate Title VII, the Supreme Court ruling, and the EEOC guidelines.[239] The race discrimination in breakdowns nevertheless continues, and there are almost no complaints—even the EEOC is silent. This suggests that a unique cultural logic is at play when it comes to entertainment employment. On discrimination in help wanted ads, the entertainment industry is, it seems, getting a pass.

There is, then, a complex, subtle, yet important factor that may affect legal interpretation and distinguishes the entertainment/media sector from others: in this sector cultural logics may trump the letter of the law. The culture may say "yes" even when the law says "no." Practices that make no sense according to the law are thus tolerated. Judges may even carve out nonsensical legal spaces for them.

This was apparent in 1964, when defenders of Title VII suggested in congressional debates that racial discrimination in the entertainment context might be acceptable, or that it would be acceptable with a simple work-around. Senators Joseph Clark and Clifford Case discussed entertainment in a long and detailed memo that explained how Title VII would work in practice. The memo muddied the waters regarding race and employment, at least in the entertainment context, by stating, "Although there is no exemption in Title VII for occupations in which race might be deemed a bona fide job qualification, a director of a play or movie who wished to cast an actor in the role of a Negro, could specify that he wished to hire someone with the physical appearance of a Negro—but such a person might actually be a non-Negro. Therefore, the act would not limit the director's freedom of choice."[240]

That leading defenders of the new legislation made this claim, and that no one seemed to notice how odd or utterly incongruous it was with the rest of the law, suggests the power of cultural conceptions of rationality or common sense.[241] Taken to its conclusion, the logic of Case and Clifford's argument would suggest that employers could specify that they wanted to hire people who have "the physical appearance" of whites, but that all races were (*ahem*) "welcome to apply." This would appear to open the door to *any* employer to defend discrimination by simply saying, "I don't prefer white people; I just prefer people who look like white people." Though that, clearly, is not what Case and Clifford meant. They *were*, however, at least suggesting that Title VII contained exceptions and certain values that were not spelled out. Not all occupations were equal and some employers could operate under separate, unspecified rules. In other words, casting was *different*.

To be sure, there have always been exceptions to Title VII's seemingly sweeping protections. For example, despite the claim of "equal rights"— that is, guarantees to each citizen—Title VII has never applied to employers with fewer than fifteen employees. Why should the employees of small businesses be unprotected from discrimination? The purpose of that explicit, statutory limitation was to protect very small businesses from liability. While arguably the fifteen-employee threshold was an arbitrary limit on employee rights claims, it was at least a clear line of liability explicitly spelled out in the law (and many state laws extended antidiscrimination law to smaller employers anyway).[242]

The claim put forward by Case and Clifford was a different matter altogether. Not only did it lack an explicit, statutory basis, but its suggestion that all employers could discriminate on the basis of color (the "physical appearance of a Negro") was explicitly contrary to the text of Title VII, which prohibited discrimination on the basis of color. Allowing a color defense in a statute that prohibited color discrimination does not make sense.

While no court has tested this color defense for casting, two have expressed some degree of approval for Case and Clifford's bizarre reasoning. In 1999, as described in Chapter 2, an Eleventh Circuit Court ruled that a firm, TPG, that assigned a black woman to call black voters for a telephone marketing campaign had made a racially discriminatory work assignment. But in a footnote, Nixon appointee Anthony Alaimo's opinion also discussed the possibility that its ruling would affect race-based casting. The ruling made a reference to Case and Clifford's argument about casting, and concluded similarly that its ruling would not affect entertainment contexts: "A film director casting a movie about African-American slaves may not exclude Caucasians from the auditions, but the director may limit certain roles to persons having the physical characteristics of African-Americans."[243]

A Fifth Circuit Court also addressed the legality of racial considerations in casting in a 1980 case involving a black undercover barbershop inspector who complained that the Texas State Board of Examiners only assigned him to inspect black barber shops. Though deciding the case on other grounds, the opinion of Lyndon Johnson appointee John Bryan Simpson considered the "business necessity" standard that can sometimes justify racially neutral employment practices that have a disparate and negative impact on a protected group. The court then extended this logic to casting: "A business necessity exception may also be appropriate in the selection of actors to play certain roles. For example, it is likely that a black actor could not appropriately portray George Wallace, and a white actor could not appropriately portray Martin Luther King, Jr."[244]

It appears likely that the senators and these judges were making allowances for a kind of culturally reasonable discrimination that nevertheless is unprincipled and has no basis in the law. If the law allowed employers to say, "We invite all to apply, but the job will go to someone with very light skin," then it would have had no effect at all, certainly not in the Deep South.

Of course, these senators and judges never meant for their reasoning to apply to employment generally. It made sense to them because they were considering it in very limited contexts: the context of casting changed their reasoning.[245] It would not be the first time that exceptions were made in civil rights law without legal justification, and also without controversy. The practice is common in sex discrimination law. When Congress passed Title IX of the Education Amendment of 1972, barring sex discrimination in any institution or program receiving federal funds, no one really meant to treat fraternities and sororities, segregated sports teams, or even segregated restrooms as instances of sex discrimination. The Office for Civil Rights, charged with the challenging task of writing regulations derived from that law, struggled for years to find meaningful rules that would implement the law but fit with widely-accepted norms of sex segregation and discrimination.[246]

In the employment context, the general rule has been that employers may not appeal to customers' discriminatory tastes to defend their own discriminatory hiring. As discussed in Chapter 1, this has extended to sex discrimination cases. Indeed, the basic rules for the use of the BFOQ defense were created when courts rejected airlines' attempts to defend preferences for female flight attendants by pointing to customers' preferences for women. These courts helped create the legal rules that required that any sex BFOQ had to be reasonably necessary to the essence of the business. These rules have been used to strike down other customer-preference-based sex BFOQs, including preferences for male waiters and bus drivers.

Yet subsequent court rulings have made allowances for gender BFOQs that violate these very rules. For example, one court allowed an employer who ran a nursing home to use customer preferences to justify limiting the tasks of male workers around female residents, particularly when those female residents might be unclothed.[247] It is difficult to imagine any part of nursing home labor that a man could not do—except for the objections of female residents. Other courts have justified sex BFOQs based on customer preferences for privacy in varied occupations, including hospital orderlies, nurses, prison guards, and janitors at a male bathhouse.[248] It is thus not surprising that one legal scholar has argued that the courts' current position toward sex BFOQs is one of "incoherence" and "instability."[249]

The "cultural logic of customer preferences" was also on display in the aftermath of a sex discrimination charge raised against the Hooters restaurant chain, which uses scantily-clad female waitresses as part of its marketing. After the EEOC supported the complaint, Hooters orchestrated a publicity campaign, and a sympathetic news media mocked the EEOC for overreaching. The EEOC relented and allowed Hooters to continue to employ exclusively women for its wait staff.[250]

So, it would seem, cultural exceptions *are* possible in sex discrimination law. Could a similar cultural exception defense support a movie or television production team in fending off an actor who sued for race discrimination based on a racially exclusive casting breakdown or casting decision? Probably not, because cultural exceptions do not travel well to the race or even national origin discrimination context.

First, consider the way the EEOC treats Title VII's BFOQ defenses for sex and national origin discrimination in the casting context. There is an echo of the culturally reasonable defense for sex discrimination in the wording of the guidelines: "Where it is necessary for the purpose of authenticity or genuineness, the Commission will consider sex to be a bona fide occupational qualification, e.g., an actor or actress."[251] The EEOC guidelines regarding BFOQ defenses for national origin discrimination, however, hardly open the door at all and give no examples. They simply state "The exception stated in section 703(e) of Title VII, that national origin may be a bona fide occupational qualification, shall be strictly construed."[252] There is no discussion of the casting context allowances, or indeed any allowances for discrimination. Of course the lack of BFOQ for race limits defenses even more for racial signaling in casting decisions.

Second, while the courts discussed above made approving comments regarding racial realism in the casting context *in dicta*, it is not at all certain that this kind of logic would hold when casting was the *focus* of an actual case before a court rather than part of some playful thought-experimenting. Cultural exceptions (that is, with no statutory basis) are very hard to find in race discrimination cases. In theory, cultural logics may carve out a space for the reasonableness of racial realism in casting, particularly if the goal is having an audience accept the authenticity of an actor, just as cultural logics have carved out spaces for "reasonable" sex discrimination. At the same time, no court has made an explicit ruling in favor of racial signaling that contradicts other rulings, as they have with some sex BFOQs in privacy or modesty contexts; nor has the EEOC authorized such discrimination. And it is unlikely that any culturally reasonable exemption could be made to extend to pro sports hiring. Unlike the slight opening for authenticity considerations in a casting BFOQ for sex, the EEOC *Compliance Manual* simply states: "Title VII also does not permit racially motivated decisions driven by business concerns—for example, concerns about . . . the negative reaction of clients or customers. Nor may race or color ever be a bona fide occupational qualification under Title VII."[253] In short, cultural exceptions exist in employment discrimination law, and some elite interpreters of the law have suggested that they are valid in the case of racial-realist casting decisions. But it appears very unlikely that courts or the EEOC could rely on such exceptions to authorize this strategy of management in entertainment and media.

Entertainment Employers, Public and Civic Roles, and the Diversity Preferences

Another possible defense may exist for some entertainment employers. It applies to TV shows (to broadcasters in particular), as well as to pro sports teams, and it might justify shows and teams matching their target demographics through racial signaling. This defense hinges on the strong links that broadcasters and sports teams may have to the public interest. This road to racial realism is likely to be blocked, given the Supreme Court's recent approach to issues of race discrimination, but it is worth exploring because it shows the complex ways that racial realism may itself be linked to public goals, even in private employment.

First, there is a Supreme Court precedent authorizing racial realism in broadcast licensing that could be extended to cover the hiring of TV show actors. The 1990 case upheld a series of court orders, FCC regulations, and statutes that in various ways gave preference to minorities seeking access to broadcast licenses. The preferences were premised on the notion of nonwhites' racial abilities (to create or broadcast programs that whites would or could not) rather than on racial signaling. As one 1987 Senate report explained, "Diversity of ownership results in diversity of programming and improved service to minority and women audiences."[254] George H. W. Bush's Acting Solicitor General (and current Chief Justice of the Supreme Court) John Roberts, however, argued that "the notion that race or ethnicity is a valid proxy for programming choices is precisely the type of racial stereotyping that is anathema to basic constitutional principles."[255]

The Supreme Court affirmed the program in 1990 in *Metro Broadcasting, Inc. v. FCC*.[256] In a five to four decision, the Court found that the preferences were substantially related to an important goal of diversity.[257] Regarding the meaning of race and why it mattered for ownership, the Court drew an analogy between the race of licensees and the diversity of races in a classroom, citing Justice Powell's famous opinion that race preferences furthered a constitutionally permissible goal of diversity in medical school admissions.[258] Writing for the majority, Justice William Brennan also quoted from FCC and House reports that emphasized that better racial representation was good for both minorities and the wider public.[259] Linking ownership to broadcasting, Brennan wrote, "A broadcasting industry with representative minority participation will produce more variation and diversity than will one whose ownership is drawn from a single racially and ethnically homogeneous group."[260]

The Court would later explicitly overrule part of this opinion; in 1995's *Adarand v. Pena*, the majority ruled that government schemes using racial preferences need to be reviewed using strict scrutiny. That is, courts should ask whether the programs are necessary to achieve a compelling goal—which is a more exacting standard. But the racial-realist logic of the opinion was not explicitly overturned.[261]

While the Court did not endorse predictions of increased profits as a rationale for racial discrimination, the Supreme Court, FCC, and Congress converged in the belief that broadcasting should serve all people and that considerations of race were relevant to this mission. A broadcaster that used racial signaling to diverse demographic groups to maximize profits from advertising revenue might use the *Metro Broadcasting* precedent to claim that her or his use of race comports with these constitutional objectives, and thus should be protected.[262] The success of this strategy might depend on whether a court would agree that a diversity of racial images is equally important and similar to the goals of the programs upheld in *Metro Broadcasting*, which emphasized diverse "viewpoints" (abilities) rather than diverse images (signaling).

Another racial realism link to the public interest figured in the Supreme Court's 2003 decision in *Grutter v. Bollinger*, which ruled that racial diversity could be a constitutionally permissible rationale to justify racial preferences, and since this conclusion was not explicitly overruled in the *Fisher v. University of Texas* case, it still may be available as a defense for certain kinds of racial meanings in employment. In previous chapters, I argued that *Grutter*'s basis in constitutional law, rather than Title VII, made it applicable only to public employment. The entertainment employers discussed in this chapter are all private employers—but arguably, they are private with a public twist.

A potentially relevant aspect of Justice O'Connor's opinion in *Grutter* was her emphasis on the "civic" benefits of diversity. She wrote, "Effective participation by members of all racial and ethnic groups in the civic life of our Nation is essential if the dream of one Nation, indivisible, is to be realized."[263] While subsequent decisions have appeared to weaken or marginalize the *Grutter* precedent (as discussed in Chapters 1 and 3), the decision has not been overruled.

A thorough search for legal authorization for racial realism in media and entertainment would force us to ask: Could these sectors be viewed as part of the civic life of the nation? Though advocacy groups have seen the image of nonwhites in advertising, movies, and television shows to be matters of grave concern, it is hard to see these purely private,

profit-making enterprises as integral to the civic life of the nation. But
sports organizations, which are named after the cities in which they are
located, would certainly seem to have a civic element.[264] As discussed
above, city governments typically pay about half of the cost of new stadiums in America, financing them, like government buildings, through
taxes on citizens. If sports teams represent their cities, should not their
employees be representative of those cities? Should not teams, either
through their players, coaches, or front offices, use "effective participation" to realize the "dream of one Nation"?

Legal scholar N. Jeremi Duru has explored the application of *Grutter*
to the construction of team rosters. He argues that in order to follow
Grutter, a team would have to avoid rigid racial quotas and use race only
as an added factor contributing to a more comprehensive review of any
particular employee. He assessed the New York Mets' mid-2000s effort
to appeal to Latinos by hiring Latino employees, including a pitcher (described above in this chapter).[265] Duru concluded that the Mets' motive
in hiring Latinos would be problematic, as their intent was to send signals
to an external constituency of potential customers. It was therefore designed to maximize profits. Duru compared it to an auto dealership that
would hire sales personnel by race in order to appeal to same-race customers and increase sales.[266] Private employers using that kind of rationale would likely be seen as catering to customers' discriminatory tastes,
and that is almost certainly a practice that the courts would disallow.

While the profit motive does seem to have been a factor in the Mets' effort to reach out to Latinos, I believe that the Mets could make some credible arguments in defense of their Latino preferences. They could argue
that there is no meaningful distinction between their goals and the goal
upheld in *Grutter*, because their attempts to improve profits actually relied
on the "effective participation" of diverse populations and sought to bring
the community together. The Mets could also distinguish their enterprise
from private businesses, such as auto dealers, on the grounds that auto
dealers do not have fans, do not represent entire cities, and do not get
billion-dollar subsidies. One might question their value, but there is little
doubt that sports teams have a very important civic meaning to millions of
people in metropolitan centers across the country. For many people, living
in or near a city is tantamount to joining the local team's fan base.

Is this line of argument likely to be pursued? Certainly not in the short
term. While *Metro* and *Grutter* remain good law, the current Supreme
Court has moved in a different direction. But it is not beyond imagination that—assuming there was litigation—a court might one day find that

Grutter created a new civic-based diversity rationale to justify racial signaling by professional sports franchises, or by other employers who could
claim to play a civic role. After all, some types of racial signaling in sports
could lead to "effective participation" and thus help to realize "the dream
of one Nation"—or at least one city.

The First Amendment as a Defense for Racial Signaling

Though cultural logics and civic roles may not provide media and entertainment employers with a pass for racial signaling, there is yet another
defense unique to this sector that needs to be considered. As suggested
in discussing the controversy over sex-segregated job ads, media producers may be able to use First Amendment defenses for racial signaling. The First Amendment guarantees free speech—the opportunity to
communicate particular ideas or messages. Courts generally understand
the purpose of free speech to be the creation of a vibrant and capable
citizenry. To use free speech as a defense for racial realism, entertainers
and advertisers would have to meet three conditions. They would have to
show: 1) that entertainment and advertising messages are protected by
the amendment; 2) that casting decisions should be considered expressive and thus covered; and 3) that Title VII's prohibition of race BFOQs
and consideration of customer discrimination do not apply to casting in
movies, television, sports, and ads.

Regarding whether these entertainment sectors are protected, the answer, at least in principle, is that they are. Courts originally differentiated
entertainment messages from other (more important) forms of expression
and allowed censorship of films,[267] but in a series of cases the Supreme
Court erased the entertainment exception, arguing in 1948 that "the line
between informing and entertaining is too elusive."[268] In 1952, the Court
elaborated: "That books, newspapers, and magazines are published and
sold for profit does not prevent them from being a form of expression
whose liberty is safeguarded by the First Amendment. We fail to see why
operation for profit should have any different effect in the case of motion pictures."[269] Subsequent rulings made imposing limits on filmmakers
even more difficult.[270]

Advertising also has moved to protected status, based on the view that
ideas are being exchanged. However, because it proposes a commercial
transaction, advertising can be more easily regulated, especially when it
is deceptive messages that are being communicated.[271]

Whether pro sports are a form of expression is trickier.[272] On the one hand, as one legal scholar has argued, the purpose of sports teams is not to communicate messages, but to win games, and the efforts of players to win would not appear to be analogous to films, TV shows, or ads.[273] At least one court has analogized pinball, chess, and baseball as "pure entertainment with no informational element."[274] On the other hand, courts do give First Amendment protection to live entertainment.[275] In addition, the purpose of *professional* sports teams is not to win but to make money. This is why pro leagues endlessly tinker with rules and team uniforms; changes are made in part to enhance entertainment value. The owners' or managers' decisions to play certain athletes, as discussed above, are sometimes calculated to communicate some message in this entertainment setting. Pro sports games are thus like many reality TV shows— staged contests designed to win viewers and make money. While no court has ruled on a sports dispute as a First Amendment issue, decisions of whom to hire in this entertainment context could have some protected expressive content.

This brings us to the second hurdle for entertainment and media employers seeking to defend their racial realism. Could casting or roster decisions be protected? The First Amendment legal rules make a distinction between protected speech and expression on the one hand, and conduct, or simple behavior, on the other. Conduct is not protected, because regulating conduct is the basic job of law.

In reality, however, speech and conduct are not always easily distinguished.[276] Courts have created a category of protected conduct, "expressive conduct," that applies when expression and behavior occur together. Could employment be expressive conduct? It is easy to imagine many employment situations with an expressive component—that is, strategic employment decisions where something about the employee is intended to send a message. Indeed, by definition all of the instances of racial signaling described in this book would seem to be expressive conduct. However, as we have seen, racial signaling has little legal authorization outside of the law enforcement context.[277]

Could an employer whose purpose is explicitly to entertain be placed in a category apart from employers in other industries or in government, so that hiring for entertainment or ads would be protected as expressive conduct?[278] There are no clear rules defining what conduct is expressive,[279] and when the First Amendment would trump antidiscrimination statutes. As legal scholar Russell K. Robinson has pointed out, the Supreme Court has sometimes ruled that laws and regulations that advance equality, including Section 1981's ban on racial discrimination in the making of contracts, can limit First Amendment rights,[280] but, he notes, more recent cases have put the First Amendment over antidiscrimination laws.[281]

One of these, *Hurley v. Irish-American Gay, Lesbian and Bisexual Group of Boston*,[282] dealt with who could or could not participate in a St. Patrick's Day parade. The Supreme Court saw parading as expressive conduct, and thus protected by the First Amendment. It broadened the definition of what was "expressive," noting that it was not necessary for expression to convey a particular message, as that narrow understanding "would never reach the unquestionably shielded painting of Jackson Pollock, music of Arnold Schoenberg, or Jabberwocky verse of Lewis Carroll."[283] The Supreme Court compared the parade organizers to a composer of music, and saw the parade as expressive.[284] The First Amendment therefore trumped a Massachusetts law banning discrimination in public accommodations, and the parade organizers had a right to choose which messages to send or not to send. While the Jackson Pollock and music composer analogies referenced high culture, there are other cases that establish the principle that speech protection must be content neutral, since "one man's vulgarity is another man's lyric."[285] All of this would suggest that casting decisions in any entertainment medium could very well be protected as expressive conduct.

After showing that decisions to fill a cast or a roster are expressive conduct, another potential hurdle for racial-realist entertainers or advertisers would be the need to show that applying civil rights law to casting decisions can violate the First Amendment. Here there are established tests for evaluating the constitutionality of laws that limit expressive conduct. The "O'Brien Test" evolved from an effort to determine the constitutionality of a law that made it illegal to knowingly destroy military draft cards. In *United States v. O'Brien*, the Court argued that "a government regulation is sufficiently justified if it is within the constitutional power of the Government; if it furthers an important or substantial governmental interest; if the governmental interest is unrelated to the suppression of free expression; and if the incidental restriction on alleged First Amendment freedoms is no greater than is essential to the furtherance of that interest."[286] If the law passes all of these tests, then its limiting of expressive conduct application is constitutional.[287]

The O'Brien Test would appear to protect racial signaling in casting. Most agree that the Civil Rights Act *is* within the constitutional powers of the federal government. The purpose of the law is to guarantee equal opportunity, and since that conforms to the basic purposes of the Fifth and Fourteenth Amendments, Title VII would pass the second part of the test as well. There would seem to be two primary purposes of Title VII, as revealed in legislative debates; namely, ending employment discrimination and alleviating minority unemployment.[288] Neither of these appears related to suppressing messages, such as the message of white supremacy. Finally, there is the question of whether there might be alternative ways to achieve equal opportunity goals that place less onerous restrictions on media producers than does Title VII. This is much trickier, but a First Amendment allowance for racial realism in entertainment and media in at least some circumstances could be a balanced, less restrictive regulation of expression than classical liberalism's ban on all discrimination.

So, what do the courts say? Does the First Amendment shield racial realism in media and entertainment? Despite the ubiquity of racial realism in these sectors, there are almost no cases to speak of, and the few decisions we have seem to go in opposite directions. In the advertising context, at least one law specifically restricts the casting of models in ads, and courts *have* upheld it, thus prohibiting racial signaling, at least as it targets whites. The law in question is limited to advertising for only one kind of business, but a very important one: real estate.[289] Section 3604(c) of 1968's Fair Housing Act states that it is unlawful "to make, print, or publish, or cause to be made, printed or published any notice, statement, or advertisement, with respect to the sale or rental of a dwelling that indicates any preference, limitation, or discrimination based on race, color, religion, sex, or national origin, or an intention to make any such preference, limitation or discrimination."[290] As described above, activists have successfully used this law to force real estate advertisers to stop preferring whites and include nonwhite models in their ads. In a 1987 decision in Virginia, a federal district court found problematic a brochure advertising a set of apartment complexes that showed sixty-eight photos of happy white residents but almost no black residents. In an opinion written by a Lyndon Johnson appointee and civil rights liberal, Robert H. Merhige, the court ruled that it was plain to anyone that the brochures were using racial signaling, and thus violating the law: "Thus, the Court finds that the natural interpretation of the . . . brochure is to indicate that [the] apartment complexes are for white, and not black, tenants, thus discouraging blacks from seeking housing there."[291] Despite the focus on expression, there was no First Amendment issue in the case: classical liberalism beat racial realism in real estate advertising.

But racial realism in an entertainment casting decision won in the only case where it was challenged as a violation of an antidiscrimination statute. The casting in question was not for a scripted performance but for the popular, long-running reality shows, *The Bachelor* and *The Bachelorette*. In these shows, an unmarried man or woman chooses a life partner from about twenty-five (opposite-sex) suitors. None of the participants in the show are typically professional actors. In twenty-four combined seasons of the two shows, every single bachelor or bachelorette had been white, and nearly every suitor had also been white. Two African-American men, Nathanial Claybrooks and Christopher Johnson, failed to be cast in 2011, and they sued the shows' producers, the American Broadcasting Companies (ABC), for intentional racial discrimination under Section 1981. More specifically, they charged that they were turned away from a casting call while white candidates were given interviews, and that news reports had claimed that the show feared loss of ratings due to the public's distaste for interracial romance. ABC and the other defendants offered a variety of defenses, including the argument that the lawsuit was not valid due to the First Amendment. They argued that by suing under Section 1981, Claybrooks and Johnson were trying to force their own preferred message into the show's content. Claybrooks and Johnson in turn pointed out that this defense proved that the show intentionally discriminated on the basis of race.

The defendants then argued that if the court sided with Claybrooks and Johnson, it would threaten entire networks that are geared toward specific audiences (including Black Entertainment Television), as well as specific shows with casts that were designed to target specific audiences (including the all-black cast of the *Cosby Show* or the all-white cast on *Jersey Shore*), as well as decisions to cast based on race or gender in productions of *Othello* or *Romeo and Juliet*. Claybrooks and Johnson responded that "identity-themed programming" should be granted an exception.[292]

A federal district court in Tennessee decided the case because the alleged discrimination occurred when the two men had shown up for a casting call in Nashville. Judge Aleta Arthur Trauger, a Clinton appointee, would be the first ever to rule on racial discrimination in entertainment casting. She ruled that the First Amendment *did* protect these casting decisions, because Section 1981 "would force the defendants to employ race-neutral criteria in the casting process, thereby regulating the creative content of the Shows."[293]

The court chose for guidance the Supreme Court opinion in *Hurley*, discussed above, where the Supreme Court viewed parade organizing as akin to music composition, and worthy of First Amendment protection from an antidiscrimination statute. The Tennessee court ruled that *The Bachelor* was similar to the St. Patrick's Day Parade, and deserved protection. Trauger rejected the idea of distinguishing "identity-themed programming" from programming where antidiscrimination statutes would apply, because in her judgment it would be difficult to decide which was which. Such a measure, she wrote, "threatens to chill otherwise protected speech," and "if implemented, would embroil courts in questioning the creative process behind any television program or other dramatic work."[294] Thus, even if *The Bachelor* and *The Bachelorette* were reinforcing negative stereotypes about which kinds of romantic relationships were appropriate in American society, casting decisions were part of the creative process, and plaintiffs could not use antidiscrimination law to force the shows to send the plaintiffs' preferred, progressive message.[295]

In a footnote, the court argued that the lawsuit would have failed under the O'Brien test as well. This was true because Section 1981 applied to casting "would impose an undue and impermissible incidental restriction on the defendants' First Amendment freedoms, thereby failing the fourth factor of the *O'Brien* test."[296]

Section 1981 rulings tend to follow the same standards as Title VII rulings, but the impact of the lone opinion on entertainment and the media is obviously unknown, nor is it possible to know whether it could be extended to other contexts where employers use racial signaling. The court provided no rule or understanding for how courts could distinguish the message-sending of a television show from the message-sending of a restaurant or any other employer. The case does make clear, however, that the First Amendment can serve as a legal basis for at least some racial realism in one employment context. In the end, racial realism in media and entertainment looks like the racial realism observed the other chapters. Though focused on signaling rather than abilities, it is like other sectors in this book in that it appears to be common in practice—advertisers, film, and television producers regularly consider their prospective audience's reaction when they choose the race of their employees, and social science evidence offers some support for these efforts. Professional sports teams use racial signaling less than they used to, but some still do, and social science also offers some support for those who choose to use race in building rosters. Though the law would seem to offer possibilities for these employers that others do not have, only one district court has used any of the options apparently available to carve out space for racial realism in media and entertainment. This court used First Amendment precedent about a street parade to rule in favor of racial realism for casting in for a television show. Yet even without more judicial support, a lack of litigation is likely to allow racial realism to flourish in this important sector of employment.

The Jungle Revisited? Racial Realism in the Low-Skilled Sector

Racial realism at the low end of the job market shows unique patterns, both in the workplace and in the law. It also presents us with some very different human dramas. In this area of employment it is not rare to find that the targets of employer preference—the workers with the most desired racial abilities—could only misleadingly be called winners in the contest for jobs.

There is no better way to introduce these issues than with a brief recap of what happened in the majority-black city of New Orleans in the aftermath of Hurricane Katrina.[1] The employment patterns during the city's rebuilding may have surprised some observers, but would not have surprised anyone who had been following shifts in employment practices since the 1980s. Central to the changes was one simple fact: employers of low-skilled workers were becoming increasingly enamored of Latinos. They valued Asian workers as well, and immigrant status seemed to be a major plus for both groups. American laborers, including whites but especially blacks, were for many employers the least desired group.

This scale of the disaster was immense. On August 25, 2005, Hurricane Katrina struck land just east of the city of New Orleans. Winds were as high as 175 miles per hour and the storm surge reached thirty-two feet. When it was all over, 1,800 people were dead, 2.5 million homes were flooded or otherwise damaged, and estimates placed the number of displaced people between 700,000 and 1.2 million.[2]

If the Katrina disaster is predominantly a story of the suffering and neglect of African-Americans, the rebuilding of New Orleans is to a great degree the story of a valorized—though to a great degree exploited—Latino workforce. The city was only 3 percent Latino in 2000, yet nearly half of the reconstruction workforce was Latino. And about half of those were undocumented. The federal government itself helped this process along by granting special waivers on immigration restrictions, easing the hiring of the undocumented. Though the wages paid to undocumented workers were considerably lower on average than for U.S. citizens and for immigrants with visas or green cards ($10 per hour vs. $16.50 per hour), and undocumented workers were more likely to face health challenges while on the job (e.g., they were far less likely to receive medications—83 percent to 38 percent), the rise of Latino labor in New Orleans was not simply a matter of dollars and cents.[3]

Employers rebuilding New Orleans sought Latino workers because they believed they were the best workers. New Orleans required not just new buildings, but also the demolition of those still standing. Workers spent their time gutting damaged structures and removing trash, as well as doing roofing, painting, and other jobs.[4] Many employers in New Orleans went out of their way for Latino labor because they believed that Latinos had abilities to do these things that the native population lacked. One contractor, Albert Stein, himself an immigrant from Colombia, explained to National Public Radio, "You hire the African-Americans, they all want the easy way out. They don't work long hours; they always want breaks; they're not loyal."[5] Demand for Latino labor skyrocketed.

Latino migrants responded, highlighting another prized ability of Latinos, at least the foreign-born Latinos: they will relocate for work.[6] According to Guatemalan immigrant Oscar Calanche, quoted in the *Los Angeles Times*, "It was like a Gold Rush. . . . In one car there'd be three up front and three or four in the back, with suitcases and tools on top. It looked like a river of people from our countries." Another migrant, Leonel Santos, was recruited by an acquaintance, a contractor doing rebuilding work, who sent a car to bring Santos and seven others from Virginia and North Carolina to New Orleans. "We were packed like matchsticks," Santos recalled.[7]

It wasn't long before some resentful locals wore T-shirts that featured a wordplay on the maligned Federal Emergency Management Agency that had tragically botched disaster relief: "FEMA: Find Every Mexican Available." New Orleans mayor Ray Nagin anticipated the whole process—and he worried about it. "How do I make sure that New Orleans is not overrun by Mexican workers?" he asked at a meeting with local businesses.[8]

Nagin's comment generated some controversy,[9] but he knew what both social scientists and journalists had been documenting since the 1980s: employers of the low-skilled commonly perceive some racial groups to have more ability than others. By "low-skilled" jobs, I am referring to jobs that involve minimal reading, math, or use of computers.[10] Typically, the desired abilities—the abilities that make Latino and Asian workers especially qualified for these jobs—include diligence, the ability to maintain a positive and compliant attitude, the ability to work through pain or injury, and the ability to do boring and/or repetitive tasks without complaining. Since some of these jobs require little thought or refined talents, it is certainly faint praise to be described as good at them or liking them.

Due to the low visibility of such jobs, racial signaling plays almost no role in the employer racial realism used to fill them. It is the management of perceived racial abilities that helps produce and maintain the observable racial patterns in the low-skilled workforce. Anyone coming to the U.S. with no assumptions or expectations about life here would surely notice widespread patterns of color in the nation's workforce: people of the same color tend to do similar jobs, there is widespread segregation, and there is a tendency toward hierarchy, with particular groups concentrated at the bottom of the job market and others at the top.

To be sure, there are dynamics in the mix that can result in some ethnic or racial groups voluntarily abandoning a niche, opening it for others, or self-segregating on the job,[11] and employers' preferences are not always or only about race. In the low-skilled employment sector, as the Katrina rebuilding shows, employers also use immigrant realism, whereby being foreign-born becomes a qualification for a job. In most cases, employment occurs through a complex amalgam of preferences for certain racial backgrounds, certain national origins, foreign-born status, and lack of documents[12]—as well as factors that are not a focus of this book, such as gender and age. There is also a dynamic of exploitation that pervades the low-skilled job market. Workers "preferred" for low-skilled jobs face some of the harshest work conditions in America, often in violation of wage and safety laws.

This is the darkest corner of American racial realism. Whether or not employer decisions are rooted in stereotypes about race, national origin, immigrant status, or even undocumented status, employer decisions are helping create a stratified workforce reminiscent of what Upton Sinclair decried in his 1906 muckraking classic, *The Jungle*.[13] As in Sinclair's time, so too today there are moral ambiguities in play, because the workers who take the worst jobs want those jobs. To close off the jobs would be to close off opportunities for them. Those who used to have these jobs and are now in many cases excluded from them, often no longer pursue them—at least with their current pay and conditions.

Another critical feature of racial realism in low-skilled jobs is that it appears to be deeply entrenched even though it is often quite clearly in violation of the most basic principle of equal opportunity and discrimination law: that we should not judge individuals based on stereotypes. However, given the seeming undesirability of these jobs, employers' hiring based on perceptions of racial or immigrant ability is rarely challenged in court. When it has been challenged, courts typically reject it, though there have been a few decisions that enable this strategy of workforce management, albeit only indirectly.

In this chapter, I first put racial realism in low-skilled jobs in historical context, showing that today's practices are an expansion and elaboration of some very old patterns. Next, I review the evidence regarding this kind of hiring, which consistently demonstrates that the practice of hiring based on racial and immigrant abilities is widespread, affecting every region of the country and both urban and rural employers. Next, I explore research that shows that there are workplace dynamics other than simple employer perceptions that contribute to create the racial patterns that prevail in the low-skilled sector, such as a tendency to rely on word-of-mouth hiring and the tendency for American workers to avoid work contexts where a language other than English is spoken. I also show how employers can manipulate these dynamics to produce their desired racial and immigrant workers. I then focus on a particularly significant case study of the low-skilled sector: the transformation of meatpacking in the last few decades, an industry where wages have plummeted and Latinos, especially Latino immigrants, have become the favored workforce. Finally, I show how Title VII and other laws, including the Immigration Reform and Control Act of 1986, would appear to forbid this racial realism except in a special circumstances, and provide some insights on why the gap between practice and court and agency rulings seems to be so great.

Immigration and the American Workplace: Plus ça change . . .

In our national folklore, America is the quintessential land of immigrants. But this portrayal usually leaves out one key fact: as long as there have been immigrants, there have been employer stereotypes about immigrants of different races and ethnicities, and there have been employer preferences based on these stereotypes.[14] Historian Theodore Hershberg and his colleagues identified patterns of immigrant employment in their comparative analysis of the Philadelphia job opportunity structure at three periods: in the years between 1850 and 1880, Irish and Germans were the major immigrant groups; in the 1930s, when Italians, Poles, and Russian Jews entered the workforce in large numbers; and the 1970s, when American-born blacks were the latest arrivals. Of course by 1970, the better jobs were disappearing. One of the more significant observations in Hershberg's account is that in 1880 and in 1930, the blacks already in Philadelphia were not getting the manufacturing jobs. To be sure, factories were rarely the sites of cushy jobs. These workers did not have collective bargaining rights, there was no Occupational Safety and Health Administration, and Upton Sinclair's *Jungle* had not yet aroused sympathy for industrial workers. But as horrific as these jobs sometimes were, they were often more desireable than the jobs that African-Americans were doing. Though 80 percent of Philadelphia's blacks lived within a mile of 5,000 manufacturing jobs, their options in this sector were limited: only 8.2 percent of blacks worked in manufacturing, while about half of all new and second-generation white immigrants worked in manufacturing, including 54 percent of Germans, 56 percent of the British, 56 percent of Poles, 33 percent of Italians, and 63 percent of Russians. By contrast, 54 percent of black workers worked in menial personal service and domestic jobs, while the percentage of white immigrants in these jobs ranged from 18 percent for the Irish to only 4.5 percent of Russians.[15] Anti-black discrimination was most definitely not restricted to the Jim Crow South.[16]

The odds of finding steady employment were better for an immigrant with a strong back. Sinclair describes the day his protagonist, Lithuanian immigrant Jurgis Rudkus, went down to the yards to get a job. Jurgis "stood there not more than half an hour before one of the bosses noticed his form towering above the rest, and signaled to him." The boss says, "Job?" to which Jurgis replies simply, "Je." The boss asks him if he can "shovel guts," and the interview is over. He is hired.[17]

In the early twentieth century, employers did not just want generic immigrants more than African-Americans; they wanted certain immigrant groups in certain jobs. Perceptions of racial abilities (and at this time, Americans commonly equated national origin with "race") could be highly specialized. At the Pabst Brewing Company in Milwaukee, Germans held the skilled jobs while non-Germans, mostly Poles, worked low-skilled jobs in the bottling department. A Scottish foreman at the International Harvester foundry preferred Poles for foundry work over his coethnic Scots. Employers in the garment industry believed German

and Polish women had a "peculiar aptitude to the work." In the ice business (this was before refrigerators), an employer told a local paper (using
a slur for Polish immigrants), "The Polacks are the best workers we have
here and the Swedes are also good men," though "a great many . . . work
a day or two and then make some excuse for drawing their pay, and we
never see them again." Not all saw Eastern and Southern Europeans as
especially qualified, however. An employer in the railroad industry looked
down on Greeks, Italians, Bulgarians, Austrians, and Hungarians, and
preferred "hoboes," who were the "best of railroad labor" because they
"do four or five times the work a gang of Greeks or Bulgarians can do."[18]

As historians James R. Barrett and David Roediger point out, both
employers' folk wisdom and the social science of the time supported beliefs about different groups' racial or ethnic abilities. These beliefs then
shaped the organization of the workplace, sometimes in elaborate if inconsistent ways. One mill saw the blast furnace as a "Mexican job," another reserved that job for "hunkies" (Hungarians or Slavs) because it
was "too damn dirty and too damn hot for a white man."[19] Sociologist
E. A. Ross argued that some kinds of dirt "that would kill a white man"
was harmless to Slavs because of their special immunity.[20] A personnel
manager at another plant pinpointed the "racial adaptability" of thirty-six
different ethnic groups for twenty-four different jobs under twelve different conditions. Views toward African-Americans tended to limit their
opportunities: some employers, for example, saw blacks as unfit for jobs
requiring exposure to cold weather or to a fast pace.[21]

A century later, American workplaces show strikingly similar employment patterns. America is again in the midst of a great wave of immigration, with the number of immigrants at an all-time high and the percentage of foreign-born near the high figures reached at the turn of the last
century. However, some key differences come to light when we look more
closely at the present situation.

As discussed in Chapter 1, the economy has changed. Many of the old
manufacturing jobs are no more, and employers often utilize mechanization to "de-skill" many of the jobs that still exist. They are now simpler to
perform than ever, with the result that the primary qualities employers
are looking for are no longer skills as traditionally understood but such
hard-to-measure qualities such as attitude, work ethic, and reliability.
The workforce has also changed over the last century, in two key ways.
First, there is today a far greater diversity of national origins, racial phenotypes, and even legal statuses. Immigrants were always a diverse lot, to
be sure, but in the past most shared European origins. In Sinclair's time,

the number of Asians was negligible due to laws barring their immigration.[22] Latino (mostly Mexican) migrants moved relatively freely across the southern border states, but except for moves to Chicago, tended to stay local in the Southwest. "Illegal" immigrants were thus not a major problem.[23] Today the foreign-born make up 12 percent of the population, and undocumented immigrants are about a third of these. In terms of racial phenotypes, the black population has grown slightly to 13 percent, and Latinos have increased from less than 1 percent of the population at the turn of the twentieth century to more than 16 percent of today's population.[24]

Another key difference is that there are now a large body of laws, regulations, and court decisions intended to bring equal opportunity to the workplace and provide a baseline of health and safety. This difference, however, is far less apparent than the new diversity of workers.

Who Is Highly-Skilled for Low-Skilled Jobs?

Since the 1980s, employers across America have lauded the superior abilities of Latinos and Asians to perform low-skilled jobs—by which is meant mostly manual labor, including jobs in manufacturing, construction, agriculture, food service, and cleaning. For these jobs, the most prized competencies are the ability to work long and hard without complaint.

"Incredibly Good Workers" and "Whining Pieces of Shit"

For employers looking to fill low-skilled positions, the antithesis of the good Latino or Asian worker is the American-born black. For many, the white worker is equally undesirable. Employers often identify particular racial groups, but sometimes they specify immigrant background; each seems to play a role in constructing the stereotype that shapes the appeal or lack of appeal of a given worker. National origin can matter as well: employers tend to group Latinos from the "islands" (usually Puerto Rico or the Dominican Republic) with African-Americans, while placing mostly positive meanings on Mexicans, Guatemalans, and others of Central and South American origin.[25] These racial rankings are widespread and remarkably uniform across cities, regions of the country, rural vs. urban contexts, and types of industries.

For example, in the late 1980s, sociologists Joleen Kirschenman and Kathryn M. Neckerman, working on a project with William Julius Wilson, conducted face-to-face interviews with almost two hundred Chicago and suburban Chicago employers. Kirschenman and Neckerman found that employers tended to praise the abilities of Latinos and Asians. As one employer explained, "When we hear other employers talk, they'll go after primarily the Hispanic and Oriental first, those two, and, I'll qualify that even further, the Mexican Hispanic, and any Oriental, and after that, that's pretty much it, that's pretty much where they like to draw the line, right there."[26]

A few years later, Wilson's book, *When Work Disappears*, reported a wealth of interview data showing a similar hierarchy in Chicago. A personnel manager at a bakery stated, "I find that the blacks aren't as hard workers as the Hispanics and—or the Italian or whatever. Their ethic is much different where they have more of the pride. The black kind of has a you-owe-me kind of attitude."[27] Similarly, a hotel manager reported, "I see far more blacks thinking the employer has the obligation to give him a check for doing nothing. There are some whites that think that way, but far more blacks. Not so much the Hispanics."[28]

A study of Brooklyn in the 1990s found similar patterns. Rather than hire the local African-American or Puerto Rican, these employers preferred to hire workers from outside the neighborhood. A warehouse manager in New York stated, "There is a friend of mine who is a carpenter and . . . (he says) that all the Mexican guys he's come in contact with are incredibly good workers. You hear that enough times and then if a Mexican guy came here for work I'd probably hire him based on that."[29] Employers in this sample, according to sociologists Philip Kasinitz and Jan Rosenberg, used "crude ethnic stereotypes" about their workers that emphasized differences in "punctuality, reliability, willingness to work hard, and to be a pliable labor force."[30]

In Los Angeles, sociologists Roger Waldinger and Michael Lichter also found unabashed lauding of the abilities of Latinos at unskilled labor. One explained, "They have a loyalty towards the company that white workers don't have."[31] Another said that Latinos are less rights-conscious and that they "like to work," even eschewing vacations.[32] Another employer focused more on specific abilities: "The Hispanic will work on a repetitive basis," and "Latinos seem to be good with their hands."[33] Another found virtue in the lack of an ambition for mobility, maintaining that Latinos are happy to work without seeking promotions.[34]

A study of the construction industry similarly found much acclaim for Latinos' racial abilities. As one employer put it, "To be honest, I love the little fuckers. I mean, they get into their work and shimmy up and down those frames of a house and jump back and forth. Man they work it. . . . And, the whole time they smile and say, 'Need anything else done?' Not, 'It's too fucking hot, I need a break,' or any of that other shit."[35] Another explained, "Many of the Mexican guys I've seen work look to be physically built to do the work. I mean, the Mexicans from the mountainous areas of Mexico are short but stout workers. They seem to pick up bags of concrete and heavy shit with little effort."[36] Many of these employers, however, distinguished Latino immigrants from American Latinos. As one employer put it bluntly, "When (they're) Americanized, they ain't worth a shit."[37]

Economists Philip Moss and Chris Tilly's study of employers (consisting of 365 interviews at 174 firms spread out between Atlanta, Boston, Detroit, and Los Angeles) found that only 5 percent of employers surveyed by telephone were willing to admit they saw differences in employee performance by race and ethnicity.[38] However, in face-to-face interviews, when they were apparently less worried about possible legal consequences for admitting their actual perceptions, 46 percent said African-Americans had both poorer soft skills (attitudes, grooming, an ability to work in groups), especially motivation, than other groups, and poorer hard skills (abilities in reading, math, and basic mechanics).[39] Others admitted to seeing positives in Latino, Asian, and immigrant identities. One manager of a Boston metal-finishing shop said, "Spanish people are more willing to work. They are willing to work longer hours. I think the ones that I've known are very dedicated to their jobs."[40] A personnel director at an Atlanta-area laundry argued that "[Hispanics] have a much higher work ethic [than blacks]. Hispanics, while they are employed with you, are very good employees. They're diligent. They do their job. They don't complain as much. [Blacks are] more vociferous than Hispanic people. If we are going to have complaints or we're going to have people not coming into work, it's going to be more predominately black than it is Hispanic."[41] Thousands of miles away, a Los Angeles garment factory manager said, "I think the work ethic for Hispanics is better than it is for blacks" and that "Asians are very good workers," while "whites, they wouldn't do the type of job in the back. That's a rarity, especially in Southern California, to see a member of the Caucasian race working in the plants. They just don't have the stamina or the, you know, humility to do that type of job."[42] An employer at a Boston factory expressed the view that the Asians' drive came from their immigrant identity: "Your Asian workforce, because it's the newest immigrant in the country, and what I've seen with them is they have a completely different work ethic. You need them for seventy-two hours a day, they'll be there for seventy-two hours a day."[43]

By contrast, as is apparent in some of the comparisons made above, employers complained that black workers did not want to stay on the job, or simply did not want to work.[44] Different studies yield different statistics, but the overall patterns are similar. When Kirschenman and Neckerman asked Chicago-area employers about work ethic, 51.4 percent said there were no differences, often observing that group differences were not racial but based on education, background, or environment. But 37.7 percent of employers ranked blacks last, while only 1.4 percent ranked Latinos last.[45] Seventy-four percent of Wilson's employers expressed negative views of black workers, revealing in various ways the perception that these workers had traits that hurt job performance, especially a poor work ethic.[46] One employer complained, "[Blacks] tend toward laziness. . . . I've seen this pattern over and over again, you know. I think people are willing to give them a chance and then they get the chance and then it's like they really don't want to work." Another said matter-of-factly, "The first chance they get, they'll slack off, they don't want to do the job, they feel like they don't have to, they're a minority. They want to take the credit and shift the blame."[47] One Chicago employer stated that the Asian worker "is much more aggressive and intelligent and studious than the Hispanic," and that native-born blacks are "the laziest of the bunch."[48] Another employer complained that "the black attitude is rubbing off on" the white workers.[49]

A study of smaller communities in the South yielded similar findings: more than 40 percent of employers reported that "blacks were poorly qualified," mainly due to a lack of motivation. Employers in these towns complained about a lack of work ethic, lack of discipline, and general laziness. One stated, "They are not dependable and don't want to work for things." Another stated, "Black attitudes are a barrier to jobs. Some blacks feel whites owe them something because of slavery."[50]

In Los Angeles, employers similarly described blacks as "lazy," or "scary" and reported that they had an "attitude." Black workers "don't try hard enough. They want everything to be handed down to them."[51] In Atlanta, Boston, Detroit, and Los Angeles, Moss and Tilly found that for every employer who said that blacks were better workers, there were twenty-five who said they were worse.[52]

In Silicon Valley, Asian workers are more prominent than in places like Atlanta and Detroit, but the racial-realism rankings are similar to those found elsewhere. According to a disk drive manufacturer:

Asians are best suited for this type of tedious and detailed work because they are very patient people—they can endure almost anything. I would not hire blacks because I think they will climb the walls after a week of sitting all day putting little screws in little holes. As a group, blacks are hardly a patient people. As for whites, they probably think that they are too good for this kind of a job. Some white person might take it because they might be desperate, but if the economy improves, they'll be gone. Then, I'll have to find someone else and that's just too much trouble.[53]

Another had similar rankings, as well as simple causal theories to explain variations in racial abilities:

Asians work hard due to their Confucian culture. They have loyalty to the company and view the company like a family. Latinos in America also work hard because they had to. Working as migrant farmers for all these years has instilled a hard work ethic in them. Whites are falling behind because they have been too comfortable. Whites would not take such a hard job for this kind of money. And blacks. I think they have lost much of their work ethic, and it's really the fault of the welfare system. Why work when you can have the same income and maybe even better benefits from the welfare office?[54]

Studies also find that employers perceive blacks to lack more specific or "hard skills." Some in Los Angeles complained that black workers, in their experience, were close to or were illiterate.[55] This was also true in Wilson's study of Chicago,[56] as well as in the study of communities in the South.[57] Moss and Tilly's sample of four cities found strong race as well as gender correlations with specific "hard skills" required in jobs. When jobs required talking with customers on the phone or face-to-face, reading instructions, writing paragraphs, doing math, or using computers, employers preferred the women within each racial group. When these kinds of skills were sought the common preference for Latinos no longer held; neither Latino nor black men tended to work in these jobs in Moss and Tilly's analysis of the four cities, and employers were usually more likely to use whites of either gender for jobs that required hard skills.[58] In face-to-face interviews, however, employers were far more likely to report that blacks lagged in hard skills than they were to report this of Latinos or Asians. For example, in Atlanta, the

percentage of employers citing poor hard skills for blacks was 28.9 percent, for Latinos 1.1 percent, and none said it of Asians. In no city did
a greater percentage say that Latinos or Asians lacked hard skills than
said this about blacks.[59]

Thus, though there was some ambiguity at the top regarding who were
the best workers, Asians or Latinos, employers were clear that African-
Americans were at the bottom—with non-Latino whites right there with
them or just above them. One employer explained, "I would say it's a
little tougher to find today white workers with as high a work ethic as
Asians. . . . I would say that twenty years ago there were [more]." Another
did not mince words: "The white factory worker is a whining piece of shit.
They [feel that they] never make enough money, they always work too
hard, they never want to work over eight hours a day and they feel that,
as soon as you hire them, you owe them."[60]

In the past, Latino workers were the pillars of the agriculture industry
in California. They remain so, but their role has since expanded to other
parts of the country and to different types of farm labor. For example,
dairy farms in Wisconsin have also become increasingly reliant on immigrant Latino labor, and employers there also laud the abilities of Latinos
while arguing that native workers are inadequate. After hiring his first immigrant Latino worker, a dairy farmer in Wisconsin gushed, "He milked
cows for 10 hours a day for 54 days straight," adding, "He wouldn't take
a day off, even though we insisted. It turned my life around."[61] Others expressed the opposite sentiment about their traditional workforce: "U.S.-
born want the money but not the work," and "They are not punctual and
work slow." Another stated "We no longer pay attention to native applications; it's not worth it."[62]

Racial Realism and Employers of Color

One may wonder whether the attitude of employers toward African-
American workers is simply a new spin on the old story of white racism.
There *is* indeed some evidence that firms where black, Latino, or female
managers are responsible for hiring tend to have more black employees.[63]
And another study found that African-American workers with African-
American supervisors experience more support and developmental op-
portunities than African-American workers with white supervisors.[64]

But the dynamics are more complex than a simple white racism story
implies. Although there is less research on the employment practices of

black employers, what evidence there is suggests that their hiring practices are not at great variance with the racial-realist strategies of white
employers. A study of construction firms in Atlanta, for example, found
no major differences in the prevalence of racial realism when comparing
firms owned by whites, Latinos, or blacks. They all tended to praise the
racial abilities of Latinos and denigrate those of blacks and whites. As
one black contractor explained, "Whites and blacks are just lazy workers, man. They kind of pussy-foot around until about 10 AM, then want
a break at 11, then lunch at 12 noon, and by 4 o'clock, their production
slows way down. I've almost decided not to hire them anymore because
they are so damn lazy."[65] William Julius Wilson's study of Chicago found
that both black and white employers felt that inner-city blacks were less
likely than other groups to have the job-related traits that they sought.[66]

In addition, the economic contributions of immigrant entrepreneurs,
who are noted by social scientists for generating jobs and revitalizing the
nation's cities,[67] have a lesser-known side: they show many of the same
preferences and aversions and the same stereotyped thinking as white
American employers. Immigrant entrepreneurs tend to run small businesses and thus are often beyond the reach of Title VII, which covers
only firms with at least fifteen employees. Not surprisingly, they often
employ family members.[68] But when they do hire outside their families,
they often hire co-ethnics—in the words of one researcher, "virtually all
immigrant employers hire primarily co-ethnic workers."[69]

This may be an exaggeration, but the pattern is real. For example,
a study of 204 Korean entrepreneurs in Los Angeles found that 37.4
percent of all of their paid employees were also Korean, while 20.6
percent were "American" and 19.6 percent were Mexican.[70] But since
the Korean population is a small part of LA's rich ethnic mosaic, these
numbers meant that Korean employers hired Koreans at a rate 47 times
higher than would be expected if Korean workers were evenly distributed
throughout the workforce.[71] The authors of the study described this ethnic preference as "nepotism and chauvinism."[72]

There may be non-racial-realist reasons why these employers hire
members of their own group—their common language is an obvious example. However, Moss and Tilly found some evidence of "chauvinism"
in their employer survey. Twenty-five percent of Latino employers said
Latinos were better workers—about double the average for all employers. Similarly, 28.6 percent of Asian employers said Asians were better workers—more than triple the average. Only 2.6 percent of black

employers said blacks were better workers, but this is still higher than the average of 1.7 percent.[73]

Still, there are limits to how much employers can rely on coethnics for employees. Ethnic entrepreneurs with larger businesses must wade more deeply into the local labor pool. And when they do, they tend to look more like their American counterparts.

Sociologist Margaret Chin explored the hiring preferences in some of the largest immigrant-owned businesses in New York City: the garment factories. Korean and Chinese immigrants own many of these firms, which typically act as subcontractors to larger enterprises that supply major retailers.[74] Though there are some differences between them (Chinese immigrants are less educated, less proficient in English, more able to hire coethnics, and more likely to organize their shops around piecework than the Koreans), both groups share other preferences in hiring. They both tend to hire women, and they hire them based on stereotypes about racial abilities.

Like other immigrant employers, these garment factory owners both tend to avoid hiring blacks.[75] Moreover, despite evidence that other employers have positive stereotypes of black immigrants,[76] their aversion to black employees extends also to black immigrants—these employers made no distinction among blacks based on their national origins. This aversion thus extends to Puerto Ricans and Dominicans as well. The problem, as they perceived it, is drearily familiar: blacks (and Puerto Ricans and Dominicans) will not work hard.

Though none of the employers that Chin interviewed had *ever* hired an African-American, they offered plenty of reasons why they would not. As one Korean employer explained, "I have friends that [sic] own stores who hire blacks, and they are just too lazy. They come to work in the beginning and work hard and then a couple of weeks later, they start coming in late, and [then they start] taking days off. I can't have that kind of person working here. We have deadlines to make. I'm not just selling things." Another explained that though blacks "never stole anything," they were not good workers because "they are not dependable. My friend had to hire someone every few months. They can't keep a job. You waste much time working with them."[77]

Others worried that having black or Puerto Rican workers would get in the way of their practice of exploiting Asians and Latinos. Some Chinese employers told Chin that they were concerned that black and Puerto Rican workers, because of their ability to speak English, posed a threat because they might complain to outsiders about work conditions and violations of law. Or as one Chinese employer explained, "I wouldn't hire any black or Puerto Rican. They would be watching everything that you do, making sure everything is fair."[78]

Do Actions Follow Words?

Most studies of employers' perceptions of racial abilities rely on interviews and surveys, as it is difficult to observe an employer actually hiring and firing, and there is reason to believe that discriminatory words and actions do not always line up.[79] The fact that black unemployment is almost always higher than Latino unemployment is certainly suggestive, but it is not in itself evidence of employers acting on racial-realist preferences.[80] There are, however, some rich ethnographic sources of evidence of employers acting on ethnic or racial preferences, and one in particular shows clearly their preference for Latino workers over African-Americans. While not generalizable, it certainly fits with everything we have described above, and it is quite eye opening.

The clearest evidence comes from sociologist Laura López-Sanders's participant observation of a South Carolina manufacturer of industrial equipment.[81] López-Sanders worked as a low-level employee for several months and witnessed firsthand how racial realism transformed a workplace. In one year, the plant's workforce of more than one thousand workers went from having only two Latinos to being fully one-third Latino.[82]

The laudatory comments López-Sanders heard regarding the racial abilities of Latinos in South Carolina are by now familiar to us. A Latino recruiter for the firm told her:

> The company cares about "the numbers" and wants people that [sic] can be fast and highly productive. The company really likes hiring Hispanics. They know that our people are here to work hard . . . they like that Hispanics are always on time for work and that they are rarely absent . . . you know how . . . if they are going to be absent they call and tell you straightforwardly why they can't make it . . . but they tell you. Hispanics are dependable and reliable and the company likes that.[83]

This firm did not simply prefer Latinos who wandered up to the application desk, or encourage those on the job to refer their Latino friends and family members. López-Sanders observed a willful effort to replace the firm's mostly black temporary workers with what (mostly white male) managers and supervisors called "enclaves" of Latinos in the firm's work teams. They even had a name for this effort: the "Project."

The Project started in the night and swing shifts and moved to the daytime. The plant managers spun-off the recruiting of the new Latinos to a temporary employment agency in order to distance themselves from a process that they knew would involve the hiring of undocumented migrants. Despite the challenge of finding Latinos with what a Latino recruiter called "good papers," López-Sanders found that "the graveyard shift changed from being 60 percent black and 40 percent white to being almost 70 percent Latino, 20 percent black, and 10 percent white over two months."[84] Another team at the plant flipped from 80 percent black to 90 percent Latino through the coordinated efforts of a new (Latino) supervisor hired for this purpose. That supervisor explained:

> They [the employers] told me overnight that I was going to start firing people, most of them black, and that I was going to bring Hispanics to replace them. . . . People didn't like the change at all. They moved the white supervisor that was in my department to a different area . . . I think . . . what happens is that the company is in the red and I think someone wanted to outsmart everyone else and decided to bring Hispanics because they know that Hispanics work hard for small pay.[85]

And so that is what he did, and the only difficulty proved to be that the staffing agency had trouble supplying enough Latinos to put on the job.

To get rid of the black temporary workers, the firm simply had to tell the recruiting agency that each temporary black worker was not needed anymore. Getting rid of permanent black workers was a bit more challenging. Strategies to motivate them to quit included speeding up the assembly line and adding tasks to existing job descriptions. Managers would also break up social groups at the plant by transferring workers to different parts of the plant, or they would add Latinos to the existing social groups of blacks. They also assigned black workers to the more unpleasant jobs at the plant, such as tasks involving a concentrated alcohol that emitted fumes that would make workers so sick they would have to leave work.[86] In short, the company engaged in a wholesale effort to change the racial composition of its workforce following perceptions of varying racial abilities.

Meatpacking: An Industry Transformed

While we have studies of employer racial preferences in particular cities and López-Sanders's in-depth study of a particular workplace, a fuller picture can emerge from a systematic study of racial realism in a particular industry. The closest thing we have to that is a series of studies of meatpacking, an industry that touches most Americans every day. What these studies find is worth exploring in some depth, because nowhere else is low-skilled racial realism on clearer display—as well as the exploitation of the "preferred" groups, who in this sector are mostly Latino immigrants.

Meatpacking has seen a massive and sometimes grisly transformation since the 1980s. The focus industry of Upton Sinclair's muckraking classic, it finds itself once again under ignominious scrutiny in the present day, for it has featured in the provocative films *Fast Food Nation* and *Food, Inc.* But since Sinclair's time, the meatpacking process has changed. It has become a hyper-rationalized, Fordist operation, with massive, vertically integrated corporations frantically butchering animals at razor-thin profit margins. Inversely proportional to the growing technical sophistication of the production process is the complexity of the work involved, which has been relentlessly de-skilled. Meatpacking today is intense, dangerous, repetitious, and poorly compensated work.[87]

To better understand the transformation, we can divide the history of this industry into three phases. Phase I was characterized by a lack of concern for worker rights and opportunities. As the large meatpacking companies developed in big cities such as Chicago near the end of the 1800s, they sought cheap workers for their dirty, dangerous, and difficult jobs, and they were happy to hire both African-Americans and immigrants in order to maximize profits. In 1929, only 57 percent of the meatpacking workforce in Chicago was native-born, and 30 percent of those were black. Poland, Lithuania, and Mexico sent the largest contingents of immigrant workers, constituting 12, 8, and 6 percent, respectively, of the local industry workforce.[88]

Many of these workers were desperate—and happy to have jobs. Sinclair captured the excitement of an immigrant through the experience of his fictional character Jurgis on his first day on the job:

It was a sweltering day in July, and the place ran with streaming hot blood—one waded in it on the floor. The stench was almost overpowering, but to Jurgis it was nothing. His whole soul was dancing with joy—he was at work at last! All day long he was figuring to himself. He was paid the fabulous sum of seventeen and a half cents an hour; and as it proved a rush day and he worked until nearly seven o'clock in the evening, he went home to the family with the tidings that he had earned more than a dollar and a half in a single day![89]

Eventually, however, honeymoons of the sort experienced by desperate workers like Jurgis ended, and attitudes soured. Pay was low and work conditions awful, but there was not much to be done about it: strikes failed in 1894, 1904, and 1921–922.[90]

Phase II in the history of meatpacking began with the passage of the National Labor Relations Act in 1935, which provided organized labor with new opportunities. The United Packinghouse Workers of America quickly became a force.[91] Wages and work conditions improved markedly—by 1960, meatpacking paid 15 percent more than the manufacturing average,[92] and work safety actually moved to a point above the average of other manufacturing jobs. These were the golden years of the industry. Meatpacking was a unionized industry, often located in cities, offering solid pay and benefits to a very diverse workforce.

Phase III began around the 1980s and continues to the present day. There were several changes. First, just a few firms (e.g., Tyson, Cargill, and ConAgra) have come to dominate the industry. Second, these firms have built mammoth new facilities in the Midwest and South. There are now sixteen different facilities that can each process one million animals annually. These plants are modern and mechanized, but there are limits to automation: the variability in the shapes of animal carcasses requires manual labor for cutting. Third, these firms and their remaining competitors have mostly eliminated unions and slashed wages.

Firms did this in the 1980s by establishing new, non-unionized plants, or by taking over unionized plants and simply getting rid of the unions. For example, IBP (now owned by Tyson) bought an Oscar Mayer plant in Iowa and reopened it with wages cut by almost $4 an hour, down to $5.80 an hour. An Arkansas City, Kansas plant shut down operations and reopened 9 months later—with wages reduced from $11 per hour to $5.[93] Other companies struggling to keep up joined the race to the bottom. The meatpacking wage as a percentage of other manufacturing wages fell from 115 percent (meatpacking used to be a high-paid job) to 82 percent.[94] Wages are so low that some full-time workers at meatpacking plants became eligible for Medicaid, the federal free-lunch program, and other forms of public assistance.[95]

A fourth characteristic of this most recent phase is that line speeds doubled and injuries increased—by the 1980s, about one third of all workers were being injured each year in what has come to be called the nation's "most dangerous industry."[96] Studies show that few workers can last very long under these conditions, and some turnover rates average 100 percent annually.[97] A sobering feature story on Tyson Foods in otherwise business-friendly *Fortune* magazine explained, "Put simply, Tyson is struggling to find enough cheap, unskilled labor to staff its processing plants. Turnover is extremely high, between 40% and 100% annually, meaning each of the company's 83 plants needs between 400 and 2,000 new workers every year." Tyson company COO Greg Lee told the magazine, "Finding enough labor is a problem the entire industry is facing."[98]

Fortune's analysis of the work in a Tyson chicken plant gave insight into why injury and turnover rates were so high. Tasks involved repetitive movements (workers sometimes perform the same motion 30,000 times a shift), and knife-wielding employees work perilously close together as they struggle to keep up with the production line. Injury statistics from the Occupational Safety and Health Administration (OSHA) for 2000 reveal that one out of every seven poultry workers was injured on the job, more than double the average for all private industries. Poultry workers were also fourteen times more likely to suffer debilitating injuries stemming from repetitive trauma—like "claw hand" (in which the fingers lock in a curled position) and ganglionic cysts (fluid deposits under the skin).[99] A Government Accountability Office report on meatpacking in 2005 found that despite improvement, the industry still had among the highest injury rates of any industry. In addition to illness caused by chemical exposure, "the most common injuries are cuts, strains, cumulative trauma caused by repetitive cutting motions, and injuries sustained from falls. More serious injuries, such as fractures and amputation, also occur . . . a worker died when he attempted to replace his knife in the scabbard hanging from his belt, missed the opening, and pushed the knife into his leg, severing his femoral artery."[100]

The fifth characteristic of Phase III in American meatpacking is a concerted move to Latino and/or immigrant labor.[101] The transition began in the 1980s, and by the end of the century it was well underway. Different studies give different figures, but the direction is everywhere the same. A 1998 federal report on the changes in and local impacts of the meatpacking industry in Iowa and Nebraska, undertaken at the request of Senators Robert Kerrey (D-NE) and Tom Harkin (D-IA), found that 25 percent of the 36,000 workers in those states' meatpacking industries were undocumented.[102] Tyson Foods said its workforce was already 40 percent Latino in the late 1990s (the union estimated the figure to be 60 percent).[103] Scholarly estimates claimed that by the early 2000s, Latin American immigrants made up about 70 percent of this workforce, and up to 50 percent of these were undocumented.[104]

Local statistics paint an even more dramatic picture. Benton County (in Arkansas) had a 9 percent Latino population in 2000, but the chicken plant was 72.5 percent Latino, and Hall County (Georgia) was 20 percent Latino, but the chicken plant was 84 percent Latino. This pattern has been repeated in other areas of the country and for other meat products. For example, McDonald County in Missouri, which hosts Simmons and Hudson Foods plants, experienced a 2107 percent growth in its Latino population between 1990 and 2000. Moniteau County, Missouri, home to a Cargill food processing plant, saw 846% growth in its Latino population.[105]

Studies of the racial-realist strategy of management in these workplaces provide us with the employers' perspective on why Latinos have become so important to the industry. One employer reported that his workforce had changed from 15 percent Latino to 33 percent Latino in six months (while blacks declined from 65 percent of the workforce to 49 percent in the same period). He explained, "They have proven to be such good, stable workers that we've been recruiting more Hispanics to stabilize the workforce." Like employers in other industries, U.S., meatpackers saw vigorous growth in the Latino or Asian segments of their workforces and also praised these groups—especially recent immigrants—while stereotyping blacks and whites negatively:

> "Koreans and Hispanics are very hard workers—but Koreans are probably the best."
> "Hispanics rate best in absenteeism and overall performance."
> "The Mexicans work every day every hour they can—we used to have a problem filling orders, but not since we got the Mexicans."
> "Vietnamese and Spanish start working hard when they first get here, but after a while they must get Americanized, because their productivity and attendance fall off."
> "Hispanics and Asians are more reliable and harder workers than blacks or whites."
> "Koreans have an excellent work ethic. We have problems with blacks, 30–40 percent do not care if they work or not."
> "A lot of blacks don't work as hard as Hispanics, but the legalized Hispanics tend to not work as well as when you could hire illegals."

"Hispanics have far better attendance and performance and attitude. Blacks and whites here about the same."

"I'll take Hispanics any day over a black or white. They don't give you no trash, just get after it. Blacks are the last pick."[106]

This marked preference for Latino workers does not necessarily translate into good treatment of these workers on the job. Some data suggest quite the opposite: a study in 2004 found that Mexican migrants were 80 percent more likely to die on the job than American-born workers.[107]

Many meatpacking plants actively recruit Latino and immigrant workers, sometimes venturing far from the local labor market to do so. Some use recruiters who travel—especially to southern Texas and northern Mexico—to seek out potential hires.[108] Meatpackers may also take advantage of federal government programs, such as one giving federal funding to refugee service providers who can provide fulltime employment to refugees. Not all recruiting methods are specifically directed toward shaping an immigrant-heavy workforce, however. To find workers, some meatpackers sign on to federal programs such as the one created by the Job Training Partnership Act (where federal funds pay for half of basic wages for disadvantaged workers during training periods) or the Targeted Jobs Tax Credit program (which allows employers to claim tax credits of up to 40 percent of an employee's first $6,000 when they hire individuals from certain categories, such as veterans, welfare or food stamp recipients, and exfelons).[109]

Perhaps more so than other industries, meatpackers have exploited gender and immigrant status, particularly the lack of documents, in their workforce. Donald Stull, a leading expert on the industry, told *Fortune* magazine, "The industry has targeted women and immigrants because they are less likely to organize, less able to find alternative [employment], and more easily manipulated."[110] In what may be a rare convergence of opinion, business magazine *Fortune*'s report is very similar to a report on the industry by Human Rights Watch, an international organization dedicated to holding "oppressors accountable for their crimes."[111] For example, one undocumented woman at the Shelbyville plant told the business magazine, "Supervisors knew who had green cards and who didn't. . . . And they used it against us. If we didn't do what they wanted, they would threaten to call immigration."[112] The human rights NGO made almost the identical claim when it quoted a Tyson poultry worker in Arkansas, who complained, "They have us under threat [*bajo amenaza*] all the time. They know most of us are undocumented—probably two-thirds. All they care about is getting bodies into the plant. My supervisor said they say they'll call the INS if we make trouble."[113] Similarly, a Nebraska Beef employee told the NGO, "[The top personnel manager] is a Mexican. He knows who is undocumented and who isn't, and he holds that over us. He says 'I know how you got here,' and 'I know you don't have papers but I'm going to take care of you.' That just makes people afraid of crossing him."[114]

A memo the company was forced to release in a Racketeer Influence and Corrupt Organizations Act lawsuit (see below) suggested that Tyson was aware of the Latino workforce being afraid to complain or report injuries. Timothy McCoy, the vice president of labor relations, authored a memo that (in the words of *Fortune*) "explicitly encouraged the hiring of Hispanics because their lack of understanding of English and of their legal rights meant they were less likely to take any action, legal or otherwise, against the company."[115]

Do Low-Skilled Workers Really Vary in Their Racial Abilities?

Are there any data to support employer perceptions of the superior racial abilities of Latinos and Asians, or of immigrants? Though there are no studies specifically comparing the work habits of different groups,[116] there are reasons to believe that black work behavior may have unique patterns. The economist Glenn Loury, for example, has suggested that negative stereotypes of black workers may be self-confirming. Operating under limited information about a black worker, an employer might well fall back on racial stereotypes. If that employer already expects to see a lack of effort in black workers, he or she may be more aware of mistakes made by blacks than by other races, and consequently may be "less willing to extend the benefit of the doubt to blacks during the training period." At the same time, a black worker's awareness that this logic is common among employers might lead to him or her to make *less* rather than more effort: "Knowing they are likely to be fired if they make a few mistakes, an outcome over which they cannot exert full control, more blacks than other workers may find that exerting high effort during the training period is, on net, a losing proposition for them."[117]

In addition, there are reasons why we might expect immigrants of any race or ethnicity to display the abilities that employers claim to perceive in them. Immigration scholars have long noted that immigrants often see their work in the U.S. as temporary, and therefore see the work conditions as temporary as well, part of the trade off for the higher wages that they earn in the U.S. when compared with their homelands.[118] Thus, Latino immigrants and African-Americans may bring two very different attitudes to the workplace. In the words of legal scholars Jennifer Gordon and Robin A. Lenhardt, the Latino immigrants have an "incentive to do whatever the boss asks in order to achieve greater economic and social status outside this country," whereas the African-Americans have a "desire to control work pace and conditions in order to ensure a modicum of dignity and respect within the United States."[119]

Observations or Just Perceptions? Evidence of the Racial Abilities of Low-Skilled Workers

Some social science theory offers explanations for why different categories of workers might bring different abilities to the job, but is there objective evidence for these differences? It is not easy to find rigorous attempts to determine whether or not there are actual differences between the abilities of blacks, whites, Latinos, and Asians, or between immigrants and natives. Studies of Latinos are rare, explicit comparisons between different nonwhite groups rarer still, and studies of Asian workers almost nonexistent. Still, there are some data that suggest that there may be variations between workers, though some of these variations are the results of the actions of the employers themselves or of the work environment.

In 1986, the National Bureau of Economic Research (NBER) sponsored a volume on *The Black Youth Employment Crisis* that contained some analysis of the workplace behavior of African-Americans. This NBER data, which unfortunately contained no information for other racial groups, showed that a quarter of youths in their survey had been fired, with absenteeism as a primary cause. Though absenteeism was unrelated to worker education or skill level, or to the general characteristics of the workplace, it *was* related to greater perceptions of discrimination. "A youth who believed his boss to be biased," economists Ronald Ferguson and Randall Filer found, "had a 50 percent greater probability of being frequently absent than one who did not hold such a belief," and "the relationship of this variable to tardiness was even stronger."[120] Though Ferguson and Filer note that this pattern could be the result of bad behavior creating strong responses from supervisors, it does not take much imagination to see here the self-confirming pattern described by Loury.

Two decades later, researchers found similar patterns. A study of black, white, and Latino workers controlled for age, income, tenure, and job satisfaction, but nevertheless found a higher rate of absenteeism for blacks than whites, but no differences between Latinos and whites. However, the black absenteeism rate was shaped in part by black workers' perceptions of whether or not their organizations valued diversity.[121] Another study found that black men are more likely to self-report that their productivity is low than are black women, white women, or white men, but this result appears to be driven by the greater likelihood of black workers having "over-the-shoulder" workplace evaluators and more negative workplace evaluations.[122]

William Julius Wilson's Chicago data suggest that the work habits of some low-skilled black workers may indeed differ from those of other workers, but this can be interpreted as a predictable result of the social isolation of African-American neighborhoods.[123] He noted: "The hard and soft skills among inner-city blacks that do not match the current needs of the labor market are products of racially segregated communities, communities that have historically featured widespread social constraints and restricted opportunities."[124]

Sociologist Frank Bean and his colleagues reported findings that offer other insights into employers' racial-realist management strategies and the rankings of low-skilled workers that put whites and blacks on the bottom. Focusing on people in the U.S. who had less than a high school education and were of prime working age, they found that both whites and blacks had higher rates of alcohol use than Latinos since 2001 (see figure 2), and that Latino narcotic use had generally been relatively low since the 1980s. By 2007, it was lower than for blacks and less than half the white rate (see figure 3). In addition, from 1996 to 2008, among men and women aged twenty-two to twenty-eight, 50 percent of Latinos and 41 percent of Asians had been arrested, compared to 60 percent of blacks and 69 percent of whites. Twenty-six percent of the Latinos had been convicted or pled guilty, and 18 percent had been incarcerated. The corresponding rates for Asians were 19 percent and 19 percent. Whites had higher rates in both categories: 43 percent convicted, and 26 percent incarcerated. Black rates were lower than whites' but still higher than Latinos': 32 percent convicted and 27 percent incarcerated (see figure 4).

Immigrants were also less likely to report having only fair or poor health or activity limitations than the native-born. For example, in 2009

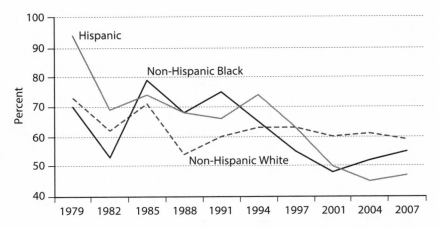

Figure 2. Percent of respondents who reported alcohol use in previous month by race/ethnicity, 1979–2007. Source: Frank D. Bean, Susan K. Brown, James D. Bachmeier, Zoya Gubernskaya, and Christopher D. Smith, "Luxury, Necessity, and Anachronistic Workers: Does the United States Need Unskilled Immigrant Labor?" *American Behavioral Scientist* 56 (2012): 1008–28; additional data supplied by Frank Bean.

9.4 percent of the foreign born with less than a high school education reported they were in fair or poor health, while 15.4 percent of whites and 16.2 percent of blacks gave those responses. In that same year, only 0.6 percent of the foreign born said their health caused limitations on activity, while 4.4 percent of whites and 4.7 percent of blacks reported health-related limitations (see figures 5–6).[125]

Another consideration that may drive employer preferences, but which is not directly related to differing abilities, has to do with wages earned. Are Latinos and Asians—or at least Latino and Asian migrants—actually cheaper to hire? Studies of racial variations in "reservation wage," or the minimum wage at which a person is willing to work, provide mixed evidence. Some studies find that Latinos or immigrants in general are willing to work for less.[126] For example, an employer in the Atlanta construction industry called Latinos "the bargain of the century,"[127] and another said, "Do I want to pay someone $20 [an hour] to do something when I can pay someone else $10 [an hour]? No, I don't have to pay $20 an hour anymore in today's market. . . . Material prices have stayed about the same, but labor has gone down. You know, the Hispanics drove that. I was paying $22 a board for drywall hanging and finishing. Now I pay $10."[128] A review of the research on the effects of immigration on wages

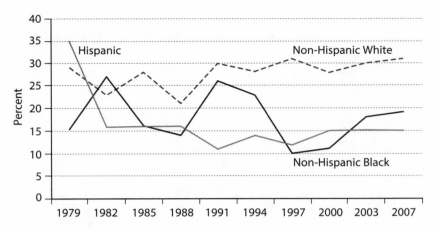

Figure 3. Percent of respondents who reported narcotics use (excluding marijuana) in previous month by race/ethnicity, 1979-2007. Source: Bean et al.; additional data supplied by Frank Bean.

has shown that immigration has reduced the wages of lower-skilled Americans by at least a small amount (about 3 percent).[129]

Other studies, however, find that the employer preferences are attributable more to perceptions of racial or immigrant ability than to dollars and cents, and that Latino wages are in reality not much lower than those earned by other groups. Looking at the four-city Russell Sage Foundation data analyzed by Moss and Tilly, economist Harry Holzer concluded that the preferences were not about wages, because Latino wages were not much lower than black wages. In his reading, employers preferred Latinos to blacks regardless of skill or experience or level of job, but the preference was strongest in low-skilled jobs (both blacks and Latinos found limited opportunities in jobs that required computers or math).[130] In the end, both perceptions of racial abilities and reservation wages are likely to be factors in shaping the racial dynamics in low-skilled jobs, though how large a part each plays in the mix varies depending on the industry and the supply of available workers.

Do African-Americans Seek the Same Jobs as Latinos and Asians?

One difficulty in any effort to assess the validity of perceptions of racial abilities is that for many firms there are few African-American applicants. The reasons for this are complex, but it is certainly the case that some of

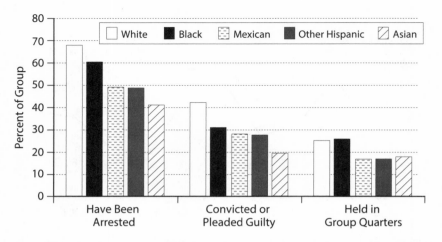

Figure 4. Criminal justice involvement by those with less than a high-school education, ages 22 to 28, 1996 to 2008 (male and female) by ethnicity. Source: Bean et al.; additional data supplied by Frank Bean.

the strategies employers use for recruitment are major obstacles for black workers especially. Recruitment methods are, in fact, both a cause and a consequence of our racially stratified workforce.

In Chicago, Wilson found that over 40 percent of employers did not even advertise their jobs, and when they did, the ads were often placed, selectively, in ethnic newspapers targeting Mexican and also Polish workers.[131] Other researchers have found that employers commonly relied on hiring by referral or "word-of-mouth," a technique that often involves tapping into current workers' personal networks or "social capital."[132] Economist Harry Holzer's analysis of the data for Atlanta, Boston, Detroit, and Los Angeles showed similar recruitment techniques, with between 25 and 30 percent of employees coming through newspaper ads and 35 and 40 percent from referrals by current employees or from other informal sources.[133] A study of the replacement of African-American farm workers in New Jersey with Cambodians found that the younger African-Americans' lack of access to crew leaders' personal networks was a major reason for the transition.[134]

Not surprisingly, word-of-mouth hiring appears to be widespread in meatpacking. Studies show that the meatpackers actively recruit immigrant workers,[135] specifically undocumented workers,[136] and often rely on the current workforce to bring in these new workers. Firms sometimes offer bonuses to workers who bring in family and friends.[137] One study

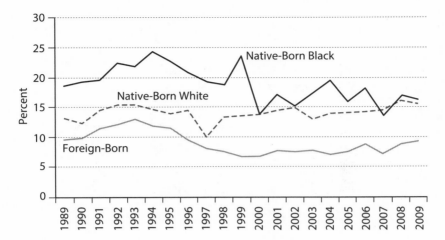

Figure 5. Percent of respondents self-reporting fair or poor health, 1989-2009. Source: Frank D. Bean, Susan K. Brown, James D. Bachmeier, Zoya Gubernskaya, and Christopher D. Smith, "Luxury, Necessity, and Anachronistic Workers: Does the United States Need Unskilled Immigrant Labor?" *American Behavioral Scientist* 56 (2012): 1008–28; additional data supplied by Frank Bean.

found that about 86 percent of the plants examined in Georgia and all of the plants in North Carolina used word-of-mouth hiring (and about 30 percent paid bonuses), with the result that between 80 and 85 percent of all workers were brought in by this means.[138] As one worker explained to Human Rights Watch, "The company pays us a bounty of two hundred dollars for a worker we recommend who stays at least three months."[139] The active nature of these efforts extends up to the federal government, as meatpacking firms lobby for continued access to immigrant Latino labor.[140]

Part of the reason that the referral mechanism is such a critical factor in the relationship between race and employment is that the members of a worker's personal networks typically share the workers' race and ethnicity, and because immigrants typically use referral recruitment very aggressively to find jobs for their relatives or friends who have recently come to the U.S. and desperately need work. African-Americans, on the other hand, do not use their networks in the same ways. In a study of the working African-American poor in southern Michigan, sociologist Sandra Smith found that those with jobs were reluctant to recruit, assist, or recommend unemployed family members and friends because they feared that those they recommended might be poor workers, abuse drugs or

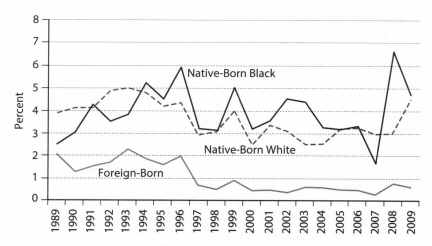

Figure 6. Percent of respondents self-reporting limited activity due to poor
health, 1989-2009. Source: Bean et al.; additional data supplied by Frank Bean.

alcohol, steal on the job, fail to show up for work, and/or generally make
the recommender look bad. Unemployed black workers know this, and
so they tend to make their job pursuit a solitary one—what Smith calls
"defensive individualism."[141] The result is that word-of-mouth hiring is
less likely to generate many black job applicants, even in workplaces with
large numbers of black employees.

Margaret Chin's study of Chinese and Korean garment factories found
that word-of-mouth hiring limited opportunities of black and Puerto
Rican employees in this industry also. The existing workforce, mostly
Asian and Mexican, hoarded information about openings, keeping workers from other groups in the dark about available jobs. For the Chinese
employer, however, this closed system also had the benefit of community
building. As one told Chin: "We hire only Chinese. It is better to work
with people who understand what you are doing and why. We're only here
for the community. . . . I like it when the women bring in new people. It
really helps me so that I don't have to look for new people. I give them
favors. We help each other."[142]

Another factor affecting the desirability of many of these jobs to blacks
and whites is the language spoken in the workplace. Once an employer
hires some Spanish-speaking workers, for example, they tend to bring
in more Spanish-speakers. There then comes a tipping point where employers have to accommodate their Spanish-speaking workforce with
more Spanish-speakers and/or with Spanish-speaking managers. Though

Spanish is widely taught in American schools, employers are obviously most likely to find Latinos to fill these jobs.[143]

Also, as the workplace becomes more Spanish-speaking, black and white workers find themselves increasingly isolated and more often in conflict with the Latino majority. One Los Angeles employer explained, "The people that are not Hispanic don't last very long." Another said, "These people don't feel comfortable working in a minority situation."[144] One employer sounded sympathetic: "When you are talking black-Hispanic differences, the black on the job will tend to feel very isolated because the Hispanic individuals cluster together, they speak their native language, and you or I or a black person would feel outside of that group automatically."[145] Language differences by themselves (without reference to feelings of isolation) can lead to management difficulties: "It's difficult to have a half-Hispanic, half-black housekeeping department, because the Hispanic employees generally speak Spanish to each other, and the black employees don't understand it."[146] It was precisely this dynamic that López-Sanders found employers using intentionally to chase off black workers.

Finally, there is some evidence that white and black American workers may avoid jobs not because of language issues, but just because certain jobs and certain workplaces have become typed or labeled as "Latino jobs," in the same way as certain jobs or workplaces become typed as "women's work." Sociologist Lisa Catanzarite calls these (in a deliberate play on the low-paying "pink collar" women's jobs) "brown collar" jobs. However, it is not easy to isolate the effect of an "immigrant job" stigma from wage effects, for like jobs dominated by women, jobs held primarily by Latinos tend to offer lower wages.[147] If blacks or whites tend to demand higher wages than Latinos or immigrants, then it is not likely that they will take jobs in these "Latino" categories even if offered them, and this will cause such jobs to shift ever more toward an immigrant workforce. Or the black or white worker might take the job, but then act in ways that show a lack of concern for keeping the job—adding more evidence to employer perceptions of whites' and blacks' lower racial abilities.

Is Racial Realism in Low-Skilled Employment Illegal?

In 1964, Congress passed Title VII with a view to preventing widespread employer preferences for whites over nonwhites—and specifically, African-Americans—from affecting hiring decisions. Lawmakers did not

consider employers' preferences for one nonwhite group over other nonwhite groups, or even over whites, and immigration was not even part
of the debate. So, are employer preferences that are based on the perceived superior abilities of Latinos, or Asians, or immigrants, illegal? And
if they are illegal—that is, if courts appear to agree that these practices
are against the law—then why do they seem to be so common?

There are two main types of employer actions here. In the first case,
employers are intentionally—but not transparently—using racial realism,
or in some cases immigrant realism, to manage their workforces. In either
case, employers are perceiving variations in abilities, rather than the effects of signaling. They perceive that blacks are not good workers, that
Latinos work longer and harder, that immigrants are more diligent workers, that the white worker is a "whining piece of shit," etc. Employers also
seem to believe that their racial realism is not supported by the law, because only rarely will they admit in court that this is what they are doing.
This means that despite these practices being intentional and sometimes
quite obvious, any litigants would have the challenge of proving that employers were using a racial-realist management strategy. This is different
from the racial realism described in Chapters 2–4, where employers are
relatively open and transparent about the ways they manage perceived
racial abilities and/or racial signaling, and the main legal issue is whether
or not the management strategies are authorized by law.

In the second case, there are employer recruitment practices in operation, whether to further racial or immigrant realist goals or not, that
produce workforces dominated by Latinos, Asians, or immigrants. The
major factor here is word-of-mouth hiring.

Before we assess the relationship between the law on the books and
these employment practices, we first need to remember how the law
works. The law grants us the right to be free from discrimination, but it
is up to *us* to assert that right. If Title VII is to function so as to end the
kinds of discrimination discussed above, a person who believes they have
lost an opportunity to work because of discrimination must go to the
trouble of making a complaint. In other words, an American worker must
be willing to *fight* for the opportunity to earn minimum or near-minimum
wages, sometimes by performing back-breaking toil that might not even
be in compliance with federal or state safety laws, and sometimes alongside immigrants who do not share the worker's language and culture.[148]
Not surprisingly, there are very few people who meet these requirements.
For these reasons, most successful cases are brought on behalf of people

who have lost their jobs, and not on behalf of the countless numbers who never were hired in the first place.[149]

We know the most about why immigrants, who are the most preferred but also the most exploited of workers, do not litigate. An interview study of Latino immigrants in the restaurant industry revealed that neither the legal nor the illegal immigrants in the study were likely to assert their rights. This was not because they did not value legal protections or because they were ignorant of them. Instead, even those with knowledge of American workplace law were still unwilling to complain for at least three reasons. First, not surprisingly, those with illegal status avoided doing anything that employers might consider making trouble. In their view, drawing attention to themselves in any way risked also drawing unwanted attention their undocumented status. Also, and mirroring their employers' beliefs, Latino workers regardless of their legal status described their work ethic as one that valorized hard work and endurance *without complaint*. Finally, as discussed above, these workers saw themselves as only temporary, as visitors to the U.S. They did not identify as dishwashers or other low-status occupations, but rather identified themselves as future business owners and homeowners, either in Mexico or in the U.S.[150]

A study of immigrant workers in the rural South yielded similar results, but with the additional finding that many Asian immigrant workers from Hong Kong or Korea were legal, on H2-B temporary worker visas, and saw their stay in a poultry plant as a short-term step on the road to a green card and greater things.[151] These workers, especially Latinos with little education, often valued the relative stability these jobs provide (relative to opportunities in the home country or in agriculture in the U.S.), the paths that they occasionally open to promotion, and the chance for at least some upward mobility.[152]

But even if black, white, or immigrant workers are willing to come forward and make a charge of discrimination (and some have, as I will describe below), theirs would be a very difficult case to make against an employer who denied that any racial or immigrant preference was occurring. One obstacle derives from the way courts have defined "discrimination" in Title VII: neither "disparate treatment" discrimination nor "disparate impact" discrimination provide an easy route to successful litigation, and for "disparate impact" discrimination that route seems to be getting more difficult due to some court decisions. Another problem regards the wording of statutes designed to prevent the hiring and exploitation of illegal immigrants. In all cases, the problem is similar: it is very difficult to *prove* a legal violation by employers acting on their perceptions of racial abilities among low-skilled workers.

The Difficulty of Proving "Disparate Treatment" Discrimination

The simplest category of discrimination claim is called a claim of "disparate treatment." This is the legal category for claims that an employer intentionally treated an individual or group differently because of race, religion, national origin, or sex. That seems straightforward enough, but complications arise when it comes to proving an employer's discriminatory *intent*, which is necessary if the court is to find that disparate treatment discrimination has taken place. Finding intent is difficult because all workplaces are basically giant selection machines. Employers make choices all the time regarding whom to hire, fire, promote, or assign to different duties—there are losers in just about every decision made—and judges are careful to avoid classifying as discrimination a work assignment that just happens to end badly for someone.

So how do judges know when there is discriminatory intent? Title VII itself says almost nothing about this. Either Congress thought that instances of discriminatory intent would be so blindingly obvious that no definition was needed, or they chose to avoid opening a can of worms that might increase opposition to the bill. But the bottom line was that judges had to make up the missing definition.

A classic case that outlined the legal rules for disparate treatment was *Slack v. Havens*.[153] The case involved a mixed-race crew at a San Diego designer and manufacturer of water desalinization products. In January of 1968, a supervisor asked some black women employees to do some difficult and dangerous clean-up work, but excused a white female member of the crew from these unpleasant duties. When the black women protested, the supervisor said they must do the work "or else," and told them, "Colored people should stay in their places." The supervisor also made a racial abilities argument, saying, "Colored folks are hired to clean because they clean better." The black women were eventually fired, but they fought back in court—and won. Major factors in their victory were the disparate treatment of white and black workers, and the supervisor's statements.[154]

These kinds of statements constitute the best evidence of intent, but they are very hard to come by. It is now very rare for an employer to be as impolitic as this supervisor and to actually make racist statements at the same time as the restriction of opportunities is taking place.

Another litigation route for a disparate treatment claim presents its own, somewhat different challenges. In this scenario, a litigant has to make a *prima facie*, or "at first look," case for discrimination. But making a prima facie case is not so easy. The first step requires showing four different things: that the plaintiff is a member of a protected class (e.g., racial group); that an employer limited her or his opportunities; that the plaintiff was treated differently from persons of a different race; and that there is some causal connection between the different treatment and the racial background of the litigant. Assuming this can be done, the employer can then give a nondiscriminatory reason for the alleged denial of opportunity, and then the plaintiff must "rebut" that explanation, showing that it was a mere pretext for discrimination.[155]

Prima facie cases can be evaded, sometimes without difficulty. The employer simply has to emphasize that the skill that he or she is looking for was the basis of the selection process—even if in the real world that employer simply uses race and stereotypes based on race.[156] Employers also could argue that they have mostly (or only) Latino and/or Asian workers because blacks and whites are not interested in the jobs that the employer has to offer. In the early years of Title VII, courts were more likely to allow the "lack of interest" defense in sex discrimination cases than race discrimination cases, but in the late 1970s this began to change.[157] Whereas during the 1967–1977 period those charging discrimination were able to win against employers who used the lack-of-interest defense 86 percent of the time, this win rate declined to 40 percent in the 1978 to 1989 period.[158] "Lack-of-interest" has the potential to be a particularly effective defense for racial-realist employers because, as we have seen, African-Americans are not likely to apply for jobs where foreign languages are spoken, or where they have little knowledge of openings, or because they live too far away.[159]

Sometimes, the Equal Employment Opportunity Commission (EEOC) will sue on behalf of workers, thus diminishing the "David vs. Goliath" feel of much individual discrimination litigation. The EEOC has had some significant losses in courts, as will be described below, but since 2008, it has, despite daunting challenges, initiated and won some cases where employers replaced current workers with Latinos. In a 2011 case, the EEOC sued an Indianapolis hotel operator that was implementing strategies similar to what López-Sanders described as the "Project" at a Carolina manufacturer. This hotel firm avoided hiring black housekeeping applicants, gave fewer hours and lower pay to black housekeepers, and fired blacks who complained about this treatment. One general manager said she wanted to bring in "Mexicans" who would clean better while complaining less. In its defense, the hotel company argued that "race discrimination under Title VII does not apply to discrimination against minorities in favor of other minorities," pointing to a federal case as a precedent.[160] An Indiana district court, in an opinion written by George W. Bush appointee William T. Lawrence, sided with the EEOC, finding that most courts viewed replacing one minority with another as a violation of the law.[161]

Other recent and successful EEOC actions include a 2010 ruling that a case involving a freight management company that preferred Latino workers over non-Latino workers at a North Carolina Wal-Mart distribution facility could go forward;[162] a temporary staffing agency's 2010 settlement requiring payment of $585,000 after the EEOC charged that the agency preferred Latinos over black workers at a Memphis, Tennessee warehouse;[163] a 2009 settlement in which a Pinehurst, North Carolina condominium support-services company that had fired six black, non-Latino housekeepers and replaced them with Latinos agreed to pay $44,700 in remedial relief;[164] and a 2008 settlement of $40,000 after a Charlotte, North Carolina supermarket chain terminated white and black workers and replaced them with Latinos after it began managing a new facility.[165] Thus, where the EEOC has chosen to act, it has found some success in recent years, enforcing the classical-liberal Title VII to halt racial-realist or immigrant-realist employment practices.

And what of the Latino immigrants themselves, including those who are undocumented? Can disparate treatment discrimination law help them? On the one hand, it would appear obvious that it can not, because employers are discriminating *in their favor* over blacks and sometimes whites. But even at the height of Jim Crow, employers preferred African-Americans for certain jobs. These were so-called "black jobs" (or labeled with a slur) that employers saw as more appropriate for blacks than for whites, and Congress sought to make this practice illegal. Specifically, Title VII made it illegal for an employer to "limit, segregate, or classify his employees or applicants for employment in any way which would deprive or tend to deprive any individual of employment opportunities or otherwise adversely affect his status as an employee, because of such individual's race, color, religion, sex, or national origin."[166] The EEOC

Compliance Manual elaborates: "Race or color should not affect work assignments, performance evaluations, training opportunities, discipline, or any other term or condition of employment. . . ."[167] When Latinos and Asians are segregated into dirty, dangerous, and/or difficult jobs, they would seem to have strong grounds for litigation.

Though this kind of segregation and discriminatory work assignments are ubiquitous in the U.S., legal scholar Leticia Saucedo has shown the magnitude of the difficulties encountered in attempting to pursue this kind of litigation.[168] The root of the problems lies in the fact that Latinos *choose* to take these jobs. Employers can therefore use the "market defense," arguing that it is not discrimination to pay the market rate for a job, and that if they are hiring a lot of Latinos for particular jobs, it is because these are the individuals who are taking what the employer is offering.

Employers have made similar arguments in sex discrimination cases. They have been able to say, in essence, "Yes, women are in the bad jobs in my workplace, but they choose that work under the terms I offer. Why should I change?"[169] Thus, if a Latino complained that he or she was relegated to the worst jobs in the meatpacking plant, along with all of the other Latinos, the employer could attempt to show that Latinos were by and large very happy to take those jobs.

In short, the law of disparate treatment discrimination would seem to prohibit racial realism as practiced across the United States. Some recent cases led by the EEOC have shown that when people get some help from the government, they can close the gap between the law and employer practice. But it is not cost effective for individuals to litigate for access to low-skilled jobs, and the judge-made legal rules for invoking the law limit its usefulness even to those whom employers deem lacking in ability because of their race or national origin. Finally, the Latino and immigrant workers who may face disparate treatment in their placement, job segregation, working conditions, and low wages also have difficulties using Title VII.

"Disparate Impact" Discrimination: New Rules Enabling Racial and Immigrant Realism?

There is another major kind of Title VII discrimination claim that rests on a very different definition of discrimination. It is possible to argue that an employer might engage in practices that, although not designed or not intended to exclude some categories of workers, nevertheless have that impact. In other words, an employer might be totally innocent of race-based, stereotypical thinking, but still be outside the law.

The Supreme Court's 1971 opinion in *Griggs v. Duke Power*, discussed in Chapter 1, is the legal basis of this "disparate impact" approach to discrimination law.[170] In that case, the Court argued that employee selection practices like an intelligence test can function as "built-in headwinds" that affect black workers much more than white workers. The case established a new rule: business practices that have even an unintentional disparate impact on protected groups are prohibited unless the employer can show that the practice measures the minimum qualifications necessary for the job.[171]

Though most of the racial realism explored in this chapter would fall under "disparate treatment" because it is based on employer perceptions of racial abilities and thus intentional discrimination, the widespread practice of "word-of-mouth" or "referral" hiring in many smaller firms, such as the garment factories run by Korean and Chinese entrepreneurs, and the meatpackers who look to hire Latinos, would seem to be "disparate impact discrimination" because word-of-mouth hiring tends to reproduce the racial makeup of the workforce. Precedents are not hard to find: in cases that involved white and black workers, several courts have ruled that word-of-mouth hiring is a violation of Title VII.[172] As one court stated, "In the context of a predominantly white work force," word-of-mouth hiring and similar practices "serve to freeze the effects of past discrimination."[173]

Because this practice so *obviously* hurts nonwhites, some courts have even equated the practice with old-fashioned disparate treatment discrimination. That is, relying on your white workers to bring in their white friends as future employees is tantamount to the employer saying that he or she simply does not like to hire black people because they are black. As one court put it, "With an almost completely white work force, it is hardly surprising that such a system of recruitment produced few, if any, black applicants. As might be expected, existing white employees tended to recommend their own relatives, friends and neighbors, who would likely be of the same race."[174] In other words, an employer's intention to avoid black workers, whether due to a belief in racial abilities or simple racial animus, sometimes can be inferred from word-of-mouth recruitment.

Even today, EEOC guidelines warn employers to avoid word-of-mouth hiring. These guidelines state, "While word-of-mouth recruiting in a racially diverse workforce can be an effective way to promote diversity, the same method of recruiting in a non-diverse workforce is a barrier to equal employment opportunity if it does not create applicant pools that reflect the diversity in the qualified labor market."[175] Similarly, the EEOC's "Q and A" document counsels employers to avoid word-of-mouth hiring: "Unless the workforce is racially and ethnically diverse, exclusive reliance on word-of-mouth should be avoided because it is likely to create a barrier to equal employment opportunity for racial or ethnic groups that are not already represented in the employer's workforce."[176] These directives are especially important for African-Americans because, as described above, this most disadvantaged group does not aggressively use an employers' reliance on word-of-mouth hiring to bring in their family and friends.

Federal courts, however, are beginning to restrict or at least send ambiguous messages about the legality of word-of-mouth hiring, and in some key cases that have involved Latino and Asian workforces, they have sided with employers. This is part of a general trend of courts siding with employers on disparate impact cases, which now account for a small percentage of the discrimination caseload.[177]

The highest-profile case that illustrates the trend to favor employers involved the Wards Cove Packing Company, an Alaskan salmon cannery that had a race-segregated workforce, with nonwhites—mostly Filipinos and Native Alaskans—working in canning, and whites in the better (noncannery) jobs. The company appeared to want nonwhite workers in the canning jobs: it hired Alaskans who lived near the canning sites, and used a predominately Filipino union, Local 37 of the International Longshoremen's and Warehousemen's union, to fill the positions. The nonwhite workers brought a disparate impact suit, saying that nepotism, separate hiring channels, subjective hiring practices, and a policy of not promoting from within prevented them from moving out of the cannery jobs. In a 5-4 decision, the Supreme Court ruled that the noncannery jobs were skilled, and required accessing a national labor market, and that there could be no assumption that the nonwhites had the appropriate skills for the noncannery jobs, or even wanted them. Moreover, the Court ruled that the challengers had to identify the specific practice that limited their opportunity, and that employers could defend themselves by simply showing that the offending practices furthered legitimate goals, rather than that the practices were necessary.[178]

Many in Congress were outraged at what they saw as the Court's brazen attack on a key component of discrimination law and responded, after a George H. W. Bush veto of an earlier effort, with the Civil Rights Act of 1991. This law attempted to restate disparate impact theory.[179] But other federal court decisions continued the trend of allowing employer practices that led to racially imbalanced workforces, making room for racial or immigrant realism in low-skilled jobs. All an employer had to do was hire some immigrant Latinos or Asians, and then let word-of-mouth hiring work its magic to bring in the desired abilities.

For example, in *EEOC v. Chicago Miniature Lamp Works*,[180] the EEOC lost its case against a small manufacturer of light bulbs on Chicago's North Side. Entry-level jobs were low paying and required little in the way of education, skills, or English ability. Between 1970 and 1981, the percentage of black workers had increased from 4.5 to 6.5 percent (though 36 percent of the city's population was African-American in 1980), while Latinos increased from 40 to 66 percent and Asians from 0 to 16.5 percent. The Latinos and Asians told their friends of the jobs and Miniature Lamp hired on the basis of these employee referrals, never using advertisements and only rarely using the state unemployment referral service. Greatly impressed by the statistical disparities, the district court, in an opinion by Carter appointee Milton Shadur, sided with the EEOC, finding that Miniature Lamp's reliance on word-of-mouth hiring was discriminatory on both disparate treatment and disparate impact grounds.[181]

But on appeal, the Seventh Circuit threw out the EEOC case, arguing that the EEOC's hiring statistics did not properly take into account the effects of commuting distance and the extra desire of immigrants to pursue jobs where English fluency was not required. Significantly, the court, in an opinion written by Johnson appointee Walter J. Cummings (known for usually liberal opinions),[182] also made a distinction that was new in discrimination law. Though African-Americans and whites were excluded from the networks, the court ruled that Miniature Lamp only *passively* relied on the word-of-mouth recruitment that the mostly Latino and Asian employees used. There was no explicit encouragement or direction from the employers. This countered any disparate treatment claim, the court argued, because a passive reliance on word-of-mouth hiring involved "no affirmative act by Miniature," and "drawing the inference of intent from 'non-action' is necessarily more difficult than drawing the inference of intent from particular actions."[183]

The court dismissed the disparate impact claim with similar reasoning, denying that *any* employment practice had actually been taken: "It is uncontested that Miniature passively waited for applicants who typically learned of opportunities from current Miniature employees. . . . The practices here are undertaken solely by employees. Therefore, disparate impact liability against Miniature must be reversed."[184]

This was a change of great significance. Given the widespread tendency of immigrants to use word-of-mouth hiring to bring in their relatives and friends, employers typically do not have to be "active" to enjoy the benefits of this recruitment method. At the same time, whether an employer asks employees to refer friends and relatives or sits back and waits for them to do so, the result would be the same. Outsiders would not only not get jobs, they would not even know of openings.

Nevertheless, the Seventh Circuit affirmed the new understanding of "passive" employment practices a couple of years later in a case involving a workforce with an even less likely racial make-up. Also a Chicago case, *EEOC v. Consolidated Service Systems*[185] involved a Korean-American-owned custodial service company. Consolidated hired a lot of Koreans. Though less than 1 percent of the Cook County workforce was Korean and barely more than 1 percent of those worked in the janitor business, in the first four years the Korean-American owner was in control of Consolidated, 73 percent of applicants for jobs and 81 percent of the people hired were Korean. Less than twenty percent of the workforce was what the court referred to only as "non-Korean." Consolidated's owner relied almost totally on word-of-mouth hiring. Though he once advertised jobs in the *Chicago Tribune*, the *Chicago Sun-Times*, and in a Korean newspaper, he never hired anyone as a result of these ads.

Could a company hire 80 percent of its workforce from one national-origin group and rely on word-of-mouth hiring to bring in new workers, and not be found to be discriminating? The answer is yes. The court ruled that the disparate impact charge was faulty because the statistics did not consider the relevant labor pool. In the court's view, that pool should have included only qualified persons interested in working for Consolidated. In making this ruling, the court did not consider the employment patterns I have described above; namely, that individuals typically avoid jobs that provide little intrinsic pleasure and that become dominated by a particular national origin or racial group, and that those who hold these jobs may hoard information so that outsiders do not even know of openings. The disparate treatment claim failed because the EEOC failed to show discriminatory intent.[186]

On appeal, the Seventh Circuit, in an opinion written by Reagan appointee and University of Chicago law professor Richard Posner, showed great sympathy for Consolidated, and the EEOC lost again. As in the Miniature Lamp case, the court ruled that Consolidated's approach was passive and thus acceptable. In fact, it was smart business, because it brought in good workers and was "the cheapest method of recruitment."[187] Because the EEOC (for unknown reasons) gave up on the disparate impact argument, Posner could ignore the question of whether or not the recruitment method was a business necessity and focus on the difficult task of showing discriminatory intent. The EEOC argued that Consolidated admitted discriminatory intent when its expert witness, sociologist William Liu, explained that it was "natural" for a recent immigrant from Korea to hire other Koreans, since they share a common culture, and that this would produce a disproportionately Korean workforce.[188] Posner rejected the notion that this was discrimination: "Well, of course. People who share a common culture tend to work together as well as marry together and socialize together. That is not evidence of illegal discrimination."[189]

While it is not clear whether the "non-Koreans" that Consolidated hired included African-Americans, case law suggests only that employers need to hire some token percentage of African-Americans—maybe even just one. Posner cautioned in *Consolidated* that if the firm had hired no "non-Koreans," then "this would support, perhaps decisively, an inference of discrimination."[190] But his ruling emphasized that national-origin or racial imbalances in a workforce—even imbalances as statistically improbable as Consolidated's—suggest nothing about intent, especially when the recruitment technique is cheap, efficient, and effective.

Because it is so hard to imagine rulings of this sort being handed down in a case where the beneficiaries of the employment practices are white, these cases appear to be motivated by a desire to enable modern-day racial realism, and not intended simply to create more room for employer discretion. The decisions would have almost certainly been more controversial, or not made at all, if the new ruling about "passive" reliance on word-of-mouth hiring was benefiting whites at the expense of blacks.[191] It is hard to imagine that Judge Posner would have said "of course" to an expert witness who said that it is "natural" for whites to share a culture and want to hang out with fellow whites. In a telling passage, Posner used vivid prose to emphasize the plight not of any business owner, but specifically of *immigrant* entrepreneurs:

> In a nation of immigrants, this must be reckoned an ominous case despite its outcome. The United States has many recent immigrants, and today as historically they tend to cluster in their own communities, united by ties of language, culture, and background. Often they form small businesses composed largely of relatives, friends, and other members of their community, and they obtain new employees by word of mouth. These small businesses—grocery stores,

furniture stores, cleaning services, restaurants, gas stations—have been for many immigrant groups, and continue to be, the first rung on the ladder of American success. Derided as clannish, resented for their ambition and hard work, hated or despised for their otherness, recent immigrants are frequent targets of discrimination, some of it violent. It would be a bitter irony if the federal agency dedicated to enforcing the antidiscrimination laws succeeded in using those laws to kick these people off the ladder by compelling them to institute costly systems of hiring.[192]

What is important about this forceful opinion from a leading jurist is that though the argument carves out a space for nonwhite employers to use recruitment techniques that exclude particular races,[193] it may have created a precedent that any employer could use. There is nothing in the legal reasoning itself that would limit its application to nonwhite employers. In this area, then, the courts are removing the gap between law on the books and employment practice by changing the law.

Firms that *only* hire from word-of-mouth hiring actually may be safer from litigation than are firms that are more open to applicants.[194] In a more recent case, the EEOC was able to prevail against a firm that made the legal mistake of advertising its openings—if only in a limited way. The case began in 2005 when African-American Jeanette Wilkins, a laid-off custodian, found a help-wanted ad placed in *Hoy*, a Spanish-language newspaper. The ad was placed by the aptly-named Scrub, Incorporated, a Chicago company providing janitorial services to large institutions, including major hotels and the massive O'Hare International Airport.[195]

Wilkins went to Scrub's offices to fill out an application. There she witnessed a Latina candidate also filling out an application, and saw that the firm immediately asked that applicant to stay for an interview. Yet Scrub told Wilkins she needed a birth certificate to apply. When she returned with her certificate, a Scrub representative told her that applications were no longer available. Wilkins submitted a resume instead and was told that the firm would call her if interested. Wilkins had told a friend, also African-American, about the jobs, and that friend had a similar experience, while watching five Latinos receive immediate interviews. Rather than simply looking for another custodial job, Wilkins complained to the EEOC, and the EEOC pulled off a significant victory.[196]

Scrub signed a consent decree agreeing to pay $3 million to approximately 550 black applicants who had failed to find employment with Scrub because, according to the EEOC, the company conducted its recruitment through media aimed at Latinos and immigrants from Eastern Europe and also used subjective decision-making that disparately impacted blacks. The company also agreed to hire some of the rejected applicants and to initiate "active recruitment" of African-American employees.[197]

In summary, though there has been a recent EEOC victory, some creative judging has tailored disparate impact discrimination law in such a way as to allow word-of-mouth hiring, even though it tends to reproduce racial disparities in the workforce. The message sent by recent cases is that employers who want to create a Latino and/or immigrant workforce and leverage their racial or immigrant abilities should rely totally on word-of-mouth hiring; they simply need to wait for their workers to do the recruiting. Word-of-mouth hiring, particularly when it is used exclusively, is now so insulated from litigation that Tyson Foods, under attack for recruiting undocumented Latinos directly from Latin America (see below), could *defend* its practices by pointing out how much it uses this previously suspect practice. The company boldly declared in a press release: "Virtually all of our immigrant laborers have come to us as a result of word-of-mouth from friends and families, not recruiters."[198]

Other Options? Using Immigration and Racketeering Law to Give Equal Opportunity in the Low-Skilled Workplace

If Title VII is of limited usefulness, are there other laws that might prevent racial realism, or immigrant realism, or that can prevent the segregation and exploitation of immigrants?

Congress passed the Immigration Reform and Control Act (IRCA) in 1986 under a cloud of controversy raised by both its restriction of and openness to immigrants. The law granted amnesty to about three million undocumented workers, made it illegal for an employer to knowingly hire one, and also made it illegal to discriminate on the basis of citizenship status.[199] Congress added this last provision to the law to balance the penalty for hiring undocumented immigrants. The idea was to protect *legal* immigrants as well as Latino Americans (in particular) from discrimination.[200]

New employees were henceforth required to present documents, such as passports, drivers' licenses, and Social Security cards, attesting to their legal presence in the U.S., and to fill out a new form, the I-9, before hiring could take place. Unlike the EEOC, which can only sue employers in court, the Immigration and Naturalization Service, and since 2002, the Department of Homeland Security, have been authorized to enforce the law, which typically involves audits of employers' I-9 forms. IRCA, which affects employers with at least four employees, also has a wider reach than Title VII, which reaches only employers with fifteen or more.[201] Another difference: the law expressly *allows* preference. It states that employers can prefer citizens over immigrants if the two are "equally qualified."[202]

On paper, the law looks like a formidable proscription against hiring undocumented immigrants, but it is difficult to show that IRCA has had much impact. Though armed with the power to perform audits and dramatic workplace raids, the federal government has used these tools only sparingly and inconsistently. Between 1990 and 2003, for example, audits plummeted 77 percent, from about 10,000 to 2200. Warnings and fines have also been inconsistent, but the numbers show a mostly downward trend.[203] Only with the Obama administration did workplace audits increase significantly.[204]

Even with strong enforcement, however, it is very difficult to use IRCA to prevent the hiring and exploitation of illegal immigrants. A case in the early 2000s, focusing on the meatpacking industry, shows why.

The Immigration and Naturalization Service, in conjunction with the Justice Department, constructed what would have seemed to be a blockbuster case against Tyson Foods. The case started in the state of Tennessee, in the mid-1990s, and began with some minor, small-town police probing. The town of Shelbyville was the site of a massive Tyson chicken processing plant—and as a consequence the town had a lot of Latino immigrants. According to William Logue, a Shelbyville police officer, "Prior to 1994, seeing a Hispanic in Shelbyville was like seeing a unicorn."[205] Logue and his partner, Donald Barber, started asking Latino migrant workers about their IDs when they picked them up for speeding or other traffic violations. "Every time we stopped one," Logue told *Fortune* magazine, "it turned out they worked for Tyson."[206] The Latino workers reported that they received the IDs from a small grocery and general store, Los Tres Hermanos, that catered to Tyson's migrant workforce.

The officers reported what they heard to the INS. The INS saw the potential to bring a major immigration law violator to justice, and they sent in an undercover agent who pretended to be a labor broker. He bought fake social security cards and talked with the owner of Los Tres Hermanos, Amador Anchondo-Rascon, about bringing undocumented workers to Shelbyville. Anchondo-Rascon, who had become very wealthy from his various businesses, told the agents that he regularly brought illegal immigrants to the Tyson plant. The INS agent then started an undercover operation, with Anchondo-Rascon as an ally, to bring down Tyson on immigration charges. The investigation would last 2.5 years; allying with the INS was the Department of Agriculture, the Social Security Administration, the U.S. Attorney's Office for the Eastern District of Tennessee, and the local police.

In December of 2001, the Justice Department slammed Tyson with a 36-count indictment. The case was much broader than Shelbyville. The government claimed that Tyson had fifteen plants in nine states that had brought illegal workers into the U.S. since 1994, and that the company was even complicit in arranging for their illegal papers. The highest levels of management were allegedly involved. The managers' goals were money for themselves and profit for the company—gained from low-cost productivity and the migrants' fear of deportation. According to the indictment, Tyson created a corporate culture that made this hiring acceptable, and top executives knew that these workers would endure quickened assembly lines and reduced bathroom breaks without complaint. Assistant Attorney General (and future Secretary of Homeland Security) Michael Chertoff announced that the Department of Justice was "committed to vigorously investigating and prosecuting companies or individuals who exploit immigrants and violate our nation's immigration laws. The bottom line on the corporate balance sheet is no excuse for criminal conduct." INS commissioner James Zigler also talked tough: "Companies, regardless of size, are on notice that INS is committed to enforcing compliance with immigration laws and protecting America's work force."[207] Justifying the effort to bring down the entire company, Assistant U.S. Attorney John MacCoon said, "Headquarters had a million red flags that things were not right."[208]

The government culled the best evidence it could from its trove of 422 undercover audiotapes, 36 videos, and 360,000 subpoenaed documents. These included written minutes from a meeting at Tyson headquarters where managers instructed those attending to "never, ever, admit hiring illegals." Recorded conversations revealed local managers saying they had to hire undocumented workers because headquarters demanded low wages. Recordings also detailed plans for recruitment in Mexico and Guatemala, including arranging transport to the plants; concerns about the potential costs of participation in a voluntary, government-run computerized identification tracking system; payments to smugglers with corporate checks labeled "recruitment"; and requests for guarantees that the illegal workers would stay for at least six months. The recordings also caught a manager from a Missouri plant saying that the verification program that Tyson joined "was a voluntary program that we put in to try and keep INS out of the place."[209]

In addition, two accused managers entered into a plea bargain that gave them lenient sentences (one year probation rather than five years of prison; fines of $2,100 and $3,100 rather than $250,000) in return for testimony. Another accused manager, however, used a gun to take his own life.[210] The surviving managers stated that they did what the company wanted. A former manager maintained that the pay of $7 an hour (with no increases for three years) was too low to attract legal workers.[211]

Tyson headquarters fought back hard, and sacrificed its lower-level managers to save the corporation. Tyson's senior vice president of human resources, Ken Kimbro, stated defiantly, "The prosecutor's claim in this indictment of a corporate conspiracy is absolutely false. In reality, the specific charges are limited to a few managers who were acting outside of company policy at five of our fifty-seven poultry processing plants." He also maintained, "We treat all team members fairly and with dignity. We're very proud of our diverse work force and encourage every team member to express freely any concerns or questions they have."[212]

Bolstering the point that Tyson did not "knowingly" hire illegal immigrants, as IRCA required, the firm's lawyers were able to point out that headquarters chose to use the government tracking system. Tyson's opening statement in trial emphasized participation in the verification program, some instances of voluntary reporting of possible violations at plants, company policy prohibiting the use of undocumented workers, a phasing out of temporary workers supplied by labor recruiters even before the indictment, and a lack of evidence that Tyson headquarters knew of the illegal actions.[213] And that was the real challenge: how could the government prove that headquarters *knew* the law was being broken?

On March 25, 2003, a jury acquitted the corporate executives of any wrongdoing. The judge's instructions to the jury emphasized that the government had to show beyond a reasonable doubt that Tyson headquarters expected managers to recruit and hire undocumented workers. In addition, in consideration of a 1996 amendment to IRCA that provided a new defense to employers, the judge told the jury that if Tyson made a "good faith" effort to prevent hiring illegal workers, and not symbolic actions that are a "sham or pretense giving a false impression of compliance with the law," then it was not liable for the managers' actions. Of course, this is an ambiguous distinction.[214] The jury's forewoman, Barbara Hailey, said after the trial, "I was appalled that the government didn't have more hard evidence than they had. . . . It was so obvious that they needed more evidence."[215] Another juror, Deborah Goldston, said, "We felt like the government didn't properly present its case. There were a lot of loopholes left in it."[216]

A final legal tool for preventing the strategy of using immigrant abilities and, specifically, undocumented immigrant abilities, is the Racketeer Influenced and Corrupt Organizations Act (RICO), part of 1970s Organized Crime Control Act. RICO allows a plaintiff to sue any enterprise engaged in a pattern (at least two acts) of racketeering activity. RICO may sound like an unlikely ally in the quest for equal opportunity, and it was until 1996. In that year, Congress expanded RICO's definition of racketeering to include "any act which is indictable under the Immigration and Nationality Act, section 274 [relating to bringing in and harboring certain aliens], . . . if . . . committed for the purpose of financial gain."[217]

In practice, however, RICO has two problematic weaknesses. Because the racketeering has to include an act indictable under IRCA, litigants still must overcome the obstacle of proving that employers "knowingly" hired undocumented immigrants. Moreover, as courts have interpreted RICO, they have developed rules that require plaintiffs to have suffered some injury, and that injury must have been caused directly by the defendant's actions.[218] In practice, showing that an illegal action caused an injury, as RICO's rules require, has been exceedingly difficult.

The potential for RICO to be a useful legal tool in preventing employer preference for undocumented immigrants is apparent from some court decisions. One case involved a custodial firm that sued a competitor because the competitor's use of poorly paid undocumented immigrant workers enabled it to undercut prices offered by the law-abiding plaintiff's company. A circuit court ruled that the illegal hiring could have allowed the underbidding and thus the injury to the firm that hired fairly, and the case therefore could proceed.[219] In a very different setting, some documented Latino farmworkers in eastern Washington sought to use RICO against their employers, the Zirkle Fruit Company and the Matson Fruit Company, charging that Zirkle and Matson knowingly hire undocumented workers so they could depress wages "below the levels they would otherwise be required to pay if they were unable to hire substantial numbers of illegal immigrants who, due to their economic situation and fear of asserting their rights due to their illegal status, can be easily exploited and who are therefore willing to work for depressed wages."[220] Reversing a lower court, an appeals court supported the case, arguing that the legal workers did not have to prove that their wages were low because of the undocumented workers in order to proceed with the case. They could prove it at trial.[221]

In an actual trial, however, plaintiffs typically have a difficult time proving a violation of RICO. Some documented workers brought a RICO suit against Tyson, claiming that Tyson's use of undocumented workers was part of a scheme to depress wages in Tennessee, Alabama, Indiana, Missouri, Texas, and Virginia. But the case ran into trouble for some of the same reasons that the Justice Department's suit had failed: the courts were not impressed with the evidence against Tyson. They demanded evidence that Tyson *knowingly* hired at least ten undocumented immigrants and were mostly unimpressed with the evidence accumulated. Plaintiffs tried to argue to a skeptical court that Tyson had a "willful blindness policy," which is tantamount to "knowingly hiring," because they purposefully ignored the legal status of their workers. But the plaintiffs also had to show that the legal workers had been injured by that policy—that is, had their wages depressed. This was also very difficult to establish, and the case stalled.[222]

Racial realism in low-skilled employment appears to be alive and well. It appears to be especially prevalent in certain industries, such as meatpacking, but it can be found in almost all sectors of the economy that rely on low-skilled labor. Racial realism, as well as the related immigrant realism, are common despite the existence of Title VII, as well as other laws that proscribe employer preferences for certain races, national origins, and legal statuses. Employers prefer Latino and Asian workers based on their perceptions of these workers' racial and immigrant abilities, and they often use various employment practices that operate to reproduce workforces that rely heavily, or in some cases almost totally, on Latino and Asian labor. The abilities in question are a combination of attitude, perseverance, docility, and reliability.

This is, without a doubt, the darkest corner of the move to racial-realist strategic management of the workforce. While all of the racial realism explored in this book prizes the usefulness of certain racial backgrounds and thus tends to exclude the less-favored backgrounds, it is only in this sector that we see the familiar American pattern of African-Americans consistently winding up at the back of the preference queue, while employers valorize other groups. It is also only in these low-skilled jobs that we see immigrant status as a major qualification, reprising patterns that existed during the last great wave of immigration, a century ago, before the existence of antidiscrimination law. Finally, it is only in this sector that employers use the racial realism strategy surreptitiously: they deny it in court, creating a burden of proof on plaintiffs.

I have argued here that the reasons Title VII and other laws often do not provide for equal opportunity are many and complex, but they can be identified. A key problem is the lack of incentive for litigation. Why fight for a low-paying job? A related problem is that few African-American workers will apply to a job in a workplace dominated by immigrants—let alone fight for that job. Existing judge-made legal rules for proving discrimination also help maintain racial realism. It is very hard to prove discriminatory intent, as demanded by disparate treatment discrimination law. Rules for proving violations of IRCA or RICO render successful litigation against employers who exploit undocumented immigrants similarly difficult. In the area of disparate impact discrimination law, judges in more recent decades have made it even more difficult to win in the current high-immigration era. In the last several years, however, the EEOC has added some federal muscle to the fight against the most pernicious aspects of racial and immigrant realism in low-skilled jobs, demonstrating that the gap between law and practice can be narrowed somewhat without changing the law.

It would take far more effort than this to create real and lasting change, however, and the EEOC's efforts have yet to touch other sectors of employment—business and the professions, government jobs, and entertainment and media. And there may be many desirable aspects of racial realism in those sectors that we would want to keep. The trick to making peace with racial realism is doing it in a way that harmonizes it with the American value of equal opportunity. This is the focus of the concluding chapter.

6

Bringing Practice, Law, and Values Together

Figure 7. President Barack Obama bends over so the son of a White House staff member can pat his head during a family visit to the Oval Office, May 8, 2009. Official White House Photo by Pete Souza, P050809PS-0264.

This book has several objectives. I have sought to offer a road map for understanding how employers and advocates for change understand race to matter or not matter in the American workplace—the strategies or cultural models they describe as the way things "are" or the way they "ought to be" in several key sectors. I have also sought to show how this emerging strategy, racial realism, fits with current American law.

To do this, I brought together existing studies in a variety of social science fields that allow us to view practices in several employment sectors, and also have examined the social science evidence regarding whether or not the assumptions that animate racial realism have empirical support. I then brought those insights to the work of legal scholars and an analysis of court opinions in order to trace the development of the rules for how employment is supposed to happen, and also to assess the size of the gap between current practice and current law.

The main argument of this book is that in significant ways the Civil Rights Act of 1964 is no longer in sync with American society. In many sectors of employment, there are great disjunctures between the law on the books, as understood by judges and administrators, and what occurs in the everyday workplace. Arguably, American employers' strategies for managing race in the workplace are, to a large extent, unregulated.

This is not a simple story of law failing to achieve its objectives. Rather, it is a story of how an alternative strategy for managing race in the workplace has taken root. Racial realism joins, but does not supplant, classical liberalism and affirmative-action liberalism. But this strategy is so different from those entrenched and legally sanctioned strategies, both of which have justice and equal opportunity as their direct goals, that it suggests something beyond them, or outside of our normal thinking about race and work. Many employers (and some employees) appear to want race to have utility or usefulness in employment in a wide variety of fields—from low-skilled jobs in basic manufacturing to professional jobs in marketing, journalism, and medicine. Even at the very top levels of government, Americans are placed in jobs by virtue of their racial abilities and signaling. In entertainment and media, this occurs openly and obviously—it even leaves a paper trail in casting breakdowns. Title VII of the Civil Rights Act of 1964, and the affirmative-action legal rules that followed it, do not provide a legal foundation for much of what is happening in today's workplace, or what various elites and advocacy groups want to happen.

In Chapter 2, I showed that there is virtually no legal support for the "leveraging" of racial diversity in American businesses where it involves preferences, either for marketing or for overall organizational dynamism. Nor is there legal authorization for leveraging the racial abilities or signaling of professionals, such as physicians or journalists. In Chapter 3, we saw that presidents—the chief enforcers of the law—and leaders of both parties, by word and deed, demonstrate their support for racial realism, even if they also say they believe in classical liberalism, racial realism's opposite. Meanwhile, support for racial realism in policing and teaching have long histories and have become only more entrenched as America has become more diverse, yet only in law enforcement is there legal authorization for these strategies. In Chapter 4, I showed how advertisers and entertainment businesses, including those producing movies, television and professional sports, have in various ways sought to use racial signaling to achieve the desired reactions from viewers. Despite the unique defenses that may be available for employers in this sector, there is only one case that has ever authorized media and entertainment racial realism. Finally, in Chapter 5, I showed that employers across the country regularly use both racial and immigrant realism to manage their workforces. However, except for some court decisions making it easier to rely on word-of-mouth recruitment in immigrant-dominated workplaces, Title VII and other statutes, as well as several court decisions and EEOC guidelines clearly prohibit these nevertheless common practices. Putting all of this together, it is difficult not to conclude that America's civil rights laws have become, in some very real and perhaps morally troubling sense, anachronisms.

There are several causes that seem to have contributed to the rise of racial realism. I have argued that demographic changes—declining native births and massive immigration—created a demand for immigrant labor, a supply of immigrant workers, and huge new markets of nonwhite consumers. Changes in the economy put pressures on firms to reduce costs and find the best workers at the lowest possible wages. Organizational dynamics in corporations created constituencies for diversity management, who argued that racial diversity, among its other benefits, boosts profits. Political efforts, at the grass roots and at elite levels, pressured some sectors to take advantage of racial abilities or racial signaling. Legal factors also mattered: there have been few lawsuits that directly challenge racial realism across sectors; and courts, using their broad powers of statutory interpretation (and absent any input from Congress in years), have carved out a few spaces for it in recruitment strategies at the low-skilled level, as well as explicit allowances for racial realism in law enforcement, especially in policing.

Classical liberalism in employment law came about after decades of debate—some have even called it "the longest debate."[1] Affirmative action was debated briefly in Congress when President Nixon introduced regulations, and in several Supreme Court cases and countless books and articles. Racial realism, by contrast, has become institutionalized without national debate. Congress has not called for hearings on the issue, and only a handful of court cases are directly on point. While we debated racial realism extensively in the very narrow context of elite university admissions, it has become deeply rooted in the national discourse and in workplace practice across the country.

Racial Realism: Mend It, Don't End It?

The empirical issues discussed in this book lead to normative questions. What kind of law should we have to achieve our goals? Does our 1964 law fit with the present day, or is it a hindrance? Of course, this begs a prior question. What *are* our goals for race in America? Equal opportunity for everyone? A diminution of racial meanings and significance in law and everyday life? Should we be celebrating diversity at the workplace? Or champion the colorblindness of classical liberalism? Should we continue to make allowance for the significance of race only to provide opportunity and justice, as is required by affirmative action? Or should we take a different route entirely, such as, for example, the libertarian stance that would give employers' discretion to hire as they see fit and let market forces work their magic? Can we trust the judgment of employers when they treat race or immigrant status as real and useful—as something to be strategically manipulated to enhance profit or organizational effectiveness?

I argue that we *will* need to change our laws to fit our racial-realist practices, but that we should not let racial realism run unchecked as it does today. It needs to mesh comfortably with our values, and if there is any value that could be said to be a consensus value in America, it is equal opportunity.[2] It is too easy for racial realism to limit opportunities, especially the opportunities of the most vulnerable people. There should be some basic principles to guide possible reforms.

There are two main reasons why we should give legal authorization for racial realism. The first is that it is simply too widespread, and there is simply too much support for it to pull back now. It is beyond imagining that corporations might forget about the value of diversity, that hospitals would for any reason ignore patient preferences and health outcomes, that police departments and school districts might begin randomly assigning officers and teachers, that advertisers would suddenly decide to pretend that all consumers respond the same way to a model, that Hollywood might stop casting without regard to race, or that employers of low-skilled could bring themselves to act contrary to their strong preferences for and business models based on immigrant labor.

The second reason that we need to authorize some version of racial realism is that it is the message we get from the top. Even as our political leaders extol the virtues of colorblindness, they act according to the logic of racial realism. The various branches of the federal government and national political organizations regularly use this strategy when they appoint individuals to positions in the cabinet, in the bureaucracy, in the judiciary, and as party leaders and spokespersons. They see race as a qualification that will enable them to reap benefits—either in the form of votes or general goodwill or legitimacy. Political leaders at the local level may be even more expert at getting value out of racial realism. For them race matters not only as a signaling mechanism, but for some jobs, especially those of police officers and teachers, racial abilities are also a consideration. In short, our political leaders do not think of the people simply as citizens or voters—they see them as Asian citizens, black citizens, Latino citizens, white citizens, etc. This will only occur more frequently and explicitly at the national, state, and local levels as the demography of the country becomes more diverse.

If political leaders believe that it is critical to be race-conscious in performing their jobs, how can they in good conscience prevent others from using race? They need to be honest. Both Republicans and Democrats should be able to agree that, whatever their thoughts about affirmative action, both classical liberalism and racial realism have their place in managing employment.[3]

What follows are brief sketches of principles for reforms in three very different sectors of employment: high-skilled jobs in business, the professions, and government; entertainment and media; and the low-skilled sector. Each presents its own challenges. Given the pernicious use of racial realism and immigrant realism in low-skilled employment and the large size of this sector, I will devote the most attention here.

In the current political environment, substantial reforms are not likely. The principles I will define are meant to be suggestive and to illuminate problem areas—to provide a blueprint for closing the gap between employment practices and the law as it is currently interpreted.

Principles for Reform for Skilled Jobs in Business, the Professions, and Government

The goals at the high end of the labor market are to adapt law and employment practices so that they are in harmony with one another and with the consensus value of equal opportunity. Racial abilities and racial signaling are most benign when we think about them as boosts for innovative thinking, or simply as means to signal fairness, openness, and modernity. More dangerous is the targeted variety of racial realism that firms apply for marketing purposes, that we can detect in the fields of medicine and journalism, and that governments use for staffing schools or deploying police officers. While racial realism can open golden doors of opportunity for racial minorities, it can also create glass ceilings. As described in Chapters 2 and 3, it can position nonwhites in dead-end jobs, relegate them to undesired work assignments (as when New York City moved cops of African ancestry to a rough neighborhood following a police brutality incident there), and in some instances can result in reduced compensation (as in the case of the managers at Walgreens drug stores). Moreover, by applying racial realism in the workplace, we may be freezing into place racial meanings instead of changing the structures that help sustain them.

High-Skilled Reform Principle #1: Keep jobs open

When employers act on the belief that a particular race is best for a particular job, especially when this results in racial matching, they can potentially erect barriers that both prevent persons of different races from moving into these jobs and make it difficult for those who want to move out of them to do so. It is important, therefore, to keep alive the possibility that people of all races might be taught the particular abilities that employers presume are linked to particular races.

I am not aware of studies looking into the effectiveness of training in the business environment as a substitute for racial abilities. Social scientists have evaluated multicultural training, but the main dependent variable there was the numbers of minorities and women hired, and not firm performance.[4]

Training has been tried, however, particularly in medicine, policing, and teaching. Medical schools routinely have required courses in multicultural medicine, and the Association of American Medical Colleges and the American College of Physicians have each advocated that "cultural competence" be integrated into medical training.[5] The federal government's Department of Health and Human Services maintains "A Physician's Practical Guide to Culturally Competent Care" on its website for those already out of medical school.[6] These efforts typically focus on a physician's ability to manage or perceive cultural variations that may impact the relationship with the patient, cultural factors that determine aspects of the patient's values and behaviors, and potential race and gender biases that may affect the care provided.[7]

Most cities now engage in various forms of multicultural training to reduce their need for hiring police officers from minority communities. In the wake of the violence of the 1960s, the President's Commission on Law Enforcement and the Administration of Justice vigorously called for "community relations programs" to improve understanding of minority communities.[8] In the 1980s, the Houston police department began to try to improve community relations by instituting programs of cultural training, increasing contacts between the police and minorities, and requiring police attendance at community meetings, classes in conversational Spanish, and classes in black culture that teach how African-Americans "live and think."[9] These efforts have expanded in more recent decades.[10]

In education, training for racial abilities goes by several names, including "culturally relevant" or "culturally responsive" teaching. Educators and advocacy groups concerned with teaching the diverse student bodies of the twenty-first century argue both that there is a need for more nonwhite teachers in education, and that, with adequate training, a person of any race can teach a student of any race. As education scholar Leonard Olguón has said, teachers do not have to know everything about a culture, but they must be sensitive: "I can't paint you brown or paint you black or make you look like an Asian," he explains, "but I need to make you know what's inside of these children so you don't ride roughshod over them without even knowing it."[11]

Can racial abilities training be a substitute for racial abilities? At this point, it is impossible to assess training as a substitute, because the benchmark of success is not even clear. Although the evidence for racial abilities in most contexts is persuasive, it is not definitive, despite the great support the concept receives. But it seems apparent that if we are to promote equal opportunities, firms or government agencies hiring and placing skilled workers according to racial abilities should consider providing optional training programs for any employee who goes to work in areas where employers believe race is a qualification.

There are some areas of employment where racial signaling plays an absolutely crucial role, and there are no training work-arounds for these. This is especially true in policing. It would require a massive and probably continuous public reeducation campaign before effective policing could be implemented minus racial signaling. A study of policing in six American cities in the 1980s found that the city of Houston, when forced by public pressure, made major efforts to train its white officers. It did all of the right things. It set up storefronts in high-crime neighborhoods so that the police would have a more visible presence, and it hired and encouraged bilingual officers. But even with white officers more visible and trained in the Spanish language and Latino culture, the study found that "Spanish-speaking people [would] sometimes wait for days until they [saw] a police car driven by an Hispanic-looking officer before filing a complaint about a crime."[12] There would seem to be limits to training, then, when racial signaling is an important part of a job.

High-Skilled Reform Principle #2: Move law closer to practice, while keeping it in line with our values

Some reform in the way Title VII is written or interpreted is also necessary to bring practice and law into alignment with one another and with our values. I do not have in mind here simply adding "race" to the list of grounds for which an employer can cite a BFOQ defense. This would not work because, as described in Chapter 1, courts have interpreted BFOQs very strictly. They almost never allow them, and so to allow the kinds of practices described in Chapters 2, 3, and 4 as BFOQs would mean having to overturn decades of precedents. Moreover, we would not want a particular racial phenotype to be an absolute *requirement* for any particular job—that would be too clearly a violation of the equal opportunity principle.

The better statutory reform would be to explicitly allow voluntary racial realism as a kind of addition and update to the voluntary affirmative-action rules already in existence. This could come in the form of an amendment to Title VII by Congress, or through the judiciary, with what legal scholar William Eskridge calls "dynamic statutory interpretation."[13] Conservative judges should like the reform because it would explicitly allow more employer freedom, which is in line with their values. Liberal judges should like it because, if done right, it could make current practices more fair.

Obviously, the hallmark of racial realism rules would not be the re-pairing of some imbalance in the workforce, but rather the instrumental use of race to achieve some organizational goal. Yet, they could share with the existing affirmative-action rules sensitivity to the opportunities of those of other races. Both could make it illegal to refuse to hire or to fire qualified people of the "wrong" race. The racial-realism rules would also prohibit *maintaining* workers in racially matched jobs against their will. Employers would need to be able to demonstrate that workers of all races could move to different parts of the organization.

There is little that is radical about this reform. Justice John Paul Stevens has pushed something similar in a set of lonely concurring and dissenting opinions, beginning with 1986's *Wygant* decision, which ruled that school districts could not hire and fire teachers for the racial signal-ing they provided as role models for minorities. In his dissent, he ar-gued that "race is not always irrelevant to sound governmental decision-making."[14] He maintained that integrated school faculties could be more effective than all-white faculties, gave examples of employee race benefit-ing law enforcement, and maintained that "the superintendent of police might reasonably conclude that an integrated police force could develop a better relationship with the community and thereby do a more effective job of maintaining law and order than a force composed only of white officers."[15]

Stevens outlined a similar approach in his concurring opinion in the 1987 case, *Johnson v. Transportation Agency of Santa Clara County*, where the Court clarified its rules for affirmative action. "The logic of antidis-crimination legislation," he argued, "requires that judicial constructions of Title VII leave 'breathing room' for employer initiatives to benefit mem-bers of minority groups."[16] Stevens noted that when passing the law, Con-gress intended that "traditional management prerogatives be left undis-turbed to the greatest extent possible."[17] He was able to cite arguments and quotations from senators (also cited in the *Weber* opinion, justifying voluntary affirmative action), that made it clear that Congress's biggest fear in banning racial preferences for minorities[18] was not employers' vol-untary efforts but rather overreaching government bureaucrats. Congress intended the law to bring justice and equal opportunity to minorities. Putting these goals together, Stevens argued that employers should be al-lowed to prefer minorities for jobs if doing so served their purposes in im-proving their functioning or creating diversity, because "statutes enacted for the benefit of minority groups should not block these forward-looking considerations."[19]

In a 1990 concurring opinion in the *Metro Broadcasting* case that upheld a federal program that encouraged minority ownership of broadcast
stations, Stevens said that the allowance for disparate treatment based on
race should be "extremely rare," but that the important thing was that it
did not stigmatize any groups.[20] He also rejected a preference for minority
contractors in the city of Richmond because it served no public interest,[21] and in 1995, insisted that a Court decision striking down a federal
preference for minority contractors did not mean that federal preferences
based on diversity concerns were always unconstitutional.[22]

Stevens' opinions, although they were never adopted by the other justices, nevertheless offer a legal roadmap for racial realism in skilled jobs. We
would need to make some modifications, however. First, Stevens said that
allowances for racial realism should be "extremely rare," but this would be
too constraining on employer practices that so many see as both practical
and beneficial. I have endeavored to show in this book that racial realism is
not "extremely rare"—it is quite common and many powerful people want
it to be more common. Since so many employers and advocates, as well as
the leaders of both parties and many races believe that race is an important
qualification, we should consider rules that allow it to be common.

But Stevens was rightfully concerned about the dangers of racial realism. One concern, explored here in Chapters 2, 3, and 4, is that employers
may segregate and ghettoize their nonwhite employees in jobs that become
typecasted for them, a practice that, the evidence suggests, affects wages
in a negative way. Once in these jobs, they might not be able to move
out. This was the concern of the black managers in Collins's study, of
the corporate workers who felt that diversity management positions were
dead-end jobs, of some journalists relegated to a racial beat, and of several
nonwhite actors and actresses. It was even litigated by black managers at
Walgreens drugstores, a woman assigned to do telemarketing based on a
presumption of her racial abilities, and several law enforcement officers.

Therefore, if the law is to remain true to the original goal of providing
equal opportunity, and if we decide to also allow racial realism, the law
must prevent jobs that have an element of racial abilities or racial signaling from becoming dead ends and career traps.

The second modification of Stevens' vision is therefore that jobs filled
through the racial-realist strategy must come with a time limit. This was
the approach taken by the New York court that upheld the transfer of
black officers to the precinct that had tortured Haitian immigrant Abner
Louima. The city's placements had to be temporary, and officers able to
transfer out.[23] Similarly, employers should be free to fill jobs where race

might be a qualification with persons of the appropriate race, as they do now, but those appointments should be time-limited to about three years maximum. Employees in any job typically have to deal with unwanted placements, work assignments, and transfers, and with denials of their requests for the placements of their choice. If we make racial realism transparent, then everyone will know which placements are the ones that everyone has to deal with, and which are based on racial realism. Non-white employees would not harbor festering suspicions that their careers are blocked due to their race (as discussed in Chapter 2), they would know which jobs are the potentially dangerous or career-limiting ones, and everyone would know that management sees whites and nonwhites alike as having value to the organization in a variety of positions. At the same time, employees who wished to stay in jobs that utilized their per-ceived racial abilities or racial signaling should be free to do so, explicitly renewing their approval of the assignment every three years.

A third reform calculated to protect employee opportunity and prevent employers from abusing racial realism would be to require employers to officially validate racial abilities and racial signaling in their jobs.[24] Racial realism need not be "rare," as Stevens suggested, but it should presuppose some effort and thought. Validation should be in the employers' own inter-ests anyway—they should not artificially limit the pool of possible workers for a job if in fact any race could do the job equally well. While it is true that social scientists with large budgets and varying research designs have not been able to definitively show the existence of racial abilities and ben-efits flowing from racial signaling in contexts such as medicine, journalism, policing, teaching, and media, this does not mean that a single organization could not validate positive results from racial realism in its own context.

There is nothing radical about requiring validation for certain employ-ment practices, and there are precedents for it in existing discrimination law. For example, courts have required governments that wish to grant preferences or set-asides to minority-owned contractors to perform "dis-parity studies" to show that the contracting process would exclude minor-ities without the racial preferences.[25] Employers also regularly use pro-fessionals to validate tests that are supposed to predict ability to perform jobs in order to prove that they actually test for ability and are not being used to exclude minorities or women.[26] Courts have already required a kind of validation of racial realism in some Fourteenth Amendment cases: they have assessed (though unsystematically) whether the argument for using race is "compelling" in the instance of a particular case. This is why a Seventh Circuit Court rejected the Chicago Fire Department's use of

diversity while accepting it in law enforcement contexts: in a fire department, the use of race was judged insufficiently compelling.

In Justice Stevens' vision, racial realism would only apply to nonwhites,
but as we saw in the previous chapters, there are some occasions, though
very rare, when employers admit to using whiteness while following racial-
realist principles. Whether or not this should be allowed is one of the more
challenging questions facing the most diverse democracy that the world
has ever seen. Given the domination of whites in all of the centers of power
in American society (at this writing, 96 percent of senators are white, none
are black; 45 of the 50 governors are white; 89 percent of all judges are
white; and in the entire history of the "Fortune 500" largest companies
in the United States, there have been only thirteen black CEOs[27]), it may
seem absurd to legally allow whiteness to be valued anywhere.

And yet, if we wish to reduce the gaps between the law on the books
and the law in practice, we need to look closely to see if there are any circumstances where racial realism for whites might be benign. If Americans
did decide to allow racial realism for whites, it should be permissible only
in very rare circumstances that mostly mirror the cases of it described
in this book—that is, situations in which employers might be able to defend the practice without being embarrassed. These would be situations
where, for example, whites are in the minority in some key context, such
as an ethnic-oriented business that wants a white interface with some
established businesses, as when Univision or Telemundo used white sales
reps to negotiate with advertisers (Chapter 2). In these instances, the
racial-realism logic is very similar to that used for nonwhites: positions
would need to be open to others, and the racial preference would need to
be validated and made temporary if the employee wished it to be. Racial
realism for whites might also be allowed where whiteness might actually
benefit nonwhites, as for example in the use of a white as diversity officer
for a firm wishing to signal to its employees that diversity was an issue of
concern to all employees and not just to nonwhites and women.

Reform Principles for the Airwaves: Raise Awareness and Maintain Our Values

In media and entertainment, the key principles relate to the need to raise
awareness that the images these industries purvey matter and shape our
culture, and that they also have the potential to harm our children. The

most potential harm can come from television, which remains an especially pervasive cultural force.

There is much precedent for thinking about the power of television images and our collective responsibility to control it, and indeed American law already provides unique opportunities to regulate racial realism in contexts related to broadcasting. Courts have been accepting of the regulation of media content in the use of public airwaves, and this suggests the possibility that racial realism in employment might also be legally regulated in television productions, under the umbrella of promoting the public good. In particular, it opens the door to racial-realist regulations that promote positive stereotypes for the benefit of young people and, ultimately, for the maintenance of a healthy and vibrant democracy.

Racial-realist reforms are possible in this context for several reasons. First, practical considerations have led to the allowance of federal regulation of broadcasting. In the interests of keeping the airwaves clear and free of crowding and interference, the federal government plays a key role through the terms of licensing for broadcasters.[28] Second, the 1934 statute that created the Federal Communications Commission (FCC) stated that the FCC was to grant licenses when the "public interest, convenience or necessity" was served.[29] Third, the protection of children has been a major focus of actions by the FCC, the Supreme Court, and Congress in limiting expression in broadcasting. In 1978, the Court highlighted broadcasting's potential impact on children when it argued, "The government's interest in the well-being of its youth and in supporting parents' claim to authority in their own household justifies the regulation of otherwise protected expression."[30]

More recently, the Telecommunications Act of 1996 fully elaborated the importance of regulating broadcast content to protect children from violent and sexual images in its Section 551, designed to provide "parental choice in television programming." This section of the law contained a list of "findings," including that "the average American child is exposed to 25 hours of television each week and some children are exposed to as much as 11 hours of television a day," that studies indicate that exposure to violence and sexuality on television has harmful effects on children, and that "providing parents with timely information about the nature of upcoming video programming and with the technological tools that allow them easily to block violent, sexual, or other programming that they believe harmful to their children is a nonintrusive and narrowly tailored means of achieving that compelling governmental interest."[31] None of this had to do with race, but it established the principle of governmental concern with children's protection from potential harm from broadcasting.

This points to a potential justification for the regulation of racial images that are broadcast—a case made most clearly by legal scholar Patricia Worthy.[32] Her argument focused on social science evidence showing the harm of negative stereotypes. Her suggested reform, however, was not to exert control over the creativity of media producers, or to ban or even limit racially stereotypical images. Instead, her strategy was to allow concerned parents to avoid the harmful effects that negative racial stereotypes would have on their children. Negative racial stereotypes, she notes, are no more difficult to identify than are excessively violent or sexual images—and Congress already regulates these. Panels of experts drawn from broadcasting, government, academia, education, and civic organizations could come together and develop a matrix for assessing the representativeness of portrayals of different racial groups.[33] Once racial images were identified, there would be at least two strategies available. Worthy suggests limiting the hours when stereotypical portrayals could be broadcast to between 9pm and 6am in order to protect children from them.[34] Another approach would be to build on to the current system of parental guidelines, perhaps through addition to the voluntary rating system created by the Telecommunications Act of 1996.[35] Currently, there are warnings regarding the suitability of violent and sexual content for younger viewers that highlight such factors to warn parents. For example, a rating of "TV-14" is designed to warn parents that programming may be unsuitable for viewers under the age of 14. An elaborate letter-code system warns parents that a program contains one or more elements of "intense violence," "intense sexual situations," "strong coarse language," or "intensely suggestive dialogue."[36] A similar rating system could warn viewers that minorities are portrayed only in marginal or low-status roles, or only in negative roles as villains or problem characters.

Worthy's suggested reforms would likely appear too heavy-handed on top of the current programs and regulations relating to violence in broadcast media. But her reforms are provocative and capture the right principles for this sector. They fit with our values of protecting children and ensuring a vibrant democracy where people of all backgrounds would be equally expected to have high aspirations. At the very least, a public debate regarding a rating system such as this might change the calculus in Hollywood that tends to make whiteness the default in casting and the choice most likely to generate profits.

Principles for Reform in the Low-Skilled Sector

Racial realism is least defensible in the low-skilled employment sector. There are two main problems here. First, for many jobs African-Americans are the least favored workers; second, the Latino and Asian workers as well as the immigrants whom employers prefer for their racial or immigrant abilities are often exploited, subjected to poor working conditions and low wages. For complex demographic reasons, however, America will remain dependent on at least some immigrant labor for low-skilled jobs, as Frank Bean and his colleagues have argued.[37] So what is to be done?

Though racial discrimination is a big part of the problem in this sector, eliminating it is not necessarily the centerpiece of the solution. As I showed in Chapter 5, the laws on the books—Title VII, IRCA, and RICO—should be preventing racial or immigrant preferences and discrimination against African-Americans, but as currently interpreted, unless pushed by the EEOC, they are clearly failing to do so.

Yet there is a place here for considerations of equality. William Julius Wilson is right to argue that the best reforms should not define the problem in racial terms, but more holistically, with a focus on improving opportunity.[38] This means that rather than maintaining a singular reliance on the utilitarianism favored by many economists (emphasizing growth, wealth, and efficiency, and accepting that there are losers along with winners), we need also to keep in mind the lawyers' language of fairness and justice. Most studies show that immigration is a net positive for the country, but for some workers, it leads to lost opportunities and disrupted lives. Because the government is complicit, making possible or incentivizing the racial realism in the low-skilled sector, there is a social responsibility to change these dynamics.

Understanding the Big Picture: The Decline of the Good Urban Jobs

From the perspective of low-skilled workers, and particularly low-skilled African-American workers, the good jobs used to be in manufacturing, were located in urban centers, and were often unionized. Between 1970 and 1990, however, the numbers of these jobs declined in the cities but grew in the suburbs and rural areas. Some social scientists suspected that these shifts had impacts on employment patterns—especially on the employment of African-Americans.[39] The "spatial mismatch" hypothesis proposed that inner-city blacks faced employment hurdles when jobs were very far from where they lived and that they often lacked the means to commute.[40] Simply relocating to where the jobs were was not a good option for blacks because, among all racial groups, they are the most likely to face discrimination in housing.[41] By contrast, evidence indicated that geography did not impact the hiring of Latinos.[42] In a comprehensive review of a large body of literature, Roberto Fernandez and Celina Su concluded, "This research is generally persuasive in showing that job accessibility—generally measured in spatial terms—is an important contributing factor to minorities' labor market difficulties."[43]

Much of this research focuses on firms moving from central cities to suburbs, but the decline of manufacturing in Rust Belt cities—while it has grown in the rural parts of the Sun Belt—has also had a significant impact on racial disparities in employment.[44] It was not a one-for-one trade, but the trends were unmistakable: rural and Southern states were the growth zones.[45]

In the 1980s, Japanese automakers in particular attracted unwelcome attention when they moved their assembly lines to the U.S. but avoided cities. There were many reasons for these moves,[46] but there was a significant racial story here as well. Chrysler, Ford, and GM were very friendly to African-Americans in the 1980s—fully 17.2 percent of the their workforce was black, and 8.4 percent of their white-collar employees were black.[47] But Japanese firms avoided Detroit and other urban centers. Instead, they built their manufacturing facilities in rural areas in the Midwest, South, and West. The Equal Employment Opportunity Commission (EEOC) went after Honda in 1988 for race and sex discrimination at its rural Ohio plant, and Honda agreed to pay $6 million in back pay to the workers. Honda's workforce was only 2.8 percent black while the surrounding area was 10.5 percent black.[48] In their analysis of the issue, management scholars Robert Cole and Donald Deskins found that Japanese-owned plants hired far fewer blacks than American-owned companies—in part because of their plant locations: "By siting their plants in areas with very low black populations, they, in effect, exclude blacks from potential employment."[49]

Today, there are other firms that exclude African-Americans from potential employment, either through the locations they choose, or through other factors, such as the working conditions and wages at those plants. The most obvious example is the meatpacking industry which, as described in Chapter 5, transformed its workforce in the 1980s to become overwhelmingly immigrant and Latino.

To be sure, there were good reasons for packers to leave the cities. Moving meat processing closer to the animals saved on the costs of shipping live animals. Rural land was cheaper for the massive, sprawling new plants. Rural counties lured them with tax breaks. And the meatpackers could also avoid unions and enjoy cheap, rural pay scales.[50]

But in moving, they almost guaranteed themselves labor-supply problems. As a report for Congress on the meatpacking industry remarked with perhaps a hint of sarcasm, "When operating a labor-intensive facility in a sparsely populated area, labor scarcity might be anticipated."[51] Many meatpackers built massive plants in small rural towns that already had low unemployment, thereby requiring that workers move a great distance to take dirty, dangerous, and difficult jobs. Those most willing or able to move were people without deep roots in the U.S.: in other words, recently arrived immigrant Latinos.

It is not just location that shapes the racial make-up of the workforce. Scholars who have studied the meatpacking industry are in agreement that other managerial decisions have important impacts as well. How the employer structures and organizes the workplace is critical. Not only did Tyson build its chicken processing plants far from the large labor pools provided by cities, it also created hazardous working conditions and offered very low wages (comparable to pay at McDonald's fast food restaurants)—and then asked American workers to take these jobs. The results were predictable: there weren't enough American workers to be found.[52] Meatpackers and poultry plants have steadfastly maintained these low wages even though wages, according to Smithfield Foods CEO Joe Luter, are only 10 percent of the production costs.[53]

Social scientists have observed how managerial decisions have shaped workforce dynamics. Anthropologist Michael J. Broadway argues that the "decline in wage levels" as well as the conditions in the plants "served to make meatpacking an unattractive employment option for many Americans."[54] Writing more broadly about the low-wage sector, sociologist Edna Bonacich noted that Americans would "willingly" do these jobs if the conditions were "decent."[55] Sociologist Kathleen Stanley stated, "In the case of meatpacking, the demand for immigrant labor was not the result of an absolute shortage of workers. Rather, this demand was created by the industry as firms pursued restructuring strategies which relocated jobs and made them less attractive to the established labor force. In spite of the fact that meatpacking pays foreign-born workers relatively high wages, the meatpacking firms must actively organize the migrant flow in order to acquire an adequate labor supply."[56]

A natural experiment shows dramatically what happens to workforce composition when wages are changed. The *Wall Street Journal* reported in-depth on the labor troubles of the Stillmore, Georgia chicken processor, Crider, Inc., which lost 75 percent of its 900-person workforce after an immigration raid. Suddenly desperate for new workers, Crider raised wages from $7 an hour to $9 an hour, and advertised widely. It also hired hundreds of persons sent to the company by a state employment agency, most of whom were African-American. Hundreds of applicants, also mostly African-American, came to the company in response to the wage increases and the wide recruitment. But Crider did not change workplace conditions, and many of the new workers, complaining of overbearing managers, safety violations, and inadequate treatment for injuries suffered on the job, left the company. The *Journal* story concluded with Crider seeking to find new immigrant workers, including more Latinos, and setting up an arrangement to lure Laotian Hmong laborers from other states.[57]

Low-Skilled Reform Principle #1: Encourage corporate responsibility regarding the impacts of firm locations and wages

The first possible reform principle is to think seriously about the ways management choices regarding where to locate firms and what wages to offer shape employment opportunities for workers, especially African-Americans. One way to do this would involve a novel interpretation of Title VII. Recall that one approach to Title VII considers employment practices that have a "disparate impact" on minority workers to be illegal discrimination, even if there was no intent to discriminate. Legal scholar Deborah Malamud has asked the logical question: Could the law be stretched so that plant location, wages, and even conditions are discriminatory management practices with a disparate impact on African-Americans?[58] Cole and Deskins seem to have anticipated such a claim when they noted, "Regardless of intent, [Japanese-owned automobile] plant site locations contribute to a drying up of opportunities for black workers in an industry that has traditionally supplied large opportunities to minority workers."[59]

The notion of plant location and managerial decisions as discrimination is helpful, because it highlights their significant racial impacts. It is not likely that these could be included in any disparate impact theory of discrimination, however, for several reasons.

First, disparate impact only applies to "employment practices." The Civil Rights Act of 1991 states that a disparate impact claim is made when "a complaining party demonstrates that a respondent uses a particular employment practice that causes a disparate impact on the basis of race, color, religion, sex, or national origin and the respondent fails to demonstrate that the challenged practice is job related for the position and consistent with business necessity."[60]

Perhaps the biggest problem with the place or wage claim is that placing or moving one's business, establishing wages, and the nature of work conditions are not employment practices typically at issue in disparate impact cases. These cases normally turn on ability tests, word-of-mouth hiring, subjective hiring assessments, or seniority rules (another practice that courts have seen to be discriminatory when it has a disparate impact on a protected group). Place and wage claims are instead decisions related directly to production and profit, or to managing current employees, rather than directly related to applicant hiring, placement, or promotion. If decisions regarding where businesses can locate, or what their wage levels should be, could be reviewed by the EEOC or be made subject to litigation by disgruntled former employees or job applicants, then the business owner might feel maddeningly hemmed in by regulations. He or she might begin to consider the race, sex, age, or national-origin impact of *every* business decision he or she makes. Judges concerned about "slippery slopes" would find a lot to worry them here. Moreover, as Malamud has predicted, the courts would not be "likely to apply disparate impact analysis to fundamental business decisions unless they [were] deeply enough disturbed by their effects to be willing to substantially unsettle their own background expectations about the reach of Title VII."[61]

Though litigation is not likely to be successful, a public relations campaign could have some impact. To the extent that employers are exposed for having run away from American workers and then to have exploited the immigrants desperate enough to tolerate dangerous working conditions and low pay, they might suffer damage to their image that would somewhat mitigate the financial incentives that drive such practices. No business likes to be branded in the public mind as selfish, irresponsible, or (even worse) racist. The most important principle here is to encourage corporations to take responsibility or at least show awareness of the disparate impacts that their plant location and wage structure may have.

Low-Skilled Reform Principle #2: Consider how the wider legal environment creates unequal opportunities

Another reform principle would be to move beyond civil rights and consider the role of the government in supporting firms that do not provide for worker welfare. Because rural counties use tax breaks to lure firms to relocate, taxpayers are subsidizing profit-making enterprises that provide unequal employment opportunities. Management scholars Cole and Deskins have suggested that the level of state subsidies should be determined in part by the types of jobs being created—a point that is most relevant to low-skilled and dangerous jobs, such as meatpacking. They helpfully suggest that subsidies can and should go toward upgrading plants in older areas that already hire minorities rather than building new ones. Cole and Deskins also suggested a sort of employment impact statement, analogous to the "environmental impact statement," but designed to monitor how firms affect their area employment picture, at least for firms building plants above a certain size threshold.[62] To prevent states and localities from engaging in a "race to the bottom," tax incentives could be limited to firms that will bring equal opportunities, provide living wages, and avoid exploitation.

Another approach would be to eliminate the race to the bottom by eliminating the possibility of tax variation. The notion sounds radical, but it is not. James Madison, the father of the Constitution, worried about companies moving from state to state, and argued that the federal government should "grant charters of incorporation in cases where the public good may require them, and the authority of a single state may be incompetent."[63] A national architecture for incorporation was proposed at other times as well, and supported by Theodore Roosevelt, William Howard Taft, Woodrow Wilson, and Franklin Delano Roosevelt, but has always been defeated by business lobbyists.[64]

As shown in Chapter 5, some firms were lured to rural parts of the Plains and Midwest by the offer of tax breaks. Social scientists have analyzed what happened next. Owners were more concerned about pleasing stockholders than members of the local communities and did not take responsibility for school overcrowding, linguistic challenges, increases in crime, housing shortages, and homelessness. They paid workers so little that even after working full-time, they sometimes were eligible for Medicaid, the federal free-lunch program, and other federal assistance programs. Though there is some evidence of positive wage effects in the region surrounding the plants,[65] there can be little doubt that many workers suffered from these business practices: some studies have shown that workers in the plants sometimes resorted to supplementing their low wages by overcrowding homes, drug dealing, and prostitution.[66]

On this point, it is worth recalling the words of the Supreme Court, delivered in 1937 in a case upholding a minimum wage law:

> The exploitation of a class of workers who are in an unequal position with respect to bargaining power, and are thus relatively defenceless against the denial of a living wage, is not only detrimental to their health and wellbeing, but casts a direct burden for their support upon the community. What these workers lose in wages, the taxpayers are called upon to pay. . . . The community is not bound to provide what is, in effect, a subsidy for unconscionable employers.[67]

In the spirit of the Supreme Court's *West Coast Hotel* opinion, a politically difficult but simple reform would be to stop communities from giving tax breaks to "unconscionable employers."[68]

Low-Skilled Reform Principle #3: Discourage dependence on immigrant labor

Another reform principle is to avoid creating or maintaining industry sectors that are organized around their ability to hire and exploit cheap, compliant immigrant labor. Economist Philip Martin and International Labour Organization policy specialists Manolo Abella and Christiane Kuptsch argue that employers "distort" labor markets by basing their investment decisions on the assumption that they will have a ready supply of immigrant workers. The more their business model relies on this assumption, the more they fight to maintain that access to cheap, exploitable labor. Migrants, their families, their communities, and the governments of their origin countries become dependent on these foreign jobs, leading to the continual replenishment of the migrant supply.

To minimize labor market distortion, they propose that employers pay the usual payroll taxes on migrant wages, but also pay an extra levy for hiring a migrant, with the fee rising over time "to encourage the employer to consider alternatives such as mechanization or restructuring work."[69] In areas where alternatives do not exist, they propose using the levies to fund research on mechanization that could reduce reliance on migrant labor, as has occurred in some sectors of agricultural work. To encourage migrants to go home after their visas expire rather than stay and become easily exploitable undocumented workers, Martin, Abella, and Kuptsch propose policy changes to allow their social security and other payroll taxes to be refunded to them when they depart.

In this way, employers will be incentivized to give domestic workers a closer look, rather than simply to assume that they are not suitable. In addition, it will mitigate the problems of word-of-mouth hiring closing domestic workers off from job opportunities, as well as make it less likely that domestic workers will feel isolated culturally or linguistically in immigrant-dominated workplaces. If it truly is the case that no domestic workers are available, it will incentivize innovation rather than subsidize exploitation.

Low-Skilled Reform Principle #4: Recommit to workplace safety

At the core of the racial abilities that employers perceive in Latino, Asian, and immigrant workers is their ability to endure long hours doing repetitive tasks without complaining. Some of these tasks are dangerous, and the federal government's workplace watchdog, the Occupational Safety and Health Administration, has been particularly ineffective in monitoring and correcting this situation.

To prevent the exploitation of workers, we need to recommit to the goal of safe workplaces. This can be done by better enforcement of the workplace safety laws already on the books. OSHA's problems were discussed in Chapter 5, but the problems go beyond that agency. For example, in 1975, there were 921 investigators in the Department of Labor's Wage and Hour Division who were responsible for monitoring compliance with laws regulating the minimum wage, overtime pay, and child labor, among other factors. That number fell to 773 by 2005, and the number of compliance actions fell from 58,758 to 37,872 between 1975 and 2004. At the same time, the number of workplaces covered grew approximately 112 percent.[70]

Both the Right and the Left have criticized OSHA in particular. Conservatives decry the punitive, adversarial nature of its regulations, and its misplaced attempts to find one-size-fits-all rules.[71] Scholars on the Left note that OSHA's investigations are few, and the fines for violations insignificant, giving a sense of its fading promise and mismatch with contemporary workplaces.[72]

It will not be easy to reform OSHA, but making it relevant would go a long way toward creating workplaces in line with the American values of equal job opportunities and respect for human dignity. To generate progress but avoid more regulatory hassles, OSHA should be in the business of dictating safety standards and goals, but not of prescribing the means that businesses must use to achieve those goals. At minimum OSHA needs more money, more leadership, support from the White House, and a reformed mission in line with workplace realities in a globalized world.[73]

Low-Skilled Reform Principle #5: Take responsibility for displaced workers

Economists and demographers often note that it is wrong to think of low-skilled migration as replacing the employment of low-skilled Americans, and argue that this kind of migration is more often complementary to the employment of low-skilled Americans. In their view, some economic adjustments may become necessary for some, but the overall wealth and efficiency of the system increases. The displacement of some workers may be a subplot to the main story of growth and improved efficiency—but it is not an insignificant one. As Chapter 5 showed, displacement—and discrimination—seem to be widespread, and current law makes them difficult to stop.

The policy of the federal government today is to allow immigrants to enter certain job sectors, either explicitly through guestworker programs, or tacitly through other immigration and refugee policies or through poor enforcement of IRCA's prohibitions on the hiring of undocumented workers, and then to let any displaced American workers pushed out of their jobs fend for themselves. The good news here is that there is some evidence that at least some American workers use this "push" in precisely the way economists would predict.

For example, anthropologist David Griffith's study of the impact of guestworkers found that the new challenge sometimes spurred American workers to find better jobs or to improve their skills. In the mid-Atlantic crab industry, he found that an influx of Mexican guestworkers pushed some African-Americans to move to new jobs in tourism, restaurants, and health care. The shift led to a reduction in hours for the American workers, and some—typically African-American women, who have a higher educational profile than do African-American males—used this time to go to community colleges and gain credentials for semi-skilled jobs, such as nurse's assistant.[74]

About 20 percent, however, left the crab industry and were unable to find job opportunities elsewhere, sometimes because of injuries that occurred on the job.[75] In all cases displacement was the result of government actions manipulating the labor supply, and the impact on workers' lives could be dramatic. A worker might upgrade skills—but should that decision be forced, through displacement? And should that worker have to navigate a new life without government aid? A "GI Bill" for displaced workers may not be necessary, but some government responsibility and assistance would certainly appear to be justified.

In an analogous area of worker displacement, that caused by free trade, the government has taken responsibility. In 1962, Congress created the Trade Adjustment Assistance (TAA) program as part of the Trade Expansion Act. When President Kennedy (who had sponsored a TAA bill in 1954 when he was a senator) sent the bill for consideration by Congress, he stated, "I am . . . recommending as an essential part of the new trade program that companies, farmers and workers who suffer damage from increased foreign import competition be assisted in their efforts to adjust to that competition. When considerations of national policy make it desirable to avoid higher tariffs, those injured by that competition should not be required to bear the full brunt of the impact. Rather, the burden of economic adjustment should be borne in part by the Federal Government."[76] TAA would provide a package of unemployment insurance, retraining, and relocation allowances for workers, and loan and technical assistance to firms, as well as tax deductions.

In its first decade, TAA did little besides increase support for free trade from labor groups. But eventually those same groups became disenchanted with the program because it was too hard to use. To get retraining assistance and other aid, workers had to petition and show that lowered tariffs were the "major cause" of their hardships—meaning that they were more important than all other causes combined. This was difficult and expensive, took months to complete, and rarely succeeded.[77] In 1974, the program requirements were lowered, so workers and firms only had to show that lowered tariffs "contributed importantly" to job, wage, and sales declines.[78]

Since that time, TAA has become a partisan issue, with Democrats mostly insisting that it be a part of any free trade agreement, and Republicans mostly arguing that it is wasteful spending that fails to adjust workers to new jobs but instead simply doles out aid. Despite continuing controversy, especially during budget debates, TAA lives on. It was a prominent part of the North American Free Trade Agreement (NAFTA), and despite flaws in the program, majorities in Congress continue to see aid to workers displaced by their policies as a federal responsibility and TAA as the best way to accomplish this.[79] The Obama administration has been a big supporter.[80]

The logic of TAA is transferable to disruptions created by immigration policy. In immigration, the federal policy of allowing or tolerating undocumented immigration leads to great advantages for some and benefits society overall. This is similar to the wide benefits of free trade. The federal government's *de facto* provision of low-skilled immigrant workers, who tend to be very attractive to employers for their racial and immigrant abilities, can, however, lead to the same disruptions as an influx of cheaper goods from abroad. There is little reason why those harmed by free trade and those harmed by immigration should not be treated equally.

The main thrust of an "Immigration Adjustment Assistance" (IAA) program would be the same as in TAA: to improve skills and to provide relocation assistance if needed. For decades, there have been calls to upgrade the skills of lower-income Americans, particularly African-Americans. For example, economist Harry Holzer has argued that employers perceive a lack of skills in this population, and he has called for a skills upgrade, particularly increased computer literacy.[81] Moreover, the Harvard Graduate School of Education's *Pathways to Prosperity* report notes that between 1973 and 2007, the U.S. added sixty-three million jobs, but the number of jobs held by people with no education beyond high school fell during the same period by two million. In the future, much job growth will be in the so-called "middle-skill" positions. These are jobs where the primary educational requirement involves some postsecondary education, but not necessarily a BA. An IAA program could help train workers displaced by immigrants to earn the associate degrees or other certificates of training necessary to step into this growing job market, which includes such vocations as electrician, construction manager, dental hygienist, and police officer.[82] Even manufacturing increasingly requires middle-skill workers who know how to utilize computers and other technologies. While these middle-skill jobs continue to grow (the Bureau of Labor Statistics predicts that in the future 45 percent of all job openings will be in the middle-skill categories), Americans' skill levels are not keeping pace.[83]

Civil rights laws are meant to ensure that each person can go as far as their abilities and effort allow. In America, in our public discourse, we have long assumed that for this to happen, we need to get race out of the picture, out of people's minds and thus out of decision-making. For nearly as long, we have recognized affirmative action as a legal method to acknowledge race in the workplace, but only in so far as it furthers the goals of justice and equal opportunity.

In the last few decades, as America has become more racially diverse than ever before, growing numbers of policy elites—including leaders at the very top of our national government—as well as employers and other advocates have come to see that the strategic management of racial differences is useful to achieve a variety of goals in a very wide array of contexts. We may never get rid of racial thinking, but we can take responsibility for our practices, acknowledge our choices, and align them with our values and our laws.

Chapter 1. Managing Race in the American Workplace

1. William N. Eskridge, Jr. and John Ferejohn, *A Republic of Statutes: The New American Constitution* (New Haven: Yale University Press, 2010) 16.

2. Bruce Ackerman, "The Living Constitution," *Harvard Law Review* 120 (2007): 1737–1812, p. 1742.

3. Discrimination is common, if more subtle than in the past, in employment and other spheres. Devah Pager and Hana Shepherd, "The Sociology of Discrimination: Racial Discrimination in Employment, Housing, Credit, and Consumer Markets," *Annual Review of Sociology* 24 (2008): 181–209. It is also the case that blatant racism is not difficult to find. See, for example, the discussion in James W. Button, Barbara A. Rienzo, and Sheila L. Croucher, *Blacks and the Quest for Economic Equality: The Political Economy of Employment in Southern Communities in the United States* (University Park, PA: Pennsylvania State University Press, 2009) 68–73.

4. A number of scholars have noted the rise and importance of the discourse on diversity. See, for example, Frank Dobbin, *Inventing Equal Opportunity* (Princeton, NJ: Princeton University Press, 2008); Peter Schuck, *Diversity in America: Keeping Government at a Safe Distance* (Cambridge, MA: Belknap Press of Harvard University Press, 2003); Walter Benn Michaels, *The Trouble with Diversity: How We Learned to Love Identity and Ignore Inequality* (New York: Metropolitan Books, 2006); Sanford Levinson, "Diversity," *University of Pennsylvania Journal of Constitutional Law* 2 (2000): 573–608; Ellen Berrey, *Bottom Line Diversity: Race and Productive Pluralism in the Post–Civil Rights Era* (Chicago: University of Chicago Press, forthcoming).

5. Bruce Ackerman, *We the People: The Civil Rights Revolution* (Cambridge, MA: Harvard University Press, 2014).

6. On cultural models or "policy paradigms" shaping policymaking, see Frank Dobbin, *Forging Industrial Policy: The United States, Britain and France in the Railway Age* (New York: Cambridge University Press, 1994).

7. 42 USC § 2000E–2(a).

8. See, for example, Gunnar Mydral, *An American Dilemma: The Negro Problem and Modern Democracy* (New York: Harper and Brothers, 1944) Part 4.

9. Thomas J. Sugrue, *Sweet Land of Liberty: The Forgotten Struggle for Civil Rights in the North* (New York: Random House, 2008); Myrdal, *American Dilemma*; Anthony S. Chen, *The Fifth Freedom: Jobs, Politics and Civil Rights in the United States, 1941–1972* (Princeton, NJ: Princeton University Press, 2009).

10. I explored these issues in John D. Skrentny, *The Ironies of Affirmative Action: Politics, Culture and Justice in America* (Chicago: University of Chicago Press, 1996), Chapter 2.

11. 42 USC § 1981.

12. See, for example, Emilio J. Castilla and Steve Benard, "The Paradox of Meritocracy in Organizations," *Administrative Science Quarterly* 55 (2010): 543–76; Devon Carbado, Catherine K. Fisk and Mitu Gulati, "After Inclusion," *Annual Review of Law and Social Science* 4 (2008): 83–102; Jerry Kang and Mahzarin R. Banaji, "Fair Measures: A Behavioral Realist Revision of 'Affirmative Action,'" *California Law Review* 94 (2006): 1063–1118; Lincoln Quillian, "New Approaches to Understanding Racial Prejudice and Discrimination," *Annual Review of Sociology* 32 (2006): 299–328.

13. Desmond King and Rogers Smith, *Still a House Divided: Race and Politics in Obama's America* (Princeton, NJ: Princeton University Press, 2011), Chapter 1.

14. 2012 *Republican Platform: We Believe in America*, 9;http://www.gop.com/wp-content/uploads/2012/08/2012GOPPlatform.pdf, accessed November 27, 2012. A smaller, libertarian strand of conservative thinking questions the need for civil rights protections at all. In this view, not only should race not be a part of law, but neither should prohibitions on discrimination, because labor markets work best if the law gets out of the way and gives employers discretion to choose and employees the freedom to move. Richard A. Epstein, *Forbidden Grounds: The Case Against Employment Discrimination Laws* (Cambridge, MA: Harvard University Press, 1992).

15. For a discussion, see Reva B. Siegel, "Equality Talk: Antisubordination and Anticlassification Values in Constitutional Struggles over *Brown*," *Harvard Law Review* 117 (2004): 1470–1547.

16. *Code of Federal Regulations* Title 29-Labor, § 1608; *EEOC Compliance Manual*, Section 15, Chapter 4, Part C; http://www.eeoc.gov/policy/docs/race-color.html#VIC, accessed July 6, 2012.

17. Executive Order 11246 (1965); *Code of Federal Regulations* Title 41-Public Contracts and Property Management, § 60.

18. On activist efforts, see Sugrue, *Sweet Land of Liberty*; Nancy MacLean, *Freedom Is Not Enough: The Opening of the American Workplace* (Cambridge, MA: Harvard University Press, 2006). On policy development, see Skrentny, *Ironies of Affirmative Action*; John D. Skrentny, *The Minority Rights Revolution* (Cambridge, MA: Belknap Press of Harvard University Press, 2002); Terry H. Anderson, *The Pursuit of Fairness: A History of Affirmative Action* (New York: Oxford University Press, 2004); Shannon Harper and Barbara Reskin, "Affirmative Action at School and on the Job," *Annual Review of Sociology* 31 (2005): 357–79.

19. *Griggs v. Duke Power Co.*, 401 U.S. 421 (1971).

20. *Griggs v. Duke* at 431.

21. *Griggs v. Duke* at 432.

22. Skrentny, *The Ironies of Affirmative Action*, Chapter 4.

23. *United Steelworkers v. Weber*, 443 U.S. 193 (1979); *Johnson v. Transp. Agency*, 480 U.S. 616 (1987).

24. See King and Smith, *Still a House Divided*, especially Chapter 1, on Democratic support for affirmative action; and Paul Frymer, *The Logic of Uneasy Alliances* (Princeton, NJ: Princeton University Press, 1999) on the Democrats' muted embrace of racial equality for African-Americans.

25. 2012 *Democratic National Platform: Moving America Forward*; http://www.democrats.org/democratic-national-platform, accessed November 30, 2012.

26. Democratic National Convention Committee, *The 2008 Democratic National Committee Platform: Renewing America's Promise* (Washington, DC: Democratic National Committee, 2008) 52.

27. *Regents of the University of California v. Bakke*, 438 U.S. 265, 407 (1978).

28. See the opinion authored by Justice Brennan in *Regents v. Bakke*, at 328.

29. See Chapters 2 and 3 in this book.

30. Owen M. Fiss, "Groups and the Equal Protection Clause," *Philosophy and Public Affairs* 5 (1976): 107–77.

31. Lawrence Tribe, *American Constitutional Law*, 2nd ed. (Mineola, NY: Foundation Press, 1988).

32. Cass R. Sunstein, "The Anticaste Principle," *Michigan Law Review* 92 (1994): 2410–55.

33. Derrick Bell, *And We Are Not Saved: The Elusive Quest for Racial Justice* (New York: Basic Books, 1987).

34. Catharine A. MacKinnon, *Feminism Unmodified: Discourses on Life and Law* (Cambridge, MA: Harvard University Press, 1987).

35. The focus on race, for example, tends to obscure ethnic variations within racial groupings—not all Asians, blacks, Latinos or whites are similarly situated. In addition, disability and sexual orientation are also bases of disadvantage and occupational segregation. M. V. Lee Badgett, "Beyond Biased Samples: Challenging the Myths on the Economic Status of Lesbians and Gay Men," in Amy Gluckman and Betsy Reed, eds., *Homo Economics: Capitalism, Community, and Lesbian and Gay Life* (New York: Routledge, 1997) 65–71.

36. Michael C. Dorf, "Equal Protection Incorporation," *Virginia Law Review* 88 (2002): 951–1024.

37. *Parents Involved in Community Schools v. Seattle School District No. 1*, 551 U.S. 701, 748 (2007).

38. Jack M. Balkin and Reva B. Siegel, "The American Civil Rights Tradition: Anticlassification or Antisubordination?" *University of Miami Law Review* 58 (2003): 9–33.

39. For an insightful analysis of the distinction between "the diversity paradigm" and the "corrective justice paradigm," see Daniel Sabbagh, *Equality and Transparency: A Strategic Perspective on Affirmative Action in American Law* (New York: Palgrave Macmillan, 2007). My thinking on employment issues, in particular the notion that common practices in today's workplaces present difficult questions to established civil rights law, owes much to the work of Deborah Malamud. See, for example, Deborah C. Malamud, "Diversity of Opinions: Affirmative Action, Diversity, and the Black Middle Class," *University of Colorado Law Review* 68 (1997): 939–1000; Deborah C. Malamud, "Affirmative Action and Ethnic Niches: A Legal Afterward," in John David Skrentny, ed., *Color Lines: Affirmative Action, Immigration and Civil Rights Options for America* (Chicago: University of Chicago Press, 2001) 313–45.

40. I explored the instrumental nature of this use of race in Paul Frymer and John D. Skrentny, "The Rise of Instrumental Affirmative Action: Law and the New Significance of Race in America," *Connecticut Law Review* 36 (2004):

677–723. On neoliberalism, see Stephanie Mudge, "What Is Neo-Liberalism?" *Socio-Economic Review* 6 (2008): 703–31.

41. I am indebted to Paul Frymer for a series of conversations in which we developed these concepts.

42. There is no accepted legal definition of "stereotype" in Title VII law. The term is most prominently discussed in sex rather than race discrimination cases. Perhaps the best legal definition came from the Supreme Court in a sex discrimination case, where the Court appeared to define the term as "myths and purely habitual assumptions" about group characteristics, and noted: "It is now well recognized that employment decisions cannot be predicated on mere 'stereotyped' impressions about the characteristics of males or females." *City of Los Angeles Department of Water and Power v. Manhart*, 435 U.S. 702, 707 (1978). The EEOC Compliance Manual also states that adverse employment actions based on stereotypes are prohibited. http://www.eeoc.gov/policy/docs/race-color.html, accessed January 16, 2013.

43. Employers may consider their racial-realist preferences to be rational or statistical discrimination. In each chapter, I assess what social science there is to support racial- or immigrant-realist preferences. On statistical discrimination, see Edmund S. Phelps, "The Statistical Theory of Racism and Sexism," *American Economic Review* 62 (1972): 659–61; and William T. Bielby and James N. Baron, "Men and Women at Work: Sex Segregation and Statistical Discrimination," *American Journal of Sociology* 91(1986): 759–99. On definitions of stereotypes by psychologists, see James L. Hilton and William von Hippel, "Stereotypes," *Annual Review of Psychology* 47 (1996): 237–71.

44. An early and influential use of signaling in employment processes, though from the perspective of the worker, is Michael Spence, "Job Market Signaling," *Quarterly Journal of Economics* 87 (1973): 355–74. The notion of signaling is used frequently in political science, especially in formal theories of international relations and the functioning of institutions. My use is similar: by signaling I am referring to employers' conscious, intentional efforts to communicate meanings through actions; in this case, through hiring workers of particular races. On signaling in political science, see, for example, Beth Simmons, "Treaty Compliance and Violation," *Annual Review of Political Science* 13 (2010): 273–96.

45. See, for example, the work of Tristin Green, who argues: "Title VII permits (and should permit) the use of race and sex in decisions organizing work as a means of reducing workplace discrimination, although not as a means of serving business interests alone"; and "Title VII requires (and should require) that those race- or sex-based decisions be part of an employer's broader integrative effort, an effort comprised of various structural reforms that are likely to foster functional integration and reduce workplace discrimination." Tristin Green, "Race and Sex in Organizing Work: 'Diversity,' Discrimination and Integration," *Emory Law Journal* 59 (2010): 585–47, p. 591.

46. The EEOC's *Compliance Manual* discusses "diversity" programs and contrasts them with affirmative action, but its description of acceptable diversity programs is essentially the same as what used to be called "soft" affirmative action or "outreach." Though it uses some racial-realist language about diversity being good for organizations, when discussing what is legal, the EEOC does not indicate

support for racial abilities or racial signaling, instead stating: "Title VII permits diversity efforts designed to open up opportunities to everyone," and though encouraging "diversity efforts to improve opportunities for racial minorities in order to carry out the Congressional intent embodied in Title VII," also warned that these should be undertaken carefully, noting that the Supreme Court has never ruled on the diversity rationale under Title VII. See the *EEOC Compliance Manual*, Section 15, April 19, 2006; http://www.eeoc.gov/policy/docs/race-color.html, accessed December 8, 2012. In 2011, Barack Obama issued Executive Order 13583, "Establishing a Coordinated Government-wide Initiative to Promote Diversity and Inclusion in the Federal Workforce." Despite some racial-realist language in the order's statement of "policy" (" . . . our greatest accomplishments are achieved when diverse perspectives are brought to bear to overcome our greatest challenges"), the order's specific requirements are all the stuff of affirmative-action liberalism. There are no specific directives regarding how to leverage difference on the job. Instead, the order simply uses the language of affirmative action: "The Government-wide Plan shall highlight comprehensive strategies for agencies to identify and remove barriers to equal employment opportunity that may exist in the Federal Government's recruitment, hiring, promotion, retention, professional development, and training policies and practices." *Federal Register* vol. 76.163 (August 23, 2011) 52,877–849. On outreach and "soft" versus "hard" affirmative action, see Sabbagh, *Equality and Transparency*, p. 3; and Hugh Davis Graham, "Affirmative Action for Immigrants? The Unintended Consequences of Reform," in John D. Skrentny, ed., *Color Lines: Affirmative Action, Immigration and Civil Rights Options for America* (Chicago: University of Chicago Press, 2001) 53–70, pp. 59–60.

47. *Grutter v. Bollinger*, 539 U.S. 306 (2003); Cynthia Estlund, "Putting *Grutter* to Work: Diversity, Integration, and Affirmative Action in the Workplace," *Berkeley Journal of Employment and Labor Law* 26 (2005): 1–39; Green, "Race and Sex in Organizing Work"; Rebecca Hanner White, "Affirmative Action in the Workplace: The Significance of *Grutter*?" *Kentucky Law Journal* 92 (2003): 263–78; Ronald Turner, "*Grutter*, the Diversity Justification, and Workplace Affirmative Action," *Brandeis Law Journal* 43 (2004): 199–237; Jessica Bulman-Pozen, "Note: *Grutter* at Work: A Title VII Critique of Constitutional Affirmative Action," *Yale Law Journal* 115 (2006): 1408–48.

48. The relevant passage states: "It shall not be an unlawful employment practice for an employer to hire and employ employees . . . on the basis of his religion, sex, or national origin in those certain instances where religion, sex, or national origin is a bona fide occupational qualification reasonably necessary to the normal operation of that particular business or enterprise." 42 USC § 2000E–2(e)(1).

49. "Interpretive Memorandum of Title VII of H.R. 7152 Submitted Jointly by Senator Joseph S. Clark And Senator Clifford P. Case, Floor Managers," *Congressional Record*, April 8, 1964, 7213.

50. State antidiscrimination laws vary in whether or not they allow a BFOQ defense for race discrimination, though this area of law is not well developed. See, for example, Pennsylvania's law; http://www.portal.state.pa.us/portal/server .pt/community/law___legal_resources/18980/pennsylvania_human_relations_ act/725567, accessed January 16, 2013.

51. *Congressional Record*, February 8, 1964, 2550.

52. Adam Clayton Powell, Jr. (D-NY) also said, "20 million Negroes are willing to take their chances on this bill." *Congressional Record*, February 8, 1964, 2550. As I show in Chapter 5, Clark, in a "Response to Dirksen Memorandum" to Senate minority leader Everett Dirksen (R-IL) who had asked about the Harlem Globetrotters or filmmakers doing a movie about Africa, explained that filmmakers could not demand a black employee but only someone who looked black. *Congressional Record*, April 8, 1964, 7217.

53. For an excellent analysis of the missing race BFOQ in Title VII, see Kingsley Browne, "Nonremedial Justifications for Affirmative Action in Employment: A Critique of the Justice Department Position," *Labor Lawyer* 12 (1997): 451–73.

54. See Kathleen Barry, *Femininity in Flight: A History of Flight Attendants* (Durham, NC: Duke University Press, 2007) for a discussion.

55. *Diaz v. Pan Amerocam World Airways, Inc.*, 442 F.2d 385 (5th Cir. 1971).

56. *Wilson v. Southwest Airlines*, 517 F. Supp. 292 (N.D. Tex. 1981).

57. Robert L. Nelson, Ellen Berrey, and Laura Beth Nielsen, "Divergent Paths: Conflicting Conceptions of Employment Discrimination in Law and the Social Sciences," *Annual Review of Law and Social Science* 4 (2008): 103–22, p. 107.

58. It should be clear that belief in the racial abilities and racial signaling of whites has always been with us, though this is openly defended only rarely, at least since 1964. There is further discussion on this below.

59. Susan S. Silbey, "After Legal Consciousness," *Annual Review of Law and Social Science* 1 (2005): 323–68, p. 324.

60. Roscoe Pound, "Law in Books and Law in Action," *American Law Review* 44 (1910): 12–36.

61. Eugen Erhlich, *Fundamental Principles of the Sociology of Law* (New York: Russell and Russell, 1962 [1936]) 493.

62. David Nelken, "Law in Action or Living Law? Back to the Beginning in Sociology of Law," *Legal Studies* 4 (1984): 157–174, p. 161.

63. On law as a set of institutions, see John R. Sutton, *Law/Society: Origins, Interactions, and Change* (Thousand Oaks, CA: Pine Forge Press, 2001) 8–14. An influential work examining legal consciousness is Patricia Ewick and Susan S. Silbey, *The Common Place of Law: Stories from Everyday Life* (Chicago: University of Chicago Press, 1998).

64. Susan Silbey, "After Legal Consciousness," 327.

65. On interpretive approaches to law, see Kim Lane Scheppele, "Legal Theory and Social Theory," *Annual Review of Sociology* 20 (1994): 383–406.

66. Ronald Dworkin has critiqued this "speaker's meaning" view of legislative intent, asking, "Which historical people count as the legislators? How are their intentions to be discovered? When these intentions differ somewhat from one to another, how are they to be combined in the overall, composite institutional intention?" Ronald Dworkin, *Law's Empire* (Cambridge, MA: Harvard University Press, 1986) 315–316.

67. William N. Eskridge, Jr., *Dynamic Statutory Interpretation* (Cambridge, MA: Harvard University Press, 1994) 16.

68. Skrentny, *Ironies*, 34.

69. Skrentny, *Ironies*, 120–21.

70. John D. Skrentny, *The Minority Rights Revolution* (Cambridge, MA: Belknap Press of Harvard University Press, 2002) Chapter 4.

71. Skrentny, *Ironies*, Chapter 5.

72. On human resources and personnel professionals having their own ideas of the meaning of the law, see Frank Dobbin, *Inventing Equal Opportunity* (Princeton, NJ: Princeton University Press, 2008); Lauren B. Edelman, "Legal Ambiguity and Symbolic Structures: Organizational Mediation of Civil Rights Law," *American Journal of Sociology* 97 (1992): 1531–76; and Lauren B. Edelman, Christopher Uggen and Howard S. Erlanger, "The Endogeneity of Legal Regulation: Grievance Procedures as Rational Myth," *American Journal of Sociology* 105 (1999): 406–54. On the idea of differently situated actors, both in the government and outside of it, having different interpretations of the meaning of laws, see Jeb Barnes and Thomas F. Burke, "The Diffusion of Rights: From Law on the Books to Organizational Rights Practices," *Law & Society Review* 40 (2006): 493–523, pp. 495–96.

73. Barnes and Burke, "Diffusion of Rights," 495.

74. Keith Bybee, *All Judges Are Political—Except When They Are Not: Acceptable Hypocrisies and the Rule of Law* (Stanford, CA: Stanford University Press, 2010). Legal philosopher Ronald Dworkin calls these "theoretical" disagreements about law, in cases when there is disagreement "about whether statute books and judicial decisions exhaust the pertinent grounds of law." Ronald Dworkin, *Law's Empire* (Cambridge, MA: Harvard University Press, 1986), 5.

75. Law may provide a framework, within which there may be considerable discretion. Robert H. Mnookin and Lewis Kornhauser, "Bargaining in the Shadow of Law: The Case of Divorce," *Yale Law Journal* 88 (1979): 950–97.

76. For a useful summary of the institutional logics of judicial decision-making, see Robin Stryker, Danielle Docka-Filipek, and Pamela Wald, "Employment Discrimination Law and Industrial Psychology: Social Science as Social Authority and the Co-Production of Law and Science," *Law and Social Inquiry* 37(2012): 777–814.

77. This is perhaps most glaringly obvious in the enforcement of American immigration laws, which would seem to forbid unauthorized entry or stay in the country, while millions of undocumented immigrants nevertheless live and work in the country. Kitty Calavita, *Invitation to Law and Society: An Introduction to the Study of Real Law* (Chicago: University of Chicago Press, 2010) 104–105.

78. Calavita, *Law and Society*, 114.

79. Calavita, *Law and Society*, 110; Terence C. Halliday and Bruce G. Carruthers, "The Recursivity of Law: Global Norm Making and National Lawmaking in the Globalization of Corporate Insolvency Regimes," *American Journal of Sociology* 112 (2007): 1135–1202.

80. This is a major part of the post–1964 evolution of Title VII law, as Frank Dobbin, Lauren Edelman, John Sutton and others have shown (see above). Congress passed the law, but it was vague, and firms had to decide what "compliance" actually meant. Courts then affirmed those compliance-symbolizing actions.

Other scholars have shown more explicitly the role of courts in this process, including "structuring occasions for norm development," "increasing non-legal actors' capacity" to generate workable norms, and "developing the capacity of mediating actors, such as experts and administrative agencies, to connect the domains of law and norms." Susan Sturm, "Law, Norms, and Complex Discrimination," in Brian Bercusson and Cynthia Estlund, eds., *Regulating Labour in the Wake of Globalization: New Challenges, New Institutions* (Portland, OR: Hart Publishing, 2008) 137–160, p. 153. My point here is that courts have not affirmed racial realism as compliant with Title VII , and have made only a few decisions allowing racial-realist strategies to become normalized, though they are still widely advocated and practiced.

81. Ewick and Silbey define this term as "the meanings, sources of authority, and cultural practices that are commonly recognized as legal, regardless of who employs them or for what purposes." Ewick and Silbey, *Common Place of Law*, 22; also see Silbey, *After Legal Consciousness*, 347.

82. This point is a major theme throughout Schuck, *Diversity in America*.

83. Paul Frymer, "'A Rush and a Push and the Land is Ours': Race, Population Control, and the Nineteenth Century American Expansion," paper presented to the Department of Politics, Princeton University, March 7, 2012; Hendrik Hartog, "The Constitution of Aspiration and 'The Rights That Belong to Us All'," *Journal of American History* 74.3 (December 1987) 1013–34; Rogers Smith, *Civic Ideals: Conflicting Visions of Citizenship in U.S. History* (New Haven, CT: Yale University Press, 1997); Rogers M. Smith, "Beyond Tocqueville, Myrdal and Hartz: The Multiple Traditions in America," *American Political Science Review* 87 (1993): 549–66; Desmond S. King and Rogers M. Smith, "Racial Orders in American Political Development," *American Political Science Review* 99 (2005): 75–92; Benjamin Ringer, *We the People and Others: Duality and America's Treatment of Its Racial Minorities* (New York: Tavistock, 1983).

84. See Chapter 18, "The Present and Probably Future Condition of the Three Races That Inhabit the Territory of the United States," Alexis de Tocqueville, *Democracy in America*, vol. 1 (New York: Vintage Books, 1990 [1945]; originally published in 1835/1840).

85. Drew Gilpin Faust, *This Republic of Suffering: Death and the American Civil War* (New York: Alfred A. Knopf, 2008).

86. Albert Bergesen and Max Herman, "Immigration, Race, and Riot: The 1992 Los Angeles Uprising," *American Sociological Review* 63 (1998): 39–54.

87. See, for example, Donald L. Horowitz, *Ethnic Groups in Conflict, 2nd ed.* (Berkeley: University of California Press, 2000); James D. Fearon and David D. Laitin, "Ethnicity, Insurgency and Civil War," *American Political Science Review* 97 (2003): 75–90; James D. Fearon and David D. Laitin, "Explaining Interethnic Cooperation," 90 (1996): 715–35; Susan Olzak, *The Dynamics of Ethnic Competition and Conflict* (Stanford, CA: Stanford University Press, 1992). On government discrimination against ethnic minorities contributing to political instability, see Jack A. Goldstone, Robert H. Bates, David L. Epstein, Ted Robert Gurr, Michael B. Lustik, Monty G. Marshall, Jay Ulfelder, and Mark Woodward, "A Global Model for Forecasting Political Instability," *American Journal of Political Science*, 54 (2010): 190–208, p. 201.

88. See, for example, the discussion in Frank D. Bean and Gillian Stevens, *America's Newcomers and the Dynamics of Diversity* (New York: Russell Sage Foundation, 2003).

89. *Lawrence v. Texas* 539 U.S. 558, 572 (2003).

90. This dynamic is familiar to scholars of organizations, who find more generally that a simple, focused job applicant identity can aid employers' abilities to assess the value of an applicant for a job, and this can make it easier to be hired over an applicant who has a complex background and no obvious placement. Yet just as with the dynamic of being typecast in a Hollywood film, that simple, focused background ultimately creates limitations. More complex identities can allow a worker to be plugged into many different situations, thus creating opportunities. Ezra W. Zuckerman, Tai-Young Kim, Kalinda Ukanwa, and James von Rittman, "Robust Identities or Nonentities? Typecasting in the Feature-Film Labor Market," *American Journal of Sociology* 108 (2003): 1018–74. This is similar to the typecasting in racial realism.

91. Malamud, "Diversity of Opinions," 962–63.

92. Martha Minow, *Making All the Difference: Inclusion, Exclusion, and American Law* (Ithaca, NY: Cornell University Press, 1990) 20, original emphasis.

93. Schuck, *Diversity in America*, 322.

94. Karen R. Humes, Nicholas A. Jones, and Roberto R. Ramirez, "Overview of Race and Hispanic Origins: 2010," *2010 Census Briefs*, March, 2011; http://www.census.gov/prod/cen2010/briefs/c2010br-02.pdf, accessed July 5, 2011. For an especially lucid discussion, see Chapter 4 of Jennifer Lee and Frank D. Bean, *The Diversity Paradox: Immigration and the Color Line in 21st Century America* (New York: Russell Sage Foundation, 2010).

95. William H. Frey, *Diversity Explosion: How New Racial Demographics are Remaking America* (Washington, DC: Brookings Institution, 2014); Mary Waters and Tomás R. Jiménez, "Assessing Immigrant Assimilation: New Empirical and Theoretical Challenges," *Annual Review of Sociology* 31(2005): 105–25.

96. Skrentny, *Minority Rights Revolution*, 37–57.

97. Douglas S. Massey, Jorge Durand, and Nolan J. Malone, *Beyond Smoke and Mirrors: Mexican Immigration in an Era of Economic Integration* (New York: Russell Sage Foundation, 2002) 40–51; Hugh Davis Graham, *Collision Course: The Strange Convergence of Affirmative Action and Immigration Policy in America* (New York: Oxford University Press, 2002); John D. Skrentny, "Obama's Immigration Reform: A Tough Sell for a Grand Bargain," in Theda Skocpol and Larry Jacobs, eds., *Reaching for a New Deal: Ambitious Governance, Economic Meltdown, and Polarized Politics in Obama's First Two Years* (New York: Russell Sage Foundation, 2011) 273–320.

98. Brent Eric Valentine, "Uniting Two Cultures? Latino Immigrants in the Wisconsin Dairy Industry," Center for Comparative Immigration Studies Working Paper 121 (September 2005) 76–78.

99. John C. Caldwell, "Mass Education as a Determinant of the Timing of Fertility Decline," *Population and Development Review* 6 (1980): 225–55.

100. S. Philip Morgan, "Characteristic Features of Modern American Fertility," *Population and Development Review* 22 (1996): 19–63; Jane Lawler Dye, "Fertility of American Women: 2006," *Current Population Reports*, August 2008, U.S.

Census Bureau; https://www.census.gov/prod/2008pubs/p20-558.pdf, accessed July 7, 2012.

101. William Kandel and Emilio A. Parrado, "Restructuring of the U.S. Meat Processing Industry and New Hispanic Migrant Destinations," *Population and Development Review* 31 (2005): 447–71; Frank D. Bean, Susan K. Brown, James D. Bachmeier, Zoya Gubernskaya, and Christopher D. Smith, "Luxury, Necessity, and Anachronistic Workers: Does the United States Need Unskilled Immigrant Labor?" *American Behavioral Scientist* 56 (2012): 1008–28.

102. Bean et al., "Luxury, Necessity," 1015-1016. Also see Doris Meissner, Deborah W. Meyers, Demetrios G. Papademetriou and Michael Fix, *Immigration and America's Future: A New Chapter: Report of the Independent Task Force on Immigration and America's Future* (Washington, DC: Migration Policy Institute, 2006), p. 5, showing that the percentage of workers with more than a high school education increased from 38.9 percent to 58 percent between 1980 and 2000, and those with a college degree rose from 21.6 percent to 30.2 percent in the same time period.

103. Meissner, et al, *Immigration and America's Future*, 10.

104. Barry Bluestone and Bennett Harrison, *The Deindustrialization of America: Plant Closings, Community Abandonment, and the Dismantling of Basic Industry* (New York: Basic Books, 1982). See especially Chapter 2. Also see Jefferson Cowie, *Capital Moves: RCA's Seventy-Year Quest for Cheap Labor* (Ithaca, NY: Cornell University Press, 1999).

105. William Julius Wilson, *The Bridge over the Racial Divide: Rising Inequality and Coalition Politics* (Berkeley: University of California Press, 1999) Chapter 2; Dorian T. Warren, "The American Labor Movement in the Age of Obama: The Challenges and Opportunities of a Racialized Political Economy," *Perspectives on Politics* 8 (2010): 847–60, p. 851.

106. https://www.restaurant.org/pdfs/research/2010Forecast_PFB.pdf.

107. Erin Kelly and Frank Dobbin, "How Affirmative Action Became Diversity Management: Employer Response to Antidiscrimination Law, 1961–1996," in John D. Skrentny, ed., *Color Lines: Affirmative Action, Immigration and Civil Rights Options for America* (Chicago: University of Chicago Press, 2001) 87–117; Lauren B. Edelman, Sally Riggs Fuller, and Iona Mara-Drita, "Diversity Rhetoric and the Managerialization of Law," *American Journal of Sociology* 106 (2001): 1589–1641; Frank Dobbin, *Inventing Equal Opportunity*.

108. The groups were in conflict on some immigration issues in the 1970s and 1980s. Daniel Tichenor, *Dividing Lines: The Politics of Immigration Control in America* (Princeton, NJ: Princeton University Press, 2002) and Nicolas C. Vaca, *The Presumed Alliance: The Unspoken Conflict between Latinos and Blacks and What It Means for America* (New York: HarperCollins, 2004). Black voters in California opposed rights for undocumented immigrants in the 1990s at twice the rate of Latino voters. Zoltan L. Hajnal, Elizabeth R. Gerber, and Hugh Louch, "Minorities and Direct Legislation: Evidence from California Ballot Proposition Elections," *Journal of Politics* 64 (2002): 154–177.

109. Rodney E. Hero and Robert R. Preuhs, *Black-Latino Relations in U.S. National Politics: Beyond Conflict or Cooperation* (New York: Cambridge University Press, 2013) Chapter 7.

110. Paul Frymer, "Acting When Elected Officials Won't: Federal Courts and Civil Rights Enforcement in U.S. Labor Unions, 1935–85," *American Political Science Review* 97 (2003): 483–99; Sean Farhang, *The Litigation State: Public Regulation and Private Lawsuits in the United States* (Princeton, NJ: Princeton University Press, 2010). Civil rights is not the only case where this has happened. Mark A. Graber, "The Non-Majoritarian Problem: Legislative Deference to the Judiciary," *Studies in American Political Development* 7 (1993): 35–72.

111. Paul Frymer and John D. Skrentny, "Coalition-Building and the Politics of Electoral Capture During the Nixon Administration: African Americans, Labor, Latinos," *Studies in American Political Development* 12 (1998): 131–61; Paul Frymer, *Uneasy Alliances: Race and Party Competition in America* (Princeton, NJ: Princeton University Press, 1999); John David Skrentny, *The Ironies of Affirmative Action: Politics, Culture and Justice in America* (Chicago: University of Chicago Press, 1996).

112. John D. Skrentny, "Republican Efforts to End Affirmative Action: Walking a Fine Line," in Marc Landy, Martin Levin, and Martin Shapiro, eds., *Seeking the Center: Politics and Policymaking at the New Century* (Washington, DC: Georgetown University Press, 2001) 132–71. On blame avoidance and policy retrenchment, see R. Kent Weaver, "The Politics of Blame Avoidance," *Journal of Public Policy* 6 (1986): 371–98 and Paul Pierson, *Dismantling the Welfare State? Reagan, Thatcher and the Politics of Retrenchment* (New York: Cambridge University Press, 1994). Sarah Staszak notes that even the judicial strategy of retrenchment can avoid direct confrontation, instead focusing on changing the rules of access to courts and the kinds of remedies offered. Sarah Staszak, "Institutions, Rulemaking, and the Politics of Judicial Retrenchment," *Studies in American Political Development* 24 (2010): 168–89.

113. *City of Richmond v. Croson*, 488 U.S. 469 (1989); *Adarand Constructors, Inc. v. Peña*, 515 U.S. 200 (1995).

114. *Parents Involved in Community Schools v. Seattle School District No. 1*, 551 U.S. 701 (2007).

115. Michelle Adams, "Stifling The Potential of Grutter v. Bollinger: Parents Involved in Community Schools v. Seattle School District No. 1," *Boston University Law Review* 88 (2008): 937–90.

116. *Fisher v. University of Texas*, 133 S. Ct. 2411 (2013). At the time of this writing, the Court has agreed to hear yet another admissions case, assessing the state of Michigan's amendment to its state constitution banning affirmative action in admission to state universities.

117. *Rico v. DeStefano*, 557 U.S. 557, 579 (2009).

118. Scholars have argued that the Supreme Court's limitations on permissible rationales for affirmative action have actually encouraged employers to frame their race-relevant hiring and placement practices as efforts to encourage "diversity" or other racial-realist terms. See Kelly and Dobbin, "How Affirmative Action Became Diversity Management." David B. Wilkins makes this argument in the context of law firms, in "From 'Separate Is Inherently Unequal' to 'Diversity Is Good for Business': The Rise of Market-Based Diversity Arguments and the Fate of the Black Corporate Bar," *Harvard Law Review* 117 (2004): 1548–1615, 1554.

119. 476 U.S. 267 (1986).

120. Despite the burdens of time and money involved in initiating a lawsuit, and the reduced likelihood of winning (see, for example, Silbey, "After Legal Consciousness," 335–36 and Nelson, Berrey and Nielsen, "Divergent Paths," 109), employment discrimination litigation is (after petitions from prisoners seeking to be set free) the largest single category on the federal courts' docket at 10 percent, or about 20,700 a year—and 98 percent of these are suits brought by private individuals rather than organizations or the government suing on behalf of workers too poor or distracted to fight for themselves. Sean Farhang, *The Litigation State: Public Regulation and Private Lawsuits in the U.S.* (Princeton, NJ: Princeton University Press, 2010) 3; Kevin M. Clermont and Stewart J. Schwab, "How Employment Discrimination Plaintiffs Fare in Federal Court," *Journal of Empirical Legal Studies* 1 (2004): 429–58, p. 432.

121. See their website, http://www.cir-usa.org/mission_new.html, accessed November 27, 2012.

122. One Cato Institute scholar has remarked, "In a free society, of course, employers would be perfectly free to engage in voluntary affirmative action of any kind—and would likely be encouraged to do so in certain circumstances—for the discrimination that is entailed by affirmative action is perfectly legitimate as a private act." Roger Pilon, "Discrimination, Affirmative Action and Freedom: Sorting Out the Issues," *American University Law Review* 45 (1996): 775–90, p. 786.

123. Steven M. Teles, *The Rise of the Conservative Legal Movement: The Battle for the Control of Law* (Princeton, NJ: Princeton University Press, 2008) 232.

124. The move to attack affirmative action at universities came about because the organization's leaders believed "the quotaization of the academy" was related to goals on their higher education agenda. Teles, *Conservative Legal Movement*, 235. Pursuing litigation aimed at university admissions also presented challenges. See Teles, *Conservative Legal Movement*, 260.

125. Author interview with Roger Clegg, November 29, 2012.

126. David Kairys, "Legal Reasoning," in David Kairys, ed., *The Politics of Law: A Progressive Critique* (New York: Pantheon Books, 1982) 11–17.

127. R. Shep Melnick, *Between the Lines: Interpreting Welfare Rights* (Washington, DC: Brookings Institution, 1994).

128. Eskridge, *Dynamic Statutory Interpretation*, 52.

129. Donald Horowitz, *The Courts and Social Policy* (Washington, DC: Brookings Institution, 1977) 13. In an earlier work, I showed how, in *Lau v. Nichols* (414 U.S. 563 [1974]) the Supreme Court ruled on statutory grounds that children of limited English ability had a right to some language accommodation in the schools, despite the Nixon administration's brief and the early draft of the opinion arguing for the same result based on the Consitution; Skrentny, *Minority Rights Revolution*, Chapter 6.

130. In earlier periods, the courts and civil rights agencies tended to work together in making new law. See R. Shep Melnick, "Judicial Power in the Civil Rights State: An Empirical Investigation" (July 15, 2009). Available at SSRN: http://ssrn.com/abstract=1434702 or http://dx.doi.org/10.2139/ssrn.1434702, accessed August 15, 2012.

131. I reviewed these arguments in John D. Skrentny, "Culture and Race/Ethnicity: Bolder, Deeper, and Broader," *Annals of the American Academy of Political and Social Science* 619 (2008): 59–77, pp. 66–67.

132. David A. Hollinger, *Post-Ethnic America: Beyond Multiculturalism* (New York: Basic Books, 1995).

133. On race mixing, see David A. Hollinger, "Amalgamation and Hypodescent: The Question of Ethnoracial Mixture in the United States," *American Historical Review* 108 (2003): 1363–90. The complexity of race in contemporary America is also insightfully analyzed in Jennifer Lee and Frank D. Bean, *The Diversity Paradox: Immigration and the Color Line in 21st Century America* (New York: Russell Sage Foundation Press, 2010); Jennifer L. Hochschild, Vesla M. Weaver, and Traci R. Burch, *Creating a New Racial Order: How Immigration, Multiracialism, Genomics, and the Young Can Remake Race in America* (Princeton, NJ: Princeton University Press, 2012); and Orlando Patterson, *The Ordeal of Integration: Progress and Resentment in America's "Racial" Crisis* (New York: Civitas, 1997).

134. EEOC Joint Reporting Committee, "Standard Form 100 Instruction Booklet"; http://www.eeoc.gov/employers/eeo1survey/2007instructions.cfm, accessed January 16, 2013.

135. EEOC, "Facts about Race/Color Discrimination"; http://www.eeoc.gov/facts/fs-race.html, accessed January 16, 2013.

136. In 2010, slightly more than half of those who said they were Hispanic also said they were white. Only 2.5 percent said they were black, and almost 37 percent said they were "some other race." Karen R. Humes, Nicholas A. Jones, and Roberto R. Ramirez, "Overview of Race and Hispanic Origin: 2010," *2010 Census Briefs*, March 2011, 6; http://www.census.gov/prod/cen2010/briefs/c2010br-02.pdf, accessed May 18, 2012. When given a chance to choose "Hispanic" as a racial identity, however, more do so. Steven Hitlin, J. Scott Brown, and Glen H. Elder, Jr., "Measuring Latinos: Racial vs. Ethnic Classification and Self-Understandings," *Social Forces* 86 (2007): 587–611.

137. EEOC, "Questions and Answers: Implementation of Revised Race and Ethnic Categories"; http://www1.eeoc.gov//employers/eeo1/qanda-implementation.cfm?renderforprint=1, accessed January 29, 2013.

138. EEOC, "Instruction Booklet."

139. EEOC, *Compliance Manual*; http://www.eeoc.gov/laws/guidance/compliance.cfm, accessed January 29, 2013.

140. See, for example, Wendy D. Roth, *Race Migrations: Latinos and the Cultural Transformation of Race* (Stanford, CA: Stanford University Press, 2012); Douglas S. Massey and Magaly Sánchez R., *Brokered Boundaries: Creating Immigrant Identity in Anti-Immigrant Times* (New York: Russell Sage Foundation, 2010). There is evidence that some Mexican-Americans are experiencing racialization, while others are assimilating. Richard Alba, Tomás Jiménez, and Helen B. Marrow, "Mexican Americans as a Paradigm for Contemporary Intra-Group Heterogeneity," *Ethnic and Racial Studies* [forthcoming].

141. G. Cristina Mora, *Making Hispanics: How Activists, Bureaucrats, and Media Constructed a New American* (Chicago: University of Chicago Press, 2014).

An example of the national news media constructing Latinos as a racial category was a recent headline story stating that, for the first time, "whites" do not make up the majority of births in the U.S., due primarily to the massive increase in the number of (apparently not white) Latinos. Sabrina Tavernise, "Whites Account for Under Half of Births in U.S.," *New York Times*, May 17, 2012; http://www.nytimes.com/2012/05/17/us/whites-account-for-under-half-of-births-in-us.html?_r=1, accessed May 18, 2012.

142. On the notion that Americans tend to categorize Latino immigrants as nonwhite, see Reanne Frank, Ilana Redstone Akresh, and Bo Lu, "Latino Immigrants and the U.S. Racial Order: How and Where Do They Fit In? *American Sociological Review* 75 (2010): 378–401.

143. From the perspective of cultural sociology, this slip in language is not surprising. Culture provides meanings, discourses, categorical schemes, and moral boundaries that are important in understanding how people behave and how similarly situated persons, even with similar goals, may respond differently. For culture to have these effects, culture does not have to be internally coherent, nor does it have to be deployed, or impactful, in consistent ways. This is true in informal spheres of life, and also in areas that people may care deeply about, as in religion. We may care about something deeply, and it also may not make much sense. For most of our lives, we interpret our world to the bare minimum—we muddle through, we do what it takes to get by and accomplish our goals. Sociologists have made this point in a variety of contexts, including religion (Mark Chaves, "Rain Dances in the Dry Season: Overcoming the Religious Congruence Fallacy," *Journal for the Scientific Study of Religion* 49 [2010]: 1–14, and John H. Evans, *Contested Reproduction: Genetic Technologies, Religion, and Public Debate* [Chicago: University of Chicago Press, 2010] Chapter 1); in career decisions (Mary Blair-Loy, *Competing Devotions: Career and Family among Women Executives* [Cambridge, MA: Harvard University Press, 2003]); politics (Amy Binder and Kate Wood, *Becoming Right: How Campuses Shape Young Conservatives* [Princeton, NJ: Princeton University Press, 2013] Chapter 8); and relationships (Ann Swidler, *Talk of Love: How Culture Matters* [Chicago: University of Chicago Press, 2001]). Keith Bybee shows that Americans simultaneously think of courts as both political institutions and also neutral arbiters of the law. Keith J. ByBee, *All Judges Are Political—Except When They Are Not: Acceptable Hypocrisies and the Rule of Law* (Stanford, CA: Stanford Law Books, 2010).

144. In an earlier stage of this project, I and some research assistants conducted several interviews with employers in such diverse fields as journalism, policing, and education. They varied considerably in their willingness to talk and to reveal much about their strategies. While police departments were quite open, school districts and news organizations were so reluctant to discuss their views on racial realism that I ceased relying on interviews for the empirical material in this book.

Chapter 2. Leverage: Racial Realism in the Professions and Business

1. Margaret M. Heckler, *Report of the Secretary's Task Force on Black and Minority Health* (Washington, DC: Government Printing Office, 1985). On this struggle, see Chris Bonastia, "The Historical Trajectory of Civil Rights Enforcement in Health Care," *Journal of Policy History* 18 (2006): 362–86; Alondra Nelson, *Body and Soul: The Black Panther Party and the Fight against Medical Discrimination* (Minneapolis: University of Minnesota Press, 2011); Jill S. Quadagno, "Promoting Civil Rights through the Welfare State: How Medicare Integrated Southern Hospitals," *Social Problems* 47 (2000): 68–89; David Barton Smith, *Health Care Divided: Race and Healing a Nation* (Ann Arbor: University of Michigan Press, 1999); Keith Wailoo, *Dying in the City of the Blues: Sickle Cell Anemia and the Politics of Race and Health* (Chapel Hill: University of North Carolina Press, 2001).

2. http://www.nih.gov/about/almanac/organization/NIMHD.htm, accessed January 30, 2013.

3. Sade Kosoko-Lasaki, Cynthia Theresa Cook, Richard L. O'Brien, *Cultural Proficiency in Addressing Health Disparities* (Sudbury, MA: Jones & Bartlett Learning, 2009).

4. Jordan J. Cohen, Barbara A. Gabriel, and Charles Terrell, "The Case for Diversity in the Health Care Workforce," *Health Affairs* 21 (2002): 90–102.

5. Cynthia Charatz-Litt, "A Chronicle of Racism: The Effects of the White Medical Community on Black Health," *Journal of the National Medical Association* 84 (1992): 717–25; Robert B. Baker, Harriet A. Washington, Ololade Olakanmi, Todd L. Savitt, Elizabeth Jacobs, Eddie Hoover, and Matthew Wynia, "African American Physicians and Organized Medicine, 1846–1968: Origins of a Racial Divide," *JAMA* 300 (2008): 306–13.

6. Cohen, Gabriel, and Terrell, "Case for Diversity," 93.

7. Cohen, Gabriel, and Terrell, 94.

8. Raynard Kington, Diana Tisnado, and David Carlisle, "Increasing Racial and Ethnic Diversity among Physicians: An Intervention to Address Health Disparities?" in Brian D. Smedley, Adrienne Y. Stith, Lois Colburn, and Clyde H. Evans, eds., *The Right Thing to Do, the Smart Thing to Do* (Washington, DC: National Academy Press: Institute of Medicine, 2001) 57–90, p. 58.

9. Paul Starr, *The Social Transformation of American Medicine: The Rise of a Sovereign Profession and the Making of a Vast Industry* (New York: Basic Books, 1982), 168.

10. Charatz-Litt, "A Chronicle of Racism"; Robert B. Baker, Harriet A. Washington, Ololade Olakanmi, Todd L. Savitt, Elizabeth Jacobs, Eddie Hoover, and Matthew Wynia, "African American Physicians and Organized Medicine, 1846–1968: Origins of a Racial Divide," *JAMA* 300 (2008): 306–13; Andrew H. Beck, "The Flexner Report and the Standardization of American Medical Education," *JAMA* 291 (2004): 2139–40.

11. Charatz-Litt, "A Chronicle of Racism"; Robert B. Baker, Harriet A. Washington, Ololade Olakanmi, Todd L. Savitt, Elizabeth Jacobs, Eddie Hoover, and

Matthew Wynia, "African American Physicians and Organized Medicine, 1846–1968: Origins of a Racial Divide," *JAMA* 300 (2008): 306–13.

12. James L. Curtis, *Affirmative Action in Medicine: Improving Health Care for Everyone* (Ann Arbor: University of Michigan Press, 2003), 18; John D. Skrentny, *The Minority Rights Revolution* (Cambridge, MA: Belknap Press of Harvard University Press, 2002) Chapter 6.

13. Statistics are from the American Medical Association's 2008 survey. American Medical Association, *Physician Statistics* (2010), http://www.ama-assn.org/ama/pub/about-ama/our-people/member-groups-sections/minority-affairs-consortium/physician-statistics/total-physicians-raceethnicity.page, accessed October 5, 2011. Also see Myra Croasdale, "Racial Fatigue: Minority Doctors Feeling the Pressure," *American Medical News*, July 23, 2007, http://www.ama-assn.org/amednews/2007/07/23/prsa0723.htm, accessed December 7, 2009. Other counts come up with slightly different but similarly low numbers. Blacks, Latinos, and American Indians make up more than a quarter of the population but only 6 percent of doctors and 9 percent of nurses. L. A. Cooper, D. L. Roter, R. L. Johnson, D. E. Ford, D. M. Steinwachs, and N. R. Powe, "Patient-Centered Communication, Ratings of Care, and Concordance of Patient and Physician Race," *Annals of Internal Medicine* 139.11 (December 2, 2003): 907–15.

14. Kenneth Labich and Joyce E. Davis, "Making Diversity Pay," *Fortune*, Sept. 9, 1996, 177.

15. The bill passed the Senate unanimously on October 26, 2000 and passed the House by a voice vote on October 31. For details, see http://thomas.loc.gov/cgi-bin/query/R?r106:FLD001:S61152 and http://www.govtrack.us/congress/bill.xpd?bill=s106-1880.

16. *Congressional Record*, November 8, 1999, 14,288.

17. Public Law 106–525, Nov. 22, 2000, Sec. 485F, "Centers of Excellence of Research Education."

18. Joseph R. Betancourt, Alexander R. Green, and J. Emilio Carrillo, *Cultural Competence in Health Care: Emerging Frameworks and Practical Approaches*, The Commonwealth Fund, October 2002, 17; http://www.commonwealthfund.org/usr_doc/betancourt_culturalcompetence_576.pdf, accessed December 14, 2009.

19. Sullivan Commission, *Missing Persons—Minorities in the Health Professions: A Report of the Sullivan Commission on Diversity in the Healthcare Workforce*, 2004, 20; http://health-equity.pitt.edu/40/1/Sullivan_Final_Report_000.pdf, accessed August 24, 2012.

20. Sullivan Commission, *Missing Persons*, 18.

21. Sullivan Commission, 18.

22. Sullivan Commission, 25. On racial diversity and medical organizations, also see Cohen, Gabriel, and Terrell, "Case for Diversity," 95.

23. *San Francisco Business Times*, March 19, 2004; http://sanfrancisco.bizjournals.com/sanfrancisco/stories/2004/03/22/focus2.html (accessed December 6, 2009).

24. Institute of Medicine Committee on Institutional and Policy-Level Strategies for Increasing the Diversity of the U.S. Health Care Work Force, *In the Nation's Compelling Interest: Ensuring Diversity in the Health-Care Workforce* (Washington, DC: National Academies Press, 2004).

25. Emily Friedman, *White Coats and Many Colors: Population Diversity and Its Implications for Health Care: An Issue Briefing Prepared for the American Hospital Association* (Chicago: American Hospital Association, 2005) 40–42.

26. U.S. Department of Health and Human Services, Health Resources and Services Administration, Bureau of Health Professions, *The Rationale for Diversity in the Health Professions: A Review of the Evidence*, October 2006, 3; http://bhpr.hrsa.gov/healthworkforce/reports/diversityreviewevidence.pdf, accessed August 24, 2012.

27. American College of Physicians, *Racial and Ethnic Disparities in Health Care*, A Policy Paper, updated 2010 (Philadelphia: American College of Physicians, 2010) 13; available from the American College of Physicians, 190 N. Independence Mall West, Philadelphia, PA 19106.

28. The Association of American Medical Colleges was the only major medical association that provided an amicus brief in the famous legal test of affirmative action in medical school admissions policies, *Regents of the University of California v. Bakke*, 438 U.S. 265 (1978). The UC-Davis Medical School had set aside a specific number of openings for black, Latino, American Indian, and Asian-American applicants. The Court ruled that racial quotas were illegal, but in a crucial swing vote opinion, Justice Powell wrote that race was a permissible factor in admissions if used for the goal of diversity. Arguments regarding the racial abilities or signaling of doctors are mostly absent from the opinions of the justices. The exception comes in Justice Powell's assessment of the Davis Medical School's argument that it sought to give preference to minority applicants in part because these applicants would be more likely to serve minority populations. Powell rejected this argument on the grounds that there was no evidence that race was a necessary admissions consideration to promote that goal, and that other methods were better suited to identify medical school applicants who would practice medicine in underserved populations. *Regents of University of California v. Bakke*, 438 U.S. 265, 310 (1978). On the *amici curiae* briefs in the case, see Timothy J. O'Neill, *Bakke and the Politics of Equality: Friends and Foes in the Classroom of Litigation* (Middletown, CT: Wesleyan University Press, 1985).

29. Amici curiae brief of the Association of American Medical Colleges et al., in *Grutter v. Bollinger*, 10, n.2.

30. Amici curiae crief of the Association of American Medical Colleges et al., in *Grutter v. Bollinger*, 11–12.

31. Amici curiae brief of the Association of American Medical Colleges et al., in *Grutter v. Bollinger*, 12–13.

32. Amici curiae brief of the Association of American Medical Colleges et al., in *Fisher v. University of Texas*, 14.

33. Bradly Gray, MS and Jeffrey J. Stoddard, MD, "Patient-Physician Pairing: Does Racial and Ethnic Congruity Influence Selection of a Regular Physician?" *Journal of Community Health* 22 (1997): 247–59, p. 257.

34. Keith, et al., "Effects of Affirmative Action."

35. Jason Schnittker and Ke Liang, "The Promise and Limits of Racial/Ethnic Concordance in Physician-Patient Interaction," *Journal of Health Politics, Policy and Law* 31 (2006): 811–38. In contrast to much of the literature in this area,

this study found only 22 percent of blacks and 27 percent of Latinos say they prefer a racially concordant physician.

36. Martha Harrison Stinson and Norman K. Thurston, "Racial Matching among African and Hispanic Physicians and Patients," *Journal of Human Resources* 37 (2002): 410–28.

37. For a review, see Kington, Tisnado, and Carlisle, "Racial and Ethnic Diversity among Physicians," 66–68. Black and Latino physicians are also more likely to have patients on Medicaid. S. N. Keith, R. M. Bell, A. G. Swanson, and A. P. Williams, "Effects of Affirmative Action in Medical Schools: A Study of the Class of 1975," *New England Journal of Medicine* 313 (1985): 1519–25; Kington, Tisnado and Carlisle, "Racial and Ethnic Diversity among Physicians," 69–73. Also see Miriam Komaromy, Kevin Grumbach, Michael Drake, Karen Vranizan, Nicole Lurie, Dennis Keane, and Andrew B. Bindman, "The Role of Black and Hispanic Physicians in Providing Health Care for Underserved Populations," *New England Journal of Medicine* 22 (1996): 1305–10. An excellent review of this literature can be found in Jeffrey F. Milem, "The Educational Benefits of Diversity: Evidence from Multiple Sectors," in Mitchell J. Chang, Daria Witt, James Jones, and Kenji Hakuta, eds., *Compelling Interest: Examining the Evidence on Racial Dynamics in Colleges and Universities* (Stanford, CA: Stanford University Press, 2003), 126–69, pp. 157–63.

38. Schnittker and Liang, "Promise and Limits of Racial/Ethnic Concordance"; Bernice Pescosolido, Jane McLeod, and Margarita Alegría, "Confronting the Second Social Contract: The Place of Medical Sociology in Research and Policy for the Twenty-First Century," in Chloe E. Bird, Peter Conrad, and Allen M. Fremont, eds., *Handbook of Medical Sociology*, 5th ed. (Upper Saddle River, NJ: Prentice Hall, 2000), 411–26.

39. Jason Schnittker, Jeremy Freese and Brian Powell, "Nature, Nurture, Neither, Nor: Black-White Differences in Beliefs about the Causes and Appropriate Treatment of Mental Illness," *Social Forces* 78 (2000): 1101–32.

40. Lisa Cooper, Debra L. Roter, Rachel L. Johnson, Daniel E. Ford, Donald M. Steinwachs, Neil R. Powe, "Patient-Centered Communication, Ratings of Care, and Concordance of Patient and Physician Race," *Annals of Internal Medicine* 139 (2003): 907–15.

41. Lisa Cooper-Patrick, Joseph J. Gallo, Junius J. Gonzales, Hong Thi Vu, Neil R. Powe, Christine Nelson, and Daniel E. Ford, "Race, Gender, and Partnership in the Patient-Physician Relationship," *JAMA* 282 (1999): 583–89.

42. Schnittker and Liang, "Promise and Limits of Racial/Ethnic Concordance."

43. Somnath Saha, Miriam Komaromy, Thomas D. Koepsell, Andrew B. Bindman, "Patient-Physician Racial Concordance and the Perceived Quality and Use of Health Care," *Archives of Internal Medicine* 159 (1999): 997–1004. Another study by Saha found that race matching was not associated with greater patient satisfaction, an inconsistency that the study authors attributed to either a methodological difference or to improving care from doctors across racial lines. Somnath Saha, Jose J. Arbelaez, and Lisa A. Cooper, "Patient–Physician Relationships and Racial Disparities in the Quality of Health Care," *American Journal of Public Health* 93 (2003): 1713–19.

44. Lisa A. Cooper, Debra L. Roter, Rachel L. Johnson, Daniel E. Ford, Donald M. Steinwachs, and Neil R. Powe, "Patient-Centered Communication, Ratings of Care, and Concordance of Patient and Physician Race," *Annals of Internal Medicine* 139(2003): 907–15.

45. Thomas A. Laveist and Amani Nuru-Jeter, "Is Doctor-Patient Race Concordance Associated with Greater Satisfaction with Care?" *Journal of Health and Social Behavior* 43 (2002): 296–306.

46. Lisa A. Cooper, Debra L. Roter, Raachel L. Johnson, Daniel E. Ford, Donald Steinwachs, and Neil R. Powe, "Patient-Centered Communication, Ratings of Care, and Concordance of Patient and Physician Race," *Annals of Internal Medicine* 139 (2003): 907–15, p. 911.

47. Kevin A. Schulman, et al., "The Effect of Race and Sex on Physicians' Recommendations for Cardiac Catheterization," *New England Journal of Medicine* 340 (1999): 618–26.

48. Marti Loring and Brian Powell, "Gender, Race, and DSM-III: A Study of the Objectivity of Psychiatric Diagnostic Behavior," *Journal of Health and Social Behavior* 29 (1988): 1–22, p. 17.

49. Alexander R. Green, Dana R. Carney, Daniel J. Pallin, Long H. Ngo, Kristal L. Raymond, Lisa I. Iezzoni, and Mahzarin R. Banaji, "Implicit Bias among Physicians and Its Prediction of Thrombolysis Decisions for Black and White Patients," *Journal of General Internal Medicine* 22 (2007): 1231–38. Also see Janice A. Sabin, Frederick P. Rivara, Anthony G. Greenwald, "Physician Implicit Attitudes and Stereotypes about Race and Quality of Medical Care," *Medical Care* 46 (2008): 678–85.

50. Individual black physicians did vary greatly, however. Janice A. Sabin, Brian A. Nosek, Anthony G. Greenwald, and Frederick P. Rivara, "Physicians' Implicit and Explicit Attitudes about Race by MD Race, Ethnicity and Gender," *Journal of Health Care for the Poor and Underserved* 20 (2009): 896–913.

51. The Kaiser Family Foundation, *National Survey of Physicians, Part 1: Doctors on Disparities in Medical Care* (Washington, DC: Kaiser Family Foundation, 2002); http://www.kff.org/minorityhealth/20020321a-index.cfm, accessed November 8, 2011.

52. Vence L. Bonham, Sherrill L. Sellers, Thomas H. Gallagher, Danielle Frank, Adebola O. Odunlami, Eboni G. Price, and Lisa A. Cooper, "Physicians' Attitudes towards Race, Genetics and Clinical Medicine," *Genetics in Medicine* 11 (2009): 279–86.

53. Kington, Tisnado, and Carlisle, "Racial and Ethnic Diversity among Physicians," 79.

54. Joseph A. Flaherty and Susan Adams, "Therapist-Patient Race and Sex Matching: Predictors of Treatment Duration," *Psychiatric Times* 15 (1998); http://psychiatrictimes.com/p980141.html, accessed November 2, 2007.

55. Peter B. Bach, Laura D. Cramer, Joan L. Warren, and Colin Begg, "Racial Differences in the Treatment of Early-Stage Lung Cancer," *New England Journal of Medicine* 341 (1999): 1198–1205.

56. William D. King, Mitchell D. Wong, Martin F. Shapiro, Bruce E. Landon, and William E. Cunningham, "Does Racial Concordance Between HIV-positive

Patients and Their Physicians Affect the Time to Receipt of Protease Inhibitors?" *Journal of General Internal Medicine* 19 (2004): 1146–54.

57. Somnath Saha, Miriam Komaromy, Thomas D. Koepsell, and Andrew B. Bindman, "Patient-Physician Racial Concordance and the Perceived Quality and Use of Health Care," *Archives of Internal Medicine* 159 (1999): 997–1004. Another study by Saha found that race matching was not associated with greater patient satisfaction, an inconsistency that the study's authors attributed to either a methodological difference or improving care from doctors across racial lines. Somnath Saha, Jose J. Arbelaez, and Lisa A. Cooper, "Patient–Physician Relationships and Racial Disparities in the Quality of Health Care," *American Journal of Public Health* 93 (2003): 1713–19.

58. Robert C. Sterling, Edward Gottheil, Stephen P. Weinstein, and Ronald Serota, "The Effect of Therapist/Patient Race- and Sex-Matching in Individual Treatment," *Addiction* 96 (2001): 1015–22.

59. Daniel L. Howard, Thomas R. Konrad, Catherine Stevens, and Carol Q. Porter, "Physician-Patient Racial Matching, Effectiveness of Care, Use of Services, and Patient Satisfaction," *Research on Aging* 23 (2001): 83–108.

60. Department of Health and Human Services, *Rationale for Diversity*, 3.

61. Robert K. Merton, "Insiders and Outsiders: A Chapter in the Sociology of Knowledge," *American Journal of Sociology* 78 (1972): 9–48.

62. See, for example, Merton, "Insiders and Outsiders," 13-16; Patricia Zavella, "Feminist Insider Dilemmas: Constructing Ethnic Identity with 'Chicana' Informants," *Frontiers: A Journal of Women Studies* 13 (1993): 53–76, pp. 53–54.

63. Maxine Baca Zinn, "Field Research in Minority Communities: Ethical, Methodological and Political Observations by an Insider," *Social Problems* 27 (1979): 209–19. Though more than twenty years old, Zinn's perspective is reprinted in a field methods textbook. Maxine Baca Zinn, "Insider Field Research in Minority Communities," in Robert M. Emerson, ed., *Contemporary Field Research: Perspectives and Formulations*, 2nd ed. (Prospect Heights, IL: Waveland Press, 2001) 159–66.

64. Peter R. Grahame and Kamini Maraj Grahame, "Points of Departure: Insiders, Outsiders, and Social Relations in Caribbean Field Research," *Human Studies* 32 (2009): 291–312, pp. 296–98.

65. Sarah R. Lowe, Kara Lustig and Helen B. Marrow, "African American Women's Reports of Racism during Hurricane Katrina: Variation by Interviewer Race," *New School Psychology Bulletin* 8 (2011): 46–57.

66. Wendy D. Roth, *Race Migrations: Latinos and the Cultural Transformations of Race* (Stanford, CA: Stanford University Press, 2012) 214.

67. On the black press, see Clint C. Wilson II, *Black Journalists in Paradox: Historical Perspectives and Current Dilemmas* (New York: Greenwood Press, 1991); Jason Chambers, *Madison Avenue and the Color Line: African Americans in the Advertising Industry* (Philadelphia: University of Pennsylvania Press, 2008); Jannette L. Dates, "Print News," in Jannette L. Dates and William Barlow, eds., *Split Image: African Americans in the Mass Media*, 2nd ed. (Washington, DC: Howard University Press, 1993), 369–18. On immigrant newspapers, see, for example, Robert Ezra Park, *The Immigrant Press and Its Control* (New York: Harper and Brothers, 1922); and Judith R. Blau, Mim Thomas, Beverly Newhouse, and

Andrew Kavee, "Ethnic Buffer Institutions—The Immigrant Press: New York City, 1820–1984," *Historical Social Research* 23 (1998): 20–37.

68. National Advisory Commission on Civil Disorders, *Report of the National Advisory Commission on Civil Disorders* New York: Bantam Books, 1968) 1.

69. National Advisory Commission on Civil Disorders, *Report*, 366.

70. Commission on Civil Disorders, *Report*, 385.

71. Petition for Rulemaking to Require Broadcast Licensees to Show Nondiscrimination in Their Employment Practices, 18 F.C.C. 2d 240 (1969).

72. Juan González and Joseph Torres, *How Long Must We Wait? The Fight for Racial and Ethnic Equality in the American News Media*, 2004) 12; http://www.arc.org/pdf/164pdf.pdf, accessed December 22, 2009.

73. U.S. Commission on Civil Rights, *Window Dressing on the Set: Women and Minorities in Television* (Washington, DC: The Commission on Civil Rights, 1977); U.S. Commission on Civil Rights, *Window Dressing on the Set: An Update* (Washington, DC: Commission on Civil Rights, 1979).

74. Virginia Mansfield-Richardson, *Asian Americans and the Mass Media: A Content Analysis of Twenty United States Newspapers and a Survey of Asian American Journalists* (New York: Garland Publishing, 1999); Wilson, *Black Journalists*, 110. A brief history of the ASNE's interest in diversity is on their website; http://asne.org/key_initiatives/diversity/asne_diversity_history.aspx, accessed December 19, 2009.

75. Michael Manning, "The Annual CBS Free-for-All: A Visit to a No Holds Barred Stockholders' Meeting," *Columbia Journalism Review* 25 (July/August 1986): 45–46.

76. Task Force on Minorities in the Newspaper Business, *Cornerstone for Growth: How Minorities are Vital to the Future of Newspapers* (Washington, DC: Task Force on Minorities in the Newspaper Business, 1988) 5.

77. Task Force on Minorities, 6.

78. Task Force on Minorities, 6.

79. Task Force on Minorities, 36.

80. Wallace Terry, *Missing Pages: Black Journalists of Modern America: An Oral History* (New York: Carroll & Graf, 2007) 349, n.91.

81. Ruth Shalit, "Race in the Newsroom," *New Republic*, October 2, 1995, 20–37, p. 21; "Race in the Newsroom: An Exchange," *New Republic*, October 16, 1995, 14.

82. David Carr, "Goodbye to All That," *Washington City Paper*, April 9, 1999; http://www.washingtoncitypaper.com/articles/17092/goodbye-to-all-that, accessed June 4, 2012. For a critical analysis, see Frederick R. Lynch, *The Diversity Machine: The Drive to Change the "White Male Workplace"* (New York: Free Press, 1997) 347–55.

83. "Race in the Newsroom: An Exchange," 14.

84. Specifically, ASNE data from 1994 showed that blacks were 12.5 percent of the population, 7.3 percent of college-educated Americans, and 5.4 percent of newsroom employees. The corresponding figures for Latinos were 10.2 percent, 4 percent, and 3.2 percent, and for Asians they were 3.4 percent, 6.3 percent, and 2 percent of newsroom employees. Joan Shorenstein Center on the Press, Politics

and Public Policy, *Implementation of Racial and Ethnic Diversity in the American Press* (Cambridge, MA: President and Fellows of Harvard College, 1996) 8.

85. Shorenstein Center, *Diversity*, 12–13.

86. Shorenstein Center, 20–21.

87. Shorenstein Center, 21.

88. Shorenstein Center, 21.

89. Shorenstein Center, 22.

90. http://asne.org/key_initiatives/diversity/asne_diversity_history.aspx, accessed December 19, 2009.

91. http://asne.org/key_initiatives/diversity.aspx, accessed December 19, 2009.

92. Quoted in Alfred L. Schreiber with Barry Lenson, *Multicultural Marketing: Selling to the New America* (Chicago: NTC Business Books, 2001) 145.

93. Quoted in Schreiber and Lenson, *Multicultural Marketing*, 185.

94. Quoted in Schreiber and Lenson, *Multicultural Marketing*, 186.

95. William McGowan, *Coloring the News: How Crusading for Diversity Has Corrupted American Journalism* (San Francisco: Encounter Books, 2001).

96. http://www.tribune.com/employment/diversity.html, accessed December 28, 2009.

97. April 2003, Tribune Diversity Statement.

98. http://www.nytco.com/company/diversity_and_inclusion/our_mission .html, accessed December 28, 2009.

99. http://www.nytco.com/company/diversity_and_inclusion/inside_our _company.html, accessed December 28, 2009.

100. http://www.gannett.com/section/CAREERS0602, accessed June 4, 2012.

101. http://www.gannett.com/section/CAREERS&template=cover, accessed June 6, 2012.

102. Bill Dedman and Steven K. Doig, "Newsroom Diversity Has Passed Its Peak at Most Newspapers, 1990–2005 Study Shows," June 1, 2005; http://www .powerreporting.com/knight/, accessed September 15, 2010.

103. David H. Weaver and G. Cleveland Wilhoit, *The American Journalist in the 1990s: U.S. News People at the End of an Era* (Mahwah, NJ: Lawrence Erlbaum Associates, 1996) 197–98.

104. Bob Papper, "Recovering Lost Ground," RTNDA *Communicator* (July/August (2004) 24–28, p. 28. Papper's more recent (though not dissimilar) statistics, limited to broadcast journalism, can be found at http://www.rtdna.org/uploads/ files/vv7.pdf, accessed January 2, 2013.

105. Lynn C. Owens, "Race in the Television Newsroom: Do On-Air Personalities Reflect the Communities They Serve?" *Electronic News* 1 (2007): 7–20.

106. Serafín Méndez-Méndez and Diane Alverio, *Network Brownout 2003: The Portrayal of Latinos in Network Television News, 2002* (Washington, DC: National Association of Hispanic Journalists, 2003) 4.

107. González and Torres, *How Long Must We Wait?* 2.

108. UNITY: Journalists of Color, Inc. and Walter Cronkite School of Journalism and Mass Communication at Arizona State University, *Diversity in the Washington Newspaper Press Corps 2008*, 11; http://cronkite.asu.edu/assets/ pdf/2008UNITY-web.pdf, accessed August 27, 2010.

109. UNITY and Cronkite School of Journalism, *Diversity in Washington*, 14.

110. UNITY and Cronkite School of Journalism, *Diversity in Washington*, 24.

111. UNITY and Cronkite School of Journalism, *Diversity in Washington*, 25.

112. Author interview with Latina journalist, April 5, 2004.

113. Author interview with African-American journalist, February 22, 2008.

114. Robert M. Entman and Andrew Rojecki, *The Black Image in the White Mind: Media and Race in America* (Chicago: University of Chicago Press, 1999) 84, 87.

115. Kirk A. Johnson, "Media Images of Boston's Black Community," *Research Report No. 18* (Boston: University of Massachusetts–Boston, William Monroe Trotter Institute, January 28, 1987).

116. David Niven, "A Fair Test of Media Bias: Party, Race, and Gender in Coverage of the 1992 House Banking Scandal." *Polity* 36 (2004): 637–49. Also see Jeremy Zilber and David Niven, *Racialized Coverage of Congress: The News in Black and White* (Westport, CT: Praeger, 2000).

117. Christian R. Grose, "Bridging the Divide: Interethnic Cooperation; Minority Media Outlets; and the Coverage of Latino, African-American, and Asian-American Members of Congress," *Press/Politics* 11.4 (2006): 115–30.

118. Mark Fitzgerald, "Most Blacks Upset by News Coverage," *Editor & Publisher*, August 6, 1994; http://www.editorandpublisher.com/Article/Most-Blacks-Upset-By-News-Coverage-p-15, accessed June 6, 2012.

119. UNITY and Cronkite School of Journalism, *Diversity in Washington*, 20.

120. *Diversity in Washington*, 23.

121. *Diversity in Washington*, 23.

122. *Love and Fear in the Time of Media Consolidation: A Survey of Asian American Journalists*, August 2, 2007, Report Commissioned by the Asian American Journalists Association.

123. Author interview with Latina journalist, May 10, 2005.

124. Author interview with African-American managing editor, June 22, 2006.

125. Merah Stuart, *An Economic Detour: A History of Insurance in the Lives of American Negroes* (New York: Wendell Malliet and Company, 1940); Joseph A. Pierce, *Negro Business and Business Education* (New York: Harper and Bros., 1947).

126. Jason Chambers, *Madison Avenue and the Color Line: African Americans in the Advertising Industry* (Philadelphia: University of Pennsylvania Press, 2008) 23.

127. Chambers, *Madison Avenue and the Color Line*, 36–37.

128. *Madison Avenue and the Color Line*, 37.

129. Jennifer Delton, *Racial Integration in Corporate America, 1940–1990* (New York: Cambridge University Press, 2009) 48.

130. Jannette L. Dates, "Advertising," in Jannette L. Dates and William Barlow, eds., *Split Image: African Americans in the Mass Media*, 2nd ed. (Washington, DC: Howard University Press, 1993) 461-493, p. 464; Chambers, *Madison Avenue and the Color Line*, 61.

131. http://www.careerjournal.com/myc/diversity/20070207-capparell-sb.html, accessed October 29, 2007.

132. Stephanie Capparell, *The Real Pepsi Challenge* (New York: Free Press, 2007) x, passim.

133. Chambers, *Madison Avenue and the Color Line*, 63.

134. Quoted in Chambers, 66.

135. Kenneth Labich and Joyce E. Davis, "Making Diversity Pay," *Fortune*, Sept. 9, 1996, 177.

136. Quoted in Steven A. Ramirez, "Diversity in the Boardroom," *Stanford Journal of Law, Business and Finance* 6 (2000): 85–133, 117.

137. Marlene Rossman, *Multicultural Marketing: Selling to a Diverse America* (New York: American Management Association, 1994) 120.

138. http://www.metlife.com/about/corporate-profile/citizenship/workplace -diversity/index.html, accessed November 2, 2011.

139. Quoted in Steven A. Ramirez, "Diversity in the Boardroom," *Stanford Journal of Law, Business and Finance* 6 (2000): 85–133, p. 86, n 4.

140. Kenneth Labich and Joyce E. Davis, "Making Diversity Pay," *Fortune*, Sept. 9, 1996, 177.

141. David A. Thomas, "Diversity As Strategy," *Harvard Business Review* 82 (2004): 98–108, pp. 98–99.

142. http://www-03.ibm.com/employment/us/diverse/, accessed November 2, 2011.

143. http://www-03.ibm.com/employment/us/diverse/heritage.shtml, accessed November 2, 2011.

144. R. Roosevelt Thomas, *Beyond Race and Gender: Unleashing the Power of Your Total Work Force by Managing Diversity* (New York: American Management Association, 1991) xi.

145. http://www.avoncompany.com/corporatecitizenship/corporateresponsibility/ whatwecareabout/peopleanddiversity/index.html, accessed November 2, 2011.

146. Anne Fisher, "How You Can Do Better on Diversity," *Fortune*, November 15, 2004, 60.

147. Robin J. Ely and David A. Thomas, "Cultural Diversity at Work: The Effects of Diversity Perspectives on Work Group Processes and Outcomes," *Administrative Science Quarterly* 46 (2001): 229–73, p. 244.

148. Larry Edwards and Rick Gordon, "Niche Market Focus Takes Multicultural Ad Spotlight," *Advertising Age* 69 (1998): s2–19.

149. National Urban League, *Diversity Practices That Work: The American Worker Speaks*, 20; http://nul.iamempowered.com/sites/nul.iamempowered.com/ files/attachments/Diversity_Practices_That_Work_2005.pdf, accessed January 15, 2013.

150. There are many examples that vary in the degree to which these marketers emphasize the value of having nonwhites involved in the creation of marketing plans. Tending toward the anyone-can-do-it perspective (though one of the authors is from Mexico City) is Felipe Korzenny and Betty Ann Korzenny, *Hispanic Marketing: A Cultural Perspective* (Boston, MA: Elsevier/Butterworth-Heinemann, 2005). At the other end of the spectrum is Juan Faura's *Hispanic Marketing Grows Up: Exploring Perceptions and Facing Realities* (Ithaca, NY: Paramount Market Publishing, 2006), where the author assumes throughout the text that marketers working the Hispanic market are themselves Hispanic. He titles a chapter on the early days of the business "Trust Me, I'm Hispanic," (p.

7), explains that when he says "we" he means "Hispanic marketing professionals" and cautions against letting "our Hispanicness get in the way of those things we know as marketers" (p. 13).

151. M. Isabel Valdés and Marta H. Sedane, *Hispanic Marketing Handbook* (New York: Gale Research, 1995) 177.

152. Schreiber and Lenson, *Multicultural Marketing*, 128.

153. *Multicultural Marketing*, 22–23.

154. Taylor Cox, Jr., *Cultural Diversity in Organizations: Theory, Research and Practice* (San Francisco: Berrett-Koehler, 1993) 30.

155. *Cultural Diversity in Organizations*, 30.

156. Chambers, *Madison Avenue and the Color Line*, 68.

157. *Madison Avenue and the Color Line*, 253.

158. Dates, "Advertising," 480–84.

159. Marilyn Halter, *Shopping for Identity: The Marketing of Ethnicity* (New York: Schocken Books, 2000) 49; Burt Helm, "Ethnic Marketing: McDonald's is Lovin' It," *Businessweek*, July 8, 2010; http://www.businessweek.com/magazine/content/10_29/b4187022876832.htm, accessed November 4, 2011.

160. Larry Edwards and Rick Gordon, "Niche Market Focus Takes Multicultural Ad Spotlight," *Advertising Age* 69 (1998): s2-19.

161. Arlene Dávila, *Latinos, Inc.: The Making and Marketing of a People* (Berkeley: University of California Press, 2001) 58.

162. *Latinos, Inc.*, 63.

163. *Latinos, Inc.*, 53. The organization no longer has the 65-percent Latino staff requirement. See http://ahaa.org/default.asp?contentID=31, accesssed April 18, 2013.

164. Halter, *Shopping for Identity*, 67, 69.

165. http://www.emgad.com/index3.html, accessed November 2, 2011.

166. http://www.ameredia.com/agency/index.html, accessed November 2, 2011.

167. http://www.ameredia.com/agency/profile.html, accessed November 2, 2011.

168. http://www.adcreasians.com/, accessed June 2, 2012.

169. A directory of these firms and experts can be found at http://multicultural.com/, accessed November 8, 2011.

170. Eric Grodsky and Devah Pager, "The Structure of Disadvantage: Individual and Occupational Determinants of the Black-White Wage Gap," *American Sociological Review* 66 (2001): 542–67. Also see Sharon Collins, "The Marginalization of Black Executives," *Social Problems* 36 (1989): 317–31; Sharon Collins, "Blacks on the Bubble: The Vulnerability of Black Executives in White Corporations," *Sociological Quarterly* 34 (1993): 429–48; Marlese Durr and John R. Logan, "Racial Submarkets in Government Employment: African American Managers in New York State," *Sociological Forum* 12 (1997): 353–70; Katherine Kiel and Jeffrey Zabel, "House Price Differential in U.S. Cities: Household and Neighborhood Racial Effects," *Journal of Housing Economics* 5 (1996): 143–65. Collins suggested that it was common for companies in the 1980s to match black managers with black communities. Though her statistics are ambiguous, a remark from one of her interviewees is suggestive: one executive for a major retail

company noted that he and twelve other blacks were hired at the same time and all placed in stores in the inner city. Collins, *Black Corporate Executives*, 114.

171. Cho, Holcombe and Murphy, "Multicultural Marketing," 9.

172. "Top Ad Agencies in Marketing to African-Americans, 2010." *Advertising Age*, Agency Report (annual), April 25, 2011, 33.

173. Dora O. Tovar, "Hispanic Public Relations and Its Emergence as an Industry," in Elena del Valle, ed., *Hispanic Marketing and Public Relations: Understanding and Targeting America's Largest Minority* (Boca Raton, FL: Poyeen Publishing, 2005) 233–82, p. 239.

174. Philip Moss and Chris Tilly, *Stories Employers Tell: Race, Skills and Hiring in America* (New York: Russell Sage Foundation, 2001) 105. Oddly, only twenty percent of all employers say customers or employees prefer workers of their own race or ethnic group (Moss and Tilly, *Stories Employers Tell*, 94), suggesting either that retailers are particularly interested in race matching or that employers are interested in race matching regardless of what they believe their customers' preferences are.

175. James W. Button and Barbara A. Rienzo, "The Impact of Affirmative Action: Black Employment in Six Southern Cities," *Social Science Quarterly* 84 (2003): 1–14, p. 12. Also see James L. Button, Barbara Rienzo, and Sheila L. Croucher, *Blacks and the Quest for Economic Equality: The Political Economy of Employment in Southern Communities in the United States* (University Park, PA: Pennsylvania State University Press, 2009).

176. Brief for MTV Networks as *Amicus curiae*, 2.

177. Brief for MTV Networks as *Amicus curiae*, 7.

178. Brief for 3M et al. as *Amici curiae*, 7.

179. Diane Cardwell and Stuart Elliott, "Ad Firms to Hire More Black Managers in City," *New York Times*, September 8, 2006; http://www.nytimes.com/2006/09/08/business/media/08ads.html?hp&ex=1157774400&en=5780e36e0c24cad7&ei=5094&partner=homepage, accessed January 13, 2013.

180. Craig A. Martin, "Racial Diversity In Professional Selling: An Empirical Investigation of the Differences in the Perceptions and Performance of African-American and Caucasian Salespeople," *Journal of Business and Industrial Marketing* 20 (2005): 285–96.

181. Thomas A. Kochan, Katerina Bezrukova, Robin Ely, Susan Jackson, Aparna Joshi, Karen Jehn, Jonathan Leonard, David Levine, David Thomas, "The Effects of Diversity on Business Performance: Report of the Diversity Research Network," *Human Resource Management* 42 (2003): 3–21, p. 16.

182. Tharp, *Marketing and Consumer Identity*, 77.

183. Nejdet Delener and James P. Neelankavil, "Informational Sources and Media Usage: A Comparison between Asian and Hispanic Subcultures," *Journal of Advertising Research*, June/July 1990, 45–52.

184. Wei-Na Lee, Carrie La Ferle, and Marye Tharp, "Ethnic Influences on Communication Patterns: Word of Mouth and Traditional and Nontraditional Media Usage," in Jerome D. Williams, Wei-Na Lee and Curtis P. Haugvedt, eds., *Diversity in Advertising: Broadening the Scope of Research Directions* (Mahwah, NJ: Lawrence Erlbaum Associates, Inc., 2004) 177–200.

185. Wei-Na Lee and David K. Tse, "Changing Media Consumption in a New Home: Acculturation Patterns Among Hong Kong Immigrants to Canada," *Journal of Advertising* 23 (1994): 57–70.

186. Halter, *Shopping for Identity*, Chapter 3; Marye C. Tharp, *Marketing and Consumer Identity in Multicultural America* (Thousand Oaks, CA: Sage, 2001) 76.

187. Jonna Holland and James W. Gentry, "Ethnic Consumer Reaction to Targeted Marketing: A Theory of Intercultural Accommodation," *Journal of Advertising* 28 (1999): 65–77; Chang-Hoan Cho, John Holcombe and Daniel Murphy, *Multicultural Marketing in Contemporary U.S. Markets* (Miami, FL: Insights Marketing Group, 2004); available at http://www.insights-marketing.com/ Documents/Multicultural+Marketing+in+Contemporary+US+Markets.pdf, accessed November 8, 2011.

188. Osei Appiah, "Effects of Ethnic Identification on Web Browsers' Attitudes Toward and Navigational Patterns on Race-Targeted Sites," *Communication Research* 31 (2004): 312–37.

189. Also see Tharp, *Marketing and Consumer Identity*, 196.

190. Delton, "Racial Integration in Corporate America," 47.

191. 478 U.S. 421 (1986).

192. Quoted in Harvard Law Review, "Rethinking Weber: The Business Response to Affirmative Action," *Harvard Law Review* 102 (1989): 658–71, p. 669, n.61; Erin Kelly and Frank Dobbin, "From Affirmative Action to Diversity Management," in John David Skrentny, ed., *Color Lines: Affirmative Action, Immigration and Civil Rights Options for America* (Chicago: University of Chicago Press, 2001) 87–117.

193. Bureau of National Affairs, *Affirmative Action Today: A Legal and Practical Analysis* (Washington, DC: Bureau of National Affairs, 1986) 93.

194. Quoted in Ramirez, "Diversity in the Boardroom," 95, n.47.

195. David A. Thomas and Suzy Wetlaufe, "A Question of Color: A Debate on Race in the U.S. Workplace," *Harvard Business Review* 75 (1997): 118–32, p. 130.

196. Quoted in Ramirez, "Diversity in the Boardroom," 98, n.64.

197. Cox, *Diversity in Organizations*, 31. Also see Taylor Cox, Jr. and Carol Smolinski, "Managing Diversity and Glass Ceiling Initiatives as National Economic Imperatives," *Federal Publications: Key Workplace Documents* (Ithaca, NY: Cornell University, 1994) 28–33.

198. David A. Thomas and Robin J. Ely, "Making Difference Matter: A New Paradigm for Managing Diversity," *Harvard Business Review* 74 (1996): 79–90, 3.

199. National Urban League, *Making Diversity Work: The American Worker Speaks II: 2009 Highlights*, 10; http://nul.iamempowered.com/sites/nul.iamem powered.com/files/attachments/Diversity_Practices_That_work_2009.pdf, accessed January 15, 2013.

200. Tristin Green, "Race and Sex in Organizing Work: 'Diversity,' Discrimination and Integration," *Emory Law Journal* 59 (2010): 585–647, 596.

201. Frank Dobbin, *Inventing Equal Opportunity* (Princeton, NJ: Princeton University Press, 2009) 145, 155.

202. Lauren B. Edelman, Sally Riggs Fuller, and Iona Mara-Drita, "Diversity Rhetoric and the Managerialization of Law," *American Journal of Sociology* 106 (2001): 1589–1641.

203. National Urban League, *Diversity Practices that Work: The American Worker Speaks II: 2009 Highlights*; http://nul.iamempowered.com/sites/nul.iam empowered.com/files/attachments/Diversity_Practices_That_work_2009.pdf, accessed January 15, 2013.

204. Brief for MTV Networks as *Amicus curiae*, 6.

205. Brief for 3M et al. as *Amici curiae*, 7.

206. Brief for 3M et al. as *Amici curiae*,7, n.5.

207. Brief for *Amici Curiae* Fortune-100 and Other Leading American Businesses, 2. This brief also emphasized a less racial-realist argument, stressing at several points that these firms wanted employees, presumably of any race, who had been educated in a racially diverse environment.

208. Ann S. Tsui, Terri D. Egan, Charles A. O'Reilly III, "Being Different: Relational Demography and Organizational Attachment." *Academy of Management Journal* 32 (1992): 402–23.

209. Susan E. Jackson, Joan F. Brett, Valerie I. Sessa, Dawn M. Cooper, Johan A. Julin, and Karl Peyronnin, "Some Differences Make a Difference: Individual Dissimilarity and Group Heterogeneity as Correlates of Recruitment, Promotions and Turnover." *Journal of Applied Psychology* 76 (1991): 675–89. Also see Carol T. Kulik and Loriann Roberson, "Diversity Initiative Effectiveness: What Organizations Can (and Cannot) Expect from Diversity Recruitment, Diversity Training, and Formal Mentoring Programs," in Arthur P. Brief, ed., *Diversity at Work* (New York: Cambridge University Press, 2008) 265–317.

210. Scott E. Page, *The Difference: How the Power of Diversity Creates Better Groups, Firms, Schools, and Societies* (Princeton, NJ: Princeton University Press, 2007) 324–28.

211. Thomas A. Kochan, Katerina Bezrukova, Robin Ely, Susan Jackson, Aparna Joshi, Karen Jehn, Jonathan Leonard, David Levine, and David Thomas, "The Effects of Diversity on Business Performance: Report of the Diversity Research Network," *Human Resource Management* 42 (2003): 3–21, p. 8.

212. Cedric Herring, "Does Diversity Pay? Race, Gender, and the Business Case for Diversity," *American Sociological Review* 74 (2009): 208–24.

213. Kochan, et al., "Effects of Diversity," 17.

214. "Effects of Diversity," 17.

215. "Effects of Diversity," 18–19.

216. Elijah Anderson, "The Social Situation of the Black Executive: Black and White Identities in the Corporate World," in Michèle Lamont, ed., *The Cultural Territories of Race: Black and White Boundaries* (Chicago: University of Chicago Press, 1999) 3–29, p. 18.

217. Peter Truell, "The Black Investor, Playing Catch-Up," *New York Times*, August 23, 1998; http://www.nytimes.com/1998/08/23/business/investing-it-the -black-investor-playing-catch-up.html?pagewanted=all&src=pm, accessed July 7, 2012. Also see Ramirez, "Diversity in the Boardroom." This section relies on John D. Skrentny, "Are America's Civil Rights Laws Still Relevant?" *Du Bois Review* 4 (2007): 119–40.

218. Geoffrey Colvin, "The 50 Best Companies for Asians, Blacks, and Hispanics," *Fortune*, July 19, 1999, 52.

219. Alfred L. Schreiber with Barry Lenson, *Multicultural Marketing: Selling to the New America* (Chicago: NTC Business Books, 2001) 120

220. *Multicultural Marketing*, 122.

221. *Multicultural Marketing*, 128.

222. Kelly and Dobbin, "Affirmative Action to Diversity Management"; Dobbin, *Inventing Equal Opportunity*.

223. Vadim Liberman, "Do Companies Truly Value Their Diversity Directors?" *Conference Board Review*, September/October 2006; https://hcexchange.conference-board.org/attachment/TCBR-09-2006-031.pdf, accessed May 4, 2009.

224. Liberman, "Diversity Directors," 20.

225. Sharon M. Collins, *Black Corporate Executives: The Making and Breaking of a Black Middle Class* (Philadelphia: Temple University Press, 1997) 77.

226. *Black Corporate Executives*, 82.

227. Wilkins, "Rise of Diversity Arguments," 1595.

228. "Rise of Diversity Arguments," 1596.

229. Liberman, "Diversity Directors," 21.

230. "Diversity Directors," 21.

231. "Diversity Directors," 21.

232. "Diversity Directors," 22.

233. "Diversity Directors," 22.

234. "Diversity Directors," 21.

235. Erin White, "Diversity Programs Look To Involve White Males as Leaders," *Wall Street Journal*, May 7, 2007, B4.

236. Dávila, *Latinos, Inc.*, 36–37.

237. Wilkins, "Rise of Diversity Arguments," 1594.

238. 443 U.S. 193 (1979).

239. At 208.

240. At 208.

241. At 208.

242. *Johnson v. Transportation Agency of Santa Clara County* 480 U.S. 616 (1987).

243. Roger Clegg, "The George W. Bush Administration: A Retrospective: Unfinished Business: The Bush Administration and Racial Preferences," *Harvard Journal of Law & Public Policy* 32 (2009): 971–95.

244. *Grutter v. Bollinger*, 539 U.S. 306 (2003).

245. 91 F. 3d 1547 (3rd Circuit 1996).

246. 91 F. 3d 1547, 1551-2 (3rd Circuit 1996).

247. *Regents of the University of California v. Bakke*, 438 U.S. 265 (1978).

248. 91 F. 3d 1547, 1562-3 (3rd Circuit 1996).

249. *Schurr v. Resorts International Hotel* 196 F.3d 486 (3rd Circuit 1999).

250. *Schurr v. Resorts International Hotel* 196 F.3d 486, 498 (3rd Circuit 1999).

251. *Schurr v. Resorts International Hotel* 196 F.3d 486, 498 (3rd Circuit 1999).

252. http://www.eeoc.gov/policy/docs/race-color.html, accessed October 18, 2008.

253. *EEOC v. Olsen's Dairy Queens, Inc.*, 989 F. 2d 165, 169 (Fifth Circuit 1993). A court could conceivably distinguish this from the racial-realist practice of attending to the preference of nonwhite customers (or employees in the case of hiring minorities to be diversity officers), saying this is in line with the goal of Title VII to provide more opportunities for minorities, but to date, this has not happened.

254. *Ferrill v. The Parker Group, Inc.* 967 F. Supp. 472, 473 (N.D. Ala. 1997).

255. *Ferrill v. The Parker Group, Inc.* 967 F. Supp. 472, 475 (N.D. Ala. 1997).

256. *Ferrill v. The Parker Group, Inc.* 168 F.3d 468, 473 (11th Circuit 1999).

257. *Ferrill v. The Parker Group, Inc.* 168 F.3d 468, 473 (11th Circuit 1999).

258. *Ferrill v. The Parker Group*, at 475. Here the court was quoting from *Knight v. Nassau County Civil Serv. Comm'n*, 649 F.2d 157 (2d Circuit 1981), a case involving a black man, James Knight, who complained that the Nassau County Civil Service Commission assigned him to minority recruiting positions against his wishes and that he found demeaning. The commission did this because it thought Knight would be better at it because he is black—a race BFOQ that the court rejected. At 162. See also Chapter 4.

259. Barbara Rose, "Diversity Goals, Bias Can Collide," *Chicago Tribune*, March 19, 2009; Harper Gerlach, "EEOC Says Walgreens Discriminated against its African-American Workers," *Florida Employment Law Letter* 19 (2007): 1–2, p. 2.

260. Barbara Rose, "Diversity Goals, Bias Can Collide," *Chicago Tribune*, March 19, 2007; http://articles.chicagotribune.com/2007-03-19/business/0703170021_1_walgreens-michael-polzin-diversity, accessed January 12, 2013.

261. EEOC, "Press Release: Walgreens Sued for Job Bias against Blacks"; http://www.eeoc.gov/eeoc/newsroom/release/3-7-07.cfm, accessed November 14, 2011.

262. EEOC press release, "Walgreens Sued for Job Bias against Blacks."

263. EEOC press release: "Final Decree Entered with Walgreens for $24 million in Landmark Race Discrimination Suit by EEOC"; http://www.eeoc.gov/eeoc/newsroom/release/3-25-08.cfm, accessed November 14, 2011; http://hr.blr.com/HR-news/Discrimination/Racial-Discrimination/Walgreens-to-Pay-20M-to-Settle-Bias-Lawsuit/, accessed December 17, 2009.

Chapter 3. We the People: Racial Realism in Politics and Government

1. Donald L. Horowitz, *Ethnic Groups in Conflict*, 2nd ed. (Berkeley: University of California Press, 2000 [1985]) Chapter 6.

2. Jane Mansbridge, "Should Blacks Represent Blacks and Women Represent Women? A Contingent 'Yes,'" *Journal of Politics* 61(1999): 628–57.

3. Donald J. Polden, "Forty Years After Title VII: Creating an Atmosphere Conducive to Diversity in the Corporate Boardroom," *University of Memphis Law Review* 36 (2005): 67–91, 78.

4. Michael J. Gerhardt, "Toward a Comprehensive Understanding of the Federal Appointments Process," *Harvard Journal of Law and Public Policy* 21(1998): 467–539, 475.

5. David Lublin, *The Paradox of Representation: Racial Gerrymandering and Minority Interests in Congress* (Princeton, NJ: Princeton University Press, 1997) 23.

6. Asian-Americans have also won several seats representing majority-white districts in California and one in Oregon. Pei-te Lien, *The Making of Asian America through Political Participation* (Philadelphia: Temple University Press, 2001) 90–93.

7. Harold F. Gosnell, *Negro Politicians: The Rise of Negro Politics in Chicago* (Chicago: University of Chicago Press, 1967 [1935]) 196

8. Mayor Bill Thompson, quoted in Gosnell, *Negro Politicians*, 200.

9. Desmond King, *Separate and Unequal: Black Americans and the US Federal Government* (Oxford: Clarendon Press, 1995) Chapter 3.

10. Robert C. Smith, "Black Appointed Officials: A Neglected Area of Research in Black Political Participation," *Journal of Black Studies* 14 (1984): 369–88, p. 371.

11. Harvard Sitkoff, *A New Deal for Blacks: The Emergence of Civil Rights as a National Issue: The Depression Decade* (New York: Oxford University Press, 1978) 77–78.

12. Sitkoff, *New Deal for Blacks*, 78–79.

13. An excellent guide to race and party dynamics is Paul Frymer, *Uneasy Alliances: Race and Party Competition in America* (Princeton, NJ: Princeton University Press, 1999).

14. E. Frederic Morrow, *Black Man in the White House: A Diary of the Eisenhower Years by the Administrative Office for Special Projects; the White House, 1955–1961* (New York: Coward-McCann, 1963). Eisenhower also appointed an African-American, J. Ernest Wilkins, as Assistant Secretary of Labor. Smith, "Black Appointed Officials," 371.

15. Wendell E. Pritchett, *Robert Clifton Weaver and the American City: The Life and Times of an Urban Reformer* (Chicago: University of Chicago Press, 2008) 213.

16. Pritchett, *Robert Clifton Weaver*, 215.

17. *Robert Clifton Weaver*, 264–65.

18. *Robert Clifton Weaver*, 268.

19. *Robert Clifton Weaver*, 268.

20. *Robert Clifton Weaver*, 273.

21. *Robert Clifton Weaver*, 274.

22. *Robert Clifton Weaver*, 274.

23. *Robert Clifton Weaver*, 277.

24. Christine L. Nemacheck, *Strategic Selection: Presidential Nomination of Supreme Court Justices from Herbert Hoover through George W. Bush* (Charlottesville: University of Virginia Press, 2007) 51.

25. I explored this story in John D. Skrentny, *The Minority Rights Revolution* (Cambridge, MA: Belknap Press of Harvard University Press, 2002).

26. J. Edward Kellough, "Affirmative Action in Government Employment," *Annals of the American Academy of Political and Social Science* 523 (1992): 117–30, p. 127.

27. Kellough, "Government Employment," 127.

28. Paul Frymer, *Uneasy Alliances: Race and Party Competition in America* (Princeton, NJ: Princeton University Press, 2010 [1999]). On Republican and Democratic racial strategies, see also Tali Mendelberg, *The Race Card: Campaign Strategy, Implicit Messages, and the Norm of Equality* (Princeton, NJ: Princeton University Press, 2001) 7, 15. On race and party images, see Tasha S. Philpot, *Race, Republicans, and the Return of the Party of Lincoln* (Ann Arbor: University of Michigan Press, 2007).

29. Frymer, *Uneasy Alliances*.

30. Adam Shatz, "Glenn Loury's About Face," *New York Times Sunday Magazine*, January 20, 2002.

31. Shatz, "Loury's About Face."

32. Author interview with Glenn Loury, August 8, 2008.

33. This resurgence was spearheaded by one controversial and much-debated book: Richard Herrnstein and Charles Murray, *The Bell Curve: Intelligence and Class Structure in American Life* (New York: Free Press, 1994).

34. Glenn Loury, "Going Home," *CommonQuest*, Fall 1996, 11–14, p. 12.

35. Clarence Thomas, *My Grandfather's Son: A Memoir* (New York: HarperCollins, 2007) 137–38.

36. Thomas, *Grandfather's Son*, 148–50.

37. Thomas, *Grandfather's Son*, 193.

38. Thomas, *Grandfather's Son*, 216. Clarence Thomas's experience as a judge was short but not unique. Some Republican white males currently serving on the Court had longer waits in the lower courts before being nominated: Anthony Kennedy served on the Ninth Circuit between 1975 and 1988 and Alito served on the Third Circuit from 1990 to 2006. Antonin Scalia served only four years on the DC Circuit, though he had been a law professor for many years before that, and had also worked for several years in the federal government. Chief Justice John Roberts' rise looks most like Thomas's; Roberts served two years and three months on the DC Circuit, about five months longer than did Thomas.

39. Cal Thomas, "Thomas, an All-American Nominee," *Milwaukee Journal*, July 7, 1991, J5.

40. *Milwaukee Journal*, July 7, 1991, J4.

41. Linda Diebel, "US Politics Upside Down in Court Fight," *Toronto Star*, August 1991, A1.

42. Kenneth T. Walsh, Ted Gest, Matthew Cooper, Jeannye Thornton, and Gloria Borger, "Scouting Thomas," *U.S. News & World Report*, July 15, 1991, 22.

43. Michael J. Gerhardt, "Divided Justice: A Commentary on the Nomination and Confirmation of Justice Thomas," *George Washington Law Review* 60 (1992): 969–996, 984

44. Gerhardt, "Divided Justice," 976.

45. Helen Dewar, "Democrats Accuse Bush of Stacking High Court," *Washington Post*, October 5, 1991, A12.

46. Norman Vieira and Leonard Gross, *Supreme Court Appointments: Judge Bork and the Politicization of Senate Confirmations* (Carbondale: Southern Illinois University Press, 1998) 200.

47. Vieira and Gross, *Supreme Court Appointments*, 200–201.

48. Jill Lawrence, "J. C. Watts and GOP: A Winning Combination," *USA Today*, April 16, 1998, 5A.

49. Bob Dole and J. C. Watts, Jr., "A New Civil Rights Agenda," *Wall Street Journal*, July 27, 1995, A10.

50. Watts, *What Color Is a Conservative?* Pages 194 and 196 detail the convention and state of the union speeches but say nothing about why he was selected.

51. Claire Jean Kim, "Managing the Racial Breach: Clinton, Black-White Polarization, and the Race Initiative," *Political Science Quarterly* 117 (2002): 55–79, p. 68.

52. In the 2008 election, the Republican Party appeared to make an effort to signal friendliness to whites. The number of black delegates at the Republican Convention was at a 40-year low: only 36 of 2,380. Latino representation also fell to 1996 levels. The contrast with 2000, when the party used African-American General Colin Powell, a video of a black preacher, and brought an entire gospel choir onto the dais, was stark: in 2008 the party did not have a single nonwhite speaker in prime time. Republican leaders were not sharing their political strategy with reporters, though they hinted that Obama's candidacy led to a shift to use white racial signaling to attract white voters. McCain's campaign manager, Rick Davis, shrugged off reporters' questions about it. Speaking of rival Barack Obama, however, he tipped his hand when he explained, "We can run our campaign the way we want to run it and not be in direct conflict with a lot of voter groups he is trying to get." Eli Saslow and Robert Barnes, "In a More Diverse America, A Mostly White Convention," *Washington Post*, September 4, 2008; http://www.washingtonpost.com/wp-dyn/content/article/2008/09/03/AR2008090303962_pf.html, accessed September 5, 2008.

53. Adam Nagourney, "At Key Moment, Diverse G.O.P. Leadership Choice," http://www.nytimes.com/2009/01/11/us/politics/11gop.html?_r=2, accessed April 13, 2010.

54. http://dyn.politico.com/printstory.cfm?uuid=2A1BA222-18FE-70B2-A83323D0DB01F7E4, accessed April 13, 2010.

55. Perry Bacon, Jr., "Steele Is RNC's First Black Chairman," *Washington Post*, January 31, 2010; http://www.washingtonpost.com/wp-dyn/content/article/2009/01/30/AR2009013003898.html, accessed April 13, 2010. By 2010, Steele had committed several gaffes and been connected to a party spending scandal, but party leaders predicted that Steele's race would make it difficult to replace him; http://dyn.politico.com/printstory.cfm?uuid=15A1C198-18FE-70B2-A845861B6C0CA47F, accessed April 13, 2010.

56. http://www.cnn.com/2009/POLITICS/02/23/jindal.gop/index.html, accessed April 13, 2010.

57. John Heilemann, "The GOP's New Colors," *New York*, February 22, 2009; http://nymag.com/news/politics/powergrid/54691/, accessed April 13, 2010.

58. Jason P. Casellas, *Latino Representation in State Houses and Congress* (New York: Cambridge University Press, 2011) 144.

59. Peter Wallsten, "GOP Taps Hispanics in Fall Test," *Wall Street Journal*, September 25, 2010; http://online.wsj.com/article/SB10001424052748703793804575512210776190450.html, accessed September 25, 2010.

60. Philip Rucker, "GOP Latinos Poised for Big Wins, but Party's Tough Immigration Stance Is a Hurdle," *Washington Post*, October 21, 2010;http://www.washingtonpost.com/wp-dyn/content/article/2010/10/21/AR2010102106904.html, accessed October 21, 2010.

61. Wallsten, "GOP Taps Hispanics."

62. Lamar Smith, "The GOP's Other Election Victory," *Washington Post*, November 27, 2010; http://www.washingtonpost.com/wp-dyn/content/article/2010/11/19/AR2010111905213.html?hpid=opinionsbox1, accessed November 28, 2010. The elected officials mentioned were New Mexico governor Susana Martinez, Nevada governor Brian Sandoval, Senator Marco Rubio (R-FL), and, in the House of Representatives, Bill Flores (R-TX), Francisco Canseco (R-TX), Jaime Herrera (R-WA), Raul Labrador (R-ID) and David Rivera (R-FL).

63. Sandhya Somashekhar, "In Florida, GOP Candidates Praise Marco Rubio, A Favorite for Running Mate," *Washington Post*, January 27, 2012; http://www.washingtonpost.com/politics/in-florida-gop-candidates-praise-marco-rubio-a-favorite-for-running-mate/2012/01/26/gIQAzGicVQ_story.html?hpid=z2, accessed January 27, 2012; Andrew Goldman, "Marco Rubio Won't Be V.P.," *New York Times*, January 26, 2012; http://www.nytimes.com/2012/01/29/magazine/marco-rubio-wont-be-vp.html?ref=magazine, accessed January 27, 2012.

64. Republican National Committee, *Growth and Opportunity Project* (no place or date) 14.

65. *Growth and Opportunity Project*, 16.

66. *Growth and Opportunity Project*, 32–33.

67. Maeve Reston, "Republicans Reach Out to Asian American Voters with New Hires," *Los Angeles Times*, April 9, 2013; http://www.latimes.com/news/politics/la-pn-republicans-asian-voters-20130408,0,4151919.story, accessed April 9, 2013.

68. Robert Barnes and Michael D. Shear, "Hispanics See Stars Aligned on High Court; For President, Diversity Is One of Many Factors," *Washington Post*, May 12, 2009; http://www.washingtonpost.com/wp-dyn/content/article/2009/05/11/AR2009051103503.html?hpid=topnews, accessed May 12, 2009.

69. Barnes and Shear, "Hispanics See Stars Aligned."

70. Damien Cave, "For Hispanics, Court Pick Sets Off Pride, and Some Concerns," *New York Times*, May 26, 2009; http://www.nytimes.com/2009/05/27/us/politics/27latino.html?ref=politics, accessed April 16, 2010.

71. Peter Baker and Adam Nagourney, "Sotomayor Pick a Product of Lessons from the Past," *New York Times*, May 27, 2009; http://www.nytimes.com/2009/05/28/us/politics/28select.html?pagewanted=1&hp, accessed April 15, 2010.

72. Charlie Savage, "A Judge's View of Judging Is on the Record," *New York Times*, May 14, 2009; http://www.nytimes.com/2009/05/15/us/15judge.html?gwh=36DDF7EFD01C5F8FF3FFE014E64665B2, accessed January 16, 2013.

73. Sheryl Gay Stolberg, "Sotomayor's Opponents and Allies Prepare Strategies," *New York Times*, May 27, 2009; http://www.nytimes.com/2009/05/28/us/politics/28web-court.html, accessed January 16, 2013.

74. http://theplumline.whorunsgov.com/stimulus-package/sotomayor-fight
-eroding-whats-left-of-latino-support-for-gop/, accessed April 17, 2010, citing
polls from the *Daily Kos* (blog).

75. Lee Epstein and Jeffrey Allan Segal, *Advice and Consent: The Politics of
Judicial Appointments* (New York: Oxford University Press, 2005) 65.

76. Epstein and Segal, *Advice and Consent*, 66.

77. L. Marvin Overby, Beth M. Henschen, Michael H. Walsh, and Julie
Strauss, "Courting Constituents? An Analysis of the Senate Confirmation Vote
on Justice Clarence Thomas," *American Political Science Review* 86 (1992):
997–1003.

78. Gerard S. Gryski, Gary Zuk, and Deborah J. Barrow, "A Bench that Looks
Like America? Representation of African Americans and Latinos on the Federal
Courts," *Journal of Politics* 56 (1994): 1076–86.

79. Mitchell Killian, "Presidential Decision Making and Minority Nomina-
tions to the U.S. Courts of Appeals," *Presidential Studies Quarterly*: 38.2 (June
2008) 268–83.

80. Jennifer Segal Diascro and Rorie Spill Solberg, "George W. Bush's Legacy
on the Federal Bench: Policy in the Face of Diversity," *Judicature* 92 (2009): 289–
301, p. 289.

81. On the inequality of representation, see John D. Griffin and Brian Newman, *Minority Report: Evaluating Political Equality in America* (Chicago: University of Chicago Press, 2008).

82. See, for a review, Vincent L. Hutchings and Nicholas A. Valentino, "The
Centrality of Race in American Politics," *Annual Review of Political Science* 7
(2004): 383–408.

83. Lawrence Bobo and Franklin D. Gilliam, Jr., "Race, Sociopolitical Participation and Black Empowerment," *American Political Science Review* 84 (1990):
377–93.

84. However, at the congressional level there were no signaling effects on
voter interest or likelihood of voting. Katherine Tate, *Black Faces in the Mirror:
African Americans and Their Representatives in the U.S. Congress* (Princeton, NJ:
Princeton University Press, 2003) 130, 141.

85. Claudine Gay, "Spirals of Trust? The Effect of Descriptive Representation on the Relationship Between Citizens and Their Government," *American
Journal of Political Science* 46 (2002): 717–32. There is also, however, evidence
of a positive civic effect that black representatives may have on whites: nonwhite
candidates demonstrate to white voters the competence of nonwhite leaders and
the compatibility of nonwhite and white interests. Zoltan L. Hajnal, *Changing
White Attitudes toward Black Leadership* (NY: Cambridge University Press, 2006).

86. Michael Tesler and David O. Sears, *Obama's Race: The 2008 Election and
the Dream of a Post-Racial America* (Chicago: University of Chicago Press, 2010).

87. Marisa Abrajano and Craig M. Burnett, "Do Blacks and Whites See
Obama through Race-Tinted Glasses? A Comparison of Obama's and Clinton's
Approval Ratings," *Presidential Studies Quarterly* 42 (2012): 363–75.

88. Seth K. Goldman, "Effects of the 2008 Presidential Campaign on White
Prejudice," *Public Opinion Quarterly* 76 (2012): 663–87. Also see Susan Welch
and Lee Sigelman, "The 'Obama Effect' and White Racial Attitudes," *Annals*

of the American Academy of Political and Social Science 634 (2011): 207–20; E. Ashby Plant, Patricia G. Devine, William T. L. Cox, Corey Columb, Saul L. Miller, Joanna Goplen, B. Michelle Peruche, "The Obama Effect: Decreasing Implicit Prejudice and Stereotyping," *Journal of Experimental Social Psychology* 45 (2009): 961–64; Corey Columb and E. Ashby Plant, "Revisiting the Obama Effect: Exposure to Obama Reduces Implicit Prejudice," *Journal of Experimental Social Psychology* 47 (2011): 499–501.

89. Jill E. Lybarger and Margo J. Monteith, "The Effect of Obama Saliency on Individual-Level Racial Bias: Silver Bullet or Smokescreen," *Journal of Experimental Social Psychology* 47 (2011): 647–52.

90. Angela Onwuachi-Willig and Mario L. Barnes, "The Obama Effect: Understanding Emerging Meanings of 'Obama' in Anti-Discrimination Law," *Indiana Law Journal* 87 (2012): 325–48, 327.

91. David M. Marx, Sei Jin Ko, Ray A. Friedman, "The 'Obama Effect': How a Salient Role Model Reduces Race-Based Performance Differences," *Journal of Experimental Social Psychology* 45 (2009): 953–56; Joshua Aronson, Sheana Jannone, Matthew McGlone, Tanisha Johnson-Campbell, "The Obama Effect: An Experimental Test," *Journal of Experimental Social Psychology* 45 (2009): 957–60.

92. Carol Swain, *Black Faces, Black Interests* (Cambridge, MA: Harvard University Press, 1993).

93. Vincent L. Hutchings and Nicholas A. Valentino, "The Centrality of Race in American Politics," *Annual Review of Political Science* 7 (2004): 383–408, 397. Research showing these effects includes Kerry L. Haynie, *African American Legislators in the American States* (New York: Columbia University Press, 2001), and Kenny J. Whitby, *The Color of Representation: Congressional Behavior and Black Interests* (Ann Arbor: University of Michigan Press, 1997).

94. Christian R. Grose, *Congress in Black and White: Race and Representation in Washington and at Home* (New York: Cambridge University Press, 2011).

95. Michael D. Minta, *Oversight: Representing the Interests of Blacks and Latinos in Congress* (Princeton, NJ: Princeton University Press, 2011).

96. James W. Button, Barbara A. Rienzo, and Sheila L. Croucher, *Blacks and the Quest for Economic Equality: The Political Economy of Employment in Southern Communities in the United States* (University Park, PA: Pennsylvania State University Press, 2009) 84.

97. Douglas S. Massey and Magaly Sánchez R., *Brokered Boundaries: Creating Identity in Anti-Immigrant Times* (New York: Russell Sage Foundation, 2010).

98. Rodolfo de la Garza, "The Latino Vote across Time," paper presented at the Woodrow Wilson International Center for Scholars, 2005; quoted in Matt A. Barreto, *Ethnic Cues: The Role of Shared Ethnicity in Latino Political Participation* (Ann Arbor: University of Michigan Press, 2010) 3.

99. Scott Graves and Jongho Lee, "Ethnic Underpinnings of Voting Preference: Latinos and the 1996 U.S. Senate Election in Texas," *Social Science Quarterly* 81 (2000): 227–36.

100. Adrian D. Pantoja and Gary M. Segura, "Does Ethnicity Matter? Descriptive Representation in Legislatures and Political Alienation Among Latinos," *Social Science Quarterly* 84 (2003): 441–60. A more positive assessment of the

decline in political alienation can be found in Gabriel R. Sanchez and Jason L. Morin, "The Effect of Descriptive Representation on Latinos' Views of Government and of Themselves," *Social Science Quarterly* 92 (2011): 483–508.

101. Jason P. Casellas, *Latino Representation in State Houses and Congress* (New York: Cambridge University Press, 2011) 140.

102. Barreto, *Ethnic Cues*, 83–87. Another study found that partisanship was more important than Latino candidate background, and Latinos supported a non-Latino candidate. Melissa R. Michelson, "Does Ethnicity Trump Party? Competing Vote Cues and Latino Voting Behavior," *Journal of Political Marketing* 4 (2005): 1–25.

103. Barreto, *Ethnic Cues*, p. 117 for mayoral results. Also see Barreto, *Ethnic Cues*, p. 135, for results for state and congressional races.

104. In the mayoral campaigns in the five cities (Los Angeles, Houston, New York, San Francisco, and Denver), Latino candidates made major efforts to reach and mobilize Latino voters. All of the candidates hired Latino campaign managers and Latino campaign consultants, and all them also had a Latino vote strategy, did canvassing in Spanish, held events in Spanish, used bilingual mailers, use Spanish TV and radio ads, discussed their family immigrants story, and targeted Latinos in fundraisers and for endorsements. Barreto, *Ethnic Cues*, p. 55. Opponents of all of the candidates raised the issue of the Latino candidates' background, adding to the salience of their Latino identity. Barreto, *Ethnic Cues*, p. 56.

105. Jason P. Casellas, *Latino Representation in State Houses and Congress* (New York: Cambridge University Press, 2011) 119.

106. Casellas, *Latino Representation*, 137; Rodney E. Hero and Caroline J. Tolbert, "Latinos and Substantive Representation in the U.S. House of Representatives: Direct, Indirect or Nonexistent?" *American Journal of Political Science* 39 (1995): 640–52.

107. Jane Junn and Natalie Masuoka, "Asian American Identity: Shared Racial Status and Political Context," *Perspectives on Politics* 6 (2008): 729–40.

108. L. Marvin Overby et al., "Race, Political Empowerment, and Minority Perceptions of Judicial Fairness," *Social Science Quarterly* 86.2 (2005): 444–62.

109. Nancy Scherer and Brett Curry, "Does Descriptive Race Representation Enhance Institutional Legitimacy? The Case of the U.S. Courts," *Journal of Politics* 72 (2010): 90–104.

110. The result was especially notable because Sotomayor is Puerto Rican, whereas most Latinos in Texas are Mexican American. Diana Evans, Ana Franco, James P. Wenzel and Robert D. Wrinkle, "Who's on the Bench? The Impact of Latino Descriptive Representation on Supreme Court Approval," paper presented at the Annual Meeting of the American Political Science Association, 2011.

111. Cassia Spohn, "Sentencing Decisions of Black and White Judges: Expected and Unexpected Similarities," *Law and Society Review* 24 (1990): 1197–1216. Spohn argued that the lack of evidence in racial judging differences was the likely result of the process of selecting a judge, which homogenizes the judiciary: they tend to come from the "establishment," share the same class background (upper or upper middle), attend the same schools, and ultimately share the same "subculture of justice" which, apparently, means being more harsh to blacks.

112. Thomas G. Walker and Deborah J. Barrow, "The Diversification of the Federal Bench: Policy and Process Ramifications," *Journal of Politics* 47 (1985): 596–617; and Thomas M. Uhlman, "Black Elite Decision Making: The Case of Trial Judges," *American Journal of Political Science* 22 (1978): 884–95. More recent evidence that black judges are not correlated with sentencing differences is provided by Geoff Ward, Amy Farrell, and Danielle Rousseau, "Does Racial Balance in Workforce Representation Yield Equal Justice? Race Relations of Sentencing in Federal Court Organizations," *Law & Society Review* 43 (2009): 757–806. Studies of the impact of attorney and prosecutor race have, like the studies of the impact of judges' race, yielded mixed evidence. An experimental study found that subjects were more likely to find defendants guilty when represented by a black attorney than when represented by a white; sex made no difference. David L. Cohen and John L. Peterson, "Bias in the Courtroom: Race and Sex Effects of Attorneys on Juror Verdicts," *Social Behavior and Personality* 9 (1981): 81–87. On the other hand, racial disparities in sentencing in urban counties decrease when there are more black and Latino attorneys in a county. Ryan D. King, Kecia R. Johnson, Kelly McGeever, "Demography of the Legal Profession and Racial Disparities in Sentencing." *Law & Society Review* 44 (2012) 1–32. Having a black prosecutor is correlated with a reduced chance for black defendants to go to prison; white defendants are more likely to be sent to prison if these racial conditions hold. Similar but much weaker effects were found with black judges. Ward, Farrell, and Rousseau, "Does Racial Balance in Workforce Representation Yield Equal Justice?"

113. Jennifer A. Segal, "Representative Decision Making on the Federal Bench: Clinton's District Court Appointees." *Political Research Quarterly* 53 (2000): 137–50.

114. Jon Gottschall, "Carter's Judicial Appointments: The Influence of Affirmative Action and Merit Selection on Voting on the U.S. Court of Appeals," *Judicature* 67 (1983): 164–73. Another surprising finding from this research was that black judges were more sympathetic to sex discrimination claimants than white judges, with 65 percent voting in favor compared to 57 percent of white judges voting the same way.

115. Nancy Scherer, "Blacks on the Bench," *Political Science Quarterly* 119.4 (2004): 655–75.

116. Susan Welch, Michael Combs, and John Gruhl, "Do Black Judges Make a Difference?" *American Journal of Political Science* 32 (1988): 126–36.

117. W. Marvin Dulaney, *Black Police in America* (Bloomington: Indiana University Press, 1996) 20–21. Also see Eric H. Monkkonen, "History of Urban Police," in Michael Tonry and Norval Morris, eds., *Modern Policing* (Chicago: University of Chicago Press, 1992) 547–80, pp. 560–61.

118. Leonard N. Moore, *Black Rage in New Orleans: Police Brutality and African American Activism from World War II to Hurricane Katrina* (Baton Rouge: Louisiana State University Press, 2010) Chapter 1.

119. Stephen Leinen, *Black Police, White Society* (New York: New York University Press, 1984) 13.

120. Thomas A. Johnson, Gordon E. Misner, and Lee P. Brown, *The Police and Society: An Environment for Collaboration and Confrontation* (Englewood Cliffs, NJ: Prentice-Hall, 1981) 107.

121. For a review of the crisis atmosphere created by these and other riots, see John David Skrentny, *The Ironies of Affirmative Action: Politics, Culture and Justice in America* (Chicago: University of Chicago Press, 1996) Chapter 4.

122. Skrentny, *Ironies of Affirmative Action*, 87–88.

123. *New York Times*, June 19, 1965, quoted in Nicholas Alex, *Black in Blue: A Study of the Negro Policeman* (New York: Appleton-Century-Crofts, 1969) 28.

124. *New York Times* March 24, 1966, cited in Alex, *Black in Blue*, 28.

125. *Black in Blue* 27.

126. President's Commission on Law Enforcement and the Administration of Justice, *The Challenge of Crime in a Free Society: A Report* (Washington, DC: Government Printing Office, 1967) 101.

127. President's Commission on Law Enforcement and the Administration of Justice, *The Challenge of Crime in a Free Society: A Report* (Washington, DC: Government Printing Office, 1967) 107.

128. National Advisory Commission on Civil Disorders, *Report of the National Advisory Commission on Civil Disorders* New York: Bantam Books, 1968) 315.

129. National Advisory Commission on Criminal Justice Standards and Goals, *Police: A Report* (Washington, DC: Government Printing Office, 1973) 329–30.

130. S. Rep. No. 92-415 (1971) 10.

131. H. Rep. No. 92-238 (1971) 17. For a discussion, see Jon C. Dubin, "Faculty Diversity as a Clinical Legal Education Imperative," *Hastings Law Journal* 51 (2000): 445–77, pp. 469–70.

132. James G. Kolts and staff, *The Los Angeles County Sheriff's Department: A Report by Special Counsel James G. Kolts & Staff*, July, 1992; http://www.parc .info/client_files/Special%20Reports/3%20-%20Kolts%20Report%20-%20LASD .pdf, accessed December 19, 2012.

133. Ronald Reagan stacked the formerly liberal U.S. Commission on Civil Rights with conservatives, leading that body to become highly critical of affirmative action, Reagan's real target, but it also criticized racial realism. In 1984, there was a legal challenge to Detroit's racial quotas in the police department, which the city had adopted in 1974 and defended based on its "operational needs"— maintaining that having African-American officers was necessary for better treatment of African-American citizens. The commission criticized this argument, saying it was divisive and would be a return to the "separate but equal" policy of Jim Crow. U.S. Commission on Civil Rights, *Statement of the United States Commission on Civil Rights Concerning the Detroit Police Department's Racial Promotion Quota* (Washington, DC: United States Commission on Civil Rights, 1984) 4–5.

134. U.S. Department of Justice, *Principles for Promoting Police Integrity: Examples of Promising Police Practices and Policies* (Washington, DC: U.S. Department of Justice, January 2001) 18.

135. Moore, *Black Rage in New Orleans*; Kenneth Bolton, Jr., and Joe R. Feagin, *Black in Blue: African-American Police Officers and Racism* (New York: Routledge, 2004).

136. *New York Post*, April 7, 1964, quoted in Alex, *Black in Blue*, 29.

137. *Black in Blue*, 28–29.

138. Button, Rienzo, and Croucher, *Blacks and the Quest for Economic Equality*, 100.

139. *Blacks and the Quest for Economic Equality*, 100.

140. President's Commission on Law Enforcement and the Administration of Justice, *The Challenge of Crime in a Free Society: A Report* (Washington, DC: Government Printing Office, 1967) 108.

141. Interview with black police association leader, 2003. Interview with Asian police association leader, 2003.

142. National Research Council of the National Academies, *Fairness and Effectiveness in Policing: The Evidence* (Washington, DC: National Academies Press, 2004) 289.

143. Eli B. Silverman and James E. McCabe, "Policing a Diverse Community: A Case Study," in Delores D. Jones-Brown, Karen J. Terry, and M.L. Dantzker, eds., *Policing and Minority Communities: Bridging the Gap* (Upper Saddle River, NJ: Pearson Prentice Hall, 2004) 183–203, p. 185.

144. Ronald Weitzer and Steven A. Tuch, *Race and Policing in America: Conflict and Reform* (New York: Cambridge University Press, 2006) 97.

145. Weitzer and Tuch, *Race and Policing*, 98.

146. *Race and Policing*, 100.

147. *Race and Policing*, 111–12.

148. *Race and Policing*, 116.

149. Jerome H. Skolnick and David H. Bayley, *The New Blue Line: Police Innovation in Six American Cities* (New York: The Free Press, 1986) 111.

150. Kenneth Bolton, Jr. and Joe R. Feagin, *Black in Blue: African-American Police Officers and Racism* (New York: Routledge, 2004) 65.

151. Bolton and Feagin, *Black in Blue*, 65. Also see Nicholas Alex, *Black in Blue: A Study of the Negro Policeman* (New York: Appleton-Century-Crofts, 1969) 140–41.

152. Interview with Liaison to Asian Officers, August 4, 2004.

153. David Alan Sklansky, "Not Your Father's Police Department: Making Sense of the New Demographics of Law Enforcement," *Journal of Criminal Law and Criminology* 96 (2006): 1209–44.

154. National Research Council of the National Academies, *Fairness and Effectiveness in Policing: The Evidence* (Washington, DC: National Academies Press, 2004) 82, 148–150.

155. Bolton and Feagin, *Black in Blue*, 52.

156. Bolton and Feagin, 53.

157. Bolton and Feagin, 157.

158. Davison M. Douglas, *Jim Crow Moves North: The Battle over Northern School Segregation, 1865–1954* (New York: Cambridge University Press, 2005) 49, 109.

159. Douglas, *Jim Crow Moves North*, 177.

160. Douglas, 108.

161. Douglas, 49.

162. Adam Fairclough, *A Class of their Own: Black Teachers in the Segregated South* (Cambridge, MA: Belknap Press of Harvard University Press, 2007) 62–67; 92–94.

163. Mark S. Lewis, *Supply and Demand of Teachers of Color* (Washington, DC: ERIC Clearinghouse on Teaching and Teacher Education, 1996) 2. Also see

Jack Dougherty, "That's When We Were Marching for Jobs: Black Teachers and the Early Civil Rights Movement in Milwaukee," *History of Education Quarterly* 38.2 (1998): 121–41.

164. Amy J. Binder, *Contentious Curricula: Afrocentrism and Creationism in American Public Schools* (Princeton, NJ: Princeton University Press, 2002).

165. W.E.B. Du Bois, "Does the Negro Need Separate Schools?" in Waldo E. Martin, Jr., ed., *Brown v. Board of Education: A Brief History with Documents* (Boston: Bedford/St. Martins, 1998), 91–100, p. 100.

166. W.E.B. DuBois, "The Students of Lincoln," in Henry Lee Moon, ed., *The Emerging Thought of W.E.B. DuBois: Essays and Editorials from The Crisis with an Introduction, Commentaries and a Personal Memoir by Henry Lee Moon* (New York: Simon and Schuster, 1972) 138–140.

167. Douglas, *Jim Crow Moves North*, 186.

168. *Brown et al. v. Board of Education of Topeka et al.*, 347 U.S. 483, 493 (1954).

169. *Brown et al. v. Board of Education*, 347 U.S. 483, 493–494 (1954).

170. *Brown et al. v. Board of Education*, 347 U.S. 483, 494 (1954). Footnote 11 is the subject of a fascinating historical analysis: Daryl Michael Scott, *Contempt and Pity: Social Policy and the Image of the Damaged Black Psyche, 1880–1996* (Chapel Hill: University of North Carolina Press, 1997).

171. *Brown et al. v. Board of Education*, 347 U.S. 483, 495 (1954).

172. Gerald N. Rosenberg, *The Hollow Hope: Can Courts Bring about Social Change?* (Chicago: University of Chicago Press, 1991).

173. Maike Philipsen, "The Second Promise of *Brown*," *Urban Review* 26 (1994): 257–72, p. 264.

174. Christina Collins, *"Ethnically Qualified": A History of New York City Public School Teachers, 1920–1980*, Ph.D. dissertation, University of Pennsylvania, 2006, 214–15, 236–37.

175. Collins, *"Ethnically Qualified,"* 237.

176. Rubén Donato, *The Other Struggle for Equal Schools: Mexican Americans During the Civil Rights Era* (Albany: State University of New York Press, 1997) 70–71.

177. Jack Bass, *Widening the Mainstream of American Culture: A Ford Foundation Report on Ethnic Studies* (New York: Ford Foundation Office of Reports, 1978) 2–3; also see William Wei, *The Asian American Movement* (Philadelphia: Temple University Press, 1993) and Fabio Rojas, *From Black Power to Black Studies: How a Radical Social Movement Became an Academic Discipline* (Baltimore: The Johns Hopkins University Press, 2007).

178. Task Force on Teaching as a Profession, *A Nation Prepared: Teachers for the 21st Century* (New York: Carnegie Forum on Education and the Economy, 1986) 79.

179. Patricia Albjerg Graham, "Black Teachers: A Drastically Scarce Resource," *Phi Delta Kappan* 68.8 (1987): 598–605, p. 599.

180. John Hope Franklin, "The Desperate Need for Black Teachers." *Change* 19.3 (1987): 44–45, p. 45.

181. Jody Daughtry, "Recruiting and Retaining Minority Teachers: What Teacher Educators Can Do," in Antoine M. Garibaldi, ed., *Teacher Recruitment*

and Retention with a Special Focus on Minority Teachers (Washington, DC: National Education Association, 1989) 25–28, p. 25; Livingston Alexander and John W. Miller, "The Recruitment, Incentive, and Retention Programs for Minority Preservice Teachers," in Antoine M. Garibaldi, ed., *Teacher Recruitment and Retention with a Special Focus on Minority Teachers* (Washington, DC: National Education Association, 1989) 45–50, p. 47.

182. Stanford University Committee on Minority Issues (Albert M. Camarillo, chair), *Building a Multiracial, Multicultural University Community: Final Report of the University Committee on Minority Issues* (Stanford: Stanford University, 1989) 19.

183. National Commission on Teaching and America's Future, *What Matters Most: Teaching for America's Future* (New York: National Commission on Teaching and America's Future, 1996) 8.

184. Education Commission of the States, *New Strategies for Producing Minority Teachers* (Denver, CO: Education Commission of the States, 1990). See also Judith R. James, ed., *Hot Topics Series: Recruiting People of Color for Teacher Education* (Bloomington, IN: Phi Delta Kappa Center for Evaluation, Development, and Research, 1993); June A. Gordon, *The Color of Teaching* (New York: Routledge/Falmer, 2000); Ana María Villegas and Beatriz Chu Clewell, "Increasing Teacher Diversity by Tapping the Paraprofessional Pool," *Theory into Practice* 37.2 (1998): 121–30.

185. Arthur Dorman, *Recruiting and Retaining Minority Teachers: A National Perspective*, Policy Brief no. 8, 1990, U.S. Department of Education, Office of Educational Research and Improvement. See page 5 for a "Guest Commentary" by Holmes with these points.

186. Education Code 44100-44105; http://www.leginfo.ca.gov/cgi-bin/display code?section=edc&group=44001-45000&file=44100-44105, accessed December 4, 2011.

187. Nancy Stevens, *Teacher Supply, Demand, and Quality Policy Research Project: Texas Teacher Diversity and Recruitment* (Austin: Texas Education Agency, 1994) 2–4.

188. Dorman, *Recruiting and Retaining Minority Teachers*, 1.

189. Robin R. Henke, Susan P. Choy, Xianglei Chen, Sonya Geis, Martha Naomi Alt, and Stephen P. Broughman, *America's Teachers: Profile of a Profession, 1993–94*, NCES 94-460 (U.S. Dept of Education, National Center for Education Statistics, Washington, DC: 1997) 10.

190. Richard W. Riley, "Our Teachers Should Be Excellent, and They Should Look Like America," *Education and Urban America* 31 (1998): 18–29, pp. 19–20.

191. American College of Physicians, *Racial and Ethnic Disparities in Health Care, A Policy Paper Updated 2010* (Philadelphia: American College of Physicians, 2010) 15. (Available from American College of Physicians, 190 N. Independence Mall West, Philadelphia, PA 19106.)

192. http://www.phdproject.org/aboutus.html, accessed July 7, 2012.

193. *University of California Diversity Statement*, 2010; http://diversity.univer sityofcalifornia.edu/diversity.html, accessed December 13, 2012. Also see the *Brief Amicus Curiae of the President and Chancellors of the University of California in Support of Respondents, Fisher v. University of Texas*.

194. *Brief Amherst, et al. Amici Curiae, Supporting Respondents, Fisher v. University of Texas*, 7.

195. National Collaborative on Diversity in the Teaching Force, *Assessment of Diversity in America's Teaching Force: A Call to Action* (Washington, DC: National Collaborative on Diversity in the Teaching Force, October 2004) 6.

196. Joe Klein, "Who Killed 'Teach for America'?" *Time*, August 25, 2003; http://www.time.com/time/magazine/article/0,9171,1005519,00.html, accessed December 2, 2011.

197. Abby Phillip, "Obama Thanks 'Teach for America'," *Politico*, February 12, 2011; http://www.politico.com/politico44/perm/0211/tfa_b9cd43e2-9f17-4daf-879d-d883a5d04346.html, accessed December 2, 2011.

198. http://www.teachforamerica.org/why-teach-for-america/who-we-look-for/the-importance-of-diversity, accessed December 2, 2010.

199. *Teach for America School-Based Team Conference 2005*, on file with author.

200. Data are available at http://www.ed-data.k12.ca.us/App_Resx/EdData Classic/fsTwoPanel.aspx?#!bottom=/_layouts/EdDataClassic/profile.asp?Tab=2& level=04&reportnumber=16, accessed December 4, 2011.

201. Data are available at http://www.ed-data.k12.ca.us/App_Resx/EdData Classic/fsTwoPanel.aspx?#!bottom=/_layouts/EdDataClassic/profile.asp?Tab=1& level=04&reportnumber=16, accessed December 4, 2011.

202. Richard M. Ingersoll and Henry May, *Recruitment, Retention, and the Minority Teacher Shortage* (Philadelphia: Consortium for Policy Research in Education, University of Pennsylvania and Center for Educational Research in the Interest of Underserved Students, University of California, Santa Cruz, 2011) 17. Different studies find somewhat different percentages. Also see Erica Frankenberg, *The Segregation of American Teachers* (Cambridge, MA: The Civil Rights Project at Harvard University, 2006) 10.

203. Ingersoll and May, *Recruitment, Retention*, 20. This was about the same percentage as in the early 1990s, when two thirds of nonwhite teachers were in schools where more than one half of the students were minorities. Robin R. Henke et al., *America's Teachers: Profile of a Profession*, 11.

204. Ingersoll and May, *Recruitment, Retention*, 21.

205. Frankenberg, *Segregation of American Teachers*, 13.

206. Ronald F. Ferguson, "Teachers' Perceptions and Expectations and the Black-White Test Score Gap," in Christopher Jencks and Meredith Phillips, eds., *The Black-White Test Score Gap* (Washington, DC: Brookings Institution, 1998), 273–317, 273–74.

207. Frederick Erickson, "Gatekeeping and the Melting Pot," *Harvard Educational Review* 45 (1975): 44–70.

208. Rubén Donato, *The Other Struggle for Equal Schools: Mexican Americans During the Civil Rights Era* (Albany: State University of New York Press, 1997) 70–71.

209. U.S. Commission on Civil Rights, *Teachers and Students: Differences in Teacher Interaction with Mexican American and Anglo Students*, Report 5: Mexican American Study. (Washington, DC: Government Printing Office, 1973) 43. This report also found some evidence that districts were matching Latino teachers to Latino students: half of all Latino teachers were in classrooms with at least 60 percent Latino students.

210. For a review, see Clifton A. Casteel, "Teacher-Student Interactions and Race in Integrated Classrooms, *Journal of Educational Research* 92 (1998): 115–20.

211. Ferguson, "Teachers' Perceptions," 277.

212. Jaqueline Jordan Irvine, *Black Students and School Failure: Policies, Practices and Prescriptions* (New York: Greenwood Press, 1990); also see Ferguson, "Teachers' Perceptions," 295.

213. George Farkas, Robert P. Grobe, Daniel Sheehan and Yuan Shuan, "Cultural Resources and School Success: Gender, Ethnicity, and Poverty Groups within an Urban School District," *American Sociological Review* 55 (1990): 127–42. Also see Stephen Klein, Stephen, Vi-Nhuan Le, and Laura Hamilton, *Does Matching Student and Teacher Racial/Ethnic Group Improve Math Scores?* (Washington, DC: RAND Corporation, 2001).

214. U.S. Commission on Civil Rights, *Teachers and Students*, 27–28.

215. Center for Research on Education, Diversity and Excellence, Occasional Reports, University of California, Santa Cruz, *Examining Latino Paraeducators' Interactions with Latino Students*, December 15, 2000, 4. Also see Ana María Villegas and Beatriz Chu Clewell, "Increasing Teacher Diversity by Tapping the Paraprofessional Pool" *Theory into Practice* 37.2 (1998): 121–30. I thank Tomás Jiménez for helping me to understand the concept of *cariño*.

216. Ronald G. Ehrenberg, Daniel D. Goldhaber, Dominic J. Brewer, "Do Teachers' Race, Gender, and Ethnicity Matter? Evidence from NELS88," *Industrial and Labor Relations Review* 48 (1995): 547–61.

217. Villegas and Lucas, "Diversifying the Teacher Workforce," 74; Jacqueline Irvine and Beverly Armento, *Culturally Responsive Teaching: Lesson Planning for Elementary and Middle Grades* (New York: McGraw-Hill, 2000).

218. Ana María Villegas and Tamara F. Lucas, "Diversifying the Teacher Workforce: A Retrospective and Prospective Analysis," in Mark A. Smylie and Debra Miretzky, eds., *Developing the Teacher Workforce: 103rd Yearbook of the National Society for the Study of Education* (Chicago: University of Chicago Press, 2004) 70–104, 72. Also see Alvis V. Adair, *Desegregation: The Illusion of Black Progress* (Lanham, MD: University Press of America, 1984).

219. Mark O. Evans, "An Estimate of Race and Gender Role-Model Effects in Teaching High School," *Journal of Economic Education* 23 (1992): 209–17.

220. Stephen Cole, Elinor Barber, Melissa Bolyard and Annulla Linders, *Increasing Faculty Diversity: The Occupational Choices of High-Achieving Minority Students* (Cambridge, MA: Harvard University Press, 2003) 172.

221. Cole, et al., *Increasing Faculty Diversity*, 176.

222. Mary E. Dilworth, "Recruitment: The Good News and the Bad News on the Teaching Profession," in Antoine M. Garibaldi, ed., *Teacher Recruitment and Retention with a Special Focus on Minority Teachers* (Washington, DC: National Education Association, 1989) 8–10; Sabrina Hope King, "The Limited Presence of African-American Teachers," *Review of Educational Research* 63 (1993): 115–49; Ana María Villegas and Beatriz Chu Clewell, "Increasing Teacher Diversity by Tapping the Paraprofessional Pool" *Theory into Practice* 37.2 (1998): 121–30; Mark S. Lewis, *Supply and Demand of Teachers of Color* (Washington, DC: ERIC Clearinghouse on Teaching and Teacher Education, 1996); June A. Gordon, *The*

Color of Teaching (New York: Routledge/Falmer, 2000) 69 (though Asian teachers less likely to believe race matters, p. 77).

223. Villegas and Lucas, "Diversifying the Teacher Workforce," 75.

224. Thomas S. Dee, "Teachers, Race and Student Achievement in a Randomized Experiment," *Review of Economics and Statistics* 86 (2004): 195–210.

225. Kenneth J. Meier and Laurence J. O'Toole, *Bureaucracy in a Democratic State: A Governance Perspective* (Baltimore: Johns Hopkins University Press, 2006) 84–86.

226. Robert Fairlie, Florian Hoffman, and Philip Oreopoulos, "A Community College Instructor Like Me: Race and Ethnicity Interactions in the Classroom," *NBER Working Paper No. 17381*; http://nber.org/papers/w17381, accessed December 5, 2011.

227. Title VII of the Civil Rights Act of 1964, SEC. 2000e (f); http://www.eeoc .gov/laws/statutes/titlevii.cfm, accessed December 6, 2011.

228. *Baker v. City of St. Petersburg*, 400 F.2d 294, 296 (5th Cir. 1968).

229. *Baker v. City of St. Petersburg*, 300.

230. *Baker v. City of St. Petersburg*, 301.

231. *Baker v. City of St. Petersburg*, 301. The relevant section of the Kerner Commission report stated: "Negro officers should be so assigned as to ensure that the police department is fully and visibly integrated. Some cities have adopted a policy of assigning one white and one Negro officer to patrol cars, especially in ghetto areas. These assignments result in better understanding, tempered judgment, and increased ability to separate the truly suspect from the unfamiliar." National Advisory Commission on Civil Disorders, *The Kerner Report: The 1968 Report of the National Advisory Commission on Civil Disorders* (New York: Pantheon Books, 1988 [1968]) 316–17.

232. *Ray v. University of Arkansas*, 868 F. Supp. 1104, 1126–27 (E.D. Ark. 1994).

233. In a case on the fringes of what might be considered law enforcement, a Fifth Circuit court decided a case on other grounds, but was sympathetic to the claims of the Texas Board of Barbershop Examiners, which had consistently placed a black employee as an undercover examiner in black barbershops, pointing out that it was hard to imagine a white examiner going undercover to do the job effectively. *Miller v. Texas State Board of Barber Examiners* 615 F.2d 650 (Fifth Cir. 1980).

234. *Bridgeport Guardians v. Members of the Bridgeport Civil Serv. Comm'n*, 482 F.2d 1333, 1341 (2d Cir. 1973).

235. *NAACP v. Allen*, 493 F.2d 614, 621 (5th Cir. 1974).

236. *Detroit Police Officers' Ass'n v. Young*, 446 F. Supp. 979, 1001 (E.D. Mich. 1978).

237. At 1016.

238. These included the Kerner report cited above, as well as National Advisory Commission on Criminal Justice Standards and Goals, *Police* (Washington, DC: Government Printing Office, 1973) 330; National Commission on the Causes and Prevention of Violence, *To Establish Justice, To Insure Domestic Tranquility; Final Report* (Washington, DC: Government Printing Office, 1969) 145; President's Commission on Law Enforcement and Administration of Justice, *Task*

Force Report: The Police (Washington, DC: Government Printing Office, 1967) 144–45, 167, 172.

239. *Detroit Police Officers' Ass'n v. Young*, 608 F.2d 671, 695 (6th Cir. 1979).

240. At 695–96 (6th Cir., 1979).

241. 648 F.2d 925 (4th Cir. 1981).

242. At 928.

243. At 929.

244. *Wittmer v. Peters*, 87 F 3d 916, 920 (7th Cir. 1996).

245. At 920–21.

246. *Reynolds v. City of Chicago*, 296 F. 3d 524, 529 (7th Cir. 2002).

247. At 530. The Latino officer in question was a "Sergeant Denk," who had a Latina mother.

248. At 530.

249. *Petit v. City of Chicago* 352 F.3d 1111, 1115 (7th Cir. 2003).

250. *Bridgeport Guardians, Inc. v. Delmonte*, 553 F. Supp. 601, 611 (D. Conn. 1983).

251. At 611.

252. *Patrolmen and Benevolent Association v. City of New York*, 74 F.Supp 2d 321, 329 (SD NY, 1999).

253. At 335–36.

254. At 329.

255. At 328.

256. At 329.

257. At 331–32. The court also noted that Safir did not transfer officers based on Haitian ancestry or ability to speak Creole, but instead based on race, ability, and junior seniority.

258. In a 1986 ruling that involved the Alabama Department of Public Safety, the Court acknowledged an amicus brief from the cities of Birmingham, Detroit, Los Angeles, and the District of Columbia that argued that using race in hiring and promotion helps build trust and cooperation among citizens. The NAACP Legal Defense and Education Fund, in its own amicus brief, linked present-day community distrust of the police to the Alabama's past history of support for segregation and opposition to the civil rights movement. In this case, however, the Court argued that Alabama's history of discrimination in employing officers provided a compelling enough interest to justify racial preferences in employment, and left for another day a ruling on a police department's operational needs as a justification for race-based hiring, promotion, and placement. *United States v. Paradise*, 480 U.S. 149, 167 fn 18 (1986).

259. In *McLaurin v. Oklahoma State Regents*, the Supreme Court considered the case of George McLaurin, a black schoolteacher who, despite being in his sixties, sought a graduate degree from the University of Oklahoma's School of Education. Originally denied admission because of laws denying admission to blacks, McLaurin sued and was admitted—but only after Oklahoma updated its laws, saying that blacks could attend white schools only if segregated. He had the same (white) teachers, but was forced to sit in special "reserved for colored" seats in lectures halls and reserved tables in the library, and to eat in the cafeteria at a special time and at a reserved-for-colored table. The Court ruled that the

result of this set-up was that McLaurin was "handicapped in his pursuit of effective graduate instruction," because the segregation limited "his ability to study, to engage in discussion and exhange views with other students, and, in general, to learn his profession." It therefore violated McLaurin's 14th amendment right to equal protection of the laws. The Court did not consider treatment of black students by white teachers, but did go out of its way to say that whether or not McLaurin would be treated badly by white students was "irrelevant" because the Court's job was only to prevent the state from discriminating. *McLaurin v. Oklahoma State Regents*, 339 U.S. 637 (1950). On the same day, the Supreme Court also struck down Texas's segregated state law school for blacks. In *Sweatt v. Painter*, the Court argued that though it was improving, the black law school was still unequal in many ways, including the number of professors, the size of the library, and the variety of courses offered. But the Court also emphasized that improvements here would not matter because the school functioned in an "academic vacuum, removed from the interplay of ideas and the exchange of views with which the law is concerned." Again, the equal protection mandate was violated because one could not obtain an equal education when segregated. Because the state was 85 percent white, the Court argued, no one could become a good lawyer in isolation from whites. Again, the Court did not consider the ability of whites to teach black students adequately. *Sweatt v. Painter*, 339 U.S. 629 (1950).

260. *United States v. Jefferson Country Board of Education* 372 F. 2d 836, 895 (5th Cir. 1966); *Kemp v. Beasley*, 389 F.2d 178, 189–90 (8th Cir. 1968).

261. 302 F. Supp. 726, (N. J., 1969).

262. This section relies on a discussion in Paul Frymer and John D. Skrentny, "The Rise of Instrumental Affirmative Action: Law and the New Significance of Race in America," *Connecticut Law Review* 36 (2004): 677–723.

263. At 732.

264. At 732.

265. At 732.

266. At 733.

267. At 733. A Third Circuit court affirmed the decision but did not address the racial meanings that Titus saw as important. *Porcelli v. Titus* 431 F. 2d 1254 (3rd Cir. 1970).

268. *Oliver v. Kalamazoo Board of Education*, 498 F. Supp. 732, 748 (W.D.Mich. 1980).

269. At 753.

270. At 753.

271. *Wygant et al. v. Jackson Board of Education*, 546 F. Supp. 1195 (E.D. Mich. 1982) at 1197.

272. *Wygant et al. v. Jackson Board of Education* 476 U.S. 267, 270 (1986).

273. *Wygant et al. v. Jackson Board of Education*, 546 F. Supp. 1195 (E.D. Mich. 1982).

274. *Wygant et al. v. Jackson Board of Education*, at 1201.

275. *Wygant et al. v. Jackson Board of Education*, 746 F.2d 1152, 1157 (6th Cir. 1984).

276. *Wygant et al. v. Jackson Board of Education*, 476 U.S. 267, 276 (1986).

277. *Wygant et al. v. Jackson Board of Education*, at 275–76. Here, Powell's logic was very similar to that used by judges in the early cases involving racial realism in police departments. As discussed above, one court even compared racial realism in law enforcement to slavery.

278. *Wygant et al. v. Jackson Board of Education*, 476 U.S. 267, 286 (1986).

279. *Wygant et al. v. Jackson Board of Education*, at 288 (1986).

280. *Taxman v. Piscataway Board of Education*, 91 F. 3d 1547 (3rd Cir. 1996), at 1552–53.

281. *United States v. Board of Educ. of Township Piscataway*, 832 F. Supp. 836 (D.N.J. 1993).

282. *Taxman v. Piscataway Board of Education*, 91 F. 3d 1547, 1558 (3rd Cir. 1996).

283. *Metro Broadcasting Inc. v. FCC*, 497 U.S. 547 (1990). See Chapter 4 for a discussion.

284. 91 F. 3d 1547 (3rd Cir. 1996), at 1562–63.

285. *Taxman v. Piscataway Board of Education*, 91 F. 3d 1547, 1564–65 (3rd Cir. 1996).

286. *Messer v. Meno*, 130 F. 3d 130, 138 (Fifth Cir. 1997).

287. At 136.

288. *Knight v. Nassau County Civil Serv. Comm'n*, 649 F.2d 157, 162 (2d Cir.1981).

289. At 162.

290. *Rucker v. Higher Educational Aids Bd.*, 669 F.2d 1179 (7th Cir. 1982).

291. At 1180.

292. At 1181. The court cited *Fernandez v. Wynn Oil Co.*, 653 F.2d 1273, 1276–77 (9th Cir. 1981).

293. At 1181.

294. *Grutter v. Bollinger*, 539 U.S. 306, 330 (2003).

295. At 333.

296. Education was important in the decision because, in O'Connor's view, courts should grant educational institutions freedom to pursue their goals, and because educational institutions are "pivotal" in preparing persons for work, citizenship, and maintenance of the "fabric of society." At 331. Here the Court cited *Brown v. Board of Education* 347 U.S. 483 (1954) and *Plyler v. Doe* 457 U.S. 202 (1982).

297. At 330.

298. At 331.

299. At 333.

300. For example, courts cited jury, voting, and school discrimination cases as they built the jurisprudence for affirmative action in employment. See John D. Skrentny, *The Ironies of Affirmative Action: Politics, Culture and Justice in America* (Chicago: University of Chicago Press, 1996) Chapter 6.

301. Jessica Bulman-Pozen, "*Grutter* at Work: A Title VII Critique of Constitutional Affirmative Action," *Yale Law Journal* 115 (2006): 1408–48.

302. Suzanne Eckes, "Diversity in Higher Education: The Consideration of Race in Hiring University Faculty," *Brigham Young University Education and Law Journal* 14 (2005): 33–51. Eckes (p. 47) noted that the Nevada State Supreme

Court had relied on *Bakke* and saw diversity as part of a constitutionally permissible faculty hiring plan. That court argued, "The University demonstrated that it has a compelling interest in fostering a culturally and ethnically diverse faculty. A failure to attract minority faculty perpetuates the University's white enclave and further limits student exposure to multicultural diversity." *University and Community College System of Nevada v. Farmer* 930 P.2d 730, 734–35 (Nev. 1997).

303. And subsequent decisions appeared to limit *Grutter* to higher education. Michelle Adams, "Stifling the Potential of *Grutter v. Bollinger*: *Parents Involved in Community Schools v. Seattle School District No. 1*," *Boston University Law Review* 88 (2008): 937–990.

304. Cynthia Estlund wrote perhaps the strongest argument for the impact of *Grutter* on employment. See Cynthia L. Estlund, "Putting *Grutter* to Work: Diversity, Integration, and Affirmative Action in the Workplace," *Berkeley Journal of Employment and Labor Law* 26 (2005): 1–39. Estlund saw surmountable challenges to having *Grutter* reshape the private employment workplace. Also see Rebecca Hanner White, "Affirmative Action in the Workplace: The Significance of Grutter?" *Kentucky Law Review* 92 (2003): 263–78.

305. *Petit v. City of Chicago*, 352 F.3d 1111, 1114 (7th Cir. 2003).

306. *Petit v. City of Chicago*, at 1115.

307. Five years before *Grutter*, the city of Chicago failed in court to defend its policy of hiring and placing firefighters with regard to their racial abilities and signaling. Judge Richard Posner, who had shown great openness to similar arguments in the contexts of policing or correctional "boot camps," did not see a compelling interest in the firefighting context. The city had argued that white firefighters would lack credibility and be denied cooperation in minority neighborhoods. Posner rejected this view, noting that the city had offered only conjecture and not evidence for this proposition. *McNamara v. City of Chicago*, 138 F.3d 1219, 1222 (7th Cir. 1998).

308. *Lomack v. City of Newark* 463 F.3d 303, 306 (3rd Cir. 2006).

309. At 307.

310. At 309–10.

Chapter 4. Displaying Race for Dollars: Racial Realism in Media and Entertainment

1. Richard Verrier, "MPAA Stops Disclosing Average Cost of Making and Marketing Movies," *Los Angeles Times*, April 1, 2009; http://articles.latimes .com/2009/apr/01/business/fi-cotown-mpaa1, accessed July 2, 2012.

2. Denise D. Bielby and William T. Bielby, "Hollywood Dreams, Harsh Realities: Writing for Film and Television," *Contexts* (Fall/Winter 2002): 21–27; p. 25 usefully discusses the linkages of economic risks and demographic marketing strategies to stereotypes.

3. Barclays Capital, *Internet Data Book 2011*: http://www.aaaa.org/ agency/pubs/NewEssentials/Documents/Ad%20Marketing%20and%20Media/

Barclays-Ad%20spending%20by%20medium%202007-2012.pdf, accessed April 26, 2013.

4. Marilyn Kern-Foxworth, *Aunt Jemima, Uncle Ben, and Rastus: Blacks in Advertising, Yesterday, Today and Tomorrow* (Westport, CT: Greenwood Press, 1994) 30–31.

5. Stephen Fox, *The Mirror Makers: A History of American Advertising and Its Creators* (Urbana: University of Illinois Press, 1997 [1984]) 278.

6. Jason Chambers, *Madison Avenue and the Color Line: African American in the Advertising Industry* (Philadelphia: University of Pennsylvania Press, 2008) 77.

7. Jannette L. Dates, "Advertising," in Jannette L. Dates and William Barlow, eds., *Split Image: African Americans in the Mass Media*, 2nd ed. (Washington, DC: Howard University Press, 1993) 461–493, p. 465. Also see Chambers, *Madison Avenue and the Color Line*, Chapter 3.

8. Chambers, *Madison Avenue and the Color Line*, 138.

9. Fox, *Mirror Makers*, 280.

10. *Mirror Makers*, 280.

11. Dates, "Advertising," 474–75; Kern-Foxworth, *Aunt Jemima*, 116.

12. "Advertising," 475.

13. "Advertising," 478.

14. Kern-Foxworth, *Aunt Jemima*, 121–22.

15. Harold H. Kassarjian, "The Negro and American Advertising, 1946–1965," *Journal of Marketing Research* 6 (1969): 29–39.

16. Ronald Humphrey and Howard Schuman, "The Portrayal of Blacks in Magazine Advertisements: 1950–1982," *Public Opinion Quarterly* 48 (1984): 551–63.

17. Charles R. Taylor, Ju Yung Lee, and Barbara B. Stern, "Portrayals of African, Hispanic, and Asian Americans in Magazine Advertising," *American Behavioral Scientist* 38 (1995): 608–21.

18. Robin T. Peterson, "Consumer Magazine Advertisement Portrayal of Models by Race in the US: An Assessment," *Journal of Marketing Communications* 13 (2007): 199–211.

19. Thomas H. Stevenson, "A Six-Decade Study of the Portrayal of African Americans in Business Print Media: Trailing, Mirroring or Shaping Social Change?" *Journal of Current Issues and Research in Advertising* 29 (2007): 1–14.

20. Robert E. Wilkes and Humberto Valencia, "Hispanics and Blacks in Television Commercials," *Journal of Advertising* 18 (1989): 19–25.

21. Robert M. Entman and Andrew Rojecki, *The Black Image in the White Mind: Media and Race in America* (Chicago: University of Chicago Press, 2001) 10.

22. Charles R. Taylor and Barbara Stern, "Asian Americans: Television Advertising and the 'Model Minority' Stereotype," *Journal of Advertising* 26 (1997): 47–61.

23. Hae-Kyong Bang and Bonnie B. Reece, "Minorities in Children's Television Commercials: New, Improved and Stereotyped," *Journal of Consumer Affairs* 37 (2003): 42–67. Bang and Reece performed a content analysis of commercials in television programming identified through *TV Guide* listings and Nielsen

viewer data and analyzed 42.5 hours of morning and afternoon programming on ABC, CBS, Fox, Nickelodeon, WB, and UPN. Biases or associations may have guided some casting decisions; for instance, ads rarely showed black children playing with toys. Only 17.6 of ads with blacks were for toys, compared to 33.2 percent of those having Caucasians, 33.8 percent having Latinos, and 24 percent having Asians. Instead, advertisers tended to cast blacks in food commercials: 61.1 percent of ads with blacks were for food, while 46.2 percent of ads with Caucasians were for food, 16.9 percent for Latinos, and 48 percent for Asians. In a potentially damaging pattern for ads aimed at children, blacks and Asians were less likely than Caucasians to be at home or in family relationships. Another study of ads aimed at children, this one using broadcast television plus the USA cable network, found in 1997 that whites and blacks were overrepresented while Asian-Americans, Latinos and Native Americans were underrepresented. Whites were significantly more likely to be in prominent roles, such as initiators of action or problem solvers. Meredith Li-Vollmer, "Race Representation in Child-Targeted Television Commercials," *Mass Communication and Society* 5 (2002): 207–28.

24. Roger A. Kerin, "Black Model Appearance and Product Evaluations," *Journal of Communication* 29 (1979): 123–28.

25. Tommy E. Whittler and Joan DiMeo, "Viewers' Reactions to Racial Cues in Advertising Stimuli," *Journal of Advertising Research* 31(1991): 37–46.

26. Devon DelVecchio and Ronald C. Goodstein, "Moving Beyond Race: The Role of Ethnic Identity in Evaluating Celebrity Endorsers," in Jerome D. Williams, Wei-Na Lee, and Curtis P. Haugtvedt, eds., *Diversity in Advertising: Broadening the Scope of Research Directions* (Mahwah, NJ: Lawrence Erlbaum Associates, 2004) 259–77.

27. Geraldine R. Henderson and Jerome D. Williams, "Michael Jordan Who? The Impact of Other-Race Contact in Celebrity Endorser Recognition," in Jerome D. Williams, et al., *Diversity in Advertising*, 279–97.

28. Jennifer L. Doleac and Luke C. D. Stein, "The Visible Hand: Race and Online Market Outcomes," May 1, 2010; http://ssrn.com/abstract=1615149, accessed December 19, 2012.

29. Derek R. Avery, "Reactions to Diversity in Recruitment Advertising—Are Differences Black and White?" *Journal of Applied Psychology* 88 (2003): 672–79.

30. Derek R. Avery, Morela Hernandez, and Michelle R. Hebl, "Who's Watching the Race? Racial Salience in Recruitment Advertising," *Journal of Applied Social Psychology* 34 (2004): 146–61; Leslie A. Perkins, Kecia M. Thomas, and Gail A. Taylor, "Advertising and Recruitment: Marketing to Minorities," *Psychology and Marketing* 17 (2000): 235–55.

31. Tommy E. Whittler, "The Effects of Actors' Race in Commercial Advertising: Review and Extension," *Journal of Advertising* 20 (1991): 54–60.

32. Sonya A. Grier, Anne M. Brumbaugh, and Corliss G. Thornton, "Crossover Dreams: Consumer Responses to Ethnic-Oriented Products," *Journal of Marketing* 70 (2006): 35–51.

33. Rohit Deshpandé and Douglas M. Stayman, "A Tale of Two Cities: Distinctiveness Theory and Advertising Effectiveness," *Journal of Marketing Research* 31 (1994): 57–64.

34. Tommy E. Whittler and Joan Scattone Spira, "Model's Race: A Peripheral Cue in Advertising Messages?" *Journal of Consumer Psychology* 12 (2002): 291–301. In addition, black subjects responded more positively to black endorsers they perceived to be high in black identity than to endorsers they thought low in black identity. DelVechhio and Goodstein, "Moving Beyond Race," 274.

35. Jerome D. Williams, William J. Qualls, and Sonya A. Grier, "Racially Exclusive Real Estate Advertising: Public Policy Implications for Fair Housing Practices," *Journal of Public Policy and Marketing* 14 (1995): 225–44.

36. On film, see Russell K. Robinson, "Casting and Caste-ing: Reconciling Artistic Freedom and Antidiscrimination Norms," *California Law Review* 95 (2007): 1–73, p. 7. This section and the legal analysis below owe much to Robinson's excellent article. On television and film writers, see Darnell M. Hunt, *The 2005 Hollywood Writers Report: Catching Up With a Changing America?* (Los Angeles: Writers Guild of America-West, 2005).

37. Stephanie Greco Larson, *Media & Minorities: The Politics of Race in News and Entertainment* (Lanham, MD: Rowmand & Littlefield, 2006) 37.

38. Thomas Cripps, "Film," in Jannette L. Dates and William Barlow, eds., *Split Image: African Americans in the Mass Media*, 2nd ed. (Washington, DC: Howard University Press, 1993) 131–85, p. 143.

39. See, generally, Larson, *Media & Minorities*.

40. Cripps, "Film," 135; Gordon L. Berry, "Television and Afro-Americans: Past Legacy and Present Portrayals," in Stephen B. Withey and Ronald P. Abeles, eds., *Television and Social Behavior: Beyond Violence and Children* (Hillsdale, NJ: Lawrence Erlbaum Associates, 1980) 231–48, 234.

41. Cripps, "Film," 154.

42. Larson, *Media & Minorities*, 27–29.

43. Esther Kim Lee, *A History of Asian American Theatre* (New York: Cambridge University Press, 2006) 21.

44. Lee, *Asian American Theatre*, 24.

45. *Asian American Theatre*, 182.

46. *Asian American Theatre*, 183.

47. *Asian American Theatre*, 183.

48. *Asian American Theatre*, 184.

49. *Asian American Theatre*, 190–91. On the *Miss Saigon* controversy as well as nontraditional casting, also see Lois L. Krieger, "NOTE: 'Miss Saigon' and Missed Opportunity: Artistic Freedom, Employment Discrimination, and Casting for Cultural Identity in the Theater," *Syracuse Law Review* 43 (1992): 839–66 and Bonnie Chen, "Note: Mixing Law and Art—The Role of Anti-discrimination Law and Color-blind Casting in Broadway Theater," *Hofstra Labor & Employment Law Journal* 16 (1999): 515–43. On nontraditional casting specifically, see Harry Newman, "Casting a Doubt: The Legal Issues of Nontraditional Casting," *Journal of Arts Management and Law* 19.2 (1989a): 55–62 and Harry Newman, "Holding Back: The Theatre's Resistance to Non-Traditional Casting," *TDR (The Drama Review)* 33.3 (1989b): 22–36. Activists continue to struggle for diversity on Broadway, because the numbers are not promising: of 6,639 total roles in the 2006–2011 theater seasons, only fifty-four went to Asian-American actors. Randy Gener, "Asian-Americans: Why Can't We Get Cast In NYC?" *NPR*, February 15,

2012; http://www.npr.org/2012/02/14/146890025/asian-americans-why-cant-we -get-cast-in-nyc?sc=emaf, accessed February 16, 2012.

50. Motion Picture Association of America, *Theatrical Market Statistics 2010*, 5; http://www.mpaa.org/Resources/93bbeb16-0e4d-4b7e-b085-3f41c459f9ac .pdf, accessed January 4, 2012.

51. Motion Picture Association of America, *Theatrical Market Statistics*, 10.

52. *Theatrical Market Statistics*, 12.

53. Edward Jay Epstein, "Hollywood's Profits, Demystified: The Real El Dorado Is TV," *Slate*, August 8, 2005; http://img2.slate.com/id/2124078/, accessed January 4, 2012.

54. Dawn C. Chmielewski and Rebecca Keegan, "Merchandise Sales Drive Pixar's 'Cars' Franchise," *Los Angeles Times*, June 21, 2011; http://articles.latimes .com/2011/jun/21/business/la-fi-ct-cars2-20110621, accessed January 4, 2012.

55. Motion Picture Association of America, *The Economic Contribution of the Motion Picture & Television Industry to the United States* [no date]; http://www .mpaa.org/Resources/3a76ac00-6940-4012-a6e2-da9a7b036da2.pdf, accessed January 4, 2012.

56. Arthur De Vany, *Hollywood Economics: How Extreme Uncertainty Shapes the Film Industry* (New York: Routledge, 2004) 234.

57. De Vany, *Hollywood Economics*, 220.

58. For an insightful discussion of some of these dynamics, see Bielby and Bielby, "Hollywood Dreams, Harsh Realities."

59. The novelization of the real-life story, Ben Mezrich's *Bringing Down the House* (New York: Free Press, 2003), jumped the gun on whitewashing, turning Jeff Ma into "Kevin Lewis" and Mike Aponte into "Jason Fisher."

60. Harry M. Benshoff and Sean Griffin, *America on Film: Representing Race, Class, Gender and Sexuality at the Movies* (Malden, MA: Blackwell, 2004) 86–87.

61. The most scientific star-ranking system is that of economist Arthur De Vany, who in the late 1990s calculated which actors had a statistically significant impact on whether or not a film was a hit or not (defined as earning at least $50 million in revenue). De Vany only found nineteen stars with such power. All but one (Eddie Murphy) were white, and all but four were men. Another measure that sought to identify which stars were associated with profits, added two other black males—Wesley Snipes and Denzel Washington. De Vany, *Hollywood Economics*, 93–95. *Esquire* magazine created its own measure based on a point system weighted toward star roles and "stand alone" films—those that were not sequels. Their 2008 list of top 25 "box office power" stars had two blacks (Eddie Murphy and Will Smith) and one blonde-haired, half-Cuban American (Cameron Diaz). Matthew Shepatin, "Who's the Most Bankable Star in Hollywood?" May 8, 2008; http://www.esquire.com/the-side/feature/box-office-power-052308, accessed July 12, 2008. Yet another ranking system is available on "IMDbPro," a subscription service for the entertainment industry available from Internet Movie Database. This measure, "STARmeter," is based on "proprietary algorithms" from a sampling of what fifty-seven million monthly visitors to the public part of IMDb. com are actually interested in seeing. If a lot of people are looking up and reading about a particular actor, that actor will score very highly on STARmeter; http:// us.imdb.com/help/show_leaf?prowhatisstarmeter, accessed July 20, 2008. The

"Top 25" from this system in 2010 had twelve women, but only one person of color, the half-Dominican, half-Puerto Rican actress Zoe Saldana (at number 10); http://www.imdb.com/features/yearinreview/2010/starmeter, accessed January 10, 2012. The "Top 100" was hardly better: joining Saldana were Will Smith (#27), Jessica Alba (#53), Selena Gomez (#57), Denzel Washington (#57), Keanu Reeves (#73), and Michelle Rodriguez (#92). Despite being nearly a third of the population , minorities were barely 7 percent of the top stars.

62. Harry M. Benshoff and Sean Griffin, *America on Film*, 89.

63. Robinson, "Casting and Caste-ing," 19.

64. See Robinson, "Casting and Caste-ing," 6–13, for more detail on this process. Also see Gary Williams, "'Don't Try to Adjust Your Television—I'm Black': Ruminations on the Recurrent Controversy over the Whiteness of TV," *Journal of Gender, Race & Justice* 4 (2000): 99–136, pp. 109–10.

65. Robinson, "Casting and Caste-ing,"10.

66. "Casting and Caste-ing," 10–11.

67. Quoted in Leonard M. Baynes, "White Out: The Absence and Stereotyping of People of Color by the Broadcast Networks in Prime Time Entertainment Programming," *Arizona Law Review* 45 (2003): 293–369, p. 311. Others argue that the diversity trend *has* hit Hollywood. Adam Moore, the diversity director for SAG-AFTRA (a union that joined the Screen Actors Guild and the American Federation of Television and Radio Artists) argues that a breakdown that does not specify ethnicity is not tacitly asking for a white actor, because casting directors "are looking for that diversity; they are actively seeking it out more and more, because that's what employers want." Nina Shen Rastogi, "Please Submit All Ethnicities: The Tricky Business of Writing Casting Notices," *Slate*, July 30, 2012; http://www.slate.com/articles/arts/culturebox/2012/07/casting_and_race_the_tricky_business_of_writing_casting_notices.single.html, accessed July 31, 2012.

68. Rastogi, "Please Submit All Ethnicities."

69. Rob Kendt, *How They Cast It: An Insider's Look at Film & TV Casting* (Los Angeles: Lone Eagle Publishing, 2005) 38.

70. Kendt, *How They Cast It*, 16.

71. *How They Cast It*, 79.

72. *How They Cast It*, 102.

73. *How They Cast It*, 125–31.

74. Nina Shen Rastogi, "Casting Notices, from *Friends* to *Girls*," *Slate*, July 30, 2012; http://www.slate.com/slideshows/arts/casting-notices-from-friends-to-girls.html#slide_2, accessed August 5, 2012.

75. *How They Cast It*, 47.

76. Focusing on getting parts written for nonwhites can be a successful, if ultimately limiting, strategy for nonwhite actors. See the discussion in Ezra W. Zuckerman, Tai-Young Kim, Kalinda Ukanwa, and James von Rittman, "Robust Identities or Nonentities? Typecasting in the Feature-Film Labor Market," *American Journal of Sociology* 108 (2003): 1018–74.

77. *How They Cast It*, 129.

78. *How They Cast It*, 113.

79. *How They Cast It*, 79.

80. *How They Cast It*, 65.

81. *How They Cast It*, 89–91.

82. *How They Cast It*, 142–44. Race-blind breakdowns do not always mean "white": the casting directors for *Alias* explained that for one character who would appear to be white and had the Jewish-sounding name of Larry Hirsch, "We kind of always saw that [role] as African-American." They cast black actor Carl Lumbly, p. 136.

83. *How They Cast It*, 46.

84. *How They Cast It*, 123. Boycotting can have the opposite of the intended effect. In 2002, civil rights leaders Jesse Jackson and Al Sharpton called for a boycott of the movie *The Barbershop* because they believed it contained dialogue regarding past civil rights heroes Rosa Parks, Martin Luther King, Jr., and Jesse Jackson that was overly negative. The film, which was written and produced by African-Americans, ended up making enough of a profit ($75.8 million) that it led to a sequel, *Barbershop* 2. Sherri L. Burr and William D. Henslee, *Entertainment Law: Cases and Materials on Film, Television, and Music* (St. Paul, MN: Thomson-West, 2004) 277–78.

85. *How They Cast It*,124.

86. *How They Cast It*, 124.

87. *How They Cast It*, 124.

88. Quoted in Hilary De Vries, "All that Korean Rage, Unbottled," *New York Times*, October 17, 2004; http://www.nytimes.com/2004/10/17/movies/17devr .html?_r=1&pagewanted=all&position, accessed on May 24, 2011. Rhimes made a point in casting *Grey's Anatomy* of not specifying race for any specific part, though she wanted the cast to be multiracial. Mathew Fogel, "Grey's Anatomy Goes Colorblind," *New York Times*,May 8, 2005; http://www.nytimes .com/2005/05/08/arts/television/08foge.html, accessed August 5, 2012. Interestingly, though Oh asserts the importance of casting without regard to her race, she also acknowledges in the same interview the importance of race in casting in at least some instances. She notes that she suggested that her character's mother in the hit movie *Sideways* be cast white, implying that her character was adopted. The challenges of interracial adoption might then help explain why her character was so temperamental and ungrounded.

89. David Colman, "Eva Mendes," *Interview* [no date]; http://www.interview magazine.com/film/eva-mendes/, accessed June 26, 2012.

90. Actors' Panel, San Diego Asian Film Festival, October 13, 2007. Author interview with Roger Fan, October 13, 2007. Other nonwhite filmmakers and actors believe that their opportunities would increase with more marketing in Asia and Africa. Bielby and Bielby, "Hollywood Dreams, Harsh Realities," 25.

91. Actors' Panel.

92. Robinson, "Casting and Caste-ing," 9.

93. Actors Panel.

94. Actors Panel.

95. Stephanie Siek, "Is Hollywood Whitewashing Asian Roles?" *CNN.com*, January 13, 2012; http://inamerica.blogs.cnn.com/2012/01/13/is-hollywood -whitewashing-asian-roles/?hpt=hp_bn1, accessed January 13, 2012. Racebend-ing.com sought to cast nonwhites in *The Hunger Games* (as originally written in the books on which the film was based) and successfully pressured Marvel Studios to cast a character, Nico Minoru, as Asian in the 2013 film, *Runaways*, based

on a comic of the same name. See www.racebending.com for details, accessed February 8, 2012.

96. Justin Lin, remarks made at San Diego Asian Film Foundation Members Film Forum: Better Luck Tomorrow, San Diego, California, May 24, 2011.

97. See imdb.com for details.

98. Smith was unmoved by the pitch and turned it down. Jennifer Hillner, "I, Robocop: Will Smith Raps about Busting Bot Outlaws, His Secret Geek Past, and the Future of Thinking Machines," *Wired*, July 2004; http://www.wired.com/wired/archive/12.07/smith.html, accessed February 4, 2012.

99. Cornel West, *Race Matters* (Boston: Beacon Press, 2001 [1993]).

100. Mark Miller, "Matrix Revelations: The Wachowski Brothers FAQ," *Wired*, November 2003; http://www.wired.com/wired/archive/11.11/matrix.html?pg=2&topic=&topic_set, accessed July 15, 2008.

101. Lynn Smith, "The Intellectual and The Matrix," *Los Angeles Times*, May 20, 2003; http://anti-state.com/forum/index.php?board=3;action=display;thread id=5421, accessed July 15, 2008.

102. Matthew W. Hughey, "Cinethetic Racism: White Redemption and Black Stereotypes in 'Magical Negro' Films," *Social Problems* 56 (2009): 543–77.

103. Terry Lawson, "Laurence Fishburne Praises Diverse 'Matrix' Casting," *Detroit Free Press*, May 13, 2003.

104. Pamela McClintock and Tim Appelo, "Black 'Thor' Actor Blasts Debate over His Casting," *Hollywood Reporter*, March 4, 2011; http://www.hollywood reporter.com/news/black-thor-actor-blasts-debate-164048, accessed June 24, 2011.

105. George Lucas explained the viewpoint of the studios: "'They don't believe there's any foreign market for it, and that's 60 percent of their profit. . . . I showed it to all of them and they said 'No. We don't know how to market a movie like this.'" Sofia M. Fernandez, "George Lucas: Hollywood Won't Finance an 'Expensive Movie' with an All-Black Cast," *Hollywood Reporter*, January 11, 2012; http://www.hollywoodreporter.com/live-feed/george-lucas-tuskegee-airmen-red-tails-280638, accessed January 16, 2012.

106. For historical accounts of African-Americans on television, see J. Fred MacDonald, *Blacks and White TV: African Americans in Television since 1948*, 2nd ed. (Chicago: Nelson-Hall, 1992) and Gordon L. Berry "Television and Afro-Americans: Past Legacy and Present Portrayals," in Stephen Basset Withey and Ronald P. Abeles, eds., *Television and Social Behavior: Beyond Violence and Children. A Report of the Committee on Television and Social Behavior, Social Science Research Council* (Hillsdale, NJ: Lawrence Erlbaum Associates, 1980).

107. Todd Gitlin, *Inside Prime Time* (Berkeley: University of California Press, 2000 [1983]) Chapter 1.

108. Gitlin, *Prime Time*, 31.

109. Kathryn C. Montgomery, *Target Prime Time: Advocacy Groups and the Struggle over Entertainment Television* (New York: Oxford University Press, 1989) 126.

110. Gitlin, *Prime Time*, 180.

111. *Prime Time*, 181.

112. For a review of this tradition, see Clint C. Wilson II, Felix Gutiérrez, and Lena M. Chao, *Racism, Sexism, and the Media: The Rise of Class Communication in Multicultural America* (Thousand Oaks, CA: Sage, 2003) Chapter 4.

113. Montgomery, *Target: Prime Time*, 14.

114. The FCC was created by the Communications Act of 1934, which was designed to regulate broadcast frequencies so they could be used most efficiently. The Supreme Court upheld FCC regulations in 1943, stating, "The avowed aim of the Communications Act of 1934 was to secure the maximum benefits of radio to all the people of the United States." *NBC v. U.S.* 319 U.S. 190, 217 (1943).

115. Montgomery, *Target: Prime Time*, 23; Wilson, Gutiérrez, and Chao, *Racism, Sexism, and the Media*, 249–51.

116. Larson, *Media & Minorities*, 38.

117. For details, see http://www.naacp.org/pages/naacp-image-awards, accessed January 24, 2012.

118. National Advisory Commission on Civil Disorders, *Report of the National Advisory Commission on Civil Disorders* New York: Bantam Books, 1968), 382–83. For a discussion, see Peter Braham, "How the Media Report Race," in Michael Gurevitch, Tony Bennett, James Curran, and Janet Woollacott, eds., *Culture, Society and the Media* (New York: Routledge, 2005 [1982]) 265–84, p. 268.

119. *In re* Petition for Rule Making to Require Broadcast Licensees to Show Nondiscrimination in Their Employment Practices, *Memorandum Opinion and Order and Notice of Proposed Rule Making*, 13 F.C.C.2d 766, para. 22 (1968), cited in Patricia M. Worthy, "Diversity and Minority Stereotyping in the Television Media: The Unsettled First Amendment Issue," *Hastings Communications and Entertainment Law Journal* 18 (1996): 509–67, p. 512, n.6. The Justice Department agreed that race mattered in which kind of programming would be broadcast. Because of the "enormous impact which television and radio have upon American life," ending discrimination there could "contribute significantly toward reducing and ending discrimination in other industries." 13 F. C. C. 2d 766, 771 (1968), cited in *Metro Broadcasting, Inc. v. FCC*, 497 U.S. 547, 554 (1990). The FCC has long held as policy that it cannot and should not regulate content. A 1960 statement of policy stated, "[W]hile the Commission may inquire of licensees what they have done to determine the needs of the community they propose to serve, the Commission may not impose upon them its private notions of what the public ought to hear." Network Programming Inquiry, Report and Statement of Policy, 25 Fed. Reg. 7293 (1960).

120. Caryl A. Cooper, "When Perceptions Affect Broadcasting in the Public Interest: Advertising Media Buyers as an Economic Hurdle for Black-Oriented Radio Stations," in Jerome D. Williams, Wei-Na Lee, and Curtis P. Haugtvedt, eds., *Diversity in Advertising: Broadening the Scope of Research Directions*, (Mahwah, NJ: Lawrence Erlbaum Associates, 2004) 133–49, p. 137 (citing an unpublished MA thesis).

121. Williams, "Adjust Your Television." On the protest strategy throughout history, see Larson, *Media and Minorities*.

122. Baynes, "White Out," 294–95.

123. Herman Gray, *Watching Race: Television and the Struggle for Blackness* (Minneapolis: University of Minnesota Press, 1995) 67.

124. Joseph Turow, *Breaking Up America: Advertisers and the New Media World* (Chicago: University of Chicago Press, 1997).

125. Kristal Brent Zook, *Color by Fox: The Fox Network and the Revolution in Black Television* (New York: Oxford University Press, 1999) 3.

126. Zook, *Color by Fox*, 4. At this time, the major broadcast networks of ABC, CBS, and NBC were not using black-oriented shows to win this audience. Herman S. Gray, *Cultural Moves: African Americans and the Politics of Representation* (Berkeley: University of California Press, 2005) 81.

127. Zook, *Color by Fox*, 66. On black writers, also see Zook, *Color by Fox*, 17, 24, 98. Racial abilities in writing can create limitations, however: "Hollywood executives strongly believe that black writers can only write about African Americans, while white writers can write about the experiences of any racial or ethnic minority group. This same logic leads to the near total exclusion of Latino, Asian-American and Native-American writers in Hollywood; they comprise less than 2 percent of those working in the industry." Bielby and Bielby, "Hollywood Dreams, Harsh Realities," 25.

128. Zook, *Color by Fox*, 11.

129. Darnell M. Hunt, "Black Content, White Control," in Darnell M. Hunt, ed., *Channeling Blackness: Studies on Television and Race in America* (New York: Oxford University Press, 2005) 267–302, p. 271; Bielby and Bielby, "Hollywood Dreams, Harsh Realities," 25.

130. Megan Angelo, "At TBS, Diversity Pays Its Own Way," *New York Times*, May 28, 2010; http://www.nytimes.com/2010/05/30/arts/television/30tbs.html?scp=1&sq=tbs%20diversity%20ice%20cube&st=cse&gwh=7DE966479D2FD96A8E70CE53EEE87864, accessed January 24, 2012. Narrowcasting of course continues on networks targeted to minority groups, including Black Entertainment Television and Spanish-language networks such as Telemundo and Univision. For a critical analysis of these networks' portrayal of race, see Baynes, "White Out," 327–30.

131. Berry, "Television and Afro-Americans," p. 236, citing Charlotte G. O'Kelley and Linda Edwards Bloomquist, "Women and Blacks on TV," *Journal of Communication* 26 (1976): 179–84. This study only examined morning shows and may not be comparable to prime time programming.

132. Dana E. Mastro and Bradley S. Greenberg, "The Portrayal of Racial Minorities on Prime Time Television," *Journal of Broadcasting and Electronic Media* 44 (2000): 690–703. On improvement in the number of blacks on television, also see Bradley S. Greenberg and Larry Collette, "The Changing Faces on TV: A Demographic Analysis of Network Television's New Seasons, 1966–1992," *Journal of Broadcasting and Electronic Media* 41 (1997): 1–13. On the inequality of representation of different nonwhite groups, also see Bradley S. Greenberg and Tracy R. Worrell, "New Faces on Television: A 12-Season Replication," *Howard Journal of Communications* 18 (2007): 277–90.

133. National Asian Pacific American Legal Consortium, *Asian Pacific Americans in Prime Time: Lights, Camera and Little Action* (Washington, DC: National Asian Pacific American Legal Consortium, 2005) 6.

134. Nancy Signorielli, "Minorities Representation in Prime Time: 2000 to 2008," *Communication Research Reports* 26 (2009): 323–36.

135. Screen Actors Guild, *2007 and 2008 Casting Data Reports*; http://www
.sag.org/files/sag/documents/2007-2008_CastingDataReports.pdf, accessed January 17, 2012.

136. Elizabeth Monk-Turner, Mary Heiserman, Crystle Johnson,Vanity Cotton, and Manny Jackson, "The Portrayal of Racial Minorities on Prime Time Television: A Replication of the Mastro and Greenberg Study a Decade Later," *Studies in Popular Culture* 32 (2010): 101–14.

137. Entman and Rojecki, *Black Image in White Mind*, 152–55.

138. Greg Braxton, "The Greater Reality of Minorities on TV," *Los Angeles Times*, February 17, 2009; http://articles.latimes.com/2009/feb/17/entertainment/et-realitytv17, accessed July 2, 2012.

139. Braxton, "Reality of Minorities on TV."

140. Dalton Ross, "'Survivor' Race Battle," *EW.com*, August 23, 2006; http://www.ew.com/ew/article/0,,20354695_1279451,00.html, accessed April 23, 2013.

141. National Association for the Advancement of Colored People, *Out of Focus—Out of Sync Take 4: NAACP Report* (Baltimore: National Association for the Advancement of Colored People, 2008) 6.

142. Braxton, "Reality of Minorities on TV."

143. Dana Mastro, "Effects of Racial and Ethnic Stereotyping," in Jennings Bryant and Mary Beth Oliver, eds., *Media Effects: Advances in Theory and Research* (New York: Routledge, 2008) 325–341, pp. 329–30.

144. Jana Steadman, *TV Audience Special Study: African-American Audience* (New York: Nielsen Media Research, 2005); http://www.nielsenmedia.com/E-letters/African-AmericanTVA-final.pdf, accessed January 17, 2012.

145. Mastro, "Effects of Stereotyping," 330.

146. "Effects of Stereotyping," 330.

147. "Effects of Stereotyping," 331.

148. Andrew J. Weaver, "The Role of Actors' Race in White Audiences' Selective Exposure to Movies," *Journal of Communication* 61 (2011): 369–85, p. 376.

149. Weaver, "Role of Actors' Race."

150. Jungmin Lee, "American Idol: Evidence on Same-Race Preferences," *B.E. Journal of Economic Analysis & Policy* 9 (2009): 1–21.

151. Sociologist Lincoln Quillian observed, "Although a number of studies point toward stereotypical portrayals in the media and analyze the history of these portrayals, fewer studies have compiled credible evidence linking media portrayals to individual beliefs. . . . Psychologists have done little to examine how the social structural forces of social relations, culture, and the media influence implicit prejudices through the formation of prejudice content." Lincoln Quillian, "New Approaches to Understanding Racial Prejudice and Discrimination," *Annual Review of Sociology* 32 (2006): 299–328, p. 322.

152. Mastro, "Effects of Stereotyping," 334; Entman and Rojecki, *Black Image in White Mind*, Chapters 4–8. Also see, for example, Franklin D. Gilliam, Jr. and Shanto Iyengar, "Prime Suspects: The Influence of Local Television News on the Viewing Public," *American Journal of Political Science* 44 (2000): 560–73, which shows that white but not black viewers are more likely to support punitive anticrime measures after exposure to the local television news crime "script" that focuses on violent, nonwhite criminals.

153. I am indebted to Baynes, "White Out," 326–27, and Mastro, "Effects of Stereotyping," 333–37 for their excellent reviews of the literature described below.

154. Jane Tagney and Seymour Feschbach, "Children's Television-Viewing Frequency: Individual Differences and Demographic Correlates," *Personality and Social Psychology Bulletin* 14 (1988): 145–58, pp. 145, 149.

155. Paula M. Poindexter and Carolyn A. Stroman, "Blacks and Television: A Review of the Research Literature," *Journal of Broadcasting* 25 (1981): 103–22.

156. Bradley S. Greenberg, "Children's Reaction to TV Blacks," *Journalism Quarterly* 49 (1972): 5–14, p.11.

157. Mastro, "Effects of Stereotyping," 333.

158. Jennifer L. Monahan, Irene Shtrulis, and Sonja Brown Givens, "Priming Welfare Queens and Other Stereotypes: The Transference of Media Images into Interpersonal Contexts," *Communication Research Reports* 22 (2005): 199–205.

159. Alexis Tan, Yuki Fujioka, and Gerdean Tan, "Television Use, Stereotypes of African Americans, and Opinions on Affirmative Action: An Affective Model of Policy Reasoning," *Communication Monographs* 67 (2000): 362–71.

160. Thomas E. Ford, "Effects of Stereotypical Television Portrayals of African-Americans on Person Perception," *Social Psychology Quarterly* 60 (1997): 266–75.

161. Moon J. Lee, Shannon L. Bichard, Meagan S. Irey, Heather M. Walt, and Alana J. Carlson, "Television Viewing and Ethnic Stereotypes: Do College Students Form Stereotypical Perceptions of Ethnic Groups as a Result of Heavy Television Consumption?" *Howard Journal of Communications* 20 (2009): 95–110.

162. Brooks Barnes, "Disney Finds a Cure for the Common Stereotype with 'Doc McStuffins,'" *New York Times*, July 30, 2012; http://www.nytimes.com/2012/07/31/arts/television/disneys-doc-mcstuffins-connects-with-black-viewers.html?_r=2&hp=&adxnnl=1&adxnnlx=1344110654-TddzRYFbYixGasXrzdoMgw&, accessed July 31, 2012.

163. Michael Milano and Packianathan Chelladurai, "Gross Domestic Sport Product: The Size of the Sport Industry in the United States," *Journal of Sport Management* 25 (2011): 24–35, p. 24.

164. Scott Tainsky and Chad D. McEvoy, "Television Broadcast Demand in Markets Without Local Teams," *Journal of Sports Economics* 11 (2011): 1–16.

165. "Plunkett Research Identifies 10 Major Trends in the Sports Industry," June 25, 2009; http://www.plunkettresearch.com/industry%20news/plunkett%20research%20indentifies%20sports%20trends%2006-25-09, accessed February 15, 2012. See also Kurt Helin, "Final NBA Revenue Numbers in from Last Season," *NBC Sports*, July 22, 2011; http://probasketballtalk.nbcsports.com/2011/07/22/final-nba-revenue-numbers-in-from-last-season/, accessed August 1, 2011; and Maury Brown, "MLB Revenues Grown From $1.4 Billion in 1995 to $7 Billion in 2010," *Business of Baseball*, April 14, 2011; http://www.bizofbaseball.com/index.php?option=com_content&view=article&id=5167:mlb-revenues-grown-from-14-billion-in-1995-to-7-billion-in-2010&catid=30:mlb-news&Itemid=42, accessed June 20, 2011.

166. Milano and Chelladurai, "Gross Domestic Sport Product."

167. Douglas Hartmann, "Rethinking the Relationships between Sport and Race in American Culture: Golden Ghettos and Contested Terrain," *Sociology of Sport Journal* 17 (2000): 229–53.

168. Sarah Wilhelm, "Public Funding of Sports Stadiums," *Public Policy Brief*: 04-30-08 (Salt Lake City: University of Utah Center for Public Policy and Administration, 2008) 1–11, p. 2. Also see J. Siegfried and A. Zimbalist, "The Economics of Sports Facilities and Their Communities," *Journal of Economic Perspectives*, 14 (2000): 95–114, p. 114; Dennis Coates, "Stadiums and Arenas: Economic Development or Economic Redistribution?" *Contemporary Economic Policy* 25 (2007): 565–77.

169. Neil DeMause and Joanna Cagan, *Field of Schemes: How the Great Stadium Swindle Turns Public Money into Private Profit* (Lincoln, NE: Bison Books, 2008) 4–5.

170. Neil DeMause, "Why Do Mayors Love Sports Stadiums?" *Nation*, July 27, 2011; http://www.thenation.com/article/162400/why-do-mayors-love-sports -stadiums, accessed February 13, 2012; Kevin J. Delaney and Rick Eckstein, *Public Dollars, Private Stadiums: The Battle over Building Sports Stadiums* (New Brunswick, NJ: Rutgers University Press, 2003); James Quirk and Rodney Fort, *Hard Ball: The Abuse of Power in Pro Team Sports* (Princeton, NJ: Princeton University Press, 2008).

171. N. Jeremi Duru, "Fielding a Team for the Fans: The Societal Consequences and Title VII Implications of Race-Considered Roster Construction in Professional Sport," *Washington University Law Review* 84 (2006): 375–428, p. 378.

172. Arguably, there are fans of certain companies, such as Apple, the computer maker, though besides the late Steve Jobs, that company had no human face and it is difficult to argue that race was an issue in public perceptions of the company. There are fans of certain fictional characters, particularly comic book and other fantasy or science-fiction characters, however, and this does translate into concern for race and hiring, and studios who violate fans' desires in this area may face their wrath. See the above discussion regarding *The Last Airbender*, and the controversy over casting a black actor in the movie *Thor*, based on a comic book hero who was part of Norse mythology.

173. David Swindell and Mark S. Rosentraub, "Who Benefits from the Presence of Professional Sports Teams? The Implications for Public Funding of Stadiums and Arenas," *Public Administration Review* 58 (1998): 11–20.

174. William C. Rhoden, *Forty Million Dollar Slaves: The Rise, Fall and Redemption of the Black Athlete* (New York: Crown Publishers, 2006) 14.

175. Jules Tygiel, *Baseball's Great Experiment: Jackie Robinson and His Legacy* (New York: Oxford University Press, 1983).

176. Quoted in Kenneth L. Shropshire, *In Black and White: Race and Sports in America* (New York: New York University Press, 1996) 103.

177. Thomas G. Smith, "Civil Rights on the Gridiron: The Kennedy Administration and the Desegregation of the Washington Redskins," in Patrick B. Miller and David K. Wiggins, eds., *Sport and the Color Line: Black Athletes and Race Relations in Twentieth-Century America* (New York: Routledge, 2004) 250–67, p. 254.

178. Thomas G. Smith, *Showdown: JFK and the Integration of the Washington Redskins* (Boston: Beacon Press, 2011) 151.

179. Smith, *Showdown*, 152–53.

180. *Showdown*,161.

181. *Showdown*, Chapter 10.

182. J. C. Watts, Jr. with Chris Winston, *What Color Is a Conservative? My Life and My Politics* (New York: HarperCollins, 2002) 124.

183. Daniel Buffington, "Contesting Race on Sundays: Making Meaning out of the Rise in the Number of Black Quarterbacks," *Sociology of Sport Journal* 21 (2005): 19–37.

184. This section is indebted to the excellent work in Duru, "Fielding a Team."

185. Howard Bryant, *Shut Out: A Story of Race and Baseball in Boston* (New York: Routledge, 2002) 143.

186. The Census Bureau's "Standard Consolidated Statistical Area" that included Boston and the surrounding towns had 3,170,009 whites and only 170,454 blacks. Bureau of the Census, *1980 Census of Population*, vol. 1: *Characteristics of the Population, chapter B, General Population Characteristics*, Part 23: *Massachusetts* (Washington, DC: Government Printing Office, 1982) table 16.

187. On the white reaction to school integration in Boston, see Ronald P. Formisano, *Boston against Busing: Race, Class and Ethnicity in the 1960s and 1970s* (Chapel Hill: University of North Carolina Press, 2003).

188. Bryant, *Shut Out*, 143. There was even a formal charge of discrimination, though it was about an issue in Florida, where the team held spring training, rather than in racially-tense Boston. In 1986, coach and former player Tommy Harper complained to the press that the Red Sox accepted without complaint a no-blacks policy at Florida Elks Club facilities. This meant that only the white players were invited to use the popular facilities during spring training. After complaining to the press and then being fired, Harper filed a complaint with the Equal Employment Opportunity Commission. The EEOC agreed that the Red Sox illegally fired Harper in retaliation for his discrimination complaint. Bryant, *Shut Out*, 147–50; Duru, "Fielding a Team," 385–86.

189. J. A. Adande, "The Truth Isn't Always Black and White for Celtics," *ESPN.com*, December 19, 2007; http://sports.espn.go.com/nba/columns/story?columnist=adande_ja&page=Celtics-071219, accessed June 26, 2012.

190. Duru, "Fielding a Team," 396.

191. Harvey Araton and Filip Bondy, *The Selling of the Green: The Financial Rise and Moral Decline of the Boston Celtics* (New York: HarperCollins, 1992) 56.

192. Araton and Bondy, *Selling of the Green*, 71.

193. *Selling of the Green*, 76.

194. *Selling of the Green*, 77.

195. Duru, "Fielding a Team," 396, n.150.

196. *Selling of the Green*, 61.

197. *Selling of the Green*, 121–22.

198. *Selling of the Green*, 123.

199. Duru, "Fielding a Team," 397; citing Araton and Bondy, *Selling of the Green*, 24.

200. "Fielding a Team," 421.

201. Jonathan Mahler, "Building the Béisbol Brand," *New York Times*, July 31, 2005; http://www.nytimes.com/2005/07/31/magazine/31METS.html?pagewanted =all, accessed February 17, 2012.

202. Barry Svrluga and Robert E. Pierre, "The Fading Image of the Black Ball-player," *Washington Post*, March 25, 2005; http://www.washingtonpost.com/wp -dyn/articles/A2948-2005Mar26_3.html, accessed March 25, 2005.

203. Svrluga and Pierre, "Fading Image."

204. All quotes from Svrluga and Pierre, "Fading Image."

205. Howard Beck, "From Ivy Halls to the Garden, Surprise Star Jolts the N.B.A.," *New York Times*, February 7, 2012; http://www.nytimes.com/2012/02/08/ sports/basketball/jeremy-lin-has-burst-from-nba-novelty-act-to-knicks-star .html?hp, accessed February 8, 2012.

206. Ken Belson, "Lin Soars, and So Does Stock Price for MSG," *New York Times* February 13, 2012; http://www.nytimes.com/2012/02/14/sports/basketball/ as-lins-stock-rises-so-does-msgs.html?_r=1, accessed February 13, 2012.

207. Jay Caspian Kang, "Person of Interest: A Trip Deep into the Heart of Linsanity," *Grantland*, February 13, 2012; http://www.grantland.com/story/_/ id/7570431/jeremy-lin, accessed February 13, 2012.

208. Associated Press, "With Lin's Emergence, Knicks Games Added in Asia," [no date]; http://sports.yahoo.com/nba/news;_ylt=AidNv.MkEjl8TK_ QpLaWcUe8vLYF?slug=ap-knicks-lineffect, accessed February 11, 2012.

209. Sam Dolnick, "Sharing a Heritage With a New Knicks Star," *New York Times*, February 10, 2012; http://www.nytimes.com/2012/02/11/sports/basket ball/at-soho-bar-jeremy-lins-fans-share-his-heritage.html, accessed February 15, 2012.

210. J. Michael Falgoust, "Asian Americans Energized in Seeing Knicks' Jeremy Lin Play," *USA Today*, February 8, 2012; http://www.usatoday.com/ sports/basketball/nba/story/2012-02-08/Asian-Americans-flock-to-see-Jeremy -Lin-play/53017410/1, accessed February 15, 2012.

211. Jesse Washington/Associated Press, "Asian-Americans Rejoice as Un-likely Basketball Star Jeremy Lin Smashes Stereotypes," *Washington Post*, Febru-ary 17, 2012; http://www.washingtonpost.com/sports/asian-americans-rejoice-as -unlikely-basketball-star-jeremy-lin-smashes-stereotypes/2012/02/17/gIQAwUK FJR_story.html, accessed February 17, 2012.

212. J. A. Adande, "Jeremy Lin Finds Perfect Landing Spot," *ESPN.com*, July 23, 2012; http://espn.go.com/nba/story/_/id/8176474/nba-houston-rockets-right -place-jeremy-lin, accessed September 1, 2012.

213. Lawrence M. Kahn, "Discrimination in Professional Sports: A Survey of the Literature," *Industrial and Labor Relations Review* 44 (1991): 395–418.

214. David J. Berri and Rob Simmons, "Race and the Evaluation of Signal Callers in the National Football League,"*Journal of Sports Economics* 10 (2009): 23–43.

215. Lawrence M. Kahn and Malav Shah, "Race, Compensation and Con-tract Length in the NBA: 2001–2002," *Industrial Relations* 44 (2005): 444–62. A study of salaries and skin tone similarly did not show employer discrimination. John Robst, Jennifer Van Gilder, Corinne E. Coates, and David J. Berri, "Skin Tone and Wages: Evidence from NBA Free Agents," *Journal of Sports Economics* 12 (2011): 143–56.

216. Richard Lapchick, with Francisco Aristeguieta, Wayne Clark, Christina Cloud, Anna Florzak, Demetrius Frazier, Michael Kuhn, Tavia Record, and

Matthew Vinson, "The 2011 Racial and Gender Report Card: National Basketball Association," *The Institute for Ethics and Diversity in Sport*, June 16, 2011; http://www.tidesport.org/RGRC/2011/2011_NBA_RGRC_FINAL%20FINAL.pdf, accessed February 16, 2012.

217. M. T. Kanazawa and J.P. Funk, "Racial Discrimination in Professional Basketball: Evidence from Nielsen Ratings," *Economic Inquiry* 39 (2001): 599–608, p. 607. On the economic value of white benchwarmers in the NBA, see Duru, "Fielding a Team," 397.

218. For a review, see R. C. Burdekin, R. Hossfeld, and J. Smith, "Are NBA Fans Becoming Indifferent to Race? Evidence from the 1990s," *Journal of Sports Economics* 6 (2005): 144–59, p. 145. This particular study does find a link between player race and attendance (p. 155).

219. Burdekin, Hossfeld and Smith, "NBA Fans Indifferent to Race?"

220. R. McCormick and R. Tollison, "Why Do Black Basketball Players Work More for Less Money?" *Journal of Economic Behavior and Organization*, 44 (2001): 201–19. On black fans' preference for black players, also see Orn Bodvarsson and Mark D. Partridge, "A Supply and Demand Model of Co-worker, Employer and Customer Discrimination," *Labour Economics*, 8 (2001): 389–416.

221. Burdekin, Hossfeld and Smith, "NBA Fans Indifferent to Race?" 154–55.

222. Eric M. Aldrich, Peter S. Arcidiacono, and Jacob L. Vigdor, "Do People Value Racial Diversity? Evidence from Nielsen Ratings," *Topics in Economic Analysis and Policy* 5 (2005): 1–28.

223. Craig Depken and Jon Ford, "Customer-Based Discrimination Against Major League Baseball Players: Additional Evidence from All-Star Ballots," *Journal of Socio-Economics* 35 (2006): 1061–77.

224. David Leonhardt and Ford Fessenden, "Black Coaches in N.B.A. Have Shorter Tenures," *New York Times*. March 22, 2005; http://www.nytimes.com/2005/03/22/sports/basketball/22coaches.html, accessed on June 10, 2011.

225. McCormick and Tollison, "Why Do Black Basketball Players Work More?"

226. For example, one study suggested that the race of an NFL coach was related to the racial mix in a city, though higher percentages of blacks in a city were correlated with *lower* likelihoods that an NFL team would have a black coach. Brian L. Goff and Robert D. Tollison, "Racial Integration of Coaching: Evidence from the NFL," *Journal of Sports Economics* 10 (2009): 127–40. Since there is no plausible mechanism to account for this result, it may just be a statistical aberration.

227. Janice Fanning Madden and Matthew Ruther, "Has the NFL's Rooney Rule Efforts 'Leveled the Field' for African American Head Coach Candidates?" *Journal of Sports Economics* 12 (2011): 127–42, p. 127.

228. For an analysis of the Rooney Rule, see N. Jeremi Duru, *Advancing the Ball: Race, Reformation and the Quest for Equal Coaching Opportunity in the NFL* (New York: Oxford University Press, 2011).

229. Benjamin Solow, John L. Solow, and Todd B. Walker, "Moving on Up: The Rooney Rule and Minority Hiring in the NFL," *Labour Economics* 18 (2011): 332–37.

230. Brian Collins, "Tackling Unconscious Bias in Hiring Practices: The Plight of the Rooney Rule," *New York University Law Review* 82 (2007): 870–912, p. 883.

231. Many have noted the lack of litigation on casting discrimination. See, for example, Robert Post, "The Logic of American Antidiscrimination Law," in Robert Post, ed., *Prejudicial Appearances* (Durham, NC: Duke University Press, 2001): 1, 48; Robinson, "Casting and Caste-ing"; Angela Onwuachi-Willig, "There's Just One Hitch, Will Smith: Examining Title VII, Race and Casting Discrimination on the Fortieth Anniversary of *Loving v. Virginia*," *Wisconsin Law Review* 2 (2007): 319–343; Bonnie Chen, "Note: Mixing Law and Art: The Role of Anti-Discrimination Law and Color-Blind Casting in Broadway Theater," *Hofstra Labor and Employment Law Journal* 16 (1999): 515–43.

232. On April 18, 2012, Nathaniel Claybrooks and Christopher Johnson filed a class action lawsuit against ABC and other companies related to the production of *The Bachelor* and *The Bachelorette* on behalf of nonwhites. The show explores the efforts of a field of contestants to win a promise of (heterosexual) marriage from the central male or female character. They charged the defendants with racial discrimination for never casting any race but white in the central role in twenty-three seasons of the two shows. They made the charge under Section 1981, which prohibits discriminating on the basis of race in the denial of contracts, as well as a California civil rights code. The complaint noted that other reality shows, including those with a romantic theme, have used racially diverse casts. The complaint can be found at Eriq Gardner, "'The Bachelor' Racial Discrimination Lawsuit: Read the Full Complaint," *Hollywood Reporter,* April 18, 2012; http://www.hollywoodreporter.com/thr-esq/the-bachelor-lawsuit-racial-discrimination-313734, accessed July 2, 2012.

233. Robinson, "Cast and Caste-ing," 3–4.

234. U.S. Equal Employment Opportunity Commission, "Section 15: Race and Color Discrimination," April 19, 2006; http://www.eeoc.gov/policy/docs/race-color.html#VIC, accessed June 14, 2011.

235. Duru, "Fielding a Team," 425–27.

236. John D. Skrentny, *The Minority Rights Revolution* (Cambridge, MA: Belknap Press of Harvard University Press, 2002) 115–16.

237. *Pittsburgh Press Co. v. Pittsburgh Commission on Human Relations* 413 U.S. 376 (1973).

238. U.S. Equal Opportunity Employment Commission, "Prohibited Employment Policies/Practices"; http://www.eeoc.gov/laws/practices/index.cfm, accessed on February 17, 2011.

239. Robinson, "Casting and Caste-ing," 30, 42.

240. *Congressional Record*, April 8, 1964, 7217.

241. On culture shaping what is considered "rational," see Frank Dobbin, "Cultural Models of Organization: The Social Construction of Rational Organizing Principles," in Diana Crane, ed., *Sociology of Culture: Emerging Theoretical Perspectives* (New York: Basil Blackwell, 1994) 117–53.

242. Supreme Court has stated matter of factly that Congress made the fifteen-employee limit "to spare very small businesses from Title VII liability." *Arbaugh v. Y.H. Corp.*, 546 U.S. 500, 502 (2006). There is almost no reference to the limit in the debate over the law, and at least one court has entertained the possibility that the limit stems from the constitutional authority for the law, which was the Commerce Clause's authorization of Congress to enact statutes to regulate

interstate commerce. In that view, fifteen employees is a threshold whereby it can be assumed that the business substantially affects interstate commerce. *Nesbit v. Gears Unlimited, Inc.*, 347 F.3d 72, 81-82 (3rd Cir. 2003). For a discussion, see Patten Courtnell, "Note & Comment: Employers Beware! The Supreme Court's Interpretation Of Title VII's Employee Numerosity Requirement Disadvantages Small Businesses," *Loyola of Los Angeles Law Review* 40 (2007): 793–808, p. 802.

243. *Ferrill v. The Parker Group, Inc.*, 168 F.3d 468 (11th Cir. 1999), at 474, n.10. This footnote also noted that the firm "could have legally assigned jobs based on accent, speech pattern. or dialect, but not expressly on race" because African-Americans had a speaking style that would appeal to African-Americans. This ruling would be in violation of the current EEOC Compliance Manual, which emphasizes that accent discrimination is only acceptable when the accent prevents adequate communication. http://www.eeoc.gov/policy/docs/national -origin.html#VA, accessed April 23, 2013.

244. *Miller v. Texas State Board of Barber Examiners*, 615 F.2d 650, 654 (5th Cir. 1980). Though the court did not explain how this would be possible given that Title VII outlawed race as a BFOQ, it did go on to explicitly reject the Case and Clifford strategy of having a director casting the part of Henry the VIII express himself in race-neutral way by saying that all applicants needed to have the physical traits of Henry the VIII: "It is unlikely that we would either require or be deceived by such convoluted semantical gymnastics . . ." *Miller v. Texas State Board of Barber Examiners*, 615 F.2d 650, 654 (5th Cir. 1980).

245. On the importance, complexity and incoherence of everyday distinctions, see Eviatar Zerubavel, *The Fine Line: Making Distinctions in Everyday Life* (New York: Free Press, 1991).

246. I explored the Title IX story in John D. Skrentny, *The Minority Rights Revolution* (Cambridge, MA: Harvard University Press, 2002) Chapter 8.

247. *Fesel v. Masonic Home Inc.*, 447 F. Supp. 1346 (D. Del. 1978), affirmed, 591 F.2s 1334 (3rd Circ. 1979). On the other hand, an Illinois court refused to approve a health club's wish to have a women-only rule, even though women at the club submitted a petition saying having men working there was an invasion of their privacy. *EEOC v. Sedita* 755 F. Supp. 808 (N.D. Ill. 1991).

248. For a provocative discussion of these and other cases, see Michael J. Frank, "Justifiable Discrimination in the News and Entertainment Industries: Does Title VII Need a Race or Color BFOQ?" *University of San Francisco Law Review* 35 (2001): 473–525, p. 489–92.

249. Kimberly A. Yuracko, "Private Nurses and Playboy Bunnies: Explaining Permissible Sex Discrimination," *California Law Review* 92 (2004): 147–213, p. 154.

250. Men who had sued Hooters nevertheless received $3.75 million in a private settlement. Michael J. Zimmer, Charles A. Sullivan, Richard F. Richards, and Deborah A. Calloway, *Cases and Materials on Employment Discrimination*, 5th ed. (New York: Aspen Law & Business, 2000) 312. Also see Robinson, "Cast and Caste-ing," pp. 42-43 for a discussion of the cultural logic of preferences in the Hooters case.

251. U.S. Equal Employment Opportunity Commission, 29 C.F.R. 1604.2(a) (2) (2000).

252. U.S. Equal Employment Opportunity Commission, 29 C.F.R. 1606.4 (2000).

253. U.S. Equal Employment Opportunity Commission, *Compliance Manual*, available at http://www.eeoc.gov/policy/docs/race-color.html, accessed July 2, 2012.

254. *Report of the the Senate Committee on Appropriations*, S. Rep. No. 182, 100th Congress, 1st Sess. 76 (1987), quoted in Worthy, "Diversity and Minority Stereotyping," 515, n.22.

255. Brief for the United States as Amicus Curiae Supporting Petitioner, Metro Broadcasting, Inc., Petitioner v. Federal Communications Commission, et al., http://www.justice.gov/osg/briefs/1989/sg890279.txt, accessed April 30, 2013; also see Neal Devins, "Congress, the FCC, and the Search for the Public Trustee," *Law and Contemporary Problems* 56 (1993): 145–88, p. 177–78; Damon W. Root, "Does Federal Law Trump an Oath to the Constitution?" *Reason* (March 2, 2011); http://reason.com/archives/2011/03/02/does-federal-law-trump-an-oath, accessed April 30, 2013.

256. *Metro Broadcasting, Inc. v. FCC*, 497 U.S. 547 (1990).

257. At 547, 567.

258. *Regents of University of California v. Bakke*, 438 U.S. 265, 311–13 (1978).

259. *Metro Broadcasting, Inc. v. FCC*, 497 U.S. 547, 554 (1990). On the public good, see *Metro Broadcasting, Inc. v. FCC*, 568.

260. At 579.

261. In his dissent, Justice Stevens sought to ensure that no one would treat the diversity goal as overruled: "The proposition that fostering diversity may provide a sufficient interest to justify such a program is *not* inconsistent with the Court's holding today—indeed, the question is not remotely presented in this case—and I do not take the Court's opinion to diminish that aspect of our decision in *Metro Broadcasting*" (original emphasis). *Adarand v. Pena*, 515 U.S. 200, 258 (1995).

262. The broadcaster may also point out that the Supreme Court has supported the notion of diverse content in broadcasting when it upheld the "fairness doctrine," which for a time required broadcasters to present multiple sides of a political issues. Because the regulations were geared toward producing more speech, rather than limiting speech, "fairness" rules avoided constitutional problems: "To condition the granting or renewal of licenses on a willingness to present representative community views on controversial issues is consistent with the ends and purposes of those constitutional provisions forbidding the abridgment of freedom of speech and freedom of the press. Congress need not stand idly by and permit those with licenses to ignore the problems which beset the people or to exclude from the airways anything but their own views of fundamental questions." *Red Lion Broadcasting Co., Inc. v. FCC*, 395 U.S. 367, 394 (1969).

263. *Grutter v. Bollinger*, 539 U.S. 306, 332 (2003).

264. For an opposing opinion, see Kenneth L. Shropshire, *In Black and White: Race and Sports in America* (New York: New York University Press, 1996) 73–74.

265. Duru, "Fielding a Team," 419–23.

266. "Fielding a Team," 423, citing Rebecca Hanner White, "Affirmative Action in the Workplace: The Significance of Grutter?" *Kentucky Law Review* 92 (2003–2004): 263–78, p. 277.

267. *Mutual Film Corp. v. Industrial Commission of Ohio*, 236 U.S. 230 (1915). See Paul Siegel, *Communication Law in America, 2nd ed.* (Lanham, MD: Rowman and Littlefield Publishers, 2001), p. 488 for a discussion.

268. *Winters v. New York*, 333 U.S. 507, 510 (1948).

269. *Burstyn v. Wilson*, 343 U.S. 495, 501 (1952).

270. See, generally, Laura Wittern-Keller and Raymond J. Habierski Jr., *The Miracle Case: Film Censorship and the Supreme Court* (Lawrence: University Press of Kansas, 2008).

271. For example, the Court has stated: "The commercial marketplace, like other spheres of our social and cultural life, provides a forum where ideas and information flourish. Some of the ideas and information are vital, some of slight worth. But the general rule is that the speaker and the audience, not the government, assess the value of the information presented. Thus, even a communication that does no more than propose a commercial transaction is entitled to the coverage of the First Amendment." *Edenfield v. Fane*, 507 U.S. 761, 767 (1993).

272. Michael T. Morley, "'Exceedingly Vexed and Difficult': Games and the First Amendment," *Yale Law Journal* 112 (2002): 361–68.

273. Morley, "'Exceedingly Vexed and Difficult'," 367–68.

274. *America's Best Family Showplace Corp. v. City of New York*, 536 F. Supp. 170, 174 (E.D.N.Y. 1982).

275. *Iota Xi Chapter of Sigma Chi Fraternity v. George Mason Univ.*, 993 F.2d 386, 389 (4th Cir. 1993).

276. For an insightful analysis of this issue, see Jed Rubenfeld, "The First Amendment's Purpose," *Stanford Law Review* 55 (2001): 767–832.

277. Employers rarely defend their discrimination explicitly on the basis of the message that different employees may send, but when they did so, it did not fare well in court. An influential Eleventh Circuit opinion regarding sex discrimination grew out of a case involving a restaurant that was trying to send a message to customers through its hiring: the restaurant wanted to hire only male waiters (and have them wear tuxedoes), because they thought this would add to the restaurant's "Old World" atmosphere. The court, however, concluded that the restaurant was not engaging in expressive message-sending but was instead attempting to enforce a stereotype that cast women as unable to fulfill the employer's goal of creating a "fine-dining" ambiance. *EEOC v. Joe's Stone Crab, Inc.*, 220 F. 3d 1263, 1284 (11th Cir. 2000).

278. Frank, "Justifiable Discrimination," 515–16.

279. The "Spence test," first articulated in a 1974 flag-desecration case, *Spence v. Washington*, was an early attempt. The Court noted that the flag desecration (which in this case involved displaying it upside down and attaching a peace sign to it) was not "mindless nihilism." The reasons for this conclusion supplied the two prongs of the test: first, there was intent to convey a particularized message, and second, there was a great likelihood that those viewing the message would understand it. *Spence v. Washington*, 418 U.S. 405, 410–11 (1974). By this standard, casting based *solely* on the prowess of the actor or athlete, would not be expressive. But casting for racial signaling would seem to pass the test. Race can be part of the story or the show, or in some cases, especially advertising or some sports teams, be part of an effort to send a message of inclusion, and though not

all would understand that the hiring was sending a message, it is likely that the message would be understood if viewers or fans saw the hiring in this light.

280. Robinson, "Cast and Caste-ing," 17, n.75, lists several cases. The Section 1981 case is *Runyon v. McCrary*, 427 U.S. 160 (1976).

281. Robinson, "Cast and Caste-ing," 47.

282. *Hurley v. Irish-American Gay, Lesbian and Bisexual Group of Boston*, 515 U.S. 557 (1995).

283. *Hurley v. Irish-American Gay, Lesbian and Bisexual Group of Boston*, 569. See Rubenfeld, "The First Amendment's Purpose," for a discussion.

284. *Hurley v. Irish-American Gay, Lesbian and Bisexual Group of Boston*, 574.

285. *Cohen v. California*, 403 U.S. 15, 25 (1971).

286. *United States v. O'Brien*, 391 U.S. 367, 377 (1968).

287. There are separate (but similar) rules governing commercial speech. Expression in ads can be protected from regulation if the ad is for a lawful activity and is not deceptive. The purpose of any regulation restricting ad speech must be substantial, it must directly advance that purpose, and it must not be broader than is necessary for that purpose. *Central Hudson Gas & Electric Corporation v. Public Service Commission*, 447 U.S. 557, 566 (1980).

288. John D. Skrentny, *The Ironies of Affirmative Action: Politics, Culture and Justice in America* (Chicago: University of Chicago Press, 1996) 34. *Griggs v. Duke Power Co.*, 401 U.S. 424, (1971) contains a concise statement on the purpose of Title VII: "The objective of Congress in the enactment of Title VII is plain from the language of the statute. It was to achieve equality of employment opportunities and remove barriers that have operated in the past to favor an identifiable group of white employees over other employees."

289. For a discussion, see Margaret A. Fiorino, "Advertising for Apartheid: The Use of All White Models in Marketing Real Estate as a Violation of the Fair Housing Act," *University of Cincinnati Law Review* 56 (1988): 1429–43.

290. 43 U.S.C. 3604(c).

291. *Saunders v. General Services Corporation*, 659 F. Supp. 1042, 1058–59 (E.D. Va., 1987). Also see the opinion by future Supreme Court Justice Ruth Bader Ginsburg in *Spann v. Colonial Village, Inc.*, 899 F.2d 24 (D.C. Cir. 1990).

292. *Claybrooks et al. v. American Broadcasting Companies, Inc. et al.*, 2012 U.S. Dist. LEXIS 147884, *30 (M.D. Tenn. 2012).

293. *Claybrooks et al. v. American Broadcasting Companies, Inc. et al.*, *15.

294. *Claybrooks et al. v. American Broadcasting Companies, Inc. et al.*, *32.

295. *Claybrooks et al v. American Broadcasting Companies, Inc. et al.*, *35.

296. *Claybrooks et al v. American Broadcasting Companies, Inc. et al.*, *16, n.8.

Chapter 5. The Jungle Revisited? Racial Realism in the Low-Skilled Sector

1. New Orleans had a population of 484,674 in 2000, of whom 67.3 percent were black. In 2006, the Census Bureau estimated that the population had fallen

to 223,000; http://quickfacts.census.gov/qfd/states/22/2255000.html, accessed August 12, 2009.

2. J. Steven Picou and Brent K. Marshall, "Introduction: Katrina as Paradigm Shift: Reflections on Disaster Research in the Twenty-First Century," in David L. Brunsma, David Overfelt, and J. Steven Picou, eds., *The Sociology of Katrina: Perspectives on a Modern Catastrophe* (New York: Rowman and Littlefield, 2007) 1–20, p. 2.

3. For details on differences in work terms, see Laurel Fletcher, Phuong N. Pham, Eric Stover, and Patrick Vinck, "Rebuilding After Katrina: A Population-Based Study of Labor and Human Rights in New Orleans," *Human Rights Center Reports*, Paper 2006_06 Rebuilding Katrina; http://repositories.cdlib.org/hrc/reports/2006 06Rebuilding-Katrina, accessed August 13, 2009.

4. Katherine M. Donato, Nicole Trujillo-Pagán, Carl L. Bankston III, and Audrey Singer, "Reconstructing New Orleans after Katrina: The Emergence of an Immigrant Labor Market," in David L. Brunsma, et al., *The Sociology of Katrina*, 217–34.

5. http://www.npr.org/templates/transcript/transcript.php?storyId= 92510412, accessed August 13, 2009.

6. On immigrant labor mobility, see Frank Bean and Gillian Stevens, *America's Newcomers and the Dynamics of Diversity* (New York: Russell Sage Foundation, 2003); Douglas S. Massey, Jorge Durand, and Nolan J. Malone, *Beyond Smoke and Mirrors: Mexican Immigration in an Era of Economic Integration* (New York: Russell Sage Foundation, 2002).

7. Sam Quinones, "Migrants Find a Gold Rush in New Orleans," *Los Angeles Times*, April 4, 2006; http://www.latimes.com/news/la-na-labor4apr04,0,128489 .story, accessed August 13, 2009.

8. "Tensions Persist for Blacks, Latinos in New Orleans: Transcript," *NPR*, July 14, 2008; http://www.npr.org/templates/transcript/transcript.php?storyId= 92510412, accessed August 13, 2009.

9. See, for example, Manuel Roig-Franzia, "New Orleans Mayor Apologizes for Remarks About God's Wrath," *Washington Post*, January 18, 2006; http://www .washingtonpost.com/wp-dyn/content/article/2006/01/17/AR2006011701353 .html, accessed August 15, 2012.

10. Gregory Acs and Pamela Loprest, "Job Differences in the Low-Skill Jobs Market," *Employers in the Low-Skill Labor Market,* Urban Institute Brief No. 4, February 2009; http://www.urban.org/UploadedPDF/411841_race_ethnicity_job_market.pdf, accessed May 28, 2012.

11. On ethnic and racial patterns and niches in employment, see Roger Waldinger, *Still the Promised City? African-Americans and New Immigrants in Postindustrial New York* (Cambridge, MA: Harvard University Press, 1996); and Ruth Milkman, *LA Story: Immigrant Workers and the Future of the U.S. Labor Movement* (New York: Russell Sage Foundation, 2006). An especially insightful discussion of whether immigration workers displace natives or replace them after they voluntarily leave a niche is Vanesa Ribas, *On the Line: The Working Lives of Latinos and African Americans in the New South*, Ph.D. Dissertation, University of North Carolina, 2012. Ethnic and racial grouping, particularly by immigrants, is common in residential patterns as well: John R. Logan, Richard D. Alba, and

Wenquan Zhang, "Immigrant Enclaves and Ethnic Communities in New York and Los Angeles," *American Sociological Review* 67 (2002): 299–322.

12. Immigrant penetration in certain labor markets is very uneven, constituting, for example, 17 percent of California's workforce, but 36 percent of service workers, 42 percent of factory operatives, and half of laborers: Nelson Lichtenstein, *State of the Union: A Century of American Labor* (Princeton, NJ: Princeton University Press, 2002) 267.

13. Upton Sinclair, *The Jungle* (Urbana: University of Illinois Press, 1988 [1906]).

14. I explored these issues in John D. Skrentny, "Are America's Civil Rights Laws Still Relevant?" *Du Bois Review* 4 (2007): 119–40.

15. Theodore Hershberg, Alan N. Burstein, Eugene P. Ericksen, Stephanie Greenberg, and William L. Yancey, "A Tale of Three Cities: Blacks and Immigrants in Philadelphia: 1850–1880, 1930 and 1970," *Annals of the American Academy of Political and Social Science* 441 (1979): 55–81. Also see Roger Waldinger, *Still the Promised City?* Other research shows that blacks and immigrants often worked alongside each other in the same jobs, though racial conflict was common when blacks were first introduced into workplaces. James R. Barrett, *Work and Community in the Jungle: Chicago's Packinghouse Workers, 1894–1922* (Urbana: University of Illinois Press, 1987).

16. Thomas J. Sugrue, *Sweet Land of Liberty: The Forgotten Struggle for Civil Rights in the North* (New York: Random House, 2008).

17. Upton Sinclair, *The Jungle*, 31.

18. Gerd Korman, *Industrialization, Immigrants and Americanizers: The View from Milwaukee, 1866–1921* (Madison: The State Historical Society of Wisconsin, 1967) 65–66.

19. James R. Barrett and David Roediger, "Inbetween Peoples: Race, Nationality and the 'New Immigrant' Working Class," *Journal of American Ethnic History* 16 (1997): 3–44, 16.

20. Barrett and Roediger, "Inbetween Peoples," 17.

21. "Inbetween Peoples," 17.

22. Daniel J. Tichenor, *Dividing Lines: The Politics of Immigration Control in America* (Princeton, NJ: Princeton University Press, 2002).

23. Mae Ngai, *Impossible Subjects: Illegal Aliens and the Making of Modern America* (Princeton, NJ: Princeton University Press, 2005); Douglas S. Massey, Jorge Durand, and Nolan J. Malone, *Beyond Smoke and Mirrors: Mexican Immigration in an Era of Economic Integration* (New York: Russell Sage Foundation, 2002), especially 24–29.

24. The number of Hispanics who lived in the U.S. in 1910 was only about 500,000 in a population of 92 million. Myron P. Gutmann and W. Parker Frisbie, "A New Look at the Hispanic Population of the United States in 1910," *Historical Methods* 32 (1999): 5–19, p. 5.

25. One experimental study found that Puerto Rican applicants for low-wage jobs face similar discrimination to that experienced by African-Americans, and both groups are less desired than whites. Devah Pager, Bruce Western, and Bart Bonikowski, "Discrimination in a Low-Wage Labor Market: A Field Experiment," *American Sociological Review* 74 (2009): 777–99.

26. Joleen Kirschenman and Kathryn M. Neckerman, "'We'd Love to Hire Them, but . . . ': The Meaning of Race for Employers," in Christopher Jencks and Paul E. Peterson, eds., *The Urban Underclass* (Washington, DC: Brookings Institution, 1991) 203–32, p. 228.

27. William J. Wilson, *When Work Disappears: The World of the New Urban Poor* (New York: Alfred A. Knopf, 1996) 112.

28. Wilson, *When Work Disappears*, 112–13.

29. Philip Kasinitz and Jan Rosenberg, "Missing the Connection: Social Isolation and Employment on the Brooklyn Waterfront," *Social Problems* 43 (1996): 180–96, p. 189.

30. Kasinitz and Rosenberg, "Missing the Connection," 191.

31. Roger Waldinger and Michael I. Lichter, *How the Other Half Works: Immigration and the Social Organization of Labor* (Berkeley: University of California Press, 2003) 160.

32. Waldinger and Lichter, *How the Other Half Works*, 160.

33. *How the Other Half Works*, 162.

34. *How the Other Half Works*, 163.

35. Cameron D. Lippard, "Racialized Hiring Practices for 'Dirty' Jobs," in Cameron D. Lippard and Charles A. Gallagher, eds., *Being Brown in Dixie: Race, Ethnicity, and Latino Immigration in the New South* (Boulder: FirstForumPress, 2011) 201–35, p. 219.

36. Lippard, "Racialized Hiring Practices," 222.

37. "Racialized Hiring Practices," 226.

38. Philip Moss and Chris Tilly, *Stories Employers Tell: Race, Skills and Hiring in America* (New York: Russell Sage Foundation, 2001) 92. Moss and Tilly note, however, that about 20 percent said that their customers or other employers were racially biased. Moss and Tilly speculate that employers were afraid of violating civil rights law in the phone interviews. *Stories Employers Tell*, 152–53.

39. *Stories Employers Tell*, 153.

40. *Stories*, 117.

41. *Stories*, 118.

42. *Stories*, 119.

43. *Stories*, 117.

44. Kirschenman and Neckerman, "We'd Love to Hire Them, but," 212.

45. "We'd Love to Hire Them, but," 210. Kirschenman and Neckerman's survey showed support for hiring whites, which is not found in other studies: 7.6 percent said blacks and Latinos were both at the bottom, while no employers ranked whites last.

46. Wilson, *When Work Disappears*, 112.

47. *When Work Disappears*, 118–19.

48. *When Work Disappears*, 112.

49. *When Work Disappears*, 113.

50. James W. Button, Barbara A. Rienzo, and Sheila L. Croucher, *Blacks and the Quest for Economic Equality: The Political Economy of Employment in Southern Communities in the United States* (University Park: The Pennsylvania State University Press, 2009) 59.

51. Waldinger and Lichter, *How the Other Half Works*, 171–73.

52. Moss and Tilly, *Stories Employers Tell*, 114.

53. Edward J. W. Park, "Racial Ideology and Hiring Decisions in Silicon Valley," *Qualitative Sociology* 22 (1999): 223–33, p. 229.

54. Park, "Racial Ideology and Hiring Decisions in Silicon Valley," 230.

55. Waldinger and Lichter, *How the Other Half Works*, 171–73.

56. Wilson, *When Work Disappears*, 116–17.

57. Button, Rienzo, and Croucher, *Blacks and the Quest for Economic Equality*, 58.

58. Moss and Tilly, *Stories Employers Tell*, 78–79. Also see Acs and Loprest, "Job Differences in the Low-Skill Jobs Market."

59. *Stories Employers Tell*, 97.

60. Waldinger and Lichter, *How the Other Half Works*, 158.

61. Quoted in Georgia Pabst, "Immigration Cultivation: Farmers Gain Insight on New Work Force through Program," *Milwaukee Journal Sentinel*, June 7, 2006.

62. Brent E. Valentine, *Uniting Two Cultures: Latino Immigrants in the Wisconsin Dairy Industry* (Working Paper 121, Center for Comparative Immigration Studies, University of California, San Diego, 2005) 47.

63. Button, Rienzo, and Croucher, *Blacks and the Quest for Economic Equality*, 51. This is partly a result of the fact that firms with black employers tend to have more black applicants, but they also hire a greater proportion of blacks than white employers do. Michael A. Stoll, Steven Raphael, and Harry J. Holzer, "Job Applicants and the Hiring Officer's Race," *Industrial and Labor Relations Review* 57 (2004): 267–87.

64. Sandy Jeanquart-Barone, "Implications of Racial Diversity in the Supervisor-Subordinate Relationship," *Journal of Applied Social Psychology* 26 (1996): 935–44.

65. Lippard, "Racialized Hiring Practices," 228.

66. Wilson, *When Work Disappears*, 130.

67. See, for example, Timoty Bates, *Race, Self-Employment & Upward Mobility* (Baltimore: Johns Hopkins University Press, 1997); Vivek Wadhwa, AnnaLee Saxenian, Ben Rissing, and Gary Gereffi, *America's New Immigrant Entrepreneurs*, January 4, 2007, Master of Engineering Management Program, Duke University; School of Information, U.C. Berkeley; http://www.kauffman.org/uploadedfiles/entrep_immigrants_1_61207.pdf, accessed August 16, 2012.

68. On family as a labor resource for immigrant entrepreneurs, see Jimy M. Sanders and Victor Nee, "Immigrant Self-Employment: The Family as Social Capital and the Value of Human Capital," *American Sociological Review* 61 (1996): 231–49.

69. Tarry Hum, "The Promises and Dilemmas of Immigrant Ethnic Economies," in Marta López-Garza and David R. Diaz, eds., *Asian and Latino Immigrants in a Restructuring Economy: The Metamorphosis of Southern California* (Stanford, CA: Stanford University Press, 2001) 77–101, pp. 80–81.

70. Ivan Light and Edna Bonacich, *Immigrant Entrepreneurs: Koreans in Los Angeles, 1965–1982* (Berkeley: University of California Press, 1988) 179.

71. Light and Bonacich, *Immigrant Entrepreneurs*, 186.

72. *Immigrant Entrepreneurs*, 204.

73. Moss and Tilly, *Stories Employers Tell*, 132.

74. Edna Bonacich and Richard Appelbaum, *Behind the Label: Inequality in the Los Angeles Apparel Industry* (Berkeley: University of California Press, 2000); Julie A. Su and Chanchanit Martorell, "Exploitation and Abuse in the Garment Industry: The Case of the Thai Slave-Labor Compound in El Monte," in Marta López-Garza and David R. Diaz, eds., *Asian and Latino Immigrants in a Restructuring Economy: The Metamorphosis of Southern California* (Stanford, CA: Stanford University Press, 2001) 21–45.

75. On immigrant employers' avoidance of African-Americans and placement of this group at the bottom of the racial hierarchy, also see Hum, "Promises and Dilemmas," 81.

76. Mary C. Waters, *Black Identities: West Indian Immigrant Dreams and American Realities* (Cambridge, MA: Harvard University Press, 1999) 116–19, finds many of the same laudatory comments described above for Latinos and Asians but directed toward West Indian blacks. They are, for example, described as having more "reliability," "willingness to do the job" and "a different drive" when compared to American blacks. These employers believe American blacks "don't have the self-discipline to hold the job." It is unclear from her study whether black immigrants were preferred over other immigrants, however. Also see Moss and Tilly, *Stories Employers Tell*, 118. In other contexts, employers may prefer and manage workers of varying backgrounds, including black, white or immigrant black, in order to undermine worker solidarity. Ribas, *On the Line*, Chapter 2. Immigrant entrepreneurs doing business in a different community may seek to match the race of some employees with the local client base. Sociologist Jennifer Lee found Korean storeowners in Harlem hiring blacks as "cultural brokers" to help them interact with the local clientele, though these cultural brokers were almost always black immigrants rather than native-born blacks. Jennifer Lee, "The Racial and Ethnic Meaning behind Black: Retailers' Hiring Practices in Inner-City Neighborhoods," in John D. Skrentny , ed., *Color Lines: Immigration, Affirmative Action and Civil Rights Options for America* (Chicago: University of Chicago Press, 2001). This pattern of matching client bases in retail is not uncommon. Rebecca Raijman and Marta Tienda (2003) show that Korean entrepreneurs, along with Mexicans, in a Mexican neighborhood hire Latinos with Latino cultural skills. For the Koreans, these workers "help cater to a Hispanic clientele by acting as translators and mediators." Rebecca Raijman and Marta Tienda, "Ethnic Foundations of Economic Transactions: Mexican and Korean Immigrant Entrepreneurs in Chicago," *Ethnic and Racial Studies* 26 (2003) 790. Korean merchants also hire white workers to deal with white customers. Judith Goode, "Encounters over the Counter: Bosses, Workers, and Customers on a Changing Shopping Strip," in Louise Lamphere, Alex Stepick, and Guillermo Grenier, eds., *Newcomers in the Workplace: Immigrants and the Restructuing of the U.S. Economy* (Philadelphia, PA: Temple University Press, 1994) 270.

77. Margaret M. Chin, *Sewing Women: Immigrants and the New York City Garment Industry* (New York: Columbia University Press, 2005) 86.

78. Chin, *Sewing Women*, 90. Kirschenman and Neckerman also found some employers in Chicago preferring Mexicans over Puerto Ricans. Kirschenman and Neckerman, "We'd Like to Hire Them," 210.

79. Devah Pager and Lincoln Quillian, "Walking the Talk? What Employers Say Versus What They Do," *American Sociological Review* 70 (2005): 355–80.

80. On the persistence of high black unemployment relative to other groups, see Harry J. Holzer and Marek Hlavac, "A Very Uneven Road: U.S. Labor Markets in the Past 30 Years," in John Logan, ed., *The Lost Decade? Social Change in the U.S. after 2000* (New York: Russell Sage Foundation Press, [forthcoming]).

81. Also see Vanesa Ribas's *On the Line*, where Ribas's participant observation shows more complex racial preferences, including employers using black workers strategically to pursue management goals, and also managing Haitian refugees in a meatpacking plant in the South.

82. Laura López-Sanders, *Trapped at the Bottom: Racialized and Gendered Labor Queues in New Immigrant Destinations*, Working Paper 176, Center for Comparative Immigration Studies, University of California, San Diego, 2009.

83. López-Sanders, *Trapped at the Bottom*, 15.

84. *Trapped at the Bottom*, 11.

85. *Trapped at the Bottom*, 12.

86. *Trapped at the Bottom*, 16. David Griffith found a similar process in the replacement of black workers with Mexicans in the crab industry in coastal Virginia and North Carolina, which was long dominated by black women. Black workers in his study complained that managers began to be more demanding of black workers, threatened to replace them with Mexicans, reduced their hours, and insisted on higher standards. As one worker explained, "To me personally, everything changed [after the Mexicans came]. It went down for Americans. That's why I left. Days got shorter. Crabs were scarce and there were so many extra workers that it was squeezing out the original workers. . . . They can't get new American workers because they know they won't make enough to survive." David Griffith, *American Guestworkers: Jamaicans and Mexicans in the U.S. Labor Market* (University Park: The Pennsylvania State University Press, 2006) 57.

87. Dell Champlin and Eric Hake, "Immigration as Industrial Strategy in American Meatpacking," *Review of Political Economy* 18 (2006): 49–70; Lourdes Gouveia and Arunas Juska, "Taming Nature, Taming Workers: Constructing the Separation Between Meat Consumption and Meat Production in the U.S.," *Sociologia Ruralis* 42 (2002): 370–90; David Griffith and David Runsten, "The Impact of the 1986 Immigration Reform and Control Act on the U.S. Poultry Industry: A Comparative Analysis," *Policy Studies Review* 11 (1992): 118–30; William Kandel and Emilio A. Parrado, "Restructuring of the U.S. Meat Processing Industry and New Hispanic Migrant Destinations," *Population and Development Review* 31 (2005): 447–71; Kathleen Stanley, "Immigrant and Refugee Workers in the Midwestern Meatpacking Industry: Industrial Restructuring and the Transformation of Rural Labor Markets," *Policy Studies Review* 11 (1992): 106–17.

88. William G. Whittaker, *Labor Practices in the Meat Packing and Poultry Processing Industry: An Overview* [CRS Report for Congress] (Washington, DC: Congressional Research Service, 2006). See p. 13, citing Paul S. Taylor, *Mexican Labor in the United States: Chicago, and the Calumet Region* [sic] (Berkeley: University of California Press, 1932) 40.

89. Sinclair, *The Jungle*, 42.

90. Whittaker, *Labor Practices in Meat Packing*, 12.

91. Roger Horowitz, *"Negro and White, Unite and Fight"*: *A Social History of Industrial Unionism in Meatpacking, 1930–1990* (Urbana: University of Illinois Press, 1997).

92. Donald D. Stull and Michael J. Broadway, *Slaughterhouse Blues: The Meat and Poultry Industry in North America* (Belmont, CA: Thomson/Wadsworth, 2004) 73.

93. Whittaker, *Labor Practices in Meat Packing*, 26.

94. Stanley, "Immigrant and Refugee Workers," 108.

95. Stull and Broadway, *Slaughterhouse Blues*, 74–75.

96. Champlin and Hake, "Immigration as Industrial Strategy," 58; Stanley, "Immigrant and Refugee Workers," 108.

97. "Immigration as Industrial Strategy," 54.

98. Nicholas Stein and Doris Burke, "Son of a Chicken Man: As he struggles to remake his family's poultry business into a $24 billion meat behemoth, John Tyson must prove he has more to offer than just the family name," *Fortune*, May 13, 2002; http://money.cnn.com/magazines/fortune/fortune_archive/2002/05/13/322904/index.htm, accessed September 24, 2011.

99. Stein and Burke, "Son of a Chicken Man."

100. Government Accountability Office, *Workplace Safety and Health: Safety in the Meat and Poultry Industry, While Improving, Could Be Further Strengthened* (GAO-05-96, January 2005) 4.

101. An insightful analysis of this process for the poultry industry shows the complex connections between these labor changes, the North American Free Trade Agreement, and impacts on Mexico's own poultry industry. Kathleen C. Schwartzman, *The Chicken Trail: Following Workers, Migrants, and Corporations Across the Americas* (Ithaca, NY: ILR Press, 2013).

102. General Accounting Office, *Community Development: Changes in Nebraska's and Iowa's Counties with Large Meatpacking Plant Workforces*, GAO/RCED-98-62, February 1998, 15.

103. Stein and Burke, "Son of a Chicken Man."

104. Gouveia and Juska, "Taming Nature, Taming Workers," 376; Champlin and Hake, "Immigration as Industrial Strategy," 62. An excellent description can be found in Steve Striffler, "Inside a Poultry Processing Plant: An Ethnographic Portrait," *Labor History* 43 (2002): 305–13, 305.

105. Leticia M. Saucedo, "The Browning of the American Workplace: Protecting Workers in Increasingly Latino-ized Occupations," *Notre Dame Law Review* 80 (2004): 303–32; pp. 322–23.

106. David Griffith, "Consequences of Immigration Reform for Low-Wage Workers in the Southeastern U.S.: The Case of the Poultry Industry," *Urban Anthropology* 19 (1990): 155–84, pp. 169–73. For more on the racial abilities of Latinos and Asians, and blacks' and whites' lack of ability, see Whittaker, *Labor Practices in Meat Packing*, 40.

107. Human Rights Watch, *Blood, Sweat and Fear*; http://www.hrw.org/en/node/11869/section/8#_ftnref289, accessed December 23, 2008.

108. Stanley, "Immigrant and Refugee Workers," 112.

109. "Immigrant and Refugee Workers," 112.

110. Stein and Burke, "Son of a Chicken Man."

111. Quotation taken from the Human Rights Watch website, http://www.hrw .org/about, accessed August 23, 2012.

112. Stein and Burke, "Son of a Chicken Man."

113. Human Rights Watch, *Blood, Sweat and Fear*, 8; http://www.hrw.org/en/node/11869/section/8#_ftnref308, accessed December 23, 2008.

114. Human Rights Watch, *Blood, Sweat and Fear*.

115. Stein and Burke, "Son of a Chicken Man." A Labor Department study conducted in 1997 and 1998 found problems were still common in the poultry processing industry, including workers who were made to stand too close together, leading to a tendency for them to slice each other up with their knives, and language problems that inhibited adequate training. In those years, 60 percent of surveyed plants violated laws regulating wages, hours, and safety and health standards (see Chapter 6 for more on OSHA). Whittaker, *Labor Practices in Meat Packing*, 44. On changes in injury rates, also see Government Accountability Office, *Workplace Safety and Health*, 3.

116. There is, however, a large body of research focusing on how differences in cognitive skills may explain wage differentials between racial groups. See, for example, Derek Neal and William Johnson, "The Role of Premarket Factors in Black-White Wage Differences," *Journal of Political Economy* 104 (1996): 869–95; George Farkas and Keven Vicknair, "Appropriate Tests of Racial Wage Discrimination Require Controls for Cognitive Skill: Comment on Cancio, Evans, and Maume," *American Sociological Review* 61 (1996): 557–60; James J. Heckman, "Detecting Discrimination," *The Journal of Economic Perspectives* 12 (1998): 101–16.

117. Glenn C. Loury, *The Anatomy of Racial Inequality* (Cambridge, MA: Harvard University Press, 2002) 29–30. Also see Naomi Ellemers and Manuela Barreto, "Putting Your Own Down: How Members of Disadvantaged Groups Unwittingly Perpetuate or Exacerbate Their Disadvantage," in Arthur P. Brief, ed., *Diversity at Work* (New York: Cambridge University Press, 2008) 202–61.

118. Michael J. Piore, *Birds of Passage: Migrant Labor and Industrial Societies* (New York: Cambridge University Press, 1979).

119. Jennifer Gordon and R. A. Lenhardt, "Rethinking Work and Citizenship," *UCLA Law Review* 55 (2008): 1161–1238, p. 1222.

120. Ronald Ferguson and Randall Filer, "Do Better Jobs Make Better Workers? Absenteeism from Work Among Inner-City Black Youths," in Richard B. Freeman and Harry J. Holzer, eds., *The Black Youth Employment Crisis* (Chicago: University of Chiago Press, 1986) 261–298, p. 292.

121. Derek R. Avery, Patrick F. McKay, David C. Wilson, and Scott Tonidandel, "Unequal Attendance: The Relationships between Race, Organizational Diversity Cues, and Absenteeism," *Personnel Psychology* 60 (2007): 875–902. This study claimed that while many researchers had found high black absenteeism rates, no researchers had ever found differences between Latino and white absenteeism (p. 894). Also see Patrick F. McKay, and Michael A. McDaniel, "A Reexamination of Black–White Mean Differences in Work Performance: More Data, More Moderators," *Journal of Applied Psychology* 91 (2006): 538–54.

122. Song Yang and Shauna A. Morimoto, "Why Do Black Men Suffer from Low Self-Rated Job Productivity? A Multi-Theory Approach," *Sociological Inquiry* 81 (2011): 431–53.

123. Wilson, *When Work Disappears*, 52.

124. Wilson, *When Work Disappears*, 137.

125. Frank Bean, Susan K. Brown, James D. Bachmeier, Zoya Gubernskaya, and Christopher D. Smith, "Luxury, Necessity and Anachronistic Workers: Does the United States Need Unskilled Immigrant Labor?" *American Behavioral Scientist* 56 (2012): 1008–28.

126. This research finds that migrants are willing to accept lower wages than are native workers, and employers prefer, for example, Mexican migrants because they accept low wages and unpleasant work environments. Marta Tienda, "Looking to the 1990s: Mexican Immigrants in Sociological Perspective," in Wayne A. Cornelius and Jorge A. Bustamante, eds., *Mexican Migration to the United States: Origins, Consequences and Policy Options* (La Jolla: Center for U.S. Mexican Studies, University of California, San Diego, 1989). Sociologist Roger Waldinger found in his study of LA employers in the restaurant, hotel, and furniture manufacturing businesses that these employers do not hire as many blacks and whites because these groups avoid the low wages these firms offer. Roger Waldinger, "Black/Immigrant Competition Re-Assessed: New Evidence from Los Angeles," *Sociological Perspectives* 40 (1997): 365–86. Another study of Los Angeles employers, this time in the electronics industry, found that employers claimed they had few black workers because they believed blacks had a higher reservation wage than what employers were willing to offer. Ward F. Thomas, "The Meaning of Race to Employers: A Dynamic Qualitative Perspective," *Sociological Quarterly* 44 (2005): 227–42. Also see Moss and Tilly, *Stories Employers Tell*, 117.

127. Lippard, "Racialized Hiring Practices," 218.

128. "Racialized Hiring Practices," 218.

129. David R. Howell, *Do Surges in Less-Skilled Immigration Have Important Wage Effects?* March 8, 2007; http://borderbattles.ssrc.org/Howell/printable .html, accessed August 17, 2009. Wage reductions may be the result of the excess labor supply that immigration brings.

130. Harry Holzer, *What Employers Want: Job Prospects for Less-Educated Workers* (New York: Russell Sage Foundation, 1996) 93. Wilson's research also finds more support for preferences based on race or nativity than on wages. He found that blacks' "reservation wage" (the bottom level of pay for which they would be willing to work), was lower than that of Latinos: $6 compared to $6.20 for Mexicans and $7.20 for Puerto Ricans. Whites insisted on at least $9 (Wilson, *When Work Disappears*, 140). In an interesting finding that could nevertheless support either argument, economist Linda Bailey found that Latino and Asian immigrants have an easier time getting a new job after being terminated than do other immigrants. Linda Bailey, *Do Immigrants Adapt Better to Job Loss? Evidence from Displaced Workers* (working paper, January 2006); http://www.msu.edu/~baileyl7/ bailey_displace_jan06.pdf, accessed August 17, 2009.

131. Wilson, *When Work Disappears*, 133–34.

132. The idea of social capital has disparate origins, but Glenn Loury, Pierre Bourdieu, James S. Coleman, and Mark Granovetter are understood to be pioneers. Alejandro Portes, "Social Capital: Its Origins and Applications in Modern Sociology," in Eric Lesser, ed., *Knowledge and Social Capital: Foundations and Applications* (Woburn, MA: Butterworth-Heinemann, 2000) 43–67.

133. Holzer, *What Employers Want*, 51.

134. Max J. Pfeffer, "Low-Wage Employment and Ghetto Poverty: A Comparison of African-American and Cambodian Day-Haul Farm Workers in Philadelphia," *Social Problems* 41 (1994): 9–29.

135. Champlin and Hake, "Immigration as Industrial Strategy," 54.

136. "Immigration as Industrial Strategy," 63.

137. Stanley, "Immigrant and Refugee Workers," 112.

138. David Griffith, "*Hay Trabajo*: Poultry Processing, Rural Industrialization, and the Latinization of Low-Wage Labor," in Donald D. Stull, Michael J. Broadway, and David Griffith, eds., *Any Way You Cut It: Meat Processing and Small-Town America* (Lawrence: University Press of Kansas, 1995)129–51, 141.

139. http://www.hrw.org/en/node/11869/section/8#_ftnref299, accessed December 23, 2008.

140. Gouveia and Juska, "Taming Nature, Taming Workers," 376.

141. Sandra Susan Smith, *Lone Pursuit: Distrust and Defensive Individualism Among the Black Poor* (New York: Russell Sage Foundation, 2007).

142. Chin, *Sewing Women*, 98.

143. Waldinger and Lichter, *How the Other Half Works*, 68; Helen B. Marrow, *New Destination Dreaming: Immigration, Race and Legal Status in the Rural American South* (Stanford: Stanford University Press, 2011) 69.

144. *How the Other Half Works*, 192.

145. Moss and Tilly, *Stories Employers Tell*, 107.

146. *How the Other Half Works*, 192.

147. Latino newcomers tend to follow previous immigrants and Latino natives into jobs and workplaces with the effect of wages going down for *all* in these jobs. Undocumented status has independent effects but does not explain the entire dynamic. In one study, Catanzarite and her colleague Michael Bernabé Aguilera conclude that "working at a predominantly Latino jobsite lowers pay by a factor equivalent to seven or eight years of education." Lisa Catanzarite and Michael Bernabé Aguilera, "Working with Co-Ethnics: Earnings Penalties for Latino Immigrants at Latino Jobsites," *Social Problems* 49 (2002): 101–27, p. 118. Also see Lisa Catanzarite, "Brown-Collar Jobs: Occupational Segregation and Earnings of Recent-Immigrant Latinos," *Sociological Perspectives* 43 (2000): 45–75; and Lisa Catanzarite, "Dynamics of Segregation and Earnings in Brown-Collar Occupations," *Work and Occupations* 29 (2002): 300–45. This same dynamic appears to hold true in meatpacking—the more Hispanics on the job, the lower the wages tend to be. Griffith, "Consequences of Immigration Reform," 166.

148. These forces against litigation in this context are analyzed by Deborah C. Malamud, "Affirmative Action and Ethnic Niches: A Legal Afterword," in John D. Skrentny, ed., *Color Lines: Affirmative Action, Immigration and Policy Options for America* (Chicago: University of Chicago Press, 2001) 313–45.

149. Malamud, "Affirmative Action and Ethnic Niches," 332.

150. Shannon Gleeson, "Labor Rights for All? The Role of Undocumented Status for Worker Claims Making," *Law & Social Inquiry* 35 (2010): 561–602; Shannon Gleeson, *Conflicting Commitments: The Politics of Enforcing Immigrant Rights in San Jose and Houston* (Ithaca, NY: ILR Press, 2012).

151. Helen B. Marrow, *New Destination Dreaming: Immigration, Race, and Legal Status in the Rural American South* (Stanford, CA: Stanford University Press, 2011) 66.

152. Marrow, *New Destination Dreaming*, 61–63.

153. *Slack v. Havens*, 7 FEP 885 (S.D. Cal. 1973).

154. The decision was affirmed in *Slack v. Havens*, 522 F.2d 1091 (Ninth Cir. 1975).

155. *McDonnell Douglas Corp. v. Green*, 411 U.S. 792, 802–804 (1973).

156. Leticia M. Saucedo, "The Employer Preference for the Subservient Worker and the Making of the Brown Collar Workplace," *Ohio State Law Journal* 67 (2006): 961–1021, pp. 984–85. Saucedo describes other avenues for litigants, including pattern-or-practice suits, where statistical evidence can be brought to bear on racial-realist employers, but finds obstacles to these strategies as well. Also see Tristin Green's discussion of the systemic disparate treatment law. Tristin Green, "The Future of Systemic Disparate Treatment Law," *Berkeley Journal of Employment and Labor Law* 32 (2011): 395–454.

157. Robert L. Nelson, Ellen C. Berrey, and Laura Beth Nielsen, "Divergent Paths: Conflicting Conceptions of Employment Discrimination in Law and the Social Sciences," *Annual Review of Law and Social Science* 4 (2008): 103–22.

158. Vicki Schultz and Stephen Petterson, "Race, Gender, Work, and Choice: An Empirical Study of the Lack of Interest Defense in Title VII Cases Challenging Job Segregation," *University of Chicago Law Review* 59 (1992): 1073–1181, 1098.

159. See, generally, Malamud, "Affirmative Action and Ethnic Niches."

160. *EEOC v. New Indianapolis Hotels*, 2011 U.S. Dist. LEXIS 2658 (S.D. Ind. 2011) 3. The case cited to defend the notion that replacing blacks with Latinos was not a violation is *Pollard v. Azcon Corp.*, 904 F.Supp. 762 (N.D. Ill. 1995), where confusion arose due to an overly technical application of the rules for making a prima facie case. In *Pollard*, some African-American workers in their 50s and 60s were terminated, allegedly for sleeping on the job. They sued for race and age discrimination. In assessing the prima facie case, the court ruled that the black workers had not shown they were discharged because of their race; in one case a worker was replaced by another older African-American male, though in another, the worker was replaced by a Latino. The court seemed to believe that all minorities are the same, stating that since one of the African-American plaintiffs "was replaced by another member of a protected class, he cannot meet the fourth element of the prima facie case" (773).

161. *EEOC v. New Indianapolis Hotels*, 2011 U.S. Dist. LEXIS 2658 (S.D. Ind. 2011) 4. The relevant precedents were *Griggs v. Duke Power*, which said that Title VII prohibits preference for any group, whether a majority or minority. The issue came up in other cases due to the part of the rules for making a prima facie discrimination claim that require a showing that the employer hired someone outside of the protected class: *Griggs v. Duke Power Co.*, 401 U.S. 424 (1971); *Jones v. Southwest Airlines Co.*, 99 F.Supp.2d 1322, 1327 n.2 (D.N.M. 2000); *Dancy v. Am. Red Cross*, 972 F.Supp. 1, 4 (D.D.C. 1997); *Dang v. Inn at Foggy Bottom*, 85 F.Supp.2d 39, 45 (D.D.C. 2000).

162. *EEOC v. Propak Logistics Inc.*, No. 09-00311 (W.D.N.C. Aug. 6, 2010).

163. *EEOC v. Paramount Staffing Inc.*, No. 2:06-02624 (W.D. Tenn. settled Aug. 23, 2010).

164. *EEOC v. Little River Golf, Inc.*, No. 1:08CV00546 (M.D.N.C. Aug. 6, 2009).

165. *EEOC v. E&T Foods*, LLC, d/b/a Compare Foods, Civil Action No 3:06-cv-318 (W.D.N.C. settled Jan. 28, 2008). These and other cases are listed at an EEOC website: http://www1.eeoc.gov/eeoc/initiatives/e-race/caselist.cfm, accessed September 20, 2011.

166. Section 2000e-2.

167. http://www.eeoc.gov/policy/docs/qanda_race_color.html, accessed September 1, 2009.

168. Saucedo, "Browning of the American Workplace," Saucedo, "Preference for the Subservient Worker."

169. For an analysis and critique of the market defense in sex discrimination law, see Robert L. Nelson and William P. Bridges, *Legalizing Gender Inequality: Courts, Markets, and Unequal Pay for Women in America* (New York: Cambridge University Press, 1999). In one of the more high-profile cases using a market defense, the EEOC sued the Sears department store for discriminating against women. Women sales associates at the giant retailer were concentrated in salaried positions (75 percent of salaried workers were women). They made half as much as men did, who were concentrated in the commission jobs. Sears argued that women were simply not very interested in the commission jobs, and presented surveys and interview evidence to make this case. The court sided with Sears, noting also that the commission jobs were very different (involving different kinds of items, such as major appliances rather than low-cost items, such as cosmetics). *EEOC v. Sears, Roebuck & Co.*, 839 F.2d 302 (7th Cir. 1988). In addition, the court argued that female applicants for commission jobs were not as competitive as male applicants (they tended to be younger, less educated, and had less experience).

170. *Griggs v. Duke Power*, 401 U.S. 424 (1971).

171. At 432.

172. See, for example, *Robinson v. Lorillard Corp.*, 444 F.2d 791, 798 n. 5 (4th Cir. 1971); *Barnett v. W. T. Grant Co.*, 518 F.2d 543, 549 (4th Cir. 1975); *Brown v. Gaston County Dyeing Machine Co.*, 457 F.2d 1377, 1383 (4th Cir. 1972); *United States v. Ga. Power Co.*, 474 F.2d 906, 926 (5th Cir. 1973).

173. *Thomas v. Wash. County Sch. Bd.*, 915 F.2d 922 (4th Cir. 1990) at 925. Also see, for example, *Domingo v. New England Fish Co.*, 727 F.2d 1429 (9th Cir. 1975); *NAACP v. Evergreen*, 693 F.2d 1367 (11th Cir. 1982); *Barnett v. W.T. Grant Co.*, 518 F.2d. 543 (4th Cir. 1975).

174. *Parham v. Southwestern Bell Tel. Co.*, 433 F.2d 421, 427 (8th Cir. 1970).

175. http://www.eeoc.gov/policy/docs/race-color.html#VIA2, accessed November 13, 2008.

176. http://www.eeoc.gov/policy/docs/qanda_race_color.html, accessed November 13, 2008.

177. Nelson, Berrey, and Nielsen, "Divergent Paths."

178. *Wards Cove Packing Co. v. Atonio*, 90 U.S. 642 (1989).

179. The problem was that the compromise language in the new law was itself ambiguous. It stated that employers had to show the job relatedness and business

necessity of the employment practice in question, but did not define these terms. Courts and legal scholars, therefore, are still arguing about the meaning of disparate impact theory. See, for example, Charles A. Sullivan, "The World Turned Upside Down? Disparate Impact Claims by White Males," *Northwestern Law Review* 98 (2004): 1505–65.

180. *EEOC v. Chicago Miniature Lamp Works*, 947 F.2d 292, 299 (7th Cir. 1991).

181. *EEOC v. Chicago Miniature Lamp Works*, 622 F. Supp. 1281, 1288 (N.D. Ill. 1985).

182. For example, Cummings had ruled that schools were liable for sexual harassment between students and against steel mills that had polluted Lake Michigan. Megan O'Matz, "Judge Walter J. Cummings, Jr.," *Chicago Tribune*, April 27, 1999; http://articles.chicagotribune.com/1999-04-27/news/9904270187_1_mr -cummings-appellate-court-supreme-court, accessed February 7, 2013.

183. *Chicago Miniature Lamp Works*, 947 F.2d 292 at 298–99.

184. *Chicago Miniature Lamp Works*, 947 F.2d 292 at 305. This court appeared to be influenced by the *Wards Cove* case and thus sensitive to burdens on employers—but not influenced by the Civil Rights Act of 1991, which became law less than two weeks later and sought to repeal the Supreme Court's proemployer stance in *Wards Cove*.

185. *EEOC v. Consolidated Service Systems*, 989 F.2d 233 (7th Cir. 1993).

186. *EEOC v. Consolidated Service Systems*, 777 F. Supp. 599 (N.D. Ill. 1991).

187. *Consolidated*, 989 F.2d at 235.

188. At 237.

189. At 237.

190. At 235.

191. Tobin M. Nelson, "Note: Word-of-Mouth Recruiting: Why Small Businesses Using this Efficient Practice Should Survive Disparate Impact Challenges Under Title VII," *University of Pittsburgh Law Review* 68 (2006): 449–68, p. 460.

192. *Consolidated*, 989 F.2d at 237–38.

193. See the discussion in Editors of the Boston College Law Review, "Survey: 1992–93 Annual Survey of Labor and Employment Law," *Boston College Law Review* 35 (1994): 349–542. Posner added, following the cited paragraph, another statement showing his focus on nonwhite employers: "There is equal danger to small black-run businesses in our central cities. Must such businesses undertake in the name of nondiscrimination costly measures to recruit nonblack employees?" *Consolidated*, 989 F.2d at 238.

194. Oddly, a firm that actually allowed more opportunities for interested workers unrelated to current employees to have access to the job applicant process lost in court. In a case that involved facts similar to those in Miniature Lamp and Consolidated, O&G Spring and Wire Forms Specialty Company, a Chicago light manufacturer, would lose to the EEOC. In part because O&G allowed applications from walk-ins off the street, and this group included some African-Americans, but O&G hired none (instead preferring Latino and Polish workers), it made itself vulnerable. *EEOC v. O&G Spring & Wire Forms Specialty Co.*, 38 F.3d 872 (7th Cir. 1994). The focus in the opinion on the treatment of the walk-in applicants suggests that O&G would have been better off if it had totally (but

only passively!) relied on referrals from its current workforce rather than cracking open the door of possibility to other workers. The majority dismissed a dissenting opinion that was guided by Posner's opinion in *Consolidated*, Posner's expressed sympathy toward immigrant entrepreneurs (O&G was owned by a Polish immigrant), as well as sociologically sound observations about how African-American workers would likely respond at workplaces where languages other than English were the dominant languages. The majority stated, "O&G incorrectly states (and the dissent repeats several times) that the district court found that African-Americans preferred not to work at O&G because its workers spoke Polish or Spanish. Not surprisingly, no such finding of language-based selection bias on the part of African-Americans—nor any shred of evidence that would support such a finding—exists in the record. The dissent's conclusion that the presence of Polish and Spanish speakers at O&G would, on its own, drive away African-Americans is entirely unfounded, and suggests ethnic attitudes without support in the evidence." *O&G Spring & Wire* 38 F.3d 872 at 877.

195. http://www.scrubinc.com/, accessed September 23, 2011; http://www.eeoc.gov/eeoc/newsroom/release/11-9-10c.cfm, accessed September 23, 2011.

196. http://www.eeoc.gov/eeoc/meetings/6-22-11/wilkins.cfm, accessed September 23, 2011.

197. *EEOC v. Scrub Inc.*, No. 09 C 4228 (N.D. Ill. consent decree entered Nov. 9, 2010). See http://www1.eeoc.gov/eeoc/initiatives/e-race/caselist.cfm, accessed September 20, 2011. In many ways, *Scrub* was similar to Consolidated, to which the courts gave a pass. While Consolidated was run by an immigrant from South Korea, Scrub was run by Roman Cmiel, an immigrant from Poland. But whereas Consolidated hired mostly coethnics, Cmiel told a trade magazine (before the lawsuit), "Diversity makes groups work together better," and proudly described a staff that included workers from Poland, Mexico, the Czech Republic, China, the Philippines, and Russia. http://www.cleanlink.com/cp/article/Industry-Profile-Roman-Chmiel-Scrub-Inc—6328, accessed September 23, 2011. Scrub was actually more diverse and open to different backgrounds than was Consolidated, but Consolidated was absolved of all wrongdoing.

198. https://www.tyson.com/Corporate/PressRoom/ViewArticle.aspx?id=175, accessed December 22, 2008.

199. Massey, Durand, and Malone, *Beyond Smoke and Mirrors,* 90.

200. One might think that Title VII's ban on national origin discrimination would have made preferences for or against citizens illegal, but it did not. In 1973, the Supreme Court ruled that Title VII did not protect workers from discrimination based on citizenship. *Espinoza v. Farah Mfg. Co.*, 414 U.S. 86 (1973).

201. http://www1.eeoc.gov//employers/other_issues.cfm?renderforprint=1, accessed September 24, 2011. For background on IRCA's development, see Tichenor, *Dividing Lines*, and Peter Schuck, "The Politics of Rapid Legal Change: Immigration Policy in the 1980s," *Studies in American Political Development* 6 (1992): 37–92.

202. Section 102 of Public Law 99–603; Michael Fix and Paul T. Hill, *Enforcing Employer Sanctions: Challenges and Strategies* (Santa Monica, CA: Rand Corporation, 1990) 37. The preference provision was an amendment offered by Dan Lundgren (R-CA), who explained that it would protect employer discretion, and

also protect defense contractors, who by law must employ only citizens. *Congressional Record*, October 9, 1986, 30,045–46.

203. Peter Brownell, "The Declining Enforcement of Employer Sanctions," *Migration Information Source*, September 2005, http://www.migrationinformation.org/usfocus/display.cfm?ID=332, accessed September 24, 2011. Some argue that employer sanctions against hiring undocumented workers almost never work—no matter where sanctions are tried. See, for example, Wayne Cornelius and Takeyuki Tsuda, "Controlling Immigration: The Limits of Government Intervention," in Wayne A. Cornelius et al., ed., *Controlling Immigration: A Global Perspective*, 2nd ed. (Stanford, CA: Stanford University Press, 2004) 3–48.

204. John D. Skrentny, "Obama's Immigration Reform: A Tough Sell for a Grand Bargain," in Theda Skocpol and Larry Jacobs, eds., *Reaching for a New Deal: Ambitious Governance, Economic Meltdown, and Polarized Politics in Obama's First Two Years* (New York: Russell Sage Foundation) 273–320.

205. Stein and Burke, "Son of a Chicken Man."

206. "Son of a Chicken Man."

207. Steve Striffler, *Chicken: The Dangerous Transformation of America's Favorite Food* (New Haven, CT: Yale University Press, 2005) 99.

208. http://www.cbsnews.com/stories/2003/03/26/national/main546248.shtml, accessed December 20, 2008.

209. Stephanie E. Tanger, "Enforcing Corporate Responsibility for Violations of Workplace Immigration Laws: The Case of Meatpacking," *Harvard Latino Law Review* 9 (2006): 59–89, 78.

210. Tanger, "Corporate Responsibility," 78; Striffler, *Chicken*, 100.

211. "Corporate Responsibility," 80.

212. Striffler, *Chicken*, 99.

213. Tyson's opening statement was reproduced at http://www.prnewswire.com/cgi-bin/stories.pl?ACCT=104&STORY=/www/story/02-05-2003/0001886019&EDATE, accessed December 22, 2008.

214. Tanger, "Corporate Responsibility," 86–87.

215. Sherri Day, "Jury Clears Tyson Foods in Use of Illegal Immigrants," *New York Times*, March 27, 2003, available at http://www.nytimes.com/2003/03/27/us/jury-clears-tyson-foods-in-use-of-illegal-immigrants.html, accessed December 21, 2008.

216. Bill Poovey, "Jury Acquits Tyson, Other Defendants in Immigrant Conspiracy Case," Associated Press State and Local Wire, March 27, 2003, accessed through Lexis-Nexis. If there was good to come of the government's case, it was only that it made Tyson stand up and take some action about its labor practices. According to the *New York Times*, "Since the investigation, the company said it had stopped hiring temporary workers and raised its wages to make its jobs more competitive." Day, "Jury Clears Tyson."

217. 18 USC § 1961 (1).

218. Julie Lam, "Note: Show Me the Green—Civil RICO Actions Against Employers who Knowingly Hire Undocumented Workers," *Washington University Law Review* 84 (2006): 717–45, p. 728.

219. *Commercial Cleaning Servs., L.L.C. v. Colin Serv. Sys., Inc.*, 271 F.3d 374 (2d Cir. 2001).

220. *Mendoza v. Zirkle Fruit Co.*, 301 F.3d. 1163, 1166 (9th Cir. 2002).

221. *Mendoza* at 1163.

222. The legal workers used economist George Borjas as an expert witness to demonstrate to the court that illegal workers are generally associated with lower wages for lower skilled workers in the U.S. But that, the court ruled, was irrelevant unless there was evidence that retaining illegal immigrants depressed wages at the specific plants then targeted by litigation. Plaintiffs would have to show the percentage of undocumented immigrants in the workforce, and that at least a majority were undocumented, since any figure less than that would not likely depress wages. Even if they did show this percentage, showing a direct causal link to wages would involve establishing several other facts, including that each additional undocumented worker had a measurable impact on wages; that the undocumented workers relieved Tyson from having to compete with other local businesses for low-skilled workers; that any documented workers at Tyson did not choose to work there at the low wages but were forced to given local labor demand; that undocumented immigrants were not members of local unions that negotiated wages (which would distort the link between hiring undocumented immigrants and wage depression); and that the undocumented immigrants worked for a long enough time at Tyson to depress wages. *Trollinger v. Tyson* 543 F. Supp. 2d 842 (E.D. Tenn., 2008); *Trollinger v. Tyson* 370 F.3d 602 (6th Cir. 2004).

Chapter 6. Bringing Practice, Law, and Values Together

1. Charles and Barbara Whalen, *The Longest Debate: A Legislative History of the 1964 Civil Rights Act* (Washington, DC: Seven Locks Press, 1985).

2. One poll reported that fully 98 percent of Americans agreed with the statement "Everyone in America should have equal opportunities to get ahead." Herbert McClosky and John Zaller, *The American Ethos: Public Attitudes toward Capitalism and Democracy* (Cambridge, MA: Harvard University Press, 1984), 83. A more recent poll found 87 percent of Americans in agreement with the notion of a shared responsibility to provide equal opportunity: "Our society should do what is necessary to make sure that everyone has an equal opportunity to succeed." Pew Research Center for the People and the Press, *Trends in Political Values and Core Attitudes: 1987-2009* (Washington, DC: Pew Research Center for the People and the Press, 2009), 56.

3. Even if political leaders did not use racial realism in making appointments, we might have to ask them to. President Obama kept in the White House a photo of an African- American boy feeling the top of the president's head, seemingly to confirm his perception that the president was, like him, black. It is hard to argue that racial realism in this sector is not at least in some circumstances a good thing. Jackie Calmes, "When a Boy Found a Familiar Feel in a Pat of the Head of State," *New York Times*, May 23, 2012, available at http://www.nytimes.com/2012/05/24/us/politics/indelible-image-of-a-boys-pat-on-obamas-head-hangs-in-white-house.html?_r=2&hp, accessed May 23, 2012.

4. See Alexandra Kalev, Frank Dobbin, and Erin Kelly, "Best Practices or Best Guesses? Assessing the Efficacy of Corporate Affirmative Action and Diversity Policies," *American Sociological Review* 71 (2006): 589–617.

5. Association of American Medical Colleges, *Cultural Competence Education* (Washington, DC: AAMC, 2005), available at https://www.aamc.org/down load/54338/data/culturalcomped.pdf, accessed April 18, 2012. American College of Physicians, *Racial and Ethnic Disparities in Health Care, Updated 2010: A Position Paper;* http://www.acponline.org/advocacy/where_we_stand/access/racial_disparities.pdf, accessed July 7, 2012.

6. "A Physician's Practical Guide to Culturally Competent Care"; https://cccm.thinkculturalhealth.hhs.gov/GUIs/GUI_AboutthisSite.asp, accessed April 18, 2012.

7. Sunil Kripalani, Jada Bussey-Jones, Marra G. Katz, and Inginia Genao, "A Prescription for Cultural Competence in Medical Education," *Journal of General Internal Medicine* 21 (2006): 1116–20.

8. President's Commission on Law Enforcement and the Administration of Justice, *The Challenge of Crime in a Free Society: A Report* (Washington, DC: Government Printing Office, 1967) 100.

9. Ibid, p. 89. In interviews conducted for this project with officers and representatives from leading police departments across the nation, most emphasized that any officer could police any neighborhood. Even those who argued strongly that nonwhite officers have special understandings of nonwhite neighborhoods and residents also insisted that any officer can effectively police a neighborhood.

10. National Research Council of the National Academies, *Fairness and Effectiveness in Policing: The Evidence* (Washington, DC: National Academies Press, 2004).

11. Karen Diegmueller, "Schooling Staff in the Ways of the World," *Journal of Staff Development* 13 (1992): 8–11, p. 11.

12. Jerome H. Skolnick and David H. Bayley, *The New Blue Line: Police Innovation in Six American Cities* (NY: The Free Press, 1986) 111.

13. William N. Eskridge, Jr., *Dynamic Statutory Interpretation* (Cambridge, MA: Harvard University Press, 1994).

14. *Wygant v. Jackson Board of Education* 476 U.S. 267, 314 (1986).

15. At 314–15.

16. *Johnson v. Transportation Agency of Santa Clara County*, 480 U.S. 616, 645 (1987).

17. At 645.

18. 42 USC § 2000e–2(j) states "Nothing contained in this subchapter shall be interpreted to require any employer . . . to grant preferential treatment to any individual or to any group because of the race, color, religion, sex, or national origin of such individual or group on account of an imbalance which may exist with respect to the total number or percentage of persons of any race, color, religion, sex, or national origin employed by any employer . . . in comparison with the total number or percentage of persons of such race, color, religion, sex, or national origin in any community, State, section, or other area, or in the available work force in any community, State, section, or other area."

19. *Johnson v. Transportation Agency of Santa Clara County*, 647.

20. *Metro Broadcasting v. FCC*, 497 U.S. 547, 601–602 (1990).

21. *City of Richmond v. J.A. Croson Co.*, 488 U. S. 469, 512–13 (1989).

22. *Adarand Constructors, Inc. v Peña*, 515 U.S. 200, 258 (1995).

23. *Patrolmen and Benevolent Association v. City of New York*, 74 F.Supp 2d 321, 331–32 (SD NY, 1999).

24. Legal scholar Ronald Turner made a similar point when he argued that employers' use of race "must not rest on a bald assertion and must be supported by a demonstrable business need." Ronald Turner, "*Grutter*, the Diversity Justification, and Workplace Affirmative Action," *Brandeis Law Journal* 43 (2004): 199–237, p. 237.

25. George R. La Noue, *Local Officials Guide to Minority Business Programs and Disparity Studies*, rev. ed. (Washington, DC: National League of Cities, 1994).

26. See, for example, Dan Biddle, *Adverse Impact and Test Validation: A Practioner's Guide to Valid and Defensible Employment Testing*, 2nd ed. (Burlington, VT: Ashgate, 2006).

27. On Congress, see http://www.congress.org/congressorg/directory/demographics.tt?catid=ethnic, accessed August 5, 2012. On judges, see Pat K. Chew and Robert E. Kelley, "Myth of the Color-Blind Judge: An Empirical Analysis of Racial Harassment Cases," *Washington University Law Review* 86 (2009): 1117–66. On the Fortune 500, see http://www.blackentrepreneurprofile.com/fortune-500-ceos/, accessed August 5, 2012.

28. Charles H. Tillinghast, *American Broadcast Regulation and the First Amendment: Another Look* (Ames: Iowa State University Press, 2000) xiii–xiv.

29. The Supreme Court has affirmed the public interest goal of federal regulation and has elaborated upon it. *NBC v. U.S.*, 319 U.S. 190, 226 (1943). A 1969 case upheld a regulation that required that broadcasters give fair coverage to both sides on public issues because this would further the goal of representing community views. *Red Lion Broadcasting Co., Inc. v. FCC* 395 U.S. 367, 394 (1969).

30. *FCC v. Pacifica Foundation*, 438 U.S. 726, 749 (1978).

31. http://fcc.gov/vchip/legislation.html, accessed April 22, 2011.

32. Patricia M. Worthy, "Diversity and Minority Stereotyping in the Television Media: The Unsettled First Amendment Issue," *Hastings Communications and Entertainment Law Journal* 18 (1996): 509–67.

33. Worthy, "Diversity and Minority Stereotyping," 564.

34. "Diversity and Minority Stereotyping," 565.

35. "Diversity and Minority Stereotyping," 565.

36. http://fcc.gov/vchip/#guidelines, accessed April 22, 2011.

37. Frank D. Bean, Susan K. Brown, James D. Bachmeier, Zoya Gubernskaya, and Christopher D. Smith, "Luxury, Necessity, and Anachronistic Workers: Does the United States Need Unskilled Immigrant Labor?" *American Behavioral Scientist* 56 (2012): 1008–28.

38. William Julius Wilson, *The Bridge over the Racial Divide: Rising Inequality and Coalition Politics* (Berkeley and New York: University of California Press and Russell Sage Foundation, 1999) 63–64.

39. Of course, as described in Chapter 5, blacks face significant discrimination even in the jobs close to their homes. One study of different neighborhoods

in Chicago—some with jobs and some without—noted that blacks did not do well even when there were a lot of jobs in the neighborhood. The conclusion: "The problem isn't space. It's race." David T. Ellwood, "The Spatial Mismatch Hypothesis: Are There Teenage Jobs Missing in the Ghetto?" in Richard B. Freeman and Harry J. Holzer, eds., *The Black Youth Employment Crisis* (Chicago: University of Chicago Press, 1986) 147–85.

40. This was not only an issue for manufacturing. For example, one study examined 102 hamburger restaurants in the city and the suburbs, noting that the suburban restaurants employed fewer blacks than did the city outlets. This study also found a variety of factors having an impact on black employment, including the race of the customers and the race of the manager. But this study, as well as many others, strongly confirmed the spatial mismatch hypothesis. As the restaurant's distance from the central business district grew, black employment declined, and the same thing happened when access to public transit declined. Keith R. Ihlanfeldt and Madelyn V. Young, "Intrametropolitan Variation in Wage Rates: The Case of Atlanta Fast-Food Restaurant Workers," *Review of Economics and Statistics* 76 (1994): 425–33.

41. Douglas S. Massey and Nancy A. Denton, *American Apartheid: Segregation and the Making of the Underclass* (Cambridge, MA: Harvard University Press, 1993); Devah Pager and Hana Shepherd, "The Sociology of Discrimination: Racial Discrimination in Employment, Housing, Credit and Consumer Markets," *Annual Review of Sociology* 34 (2008): 181–209.

42. Holzer, *What Employers Want*, 128. This view is not unanimous, and there is also some evidence that the spatial mismatch hypothesis also explains Latino disadvantage. See Keith Ihlanfeldt and David L. Sjoquist, "Intra-Urban Job Accessibility and Hispanic Youth Employment Rates," *Journal of Urban Economics* 33 (1993): 254–71.

43. Roberto M. Fernandez and Celina Su, "Space in the Study of Labor Markets," *Annual Review of Sociology* 30 (2004): 545–69, p. 553.

44. Frank D. Bean and Gillian Stevens, *America's Newcomers and the Dynamics of Diversity* (New York: Russell Sage Foundation, 2003), 48; John A. Kasarda, "Industrial Restructuring and the Changing Location of Jobs," in Reynolds Farley, ed., *State of the Union: America in the 1990s*, vol. 1: *Economic Trends* (New York: Russell Sage Foundation, 1985) 215–67. State government officials trying to lure businesses have reported that some businesses have requested states to remove sites from consideration that have more than 30 percent blacks in the county population. Cole and Deskins, "Racial Factors," 20; citing the *New York Times*, February 15, 1983, Reginald Stuart, "Businesses Said To Have Barred New Plants in Largely Black Communities."

45. "Between 1980 and 1990, the Frostbelt (Northeastern and Midwestern census regions) lost 1.5 million manufacturing jobs and $40 billion (in constant 1989 dollars) in aggregate manufacturing worker earnings, whereas the Sunbelt (South and West) added 450,000 manufacturing jobs and gained $21 billion in manufacturing worker earnings. . . . During the 1980s, the central counties of the Frostbelt's 28 largest metropolitan areas lost nearly 1 million manufacturing jobs and over $28 billion in manufacturing worker earnings." Kasarda, "Changing Location of Jobs," 215.

46. For example, one study of the placement of Japanese car manufacturing plants in rural areas argued that the main reason for the placement of these plants was the implementation of "just-in-time" manufacturing practices—parts suppliers were already rural, and the Japanese sought proximity to ease deliveries to their new plants. Andrew Mair, Richard Florida, and Martin Kenney, "The New Geography of Automobile Production: Japanese Transplants in North America," *Economic Geography* 64 (1988): 352–73. They found no evidence for or against the argument that race is also a factor (366).

47. Robert E. Cole and Donald R. Deskins, "Racial Factors in Site Location and Employment Patterns of Japanese Auto Firms in America," *California Management Review* 31 (1988): 9–22.

48. Cole and Deskins, "Racial Factors," 15.

49. Cole and Deskins, "Racial Factors," 13. A Canadian auto industry consultant who advised Japanese companies, Dennis de Rosiers, stated that the executives he talked to expressed a desire to avoid unions, but noted also that they asked about the ethnic makeup of the areas where they were thinking about locating: "They like a high German content. Germans have a good work ethic—well-trained, easy to train, they accept things. . . . [The Japanese] probably don't like other types of profiles" (17). An official working for the government in a state that was recruiting Japanse firms said to Cole and Deskins, "Many Japanese companies at the time specifically asked to stay away from areas with high minority populations" (18). Moreover, the Japan External Trade Organization enabled this kind of discrimination by making census data available that listed racial breakdowns of different areas, and offered a publication that advocated plant locations in California because that state had many Asians who are "high quality employees" (18).

50. Kathleen Stanley, "Immigrant and Refugee Workers in the Midwestern Meatpacking Industry: Industrial Restructuring and the Transformation of Labor Markets," *Review of Policy Research* 11 (1992): 106–17, p. 108.

51. William G. Whittaker, *Labor Practices in the Meat Packing and Poultry Processing Industry: An Overview* [CRS Report for Congress] (Washington, DC: Congressional Research Service, 2006) 39.

52. Nicholas Stein and Doris Burke, "Son of a Chicken Man," *Fortune*, May 13, 2002; http://money.cnn.com/magazines/fortune/fortune_archive/2002/05/13/322904/index.htm, accessed September 24, 2011.

53. Luter told *Fortune* that the best solution to the difficulty in finding workers is to offer higher wages. He explained that offering wages attractive to American workers would only add a small amount to the cost of meat. "But in a business in which two cents a pound can mean the difference between winning or losing a deal with a retailer," the business magazine explained, "no company seems willing to make the first move." Stein and Burke, "Son of a Chicken Man."

54. Michael J. Broadway, "Beef Stew: Cattle, Immigrants and Established Residents in a Kansas Beefpacking Town," in Lamphere, *Newcomers in the Workplace*, p. 25, cited in Whittaker, *Labor Practices in Meat Packing*, 41.

55. Edna Bonacich, "Advanced Capitalism and Black/White Race Relations in the United States," *American Sociological Review* 61 (1976): 34–51, 48; cited in Whittaker, *Labor Practices in Meat Packing*, 41.

56. Stanley, "Immigrant and Refugee Workers," 115.

57. Evan Perez and Corey Dade, "Immigration Raid Aids Blacks for a Time," *Wall Street Journal*, January 17, 2007; also see NPR's follow-up story on the Hmong workers at http://www.npr.org/templates/story/story.php?storyId=10461104, accessed October 16, 2009.

58. Deborah C. Malamud, "Affirmative Action and Ethnic Niches: A Legal Afterword," in John D. Skrentny, ed., *Color Lines: Immigration, Affirmative Action and Civil Rights Options for America* (Chicago: University of Chicago Press, 2001) 313–45, p. 335. For the point that work conditions may lead black workers to leave, also see Jennifer Gordon and R. A. Lenhardt, "Rethinking Work and Citizenship," *UCLA Law Review* 55 (2008): 1161–38, p. 1178.

59. Cole and Deskins, "Racial Factors," 19.

60. 42 USC § 2000E–2(k).

61. Malamud, "Legal Afterword," 336.

62. Cole and Deskins, "Racial Factors," 19.

63. Alex Marshall, "How to Get Business to Pay Its Share," *New York Times*, May 3, 2012; http://www.nytimes.com/2012/05/04/opinion/solving-the-corporate -tax-code-puzzle.html?_r=1&hp, accessed May 3, 2012. Alex Marshall, *The Surprising Design of Market Economies* (Austin: University of Texas Press, 2012).

64. Marshall, "Business Pays Its Share." Also see Charles Cray, "Revisiting Corporate Charters: Reviving Chartering as an Instrument for Corporate Accountability and Public Policy," *2007 Summit on the Future of the Corporation, Paper No. 7*; http://www.corporatepolicy.org/pdf/charters.pdf, accessed July 7, 2012.

65. Örn Bodvarsson and Hendrik Van den Berg, "The Impact of Immigration on a Local Economy: The Case of Dawson County, Nebraska," *Great Plains Research* 13 (2003): 291–309.

66. David Griffith, Michael J. Broadway, and Donald D. Stull, "Introduction: Making Meat," in Donald D. Stull, Michael J. Broadway, and David Griffith, eds., *Any Way You Cut It: Meat Processing and Small-Town America* (Lawrence: University Press of Kansas, 1995) 1–16; Lourdes Gouveia and Donald D. Stull, "Dance with Cows: Beefpacking's Impact on Garden City, Kansas and Lexington, Nebraska," in Stull, Broadway and Griffith, eds., *Any Way You Cut It*, 85–107; Donald D. Stull and Michael J. Broadway, *Slaughterhouse Blues: The Meat and Poultry Industry in North America* (Belmont, CA: Thomson/Wadsworth, 2004).

67. *West Coast Hotel Co. v. Parrish*, 300 U.S. 379, 399 (1937).

68. On this point, also see Greg LeRoy, *The Great American Jobs Scam: Corporate Tax Dodging and the Myth of Job Creation* (San Francicsco: Berrett-Koehler Publishers, 2005); Peter K. Eisinger, *The Rise of the Entrepreneurial State: State and Local Economic Development Policy in the United States* (Madison: University of Wisconsin Press, 1989); Katherine S. Newman and Rourke O'Brien, *Taxing the Poor: Doing Damage to the Truly Disadvantaged* (Berkeley: University of California Press, 2011).

69. Philip Martin, Manolo Abella, and Christiane Kuptsch, *Managing Labor Migration in the Twenty-first Century* (New Haven: Yale University Press, 2006) 126.

70. Doris Meissner, Deborah W. Meyers, Demetrios G. Papademetriou, and Michael Fix, *Immigration and America's Future: A New Chapter—Report of the*

Independent Task Force on Immigration and America's Future (Washington, DC: Migration Policy Institute, 2006), 96, n.37. Also see Jennifer Gordon, *Suburban Sweatshops: The Fight for Immigrant Rights* (Cambridge, MA: The Belknap Press of Harvard University Press, 2005), and Edna Bonacich and Richard Appelbaum, *Behind the Label: Inequality in the Los Angeles Apparel Industry* (Berkeley: University of California Press, 2000), for the inadequacies of OSHA and other worker protections.

71. Robert A. Kagan, *Adversarial Legalism: The American Way of Law* (Cambridge, MA: Harvard University Press, 2001); Philip K. Howard, *The Death of Common Sense: How Law is Suffocating America* (New York: Random House, 1994).

72. Michael Silverstein, "Getting Home Safe and Sound: Occupational Safety and Health Administration at 38," *American Journal of Public Health* 98 (2008): 416–23.

73. Thomas McGarity, Rena Steinzor, Sidney Shapiro, and Matthew Shudtz, "Workers at Risk: Regulatory Dysfunction at OSHA," *Center for Progressive Reform White Paper #1003*, February (Washington, DC: Center for Progressive Reform, 2010).

74. Griffith does not clearly explain why women were the ones pursuing an upgrade in skills when faced with an immigrant-related job loss, though this finding reflects larger patterns nationwide where women are more likely to go to college. See Thomas A. DiPrete and Claudia Buchman, "Gender-Specific Trends in the Value of Education and the Emerging Gender Gap in College Completion," *Demography* 43 (2006): 1–24; Claudia Buchman and Thomas A. DiPrete, "The Growing Female Advantage in College Completion: The Role of Family Background and Academic Achievement," *American Sociological Review* 71 (2006): 515–41.

75. David Griffith, *American Guestworkers: Jamaicans and Mexicans in the U.S. Labor Market* (University Park: The Pennsylvania State University Press, 2006) 54–55. Laura López-Sanders also found some movement toward skill upgrading by displaced workers, mostly women. Laura López-Sanders, *Trapped at the Bottom: Racialized and Gendered Labor Queues in New Immigrant Destinations*, Working Paper 176, Center for Comparative Immigration Studies, University of California, San Diego, 2009.

76. John F. Kennedy, "Special Message to the Congress on Foreign Trade Policy," January 25, 1962, in *John F. Kennedy: XXXV President of the United States, 1961–1963*, American Presidency Project; http://www.presidency.ucsb.edu/ws/?pid=8688#axzz1sP9jhpeV, accessed April 18, 2012.

77. J. F. Hornbeck and Laine Elise Rover, "Trade Adjustment Assistance (TAA) and Its Role in U.S. Trade Policy," *Federal Publications* Paper 867, Congressional Research Service, 2011, 7; http://digitalcommons.ilr.cornell.edu/key_workplace/867, accessed April 18, 2012.

78. Hornbeck and Rover, "Trade Adjustment Assistance," 8.

79. See, for example, Ethan Kapstein, "Trade Liberalization and the Politics of Trade Adjustment Assistance," *International Labour Review* 137 (1998): 501–516.

80. See the White House "Fact Sheet" on TAA; http://www.whitehouse.gov/sites/default/files/email-files/TAA_Fact_Sheet.pdf. Also see the defense of TAA at

http://www.ustr.gov/aboutus/press-office/blog/2011/june/truth-about-trade
-adjustment-assistance.

81. Harry J. Holzer, *What Employers Want: Job Prospects for Less-Educated Workers* (New York: Russell Sage Foundation, 1996) 129–30.

82. Pathways to Prosperity Project, *Pathways to Prosperity: Meeting the Challenge of Preparing Young Americans for the 21st Century* (Cambridge, MA: Harvard Graduate School of Education, February 2011) 2–3.

83. Harry J. Holzer and Robert I. Lerman, *America's Forgotten Middle-Skill Jobs: Education and Training Requirements in the Next Decade and Beyond* (Washington, DC: Urban Institute, 2007) 3–4; http://www.cof.org/files/Documents/Conferences/2008Summit/PathwaytoSharedProsperityWhatWorks1.pdf, access April 18, 2012.

INDEX

ABC television, 213–14, 355n231
Abella, Manolo, 285
absenteeism rates, 239, 367n121
Acker, William, Jr., 87
Ackerman, Bruce, 3
Actors Equity Association (AEA), 164, 165
Adams, Ed, 64
Adarand v. Pena, 207, 357n260
adCREASIANS, 68
Advertising Age, 65, 67
AEA (Actors Equity Association), 164, 165
affirmative-action liberalism strategy, 3–4, 6–10, 15. *See also specific topics, e.g.,* EEOC; political appointments, racial realism practices
affirmative-action plans, court rulings, 7–8, 9, 28–29, 81–82, 84–86, 137, 301n118, 320n253
African Americans, statistics: advertising models, 158–89, 340n23; alcohol/narcotics use, 239; consumer market, 156; crime rates, 239; entertainment industry, 180, 181–82, 348n126; journalism profession, 311n84; Kaiser's affirmative action plan, 81; manufacturing sector, 220, 232, 254, 280; marketing profession, 70; medical profession, 41, 46, 306n13, 307n35; policing profession attitudes, 117; population share, 24, 221; professional sports, 192; Republican National Convention, 323n52; teaching profession, 129–30, 144; Walgreens' employment practices, 87. *See also specific topics, e.g.,* low-skilled jobs, racial realism practices; political appointments, racial realism practices; teaching profession, racial realism practices
African Nationalist Pioneer Movement, 115–16
Aguilera, Michael Bernabé, 369n147
Alabama, 86–87, 137, 336n258
Alaimo, Anthony, 87, 203
Alba, Jessica, 168
Alias, 172
Alito, Samuel, 146, 322n38

AMA (American Medical Association), 41
Améredia, 68
American Association of Advertising Agencies, 157
American Association of Medical Colleges, 41
American College of Physicians, 43–45, 128
American Hospital Association, 44
American Idol, 184
American Medical Association (AMA), 41
American Society of News Editors (ASNE), 53, 55
American Tobacco Company, 62
Amos and Andy, 177
Amsterdam News, 51
Ana role, in *Real Women Have Curves*, 172
Anchondo-Rascon, Amador, 259–60
Anderson, Elijah, 76
anticaste principle. *See* affirmative-action liberalism strategy
anticlassification principle, 6, 10. *See also* classical liberalism strategy
antisubjugation principle. *See* affirmative-action liberalism strategy
antisubordination principle. *See* affirmative-action liberalism strategy
Apple advertising, 160
appointments, government. *See* political appointments, racial realism practices
Aragorn role, in *The Lord of the Rings*, 172
Are We There Yet?, 180
Arizona, immigration law, 103
Arrington, Richard, 86
Asano, Tadanobu, 176
Asian Americans, statistics: acting profession, 342n49; advertising models, 159, 340n23; entertainment industry, 181–82, 348n126; journalism profession, 57–58, 60, 311n84; manufacturing sector, 254; medical profession, 41–42, 49; population share, 24; teaching profession, 129–30; voting patterns, 92, 104. *See also specific topics, e.g.,* business sector, diversity practices; entertainment